T0354517

OLD SCHOOL

OLD SCHOOL

The Evolution of America's Pastime

Ted Kubiak

OLD SCHOOL
THE EVOLUTION OF AMERICA'S PASTIME

iUniverse books may be ordered through booksellers or by contacting:

iUniverse
1663 Liberty Drive
Bloomington, IN 47403
www.iuniverse.com
1-800-Authors (1-800-288-4677)

ISBN: 978-1-5320-8455-3 (sc)
ISBN: 978-1-5320-8456-0 (hc)
ISBN: 978-1-5320-8457-7 (e)

Library of Congress Control Number: 2019916543

Print information available on the last page.

iUniverse rev. date: 12/13/2019

Contents

Dedication

Old School is dedicated to the two greatest legacies of my life, my daughter, Kristi, and my son, Justin, both of whom I could not love more, or be prouder of. My hope is that it will provide them with a better understanding of who I am, and allow them to experience some of this other wonderful world in which I lived.

Foreword

Ted Kubiak's book, *Old School,* is a narrative that tracks his life-long affair with baseball from childhood, through his minor- and major-league years, and finally his decades-long career in player development. Forty-plus years in the game are qualifications enough for him to give the reader a revealing view of baseball's most critical current issue—the transformation of the game from its traditional, or old school methodologies, to one dominated by statistical analyses and sabermetric findings. Front offices now have a stable of talented and pedigreed innovators who, with a flurry of metric-based formulas, have applied their new technological concepts to the game, replacing the traditional standards and practices that have served it for more than a century.

The media have been solidly supportive of this renaissance, but recently, and with noticeable frequency, questions have surfaced about the computational conclusions being relied upon as end-all answers. The complete about-face that baseball has taken has aroused many concerned that its impact has been detrimental to the quality of play. Whether it has or not puts *Old School* in a perfect position to contribute to this discussion because Ted Kubiak is the first author to write from the perspective of a ten-year major-league career, three World Championships with the Oakland A's in 1972, 1973, and 1974, and twenty-five years as a minor-league player development manager, coach, and coordinator. The quality of his writing is so impressive that after reading a draft of *Old School,* I asked him who his collaborator, or ghost writer was. His answer was even more impressive. Ted wrote every word assisted by an editor whose sole purpose was to review his manuscript for its continuity and clarity of thought, and, if necessary, to correct his grammar, punctuation, and use of tenses to keep it reading smoothly.

The timing and substance of the attention that *Old School* gives the present analytical system that has redefined America's pastime is so thought provoking it should be placed in conversations with the most important baseball books ever written. This high praise is well earned. Its urgency to the state the game is in today is not exaggerated, and neither are Ted's credentials to comment on the difference between the two philosophies.

Bill James, in the late '70s and into the '80s, was an early pioneer of the concept of applying statistical analyses to baseball records to evaluate individual performances. The process came to be known as sabermetrics, a term coined from the acronym SABR—the Society for American Baseball Research. James's work inspired a legion of followers who have, themselves, developed formulas that challenged the traditional pillars of baseball's operations: scouting, player development, roster construction, game leadership, and strategy. The number of practitioners has grown geometrically, and with renewed intensity. None of their motivations can be considered evil because they are fueled by a sincere interest in the game, and the belief that what they are doing can improve it.

Professional baseball has been known for its resistance to change, and though moving at a glacier-like pace when it does, it has lately become more proactive. Never has it experienced anything like the growth of this scientific approach that has caused a tsunami-like surge of its applications throughout the game. Consider how many areas of the game have been challenged by a surging bevy of analysts who have gained access to a number of positions of impact. Literally, they have targeted every area of decision making in Baseball Ops.

How serious is this? The game's core has been drastically changed. What this has done is put some very astute baseball minds into competition as to which philosophy is superior.

From the game's inception, players chased the money. Many moved from team to team, year after year. Ownership eventually put a stop to the annual migration by adopting the reserve clause. It took more than one hundred years before the players fought back against the servitude under which they played, and were able to unravel the stranglehold the monopolistic owners had on them. The battle to gain their freedom, with Curt Flood as an early leader, was a difficult undertaking, but through it all, their play on the field never wavered. It remained excellent.

The initial upheaval to the structure of the game came from the resolve of Andy Messersmith and Dave McNally, who fought the contractual restraint they were under. In 1975, they won an arbitration hearing that awarded them free agency. The Major League Baseball Players Association (MLBPA) and the major-league team owners negotiated a settlement that gave the players their freedom under certain conditions. Nothing like this monumental achievement had ever occurred in the game's history. Its major consequence has been the "financial" effect it has had on players and owners alike.

But now, with the acceptance of an analytical and scientific approach to evaluate every aspect of Baseball Operations, the stakes are much higher. The New versus Old issue has moved to the top of the most monumental change list. This issue is not about how much is earned and who pays, but who plays, and how the game is played. With the heart and guts of the game directly impacted, baseball executives cannot afford to make mistakes with respect to maximizing Baseball Ops decision making.

The essence of the game does not change. Scouting departments find the talent, management acquires them and constructs rosters, experts in player development coach talent into skills, and major-league staffs mold an assemblage of players into a championship style of play. What does change is how the "basics" of each department are implemented. Possibly, they can be improved by combining the best of the Old and New approaches. At their extremes, though both sides share the same challenges, the supporters of each side value its own methods, and disrespects the other's.

The analytical approach is more corporate-like, run by individuals with lofty educational backgrounds that emphasize computers and technology. They move immediately into front-office positions with no exposure to the heartbeat of professional play. Analysts have introduced many formulas that benefit many areas of the game and accept no limits to their application and influence, but they have found no way to measure the intangibles.

Those in uniform who are considered to be in charge are looked upon as functionaries. Their value is relaying front office mandates to the players. That they are easily replaceable speaks directly to a lack of confidence in coaching and in-game decision making. The effect diminishes game competition by lessening coaching adjustments and strategies. It also damages the traditional respect earned by the manager and the coaching staff by diverting it to the front office personnel. Respect goes to the decision maker.

The old-school approach recognized the value of an education, but preferred step-by-step advancements. The game was learned in progressive pieces then combined to equal the basics. An analysis of prepared material was valued, but emphasis was reserved for insights obtained by "observational" analyses. It was an accumulation of expertise through experiences and relationships. Special attention and value were given to intangibles such as accountability, competitiveness, and toughness.

The approach taken decades ago has an advantage when contrasted to today's functionaries because it relied on the manager's and staff's abilities to react to the in-game dynamics of a competition between men, not machines. Baseball has had a historic understanding that those who make adjustments during the contest win, and those who do not lose. In that era, respect and trust of leadership was not automatic; it had to be earned. When they reside in the dugout, they are game changers.

The divide between the old and new approaches has serious consequences for the health and prosperity of our game. Baseball's decision makers, Major League Baseball, the MLBPA, owners of the thirty organizations and their executives, are all responsible for selecting the best approach. Perhaps a blend of both philosophies is best.

Old School has two major themes that are seamlessly connected throughout the book by their relevance to baseball as a game and as an industry. One is intensely professional and thought provoking; the other is highly personal with insights that are entertaining and revealing. Ted does not hesitate to express himself on either of those issues. His candidness, especially when it is self-directed, is appreciated and trust inspiring. His candid style of writing earns the readers' trust. It helps them appreciate the personal parts of his story, and the seriousness of the analytical issue now facing baseball's decision makers.

Ted's introduction to America's pastime is classic. As part of growing up in Highland Park, New Jersey, he attended games at Yankee Stadium, became a Yankees fan, and especially one of Mickey Mantle. Baseball became a passion by playing on neighborhood playgrounds. Ultimately that led to the possibility of a baseball career. In areas where young prospects have limited game opportunities to attract attention from professional scouts, organizations would conduct tryout camps. Amateur players with suspected big league ability were invited to these workouts by the area scouts of the major-league clubs. It was very difficult to show enough talent to be offered a contract in such makeshift environments.

At a local tryout, the Kansas City A's led by Tom Giordano, a well-respected scout, were impressed with Ted's workout and offered him a contract. He had a choice between two professions, baseball being one, and the other, becoming an architect. Ted as a potential architect helps us appreciate the intelligence and attention to detail that he has as an author devoted to *Old School*.

Ted's playing career, beginning in 1961, included six years in the minor leagues and ten in the major leagues. In *Old School*, most of Ted's references to his playing career involve his minor-league days. His instincts resonate with the majority of baseball fans over the years. They have had a fascination with the reality of life in the minors. Maybe it's because the conditions in the major leagues are better known and have a Fantasy Island type of life. Minor leaguers deal with more of a normal life of toughness and challenges.

Modern minor-league conditions have definitely improved compared to what they were. They were so basic, tough, and lacking conveniences that they fit the saying where adversity exists: "Someday we will all look back and laugh at what we went through." The lack of just about everything and enduring it was part of the minor-league experience. The opportunity to experience professional baseball and its brotherhood made those years worth the hardships.

In *Old School*, Ted has several wonderful references about life in the minor leagues. Some examples were the awful conditions of the playing fields, the unusable locker rooms, the difficult travel and accommodations, and the lack of suitable equipment. However, it more than worked to save the great experiences of being together with teammates. One of my favorite chapters was Ted's devotion to his Rawlings model "XPGS" glove!

Part of Ted's reflections as he began pro ball and struggled through the minors to become a major leaguer are powerfully personal. His willingness to share self-evaluations demonstrate his commitment to truth throughout the book. He confronted his neuroses, insecurities, emotional stresses, and immaturity, and found the means to overcome them. Ted's inner strength was a part of the process. He also credits a couple of dramatic negative experiences that helped him grow emotionally. The deaths of his parents and teammate Catfish Hunter, and an attention-getting conversation with his original mentor, Tom Giordano. Tom alerted him that his release was being discussed and he needed to feel the urgency to save his career.

As I read *Old School*, I had lots of impressions. Depth was one that often came to mind. It was triggered by the subjects and experiences included in the book. Ted got into nothing superficially. When depth is relevant in baseball, Earl Weaver's presence is felt. One of Earl's keys to winning was to construct a roster so deep that it could deal with the competition of a 162-game season and the postseason. His objective was "deep depth." Earl would have enjoyed reading *Old School* because it has the same objective regarding the Old versus New issues confronting the game today. A pioneer in understanding how valuable statistics were to a manager, Earl's active mind would have embraced how to reconcile the two approaches.

When I asked Ted for input on what he expected of the foreword I would write, he answered "just read the manuscript and write what you think." What made sense to me was to compare *Old School* to how we managed and prepared for each game. Our teams divided a game into three-inning segments. We wanted to score early and often in innings one through three. In innings four, five, and six we reacted to the scoreboard by either adding runs or coming from behind. And because most games are decided in innings seven, eight, and nine, we sharpened our focus to a single run, scoring one or preventing one, with the goal of our closer completing the win. Defensively, the objective of each inning remained the same, put up a zero, or limit scoring to as few runs as possible. Push the starting pitcher and finish with the relievers setting up the closer.

I looked at *Old School* the same way. This foreword's beginning highlights the importance of the Baseball Ops Old versus New methodology. The middle establishes Ted's credentials to comment on the Old versus New issue by presenting his candid account of his life and career, and the closer is the challenge to solve the issue, whereby the winner is Major-League Baseball and extends to all that enjoy and work for it. The end suggests that those responsible for reconciling this critical issue embrace the teachings of a legendary baseball coach and mentor, George Kissell.

George has all the qualifications of a game-changing closer. He wore a St. Louis Cardinals uniform for sixty-nine years. He impacted the baseball lives of thousands in organizations besides the Cardinals. He was famous for developing techniques that featured simplicity and effectiveness. One of his best was preaching adherence to Baseball's Golden Rule and his "Love and Learn Test" to insure compliance.

That George combined the Golden Rule with his Test applies directly to those entrusted with finding the solution to the Ops issue that serves the best interests of the game. Honor the Golden Rule by passing his Test! The Rule requires that everyone who chooses to work for baseball pledges to do his best while understanding his first priority is what's best for the game. The two sides that are passionately analyzing the game from their different ideologies must structure their thinking and work within the priority attached to the Rule. What is the best way to scout and acquire talent;

develop talent into skills; construct rosters; and impact the action and strategies of the game competition? How best can the two different methodologies come together? George would have insisted that "knowledge" could supply the answer.

His "Love and Learn Test" states that you must love baseball enough to continually learn as much as you can about it. That commitment not only raises your baseball IQ, but activates a rewarding cycle. The more you learn, the more you will love the game, which will whet your appetite for more learning. It's a reliable cycle as long as the commitment is sincere and well intentioned.

And this is what I find thoughout Ted's book. He was a constant learner. From one appearance to the next in the batter's box, from each fielded play, inning to inning, town to town, season to season: Ted was learning baseball every day, if he failed to learn when he should have, he worked that much more to compensate for what he considered a missed moment.

George would urge the Old and New Baseball Ops sides to recognize more about the other, and use the best of both to construct the ideal methodology that honors the Golden Rule.

In 1977, when I asked George if I had the potential to be a baseball manager, he challenged me with the Rule and the Test. He explained that an unwillingness to honor one and pass on the other meant I did not deserve a position in baseball. Consistent with his excellence as a coach/teacher, George would add a positive comment of confidence that I would qualify.

George would give the Old and New sides the same blunt opinion, and the same expectation that they cared enough about the game to fulfill their obligations.

TONY LA RUSSA

Preface

Neither of my children knew much about my career, or what it took to become a major-league player—they were eight and four years old when I retired—and only little about my twenty-five years as a minor-league manager and infield instructor. So often, as the years passed, did I think how wonderful it would be to leave them some sort of accounting, journal, or memoir, something that could be considered a legacy of what I experienced during my forty-plus years in the game. With each passing year, that they knew me a little better became more and more important. Not having questioned my own parents more about their lives was something I wish I had done.

Carving a career in professional baseball, a vocation that can be glamorous, is a difficult pursuit not only because of how hard the game is to play, but the constant negativity that must be dealt with can be overwhelming. The game is a physical and mental challenge, and if there is even the attempt to make it your life, it has to be loved. Leaving my children something that might explain the fascination I had with its challenges made sense to me as their father; it actually became an obsession. I also wanted to expose the game as it changed from the one I knew into one that I had a hard time recognizing. Examining this transformation, and how a new breed of executives who, whether the rest of us liked it or not, were molding it to their unique specifications, seemed worthy of my attention.

Scripting my own story would be easy, I only had to be vulnerable, but it would take some soul searching to expose what was happening, not so much on the field, but in the offices of the executives who were reinventing the game because they believed they knew better.

What I hoped would be an inspirational project was harder than expected. My thoughts or ideas of where to start either ran wild or not at all, and, when in front of the computer, assessing what it was I was trying to say, my lack of literary skills became glaringly apparent.

Every attempt at just an opening sentence was frustrating. Nothing seemed appropriate, worthy of print, making it more clear with each session that if I was to do this, someone was going to have to help me. That every word in this book has ultimately been drawn from my shaky literary expertise surprises even me.

Once begun, the entanglement of grammatical and syntactic possibilities, the misuse of tenses, punctuation, and cliches, and too many words gratuitously penned that stretched sentences into lengthy and boring paragraphs defined much of my early efforts. My work was at times monosyllabic, dull, and non-descriptive, then rambling and incoherent, often childish, very often confusing, and sometimes illogical and incomprehensible. This was more than a formidable undertaking.

After toying with the idea off and on for a few years with no appreciable success, I gave up with a new found respect for anyone who could take on authorship of anything.

The fact that, at the time, I was constantly on the lookout for ways to improve my teaching methods as a minor-league infield instructor led me to another, and similar, project. It dawned on me one day that it might be interesting to put down on paper what I had painstakingly taught myself about fielding a ground ball early in my professional career.

Where this new exercise would lead I wasn't sure, but being more than satisfied with the depth of my study of the fielding process, and what I had taught myself—instructors were somewhere in the future—organizing an instructional essay that included all of my findings had merit. Despite my previous literary confusions, the construction of this "defensive" document would not be as troublesome because its content would be more linear, the information more clearly defined.

What I never realized was how thoroughly I had examined, and dissected the movements and actions that were required to perform the simple act of fielding a ground ball. It took the better part of a year of sporadic on-again-off-again work to put my defensive discoveries, and each individual step, into a sequential methodology that had a flow and continuity to it that was equally coherent and readable.

The results were an incredibly comprehensive twenty-eight pages of information. This reestablished hope that, maybe, just maybe, I could one day put something worthwhile together about my baseball life for my children. Pleased with this latest work, but not knowing exactly what to do with it, I put it aside, proud of what I had done.

Some months later, I realized that handing my infielders something to read that reinforced my verbal instructions might have a significant benefit. Believing that to be a worthy idea, I drew up a simple outline for what I hoped would be a thorough and comprehensive manual on infield play.

It took two years to complete what I titled *Fundamental Infield Play.* The cornerstone of this instructional 300 page effort was the document I had written detailing all of the movements and actions that I considered part of the process of fielding a ground ball. Having smartly titled that work, "How to Field a Ground Ball," it became the lead chapter of the manual which was given to each of the organization's new infielders every spring. Staff members also received one; there was no excuse for everyone not knowing what was expected of them.

Once *Fundamental Infield Play* was copyrighted, anything I might do as a journalist/author, except to sign autographs, effectively ended. Though haunted by my earlier inept attempts to tell my life story, giving it another try was pretty much forgotten.

During the following summer, while managing the Cleveland Indians farm team in Kinston, North Carolina, Chris Kline, a sportswriter covering the team, and a very close friend, shocked me, when out of the blue, he said he would like to write a book about me. I was humbled by his suggestion, and though I saw little value of me being in print, it did make me think.

In discussing the possibilities of a book with Chris, and why he suggested such an ambitious undertaking, he convinced me that it had merit. It was then a matter of how best to effectively make the work a worthwhile reality from my perspective. If this was to be, there was one thing on which I would not waver. It could not be the typical baseball diary that recounted the days of their author spiced by the offbeat shenanigans of his teammates. Too many pat-me-on-the-back, tattletale, unimaginative sports biographies were stagnating on bookstore shelves, offering nothing with emotional impact or depth. And for me to consider that my life story could in any way compete with those presented by Ted Williams, Joe DiMaggio, Babe Ruth, and other true stars of the game, was unrealistic. Only if Chris or I could come up with an interesting format, a style of presentation that would give greater significance to my baseball life, would I be willing to consider moving forward.

Remembering the futility of my previous attempts to record something of my baseball life, and that nothing had happened since to make me feel that another attempt would be any better, it made sense to leave this project in Chris' hands. Months passed with neither of us coming up with a format that met my parameters until after dinner one evening the following spring, Chris suggested doing something of a biographical nature. That by itself was nothing to get excited about, but when he suggested that we use my 300 page *Fundamental Infield Play* manual as the guide, I saw its possibilities. How he intended to rework my instructional treatise into a book I had no idea, but no sooner had the words left his mouth, I thought he'd come up with the perfect format, one that would allow me to recount my early years in the game, my struggles with it, and myself in the process, while turning most of the instructional information into what I had seen happen to the game.

Chris was not only a good writer, he had an eye for baseball talent that had always impressed me. He saw things as a sportswriter that not many scouts did. The many conversations we had about players convinced me of that time and time again. It was not long after we had decided to proceed using the format he'd suggested, that he was given the opportunity to put his notepad aside and become a baseball scout himself, something he told me he long wanted to do. Since making the change he has more than proven his worth by securing several high-round picks for two organizations, the Pittsburgh Pirates and the Toronto Blue Jays. His change of heart, however, significantly altered any future there was of us collaborating on a book. Nevertheless, his original intent had excited me so much that I decided to sit down again, and do it by myself, or at least try.

So, with only Chris's advice and the encouragement his suggested format provided, without knowing what I was doing, I began to pile up hours on the computer trying to capture the essence of my life in baseball, but it wasn't working. The attempt to turn my instructional manual, and its step-by-step rigidity into an autobiography with emotions and feelings, was going nowhere fast.

But, with a slight change of direction, I grew more and more satisfied with what I proudly began calling "my book." The more I wrote, however, the more I knew that I was not going to be able to complete it by myself. Putting my thoughts in writing has always been easier than verbalizing them, but this project required more scholarly expertise than what modest academic and poetic skills I had, skills that peaked at penning letters and notes to friends. I was in a literary morass, trapped by my own ineptitude.

Occasionally we have the good fortune to meet people with whom we connect in one way or another. Some inspire, some educate, some become nothing more than friends, some are mere passers-by. Just such an encounter fell my way one day through an off-the-wall circumstance involving my relationship with a longtime close friend, Doug McWilliams, that was perfect in its timing.

Doug was a photographer whom I first met in 1968 when my Athletics arrived in Oakland from Kansas City, the franchise having been uprooted and moved by our enigmatic owner, Charles O. Finley. Doug was just beginning his career as an on-field photographer, a career that would span decades with the Topps Company, and his phenomenal collection of baseball photographs was now being sought by the Baseball Hall of Fame in Cooperstown. Through a circuitous connection, I was contacted by an attorney from Washington, D.C., who was looking into Doug's background seeking what information I might share about his work and his legitimacy.

Satisfied with my résumé of Doug and the quality of his work, our conversation morphed deeper into baseball memorabilia, and when I mentioned that I had some items I needed to have authenticated, he put me in touch with a gentleman by the name of Kevin Keating, recommending him as someone with the expertise I needed.

Believing that Kevin and I had never met, once we began communicating, I found that was not the case. As an eleven year old, living in Lake in the Hills, Illinois, about fifty miles northwest of downtown Chicago, Kevin was making long trips on holidays and weekends to the heart of the "Windy City," either by car with his father or by Northwestern train service, from nearby Crystal Lake. His mission was to meet as many major-league players that he could during the baseball season.

He would spend all day at the Executive House in Chicago. This hotel on Wacker Drive was home to my Oakland A's when in Chicago, as it was to almost all the other major-league teams from both the American and National Leagues when playing the Cubs or the White Sox. Stationed outside the hotel entrance, Kevin was a young autograph seeker, getting as many as he could from the players either leaving or returning to the hotel. Some of them, he said, were kind enough to stop and talk to him for a few minutes.

I had no specific recollection of who I might have signed things for at the time, but do remember a young man getting autographs at the hotel. Kevin informed me that he was that boy, and, yes, I had signed something for him. He also told me that in all those years of his collecting autographs at the hotel, and mailing the signers notes of appreciation, I was the only player to reply to one of his "thank you" notes with an unsolicited response. I had sent him an autographed postcard—which he still had!

Kevin was a starry-eyed teenager who was on a passionate and militaristic-type mission to collect as many signatures as he could. His trips were well-planned and organized. Not only was he armed with pen and paper, he had a bagful of baseballs, pictures, magazines, and baseball cards of all the players for the particular team that was in town, all alphabetically filed for quick reference and selection. As he waited patiently, fearful of losing a potential signee should he fumble with all he'd brought with him, he practiced rifling through his cache so he knew the exact location of the various items and could instantly find the piece he wanted. He did not want to be caught off-guard and miss an opportunity. The ingenuity and persistence of his trips so impressed a writer from the *Chicago Sun-Times* that he posted an article about Kevin's initiative, making him an instant celebrity at Algonquin High School. By the time Kevin graduated, he had amassed over 10,000 signatures.

Collecting autographs remained a big part of Kevin's life. His passion grew, so much so that it became a livelihood for him. Over the years he obtained the signatures of an untold number of famous people in the sports and entertainment fields, including US presidents, and had a sphere of celebrity friends that was astonishing with a story for each of their meetings that was more interesting than the fact that he had gotten them to sign.

His life was as impressive as his collection. After graduating from the West Point Military Academy where he excelled as a Chinese major, he became an Airborne Ranger and Infantry Officer. He lived in Japan for two years while his father taught English at Niigata University, and at the ages of seven and eight, for two years, attended an all-Japanese elementary school, learning the Japanese culture and language.

He later earned a Master's Degree in International Public Policy from Johns Hopkins University, worked with the FBI to help prosecute autograph forgers, traveled internationally, and wrote a couple of books. He is a certified autograph authenticator, has run a well-known sports autograph business, is now the prime authenticator for PSA/DNA—the country's leading autograph certification company—and annually attends the Colorado Rockies Fantasy Baseball Camps while still finding time for his wife and twin sons.

In one of our earliest conversations, when I mentioned that I was writing a book, he offered that his father, James Keating, was an editor who, should I be interested, might be able to help me. With no others in mind at the time, I had to, at least, look into that possibility.

Learning of Jim's own extensive and imposing intellectual background from a conversation or two that we had, and realizing that he was the force behind Kevin's success, there was no reason for me to look any further for an all-encompassing teacher/editor.

Jim and I would not only become business associates, but good friends, and I had the opportunity to visit him and his wife, Noriko, at their home in Lafayette, Indiana, during the time he was cleaning up my work. With my interest in architecture, seeing their historic 1880 Victorian house was a special aside to what was a great visit.

After seven years of working together, Jim, unfortunately, passed away in 2019. I lost a wonderful friend and mentor. He and Noriko had grown to be important to me, as they were to their wide circle of friends. Jim lived in an incredible sphere of educated people all of whom I was introduced to when he and Noriko graciously hosted a dinner in my honor on my visit. That gesture alone tells what wonderful people they were. Meeting a dozen or so of their friends turned out to be an education for me, and an evening not to be forgotten.

Jim's own history was no less remarkable than Kevin's. A graduate of Purdue University in creative writing, he lived in Japan for about twenty-five years, three as an Air Force crypto-analyst, two teaching at the university in Niigata, and twenty overall in Tokyo where he was the Editorial Manager at the headquarters of Daiwa Securities. He also did some freelance work for the government and many of Japan's top industries. Before his career move to Tokyo, Jim was a copy editor at *Business Week* magazine in New York City.

A writer himself, he published a stylebook, entitled *Writing Modern English,* in Japanese and English that was a long-running No. 1 Amazon-Japan best seller for several consecutive weeks. It even topped a Harry Potter best-seller translation for more than a year.

Jim had his hands full with me, but with an absolute passion for constantly reviewing and correcting the written word, he gently warned me about inconsistencies, overstatement, rhythm, continuity, negativity, useless words and unnecessary content. What he rephrased, suggested, and repaired often came with the rules, the reasons why, and an acceptance of my ignorance for which he could not have been more tolerant.

Whether it was a paragraph or a chapter, my first effort was always personally satisfying. It seemed clear, accurate, and coherent, but in a reread, expecting a gloating corroboration of my proficiency, I, instead, found a surprising incompetency, and a discouraging lack of accomplishment. I could not believe what I was reading. Jim would fix it, put it all in perspective. He so often recognized the utter confusion of what I was trying to say, and gently redirected me toward the perfection I thought I had submitted. It was baffling how this continued to happen no matter how careful I was in my construction. Things like misspelled words, and the constant omissions and repetitions had me questioning my eyesight. Punctuation was left to him; I never did understand how to correctly use a comma.

Another phenomenon was how often my best efforts came at three or four o'clock in the morning; I have no idea why. I could only wonder about writers and columnists such as David Halberstram, Marty Appel, John Feinstein, Peter Golenbock, Phil Pepe, Dick Young, et al., a select group who make their pages of sports prose and reporting dance and sing in a way I could never dream of duplicating. Was it possible that at some point they too had misgivings about their own work?

Have my efforts been successful? For me, there is no doubt they have been. Once I understood more about what I was doing, there was something fun about spending days on a couple of paragraphs, weeks on a specific chapter. Sitting at the computer was an education. I was constantly amazed at how my thoughts would so often be alive, flowing and meshing perfectly, then all of a sudden crash so violently that I had to get away from the keyboard.

What is herein published reveals the scope, depth, and tenaciousness of Jim's efforts. There are not enough thank-yous to express the gratitude I have for all he did for me. Having had his expertise and, most important, his friendship makes this work more satisfying than I could have imagined. When I think of *Old School*, the Keating name, and of course Jim, always comes to mind.

Completing this work took years. It was more difficult than I had anticipated, but it was an absolutely enjoyable experience. I am very proud of what I've done. For me, it is all I hoped it would be. For you—well, make the call as you see it.

Introduction

The Knickerbocker Club of New York City was a social club of elite New Yorkers that is credited with reinventing the game of baseball in the 1840s when a couple of the club's executives, one being Alexander Cartwright, imposed twenty new rules of play. The new regulations were meant to bring uniformity to a game whose popularity was quickly spreading. Teams were being formed in any number of cities and towns. In the late 1850s, to more formally govern the sport, sixteen teams around New York joined to form the National Association of Base Ball Players, and in the late 1860s, with some clubs beginning to recruit and pay players, baseball became professionalized.

Almost 200 years later, the game is an established billion-dollar-a-year industry ripe with unforeseen technological expertise, scholastic intelligence, and algorithmic pioneering. Baseballs are being thrown with a rocket-like consistency, and hit to unheard of distances by even the smallest of its competitors whose imposing physical presence belies a perplexing fragility that is being accommodated by rule changes that protect against modern day incompetencies.

What follows in this text are the struggles of one man who, for almost two decades, tried to understand and make sense of himself while battling the game he loved. Many more years would pass before his personal discoveries and homespun analyses allowed him to make better sense of his life. Had that clarity occurred earlier, it might have altered a career, and kept a beautiful family intact.

Written with a reverence, and the greatest respect for what has happened to professional baseball over the past fifty years, this book catalogs the dedication and commitment that built a career while keeping alive the game's glorious past; it pits the game's history against its present condition. There was no intent to be critical, but it was impossible to ignore the questions that have been raised regarding the efficacy and worth of baseball's scholarly revolution over the past few decades.

Some will say I'm just another old guy complaining and whining about how much greater the game once was, that my goal was to venerate the days prior to free agency, ESPN, 24-hour-a-day talk shows, and Ron Blomberg stepping in to the batter's box as the game's first-ever designated hitter in 1973. I cannot deny that possibility, but it is difficult to erase the memories of something I love so much while watching its reconstruction occur without the forethought or recognition of what effects the changes being made were having.

This book is about change which, for the most part, is inevitable while also being unpredictable. The hope is that it inspires productivity and improvement, not incredulity and disappointment. If intelligently proposed, properly developed, and reasonably implemented, innovation can be positive, but that is never guaranteed. Surely, no one could foresee the outcome of the scholarly reincarnation that has descended on the game of baseball and transformed its core.

That the game needs its present-day young, brilliant minds goes without saying, but those minds work best when unraveling the game's financial and legal craters, and their contingent complexities.

With regard to the game itself, the new executives stumble on a competence borne only from a theoretical knowledge of the game which is what they've seen as the fans they once were. They know little or nothing about what the game truly encompasses as evidenced by some of their decisions. In their well-intentioned attempts to remodel that which inspires and arouses millions with the cry of "Play Ball," their efforts merely serve to overshadow an unintentional disregard for the type of play that was so important to us old guys.

These new guardians have embraced their roles with an unmatched intensity. What they have done to the game may be thought misguided, but that faults their efforts which is unfair. It is more a lack of comprehension that is behind the ill-informed direction in which they are moving. While abandoning too much of what produces wins, they have analyzed and reduced the game to a plethora of numbers and categories as if there is some magical secret to ensure a successful season, and a championship. Today's athlete is different, but the game requires nothing more than what has been successful for a very long time; it hasn't changed.

With each passing season I grow prouder of the era in which I played. There were few similarities, and only slight equality, when comparing my abilities to those of the competition. It was all I could do to compete against some of the game's most skilled players ever, but, more important, was the comfort I felt in their company.

My memories are incredible, and many. I feel privileged to have been on the same field with so many of the greats, including countless members of the Hall of Fame, the special three being Catfish Hunter, Rollie Fingers, and Reggie Jackson from my Oakland club. They hold significance because we grew up together in the same organization. But others such as Lou Brock, Bob Gibson, Steve Carlton, and Joe Torre from the St Louis Cardinals, and Willie McCovey and Dave Winfield of the San Diego Padres, are held in the same admiration for their accomplishments.

Other Hall of Fame players, such as Mickey Mantle, Jim Palmer, Frank and Brooks Robinson, Tom Seaver, Roberto Clemente, Carl Yastrzemski, Johnny Bench, Joe Morgan, Ernie Banks, Harmon Killebrew, and Willie Mays, to name a few, were wonderful to watch, though sometimes discouraging because of how they effortlessly made the game look so easy. How could the rest of us not admire their talents? They played the game the way we wished we could.

Baseball junkies agree that the '60s and '70s were some of the best years in baseball. I can vouch for that in one respect; the quality of play in those days is not seen today. What play was like before then I can't say, but today's bigger and stronger athletes, who show strength and agility never seen in earlier years, have not kept pace with the sound fundamental play that preceded them.

The record books boast of many great individual accomplishments, some that may never be surpassed. A couple of contemporary pitchers have no more than a remote chance of challenging the magic 300-win mark, but no one will ever surpass Nolan Ryan's 5,714 strikeouts. Should anyone hit in fifty-seven consecutive games to eclipse the long-standing mark of fifty-six by "Joltin" Joe DiMaggio, it will be accomplished with the help of today's liberal scoring.

If not for the steroid era, Henry Aaron would still be the all-time home run king, and Babe Ruth the Sultan of Swat. As for the strikeout which is no longer the bane of a player's career, no one will ever strike out only three times playing a full season as Joe Sewell did in 1932. And I see no one coming close to his career record of striking out an average of only once in every sixty-three at-bats.

Individual records make the game fascinating, but many teams have amassed their own collective honors, and what a phenomenal achievement it would be if one team could match or pass the total of the twenty-seven World Championship titles won by the New York Yankees. With the present shuffling of rosters from year to year, an equally difficult accomplishment would be to duplicate their five consecutive titles from 1950 to 1954, and four in a row earlier, from 1936 to 1939. The rarity of three in a row isn't easy either, but the Bronx Bombers did that not long ago in 1998, 1999, and 2000. The only other three-peaters have been the Boston Red Sox in 1914, 1915, and 1916, and my Oakland A's in 1972, 1973, and 1974.

Times and circumstances have significantly altered society, life in general, and every vocation, causing every sport to evolve in ways that make attaining certain milestones impossible while others remain simple cakewalks. It is the quest to equal or better them that keeps many of the games followers interested in their pursuit.

Few would dispute that pitching and defense wins games. Their combination was largely responsible for the championships won by my Oakland Athletics teams. Our pitching was exceptional, but the pitching in both leagues during my career made hitting a much greater challenge.

Long remembered will be my first major-league at-bat, and the calm, prophetic admonition given me by veteran home plate umpire Ed Runge as I approached the batter's box to "swing the bat." That was not just a greeting, he meant it. Positioning himself in what he may have considered a safety zone a couple of feet behind the catcher, and wearing the old "balloon" chest protector, he never saw a pitch he didn't like. His strike zone was huge, and his definition of it, were he asked, might have been the same simple and succinct advice he had given me: "Swing the bat!"

Despite my struggle to compete with outstanding players, I played in the big leagues for a relatively long time. Little did I know as a high school senior that major-league baseball was to be my future when I was surprisingly named the Most Valuable Player of my Highland Park High School baseball team. Startled when my name was announced, I realized in later years that my reaction was typical of the lack of self-esteem and belief I had in who I was, or would become. I lived with a disappointing lack of confidence that consumed far too many years of my life.

The best way to describe my childhood is that I was neurotically happy, but unable to enjoy who I was. It took many years and the utterance of the most frightening word any aspiring young professional baseball player could hear, "RELEASE," to bring me to gain some sense of myself. Realizing that my career might end prompted an immediate examination of who I was, what I was doing, and what I wanted. This triggered a fearful confrontation with maturity that was long overdue. One little terrifying word inspired a much-needed awakening to who I was, and what it was I was doing to sabotage my life and career.

● ● ●

Not the typical sport biography, *Old School* documents the emotions that dictated a life within a life. It lays bare the ambivalence that dominated both for far too long while openly exposing the emotional underpinnings that controlled everything. It is an appraisal of discoveries and concerns, an honest in-depth look at my life and baseball's effect on it, a psychological self-analysis of what I didn't understand about myself while passionately trying to make sense of the career I was trying to fashion in the sport I loved.

It is also a critical, deprecating, but sincere examination of the game itself from inside the clubhouse. Meant to be non-scathing in its truths, it questions why it was thought that changing it to mimic societal transformations, or complying with technological dictums, would be beneficial.

Writing it freed me from a naive acceptance of life as I began to understand the power of being vulnerable to my own truths. It underscored how selfish and egotistically thoughtless my responses were too many times, how I acted blindly and ignorantly, and not at all with the compassion and consideration I should have. Those situations have not been neither defined nor detailed herein because their mention is the only thing of importance to the purpose of this book, and enough for the reader to realize the areas in which I needed to grow.

I made mistakes, but with the same determination and perseverance that I conquered the difficulties of the bouncing ball, so I did with life, always buffered by three self-imposed rules: remain resilient, always look for a better way, and never quit.

An Undignified Exit

Every athlete rues the day when he will no longer be able to move with the same ease, react as quickly, run as fast, or depend on strength that was once taken for granted. Realizing that your career is ending can be frightening. The last competitive day is an uninvited inevitability that hurts. Some exits occur suddenly, often mandated, some not soon enough. Only a few receive the pageantry expected. But no matter the circumstances, the end of a career is regrettable, disheartening, and, for many, depressing. It was for me. I would have done anything to prevent seeing the end of mine bearing down on me, but it was unavoidable.

However the transition to a second life occurs, the retired athlete finds little solace in its reality because this change of life is not easy. It is not into a society that has completely forgotten him, but one that seems to share more of a "Where-did-he-go?" attitude. Except for family and an immediate circle of close friends, no one truly cares. Exploits left behind are to be proud of, for sure, but even before their glow fades, the next generation has begun taking its turn.

Whether my retirement would upset anyone in baseball didn't matter; the only ones to be affected by it would be my family. There was good reason for me to chronicle my departure in this work, including the circumstances leading up to it, but ashamed and embarrassed about how I handled the situation, there were enough justifications for me not to. It was not hard to convince myself that the ugly details of my quitting would add nothing informative, or meaningful, to this book, but the truth for avoiding its inclusion was simply that I did not want to see my exit exposed in black-and-white for everyone to read.

After numerous reviews and edits of the content of each of the chapters I'd written, correcting syntax, flipping tenses, and untangling thoughts that wrongfully conveyed my intentions, I was impressed with what I thought was finally my decent use of the English language, and the clarity of my work. Everything read well, but haunting me were the events that prompted my decision to retire, and whether they should be included. Having been forthright with every word I had written, it was only after accepting that I was trying to conceal the reasons, bury the truth, and avoid the humiliation of how I so abruptly walked away from the game, was I able to expose what I had done. How I handled my exit was not one of my proudest moments. An explanation of why I quit seemed appropriate.

The mechanics of my decision remain personally embarrassing, and I don't have a suitable answer for what I did, or if I should have handled it differently. Perhaps it was the pairing of my Taurean and Polish obstinacy that overrode any sense of reason I should have had, but to squeeze even one more year out of my fading skills would have been an onerous undertaking. With everything that was going through my mind, the one question that deserved consideration was whether I should swallow my pride, try to turn things around, and see how much longer I might be able to play. But that was something I could not do. The simple act of successfully catching a thrown ball, that for a long time had presented no problem, was now becoming a challenge; how hard they were being thrown was beginning to matter. Ground balls that I once danced around were in need of a new choreography. Plays that I had matter-of-factly made for so long were now more than a concern.

Even worse, my heart was no longer in the game. After sixteen years, time at the ballpark was no longer the good time it had always been. The game's appeal was gone, and nothing I tried was rekindling the love for it that I once had. The inner drive that had been so naturally a part of me was fading, and recognizing that I had no control over anything anymore was frightening.

It wasn't easy to accept that I was no longer the player I had been, but my dilemma, and what worried and panicked me more than anything, was that I didn't know what I would do with the rest of my life.

My career ended early one morning in March of 1977. Spring training had been a nightmare. Nothing was going right. My anxiety was building, and I was a nervous wreck realizing what I was about to do.

Up early that day—I had not slept much all night—I packed what little I had, checked out of the team hotel, and drove to the clubhouse in Yuma, Arizona, the spring home of the San Diego Padres. Making sure to arrive before any of the other players, I cleaned out my locker hoping to avoid questions from a couple of young clubhouse attendants who had to be wondering what I was doing, and made a sad, dazed, and glassy-eyed eight hour drive to my home in Piedmont, California. That was it, no ifs, ands, or buts! My wife was shocked to see me, and her only response as I walked through the door was: "What are you doing here?"

My answer was simply, "I quit!"

What was I doing there? I was bitter and frustrated, feeling that my life had just ended. My stomach had been in knots ever since my contract had arrived in January, and my couple of month's battle dealing with the shock of how much my salary had been slashed only compounded and confused my thinking. Was what I had done a knee-jerk reaction to that? I was an emotional wreck.

The twenty percent pay cut may have added fuel to the fire, but I don't honestly believe it was responsible for my quitting as I did. Baseball had been slowly becoming the job I never considered it being. I was almost 35 years old, and though I had just endured my last battle with ownership, I was not the player I had been. Even with free agency about to overhaul the financial structure of the game, fighting another day under the final vestiges of servitude while waiting for the questionable results the new system might bring was something I no longer had time for.

My first three major-league seasons were years of inactivity that set the tone for my career, making it more difficult than perhaps it should have been. I sat on the bench for nine of my ten big-league seasons, but it was the first three, more specifically the first one, that shaped my future. Sitting on the sideline was not fun. I'd never been relegated to the bench before, anyplace, and I was not happy. The most punishing thought, and what scared me, was knowing that without regular playing time, keeping my defensive skills honed was going to be impossible. They were as good as they were going to get when my AAA season ended in 1966, and were the reason why I even had a major-league career, eventually being in a class of those considered the game's best defenders. But without the innings of work I knew I needed, maintaining what I had worked so hard to achieve was going to be a challenge. As the season progressed, the devastation of feeling my ability ebb, slowly as it was, wore on me. Knowing that my skills were fading, and that there was nothing I could do about it, was a horrible feeling. This was no way to start a career.

It took an increasingly greater effort each year to maintain a respectable level of play. It was about my seventh or eighth year that I could feel the end coming, how quickly it would I didn't know. Each day was more difficult than the day before. The game was never easy, but it was beginning to become harder than it should have been. My body was no longer responding as it had for so long. Add to this an unhappy trade, a new environment, what I thought was disrespect from management, a never-before shocking contractual battle, and I could see no other obvious outcome. I had to quit. The game had been a constant struggle, physically and mentally, and I was losing the battle to put up with it.

The downward spiraling of my ability was frightening. Not only was I concerned about how much longer I would be able to play, I had to begin considering what I would do when I no longer could. I would need another job; I was going to have to go to work. But what would I do? What could I do? I wasn't prepared for anything. When life after baseball began to consume my every waking thought, instead of thinking baseball all day, every day, I began to wonder, and worry, what my days would be like without it. The game no longer seemed important.

When I first decided on a professional baseball career, I fully intended to enroll in college, and pursue an architectural career in the off-seasons. It would have taken a few more years than what would have been normal, but it could be managed. Invitations to the instructional and winter leagues postponed the start of my schooling for a few a few years, but it was a conflict with the baseball season and the scheduling of classes—even with a concession for being late from the school's admissions office— that became the real problem. A semester of school started before the season ended in the fall, and ended after baseball began the following spring. It was not possible to coordinate both.

When baseball was not consuming my winters, I found work in a bank trying my hand at a financial career, sold a few properties after getting a real estate license, and spent one off-season working for Charles O. Finley doing public relations work for the club; none of which would suitably sustain a life after baseball.

One thing that didn't have me concerned was the amount of money I would need to maintain my family's lifestyle. I absolutely believed I would have no problem making at least what I did as a player, no matter what I did. I wasn't making that much. Staying in the game for what most people thought were the riches it afforded was simply a myth. Losing my salary was nothing to fear.

● ● ●

During the 1974 and 1975 seasons, the Yankees were forced to shift their home schedule of games to Shea Stadium, home of the New York Mets. Yankee Stadium, first opened in 1923, was badly in need of repairs. Chunks of concrete were randomly breaking away and falling, putting fans in serious jeopardy, so it was closed for renovation at the end of the '73 season. In early May 1975, when told during batting practice at Shea that Mr. Finley was on the phone and wanted to talk to me, I knew immediately that I had been traded. What other reason could there be for me to be called off the field by the owner of the ball club? A minute or two later in the manager's office, I could not have felt worse when told that I was now a member of the San Diego Padres. This was my ninth major-league season.

He had traded me once before in 1969, but had reacquired me in 1972. This time there would be no return. The earlier trade had an upside because of my age, but being shopped to other clubs nearing my mid-thirties meant my career was winding down. After "San Diego Padres," I didn't hear much of anything else Mr. Finley said. How I found the strength not to tell him that I was going to retire rather than accept the trade, I don't know, but somehow I held my tongue knowing that would have been stupid and rash.

Plus, I was numb. I needed time to understand what had just happened.

In just an instant, everything I had ever done for the A's or felt about them lost all relevance. Whatever ties I had to the organization—a total of thirteen years— were instantaneously severed, and I felt strangely alienated from teammates with whom I'd been laughing five minutes earlier. My mind was a whirlwind of confusion as I sadly removed the A's green-and-gold uniform for one last time and began to pack. I was leaving a championship team, one I felt truly part of, a city I considered home, players who were like family, and going to a perennially struggling ball club that showed not much of a future either for itself or me. I had hoped to end my career in the gaudy Oakland colors, but, instead, my exit would be made in one as drab in color as the team I was joining.

After fifteen professional seasons, some good, some bad, this trade was the low point. At age thirty-four I obviously had little playing time left, but now on a team going nowhere, any longevity I might expect to have was considerably shortened. I had to seriously regroup mentally, take stock of what remained of my ability, and determine how much longer I wanted to play, or could play, while facing the reality of my eventual retirement.

After three consecutive World Championships, Oakland was poised for a run at number four in 1975, but there was something not right with the ball club that spring. Everyone was going about their business in a way that was strange and unsettling. I sensed a lackadaisical attitude that was unprecedented. I wasn't sure how concerned I should be, but something was different. Finley's phone call substantiated the uneasiness I felt.

Whether it was an overconfidence that had been well-tamed for the previous five years, or simply a brief period of earned complacency, what I sensed was that the club was not going to be intact much longer. The camaraderie, the familiarity, and the closeness I had come to know for more than a decade was about to be dismantled. My instincts were telling me that change was coming, and with my trade as a first step, my intuition signaled that some of my teammates would also be moved, and quickly.

How right I was.

The good years for the A's were over, and though I wasn't a main cog on a great team, I believed my role was important even in its limited capacity. By trading me for a pitcher he felt he needed, Finley was leaving unprotected the role of utility infielder that I had ably filled. My departure was going to trigger a change in the dynamics of an Oakland A's team that had been one of the game's best ever for half a decade.

Oakland won the division title again in 1975, but the breakup began after the 1974 season when Catfish Hunter was declared a free agent over a contract technicality, and signed with the Yankees. Reggie Jackson and Ken Holtzman were traded before the 1976 season, and with free agency beginning to severely alter the landscape, Finley went to work paring his roster of stars, attempting to generate trades with Boston, New York, and other interested clubs.

When nothing developed to his liking, he sold Joe Rudi and Rollie Fingers to Boston for $1 million each, and Vida Blue to New York for $1.5 million, but the Commissioner of Baseball, Bowie Kuhn, nullified the sales "in the best interest of baseball." By the end of 1976, the true core of the club had been decimated through trades or free agency, and in 1977, only two years after winning another division title, Oakland fell into last place, one rung below where my San Diego Padres would finish in the National League West Division.

Leaving Oakland was difficult. My teammates might have been shocked to know that not only would I miss them because I would never again play for such a great group known as the "moustache gang," but that I also had misgivings about leaving their owner. We had been together for years, and though Finley's abrasive and sometimes eccentric personality could grate on you, he had a side that was genuine and likable that I respected. Despite his shenanigans, he was responsible for the collective continued drive for excellence by each individual, and it was a lesson not to be forgotten.

In no way would the San Diego Padres come close to offering the legacy I was leaving.

More pointedly to my future, going to a losing club didn't bode well for the balance of whatever career I had left. Teams like the Padres were always looking to make any move that might right their situation, and I was the type of player who would be fodder for another swap in the future.

I had experienced collective failure with teams in two previous major-league seasons, once in Kansas City and another in Milwaukee. Joining the San Diego franchise from an Oakland club that knew where it was going, and what it had to do to be successful, was frustrating. San Diego was disorganized, had no direction, and from my experience no leadership. Despite some well-known and great players, such as Willie McCovey, Randy Jones, Dave Winfield, Doug Rader, John Grubb, and Tito Fuentes, the organization was in a state of confusion, looking for solutions.

Their lack of direction was immediately evident when on the very first night I walked into the San Diego clubhouse I was told I would be playing third base. That made no sense, and was another pronouncement of the organization's ineptitude. I was not a third baseman, never was. My time at the position after eight big-league seasons amounted to maybe a handful of games, and my bat did not have the thunder expected from a third-sacker. The club was desperate for something or someone else, but I was not the answer. With Oakland my role was defined. With San Diego I wasn't quite sure what it was; really, why did they want me?

I was unaccustomed to losing and the humiliation of it. One of the team's regulars was having personal issues that were affecting the club, and he and I had many long talks. My understanding was that the organization wasn't helping him. I didn't know if I was or not. On a bright note, Randy Jones was beginning a comeback and would have his utterly remarkable Cy Young season in '76. When he didn't pitch, we got pounded. Randy was the only one who could tame the Cincinnati Reds, the Big Red Machine, who wore us out much as did the Phillies and Mike Schmidt.

About a week before the 1975 season ended, I met with General Manager Buzzy Bavasi to see what plans the organization had for me. Were they pleased with what I had done? Was I even in their plans, or might I expect to be traded again, or possibly released? I was up in age and wanted to have some idea going forward about what to expect.

Bavasi assured me that they were pleased with my contribution and that I would be back in '76. I left his office relieved knowing I would be adding another year—my tenth— to my pension. But after a not-so-stellar 1976 from me or the team—we lost 89 games, two less than in 1975—the contract I received for 1977 showed a hefty twenty percent salary cut, the maximum amount allowable. I had not met with Bavasi as I had the previous winter because I expected it would not go very well. I had reservations about my future, and wanted to avoid what may have been an unpleasant conversation, leaving me at least some semblance of a relaxed off-season. I saw what was coming, but not the severity of it until my contract arrived. Had my year been that bad? Negotiating my way out of this was not going to be easy.

The club was within its rights to impose the cut. It made sense for them financially, but it was screaming something about their opinion of me. I had been around the game long enough to know when something wasn't right, and this was one of those times.

What I had not expected was that there would be no negotiating my contract. Numerous telephone calls and letters to Bavasi drew nothing in response, and I reported to spring training unsigned. Further attempts to meet or talk to him during the camp were similarly rebuffed. Not talking to a player about his contract was an often used tactic to get the player to capitulate. Year after year it had become increasingly difficult to go through the archaic song-and-dance routine for a few extra thousand dollars, but this standoff with Bavasi was something I had never before experienced.

Stonewalling any talks with me as he did was in stark contrast to what I considered the respect I had received from Charlie Finley during ours. Regarded as a bombastic, egotistical renegade among the owners, and with many of my teammates having no trouble throwing around various expletives at the mention of his name, Finley was nevertheless deferential during our yearly negotiations. With both of us holding our ground through a handful of emotional sessions, never did he do what San Diego was doing to me. I found him interesting and honest, and subsequent meetings with him over other issues showed a vulnerable side that I'm not sure many others had seen, ever.

Bavasi's strategy of silence was no doubt his way of getting me to cave in to his offer, and though he eventually rescinded the twenty percent reduction, by then it didn't matter. Were he able to wear me down, and have me agree to such a large pay cut, he would have successfully done what he was hired to do, which was to save the club money. His tactics, however, did not wear me down, they wore me out. They were nothing more than what was typically frustrating about the game, except that they had come at what was now a critical juncture in my baseball life.

Well before this Bavasi fiasco took place, my focus during the last months of the 1976 season was more on the future financial status of my family than on the game, and how I was playing. My mind wandered and my game preparation was horrible. I wasn't sure if it was because I was losing my skills, or that I was unable to steel myself against the game's pressures any longer, but my final days were nearing.

With each day no better than the previous one, an incident late in the season was more than a sign that my career was nearly over. It happened versus the Chicago Cubs in iconic Wrigley Field in Chicago. Its ivy covered walls, minuscule dugouts, and second-floor closet-sized locker room made it one of baseball's historic and memorable ballparks, and I was glad to have seen and played in this National League treasure. On a warm, sunny afternoon, we were again customarily behind by ten runs when the uncertainty of my future hit me with an abruptness and a suddenness I didn't expect. Being beaten as badly as we were, I was looking ahead to getting on the plane after the game and leaving the Windy City.

There was no good reason for me to be sent in to play shortstop in the bottom of the eighth inning with only three outs to go as I was. Depressed with how things were going that season, it was a slap in the face, and a blow to my ego. Should the substitution have had a specific purpose, as my late-inning substitutions did with a winning Oakland club, it would have made perfect sense. With Oakland, though I was often the final substituted infielder for defensive purposes in many important games—not just to finish one off—I felt I was contributing something to our success, and that the organization trusted me in what were the crucial late innings.

Standing at the shortstop position in one of baseball's cherished venues with my mind on everything but the game, upset and completely distracted by other thoughts, I was hoping we could get the three outs without my having to do anything, but, of course, someone hit a ground ball directly at me. Under normal circumstances, it would have been an easy play, but I approached it with two left feet. They seem tangled up as if I was back in high school. I had never been that unprepared for a ground ball in my life.

I saw the ball, but don't remember even touching it as it went through me into the outfield. I could not have been more humiliated and embarrassed. Whether that play triggered Bavasi to cut my salary the next spring, I didn't know, but it was a defining personal moment for me, and my future.

● ● ●

It took me no more than five minutes to clean out my locker that early spring morning in 1977. I was out of the Padres clubhouse, and on the road back to Piedmont by 6:30 AM. I had eight hours to think about what had just happened, and that was all I could think about. I had just quit; sixteen years, ten major-league seasons, some good, some bad, championships, trades, teammates, fans, family, friends, so many memories were now just that, gone, over; and so many questions; my wife, kids, future, job—what job? I was a mess. My thoughts were about as clear as the mirage of heat radiating from the highway; they made no sense, yet they pestered me through every mile of the Sonoran and Colorado deserts back to the Bay Area. What reaction would the Padres have? I rightly figured none.

What somewhat surprised me was that I did not hear from the manager. I considered John McNamara a friend of sorts, if only because he had guided me through several previous seasons in the minors and the major leagues when I was with Oakland. It was possible he may have even been instrumental in my being traded to San Diego, I didn't know. He had every right to be angry with my decision, but I never knew what his reaction was. To have confided in him may have been the mature thing to do, but with the game still confrontational between players and owners, I saw nothing good to result by letting him know what I was going through. Someone of my status had little bargaining power, and confiding in him would have only hurt my position. There was no need for him to know what I was feeling; he would have been no help.

About a month later I received the standard written notice from the Padres front office telling me that I had been placed on major-league baseball's disqualified list. I am not up-to-date on all the legalities, but I believe I remained a Padre for a few years until I was put into some kind of permanently retired category.

My decision to quit the game I loved was something I wished I never had to consider, and, yes, I should have been better prepared. I spent months trying to make sense of what I was going through, agonizing over what I knew was the right thing to do, but wondering if I should. My stomach was in knots; I couldn't sleep or eat. The bottom line was that as disappointed I was in my play, I was not able to do a thing about it. I was no longer able to play the game and meet even my own acceptable standards. Neither the trade to San Diego nor the Bavasi episode, though they offered nothing positive, had any influence of my decision to quit. I had just gotten too old to perform, and that hurt…a lot!

2

FREEDOM AT LAST

Trap ball, goal ball, fetch ball, one-eyed cat, and round ball were just some of the earliest primitive games that we call baseball. They were fun diversions from the tedium of everyday living when first played in the nineteenth and early twentieth centuries. As their popularity increased, numerous countries around the world played their own unique versions of the sport. The British game of stool ball is considered to be the basis for a game called rounders, supposedly the precursor to what is now America's pastime.

Baseball grew to have historical significance even as it suffered an obvious entanglement of opinions regarding its place of origin and true architect, both of which remain guesswork at best. The uncertainty and debate surrounding those findings have caused similar turmoil, and fall comfortably in line with other controversies the game has known. Ever since its inception, baseball has been rocked with disagreement and strife on and off the field while its followers have remained enthusiastically dedicated and passionate toward their chosen teams and players.

To put an end to the controversial speculations concerning the game's birthplace and its creator, in 1905 Albert Spalding appointed his friend, Abraham G. Mills, National League president in 1883 and 1884, the head of a fact-finding commission seeking answers that he hoped would end the ongoing uncertainties once and for all. Impassioned about wanting the game to have an American birthright, Spalding cleverly stacked the commission with members who believed baseball had an American birthright to counter those who supported the contention of Britain's Henry Chadwick that it had evolved from the English game of rounders.

The commission's ultimate finding was that a gentleman by the name of Abner Doubleday was the mastermind responsible for the game's genesis in 1839. It was of no concern to Spalding that no discovery specifically substantiated or legitimized that presumption, or that the commission's conclusion was never corroborated. The conflict of that decision was that the sparse evidence conveying that honor to Doubleday, who was born a New Yorker, and later became a career Army officer and General in the Civil War, came from only one brief mention of baseball in his letters and diaries of him reportedly asking for some baseball equipment. Exactly why he did, or what it was he wanted, no one knew. Nothing else was found to indicate that he had the slightest interest in the sport, and even his New York Times obituary in 1893 made no mention, or contained any references connecting him to the game.

Other prominent men such as Chadwick, John Montgomery Ward, Harry Wright, and the preeminent author of the game's rules, Alexander Cartwright, though more responsible for the growth of baseball in America, were overlooked and given no consideration for the honor. Like many others, they opposed the Commission's finding of Doubleday being the game's mastermind, but his dubious nomination received validation primarily from a supposedly fabricated story by an elderly gentleman, Abner Graves. In a letter to the commission, Graves told of seeing Doubleday assemble two teams in 1839, and make a drawing of a ball field in the dirt with a stick.

That Graves was five years old at the time of this alleged sighting, and Doubleday, who did live in Cooperstown as a young boy, would have then been twenty, places more doubt on Grave's submission. Moreover, Doubleday's family was known to have moved from Cooperstown the year before Grave's written testimony. Further confusion surrounds the doubtful conclusion because Graves, who spent time in an insane asylum later in life, could have mistaken a cousin, Demas Abner Doubleday, for Abner Doubleday, who was also in Cooperstown at the time, as the man he saw drawing in the dirt. None of this was ever fully investigated by the Mills Commission.

Stronger evidence against bestowing such a glorious honor on Doubleday was that he was attending the United States Military Academy at West Point, New York, in 1839 when the commission made its decision.

The ambiguity surrounding Doubleday's selection as the game's founder held until 1953 when the U.S. Congress declared Alexander Cartwright the father of the game of baseball. It was Cartwright who was more reasonably thought to have diagrammed what may have been the first baseball diamond, and proposed many of the rules on which the game is based.

● ● ●

Discovered hieroglyphics have proven that the game of baseball, or something similar, was known to have existed back in the days of ancient Egypt. England, Russia, Romania, and Germany are among the many countries that played a semblance of the game a century or two ago, but no matter to whom or from where the honor of its beginning rests, the game has been enjoyed by several cultures worldwide.

The first game of baseball is reported to have been played in Pittsfield, Massachusetts, in 1791. In time, what was known as "the Massachusetts game" would acquiesce to rule changes, and give way to "the New York game." The game's growth was unstoppable, and continued until it blossomed into the entertaining and financial monster it is now while finding cures for the many problems it experienced on and off the field.

In the late 1800s, owners fought with and against each other trying to get the upper hand not only on the players, but also on some of their own. Players signed contracts at will, jumping from team to team, and/or league to league, moving to wherever the most money would take them. The owners were compliant and complicit, and it was not inconceivable that the stealth and greed of both parties would have one player surreptitiously under contract to two teams at the same time in one year.

Gambling was an uncontrollable habit for more than one player, and multiple paychecks were usually needed to defray the accumulated losses. The number of hits, runs, and errors that might be made in a game were only a few of the outcomes that drew eager bettors, and there was no shortage of needy players who worked willingly with gamblers to throw or fix a game. In a similar stance taken by today's free agents, loyalty was often where the most money could be found.

In 1901 Ban Johnson organized and pushed the American League into existence with a concerted lean toward improving conditions, instilling a decency within the game that was unknown, and bringing more respect to its unruly nature. With gambling, bribery, and scandals the order of the day, his objective was to provide a more family- and female-friendly game.

As president of the Western League in the minor-league system, Johnson fought to gain respect for the umpires, and reduce the abuse they were taking from players and owners. He wanted decorum on the field, fined or suspended players who used foul language, and sought a reversal of the rough-and-tumble image for which the game had become known.

As Johnson's more dignified game gained favor, interest in it grew uncontrollably. Small towns began forming teams, and larger cities organized baseball clubs. Proving to be a competitive and emotional outlet for much of the country, it was soon considered "America's" sport, thanks in large part to it being recognized as our National Pastime by the same Albert Spalding who had honored Abner Doubleday.

The players ran the earliest baseball games themselves, but seeing the possibility of a lucrative investment, businessmen moved in and took control. One of their first concerns was to control the gamblers, and the sale of liquor, both of which were driving down attendance and affecting income.

Amateur and raucous play slowly took on a more genteel look, and as more and more teams were established, more exacting playing rules were formulated, and the game's organizational structure improved. Alexander Cartwright is credited with having established a new set of guidelines for play in 1845. His own team that year, the New York Knickerbockers, played the first game under his new directives, only to lose 23-1 to the New York Baseball Club. Cartwright established a list of twenty new rules, the chief change being that no longer could a runner be 'soaked," or put out by opponents throwing at, and hitting him, with the ball. He proposed that a batter would be out should his fly ball be caught on one bounce, that a game would be decided by the team that first got "twenty-one" aces or runs, and that the base paths would remain at a distance of seventy-five feet each. It would be a few years before nine innings would determine the length of a game, and almost ten years before the bases would be pushed to their present ninety-foot distance.

Other rule changes occurred when it was thought their implementation would improve the sport. The flat bat, used primarily for bunting, was outlawed in the late 1800s. The batsman, who at one point was given his base after eight "unfair" balls by the pitcher, had that count reduced to four for the "walk," or "base on balls," as a new century began. Rule changes sparked public interest, and to further increase attendance, teams resorted to raiding the better players on other teams with under-the-table money. To ensure that better talent could be recruited, and to allay rising costs and travel expenses, owners sought donations and sponsors. Admission fees went from a nickel to the unheard of amount of twenty-five cents!

One definition for the term "dead-ball," as this early period was called, referred to the practice of a pitcher intimidating the batter by hitting him, or his bat, without a swing being made. The batter was not awarded first base even though he'd been hit, the ball was simply ruled "dead." With that in effect, pitchers threw at hitters hoping to lessen the effectiveness of their swings. The ball was also ruled dead should it strike the umpire.

The awarding of a base to the batter being hit was not mandated until the American Association used it as a penalty against pitchers in 1884. Before that, a pitcher was fined from ten to fifty dollars when judged to have intentionally thrown at a hitter, but no other penalties were imposed.

The more easily understandable reason, and the one historically accepted for this period of baseball to be referred to as the "dead ball" era was the ball itself. At the end of the nineteenth and into the twentieth centuries, it was common that an entire game would be played using only one ball, after which the victorious team received it as a trophy. Darkened by spit, tobacco juice, and dirt made it almost invisible to players as the game progressed, and it was softened by the pounding it had taken to the point of unraveling. With the increased difficulty to then hit it with any authority, it was considered "dead." This gave rise to a period of "small-ball" strategies. Bunting, stealing bases, the hit-and-run, and place hitting became popular. To exacerbate the issue and save the expense of a new three dollar baseball, the tightfisted owners required the players to retrieve balls hit into the stands and return them to play.

It was the construction of a livelier, cork-center ball around 1911 that brought a change to the game and its strategies, and in a few years the game had an altogether different look, in large part because of the emergence and influence of Babe Ruth. A superb pitcher turned superb hitter, he transformed the sport, bringing the home run and the long ball into prominence, making the game much more exciting, and entrenching it deeper into the hearts of the American public. When he walloped a season high twenty-nine home runs in 1919, the "dead-ball" era was all but over.

Baseball has since had a history that is both stored and storied. Year after year, statistics are compiled that have provided a litany of notable achievements and disappointments, giving baseball junkies a continual flow of data to devour and argue. Some players are remembered for the numbers they produced, and some numbers remind us of the players who produced them. Records continue to be broken, some with a purity that is unquestioned, others with a criminality that severely taints their accomplishment, yet the game remains a continuous source of pleasure for the historically minded.

As baseball grew in popularity, it was marred by battles on and off the field between players and owners and fans, in no particular order or combination. It has survived societal, cultural, and financial upheavals, even criminal activities. None other than one of the game's greatest, Ty Cobb, had long been accused of pistol-whipping an African-American man to death. This was never proven nor was it ever determined that he and another Hall of Famer, Tris Speaker, were members of the Ku Klux Klan, as had been rumored. Cobb and perhaps the game's greatest player, Babe Ruth, were let off the hook more than once because of their spirited shenanigans. In more recent times, a prominent major-league pitcher spent seven years in prison for his alleged attempt on someone's life, and numerous others have spent time incarcerated for their disreputable associations, or other unlawful actions.

Quite possibly the most prominent black eye the game would ever receive was the Black Sox scandal, and the throwing of the World Series in 1919. Despite a court's acquittal, Judge Kennesaw Mountain Landis banned the bribed culprits for life. His decision set a standard, and some seventy years later when Pete Rose, baseball's all-time hit leader, violated baseball's one stringently written rule that forbids betting on games, he too was banned. Whether he will ever be honored by membership in the Hall of Fame is now one of the game's more-controversial issues.

Google "baseball criminal" for an interesting read. You will find that the sport is no more than an extension of society. Players were far from exemplary citizens before and after the turn of the twentieth century, but from its inception and for decades thereafter, playing professional baseball was a handsome living for those who could. Not considered the noblest of vocations, baseball attracted many young men who followed their dreams when given the opportunity. The game has not been pure, and never will be, but its entertainment value has continued to capture and captivate its fans.

Even in these modern times, when more well-reasoned individuals and decorum are expected, official police records show the many indiscretions amassed by players and managers, including a variety of illicit acts such as drug possession, sexual assault, drunkenness, and paternity suits. Who really knows how many federal tax and IRS difficulties, marital problems, spousal attacks, DUI arrests, and fights among teammates and their managers on and off the baseball field there have been.

Present-day baseball has survived its controversial drug years with an array of players getting caught with powdered noses, bloodshot and glazed eyes, tainted urine, and punctured backsides. There are players who have been combative with fans, a la Ty Cobb, and others who have torn up clubhouses, or just been thorns in the sides of team owners. Today's powerful Major League Baseball Players Association will stand up and fight back whenever punishment is internally placed on one of its own, much like when Cobb's teammates refused to play after he was legitimately suspended for his attack on a fan whose handicap was having lost eight of his fingers in an industrial accident. Cobb's combative on-field behavior saw him wrongly accused of certain other physical attacks and racial indiscretions throughout his career.

Maybe little or nothing has changed. The game continues to find itself enmeshed in one legality or another. Much of what today's problem athletes errantly do never hits the papers. Organizations silence reports of internal problems and extreme behavior because of the talent at fault, and the embarrassment these outbreaks might bring should they be made public. Whether that silence is justifiable can be questioned, but of the 1200 players on today's major-league rosters, few cause significant disruptions.

That baseball might distance itself from its legal problems is unrealistic. Players have been given second and third chances and leniency has taken the sting out of punishment. In my day, when drugs first appeared and questions were raised about what penalties should be imposed, one of my Oakland teammates opined that, "The first time you get caught, you should be done." Righteous as that might have been, it was somewhat reactionary, but three such strikes before you were banned from the game seemed reasonable, and more appropriate.

The actions of the executive director and his assistants of the Major League Baseball Players Association, one of the most powerful unions in the country, have saved many a player. One pitcher was given seven reprieves and never did get straightened out. There's no doubt that being left-handed with a 94-mph fastball influenced his catlike existence. I spoke to him after his fifth fall off the wagon, and he assured me that he had learned his lesson. It was only a month or two later that he disappeared—for days. No one knew where he was, and neither could he recall his whereabouts when he finally reappeared. His career was thereafter short-lived. It is noble to give someone a second chance, but the owners fool no one about why they protect the "better" players; they have no other choice, they need them.

The modern era has seen a toning down of the quarreling, brawling, cheating, gambling, and dishonesty of baseball's early years, and the game has taken on a more civilized demeanor, but it hasn't completely lost its dark moments. Lively personalities and interesting teams remain to provide additional entertainment in one way or other. An interesting read would be *The Mustache Gang*," an overblown recounting of what were considered the uncivilized exploits of my Oakland A's teams. Our in-house fighting and turmoil with Charley Finley made for colorful reporting, but no more than what other teams did that followed in our footsteps.

There is no comparing some of the behavior of my shaggy-coiffed teammates to the raucous, uncouth, drug-riddled, and often unprincipled deportment of the New York Mets teams of the mid-1980s. Many notable members of the Pittsburgh Pirates during that same decade confessed to drug use inside the clubhouse for which the Commissioner of Baseball lightly slapped their wrists with suspensions. For testifying against their drug providers the players received immunity from prosecution. Sexual exploits by major-league players have also been known to occur after the playing of the National Anthem in locations not far from home plate, but out of sight.

The most recent scandal, the use of performance-enhancing drugs and the congressional hearings it has provoked, has embroiled baseball in a battle over who truly is the game's rightful home-run king. A couple of bloated individuals wrestled that crown from Henry Aaron, though many hardliners do not consider them fit to wear it. In that same context, other star players have seen their own offensive exploits diminished by the investigations, and will not know their place in history for a long time, if ever. The game has survived the PED scandal as it has all of its other problems, and will continue to do so.

Not to be ignored, even umpires have been involved in their own unhealthy confrontations. The behavior of today's players shows respect for these arbiters unlike that seen around the turn of the twentieth century when the men in blue would sometimes be unexpectedly attacked by players or fans, maybe both, for what were considered errant calls. One might have very easily been spit on a la the 1996 Roberto Alomar incident when he intentionally spewed in the face of Umpire John Hirschbeck over a called third strike. Claims have been raised that Alomar's action was precipitated by the umpire mocking his ethnicity, but whether true or not, his nasty reprisal was a disrespectful and unsanitary form of retaliation.

Being physically attacked, called every nasty name available, chided and ridiculed, and forced to hide in a hotel room to escape a rowdy crowd was nothing odd to deal with. It was all in a day's work for the game's earliest officials. They were abused by players, fans, and owners with such treatment further encouraged because each game had but one decision maker, compared to the quartet that monitor every game today. One vintage umpire is known to have taken it upon himself to return the abuse he received by attacking a player with a bat, only to have to quickly run for his life.

Today's players are choir boys compared to the wild jocks of old who pulled out all the stops in their attempts to win. When an umpire was distracted by the game's action, a baserunner might have been held by the belt to prevent him from scoring, or thinking he was unnoticed, purposely cut the corner without touching the bag as he rounded the bases instead of following the required route. It wasn't uncommon at all for players to do things that were unsportsmanlike simply because they could. Cheating was a healthy part of the game, and if a cheater was not caught in the act, why wouldn't he do so again? Would it not be right to then say that the recent steroid scandal was simply another chapter in a long line of the game's insolence?

Baseball's growth has often been challenging. Immigrants arrived and fought their way onto teams; players jumped teams for more pay; owners raided rosters, and the Negro Leagues that began in the 1920s, remained isolated, ignored for decades, not because of inferior play, but because of the contempt for black players. Gamblers polluted the game, and despite the 1919 Chicago Black Sox scandal, betting on games continued. When the impact of a world war turned hundreds of players into patriots, the game was left in the care of women. The All-American Girls Professional Baseball League kept the game alive. And, in 1994, after decades of squabbling with players, the owners padlocked the stadiums over their differences, and went so far as to cancel that year's World Series.

When the Dodgers and Giants decided to take their bats and balls westward, giving rise to new cities gaining major-league status, the owners relinquished none of their domination and control of the game, or its players. Both sides got along because they had to, but the pot had begun to boil. Nothing in the game's history that involved money had gone smoothly, but what was about to happen would dwarf earlier problems. Believing they had been held captive and under the owner's authority far too long, the players banded together in the '60s and went after what they'd been denied. The game would enter a period of transformation that would be unprecedented.

The treatment of players in today's financially exorbitant world is monumentally unlike the imprisoning monopolistic hold exerted by the earliest owners, and those who followed, until the mid-1970s. My teammates and I played under their giant proverbial "thumb." Standing as one during the 1972 Collective Bargaining Agreement discussions, we boldly voted to go out on strike when negotiations stalled over owner contributions to our player benefit plan. Our walkout was an epoch-making response to an apathetic and condescending group who misjudged the seriousness of our resolve, the first in modern professional sports. It lasted one day short of two weeks.

Changes came quickly, though the initial concessions were small. The minimum salary jumped to $16,000. The owners conceded to a huge increase in their contributions to our pension fund, and accepted the practice of salary arbitration which has been an unabashed boon to the players while adversely affecting their bottom line.

Today's player has much to say about his future, even to the point of dictating the team or teams for which he will play. Owners control little and have abdicated their throne, but they freely negotiated the present position in which they find themselves. It was amazing to see how the pendulum constantly swung in our favor with every negotiation after years of involuntary bondage. Ownership gave away the store in every work stoppage, which emphasized the health of the industry despite their constant denial to the contrary.

But the owners were not without their wiles. They deftly manipulated city and state governments into building new stadiums; developed new marketing and advertising strategies; contracted profitable licensing and merchandising agreements, and negotiated lucrative television, cable, and Internet contracts. They shrewdly made the game more enjoyable, fan friendly, and exciting by lowering the pitching mound, shrinking the strike zone, and introducing the designated hitter. World Series night games, and inter-league play sparked attendance and greater followings, as did smaller playing fields, and a Disney-kind of experience in beautiful new ballparks.

Until free agency in 1976 restructured the game, early ownership bordered on the miserly. Several owners, if not all, were known to be very tightfisted. Many were penny-pinchers simply because they could be. Charlie Finley's penurious ways were well documented by everyone under his employ, and when he saw how free agency was going to affect his bottom line, he moved to protect himself by selling his higher-priced players. Commissioner Bowie Kuhn intervened and nullified the transactions. Considered by many to be a renegade for his off-the-wall suggestions and proposals, Finley proposed contractual innovations that if adopted would have positively affected every owner's financial position.

Known to be the notorious lone wolf among the owners, he suggested freedom for every player every year because he saw the potential destruction that free agency would have on his finances. His proposition was given cursory scrutiny by his colleagues, much in the same way they viewed his other ideas. Permitting free agency every year was a radical position to take at a time when it was undecided just how this new contractual system would affect salaries. Being ever the businessman who had turned his idea of selling group disability insurance to doctors into an income of millions of dollars, Finley foresaw the sound reasoning behind the one-year deals. He thought it the only correct and sensible way to pay players.

Paying everyone on a year-to-year basis dependent on what they had done the year before made perfect sense to him. Had it been adopted the multiyear abyss in which many owners now find themselves while hoping a player will duplicate his most-recent performance might have been avoided. The other owners were deathly afraid of what the game would look like under free agency. They found themselves at a loss, but what could they do? Their fears were well founded, yet they disregarded the wisdom of Finley and agreed to, and approved, a financial structure that dug deeply into their pockets.

A close and realistic look at Finley's proposal revealed its practicality for the owners, but negotiating its final composition with the players may not have been easy. There would have been two major obstacles the employers would face, the solidarity of the players union and Marvin Miller, its executive director. Both would have fought this, and any similar proposal, for sure. The idea of having players moving every year could very well have become unwieldy and chaotic, but it would have saved the owners millions of dollars. Players would have bought into this singular system if it was their only avenue, but the union, luckily headed by Miller, might have just as easily out-slugged their bosses on that issue too. No one knew just how high salaries would go, but with what they are now, one-year deals could have been a godsend to the owners.

Had Finley's proposal been enacted, some owners might still have sought long-term contracts in retaliation, triggering a court battle or two. What then? What would the courts decide? Under one-year contracts, would the present arbitration process have been instituted? Would the owners have abided by whatever the new policies were, or would they have continued to operate with the greed and infighting they had exhibited among themselves in the past? Would there have been a signing frenzy? No one will ever know what that different scenario might have produced.

One well-known owner in his trading wars with the late George Steinbrenner, decades removed from Finley's initial attempt to reform the system, had this to say about all the owners in general: "Everyone is out to screw everyone else."

The historical avarice among owners indicates that compliance would not have been easy, no matter what was negotiated. Who knows if Finley's concept would have been better than the policy put in place. It was an interesting idea from a man who had many. Because he had a mule for a mascot, several of his contemporaries probably considered him, and the animal, appropriate companions.

The idea of one year ownership of a player by the owners was viewed with trepidation by the head of the players union, Marvin Miller. He saw its validity. He understood how it would have definitely held down salaries for his players. Very relieved that the owners didn't see how its adoption would benefit them, Miller negotiated servitude of six years, rather than the ten sought by the owners, before the players could walk free. With that victory, and the other being salary arbitration, salaries have reached magical heights.

There was a day when it was considered inconceivable that a player would make $100,000 a year. The public was outraged that a player had the nerve to ask for that much, but today that amount is given without hesitation, and in a strange twist of reality, there are rabid followers of the game who now believe that "so-and-so" deserves upward of $20 million! The man on the street is now siding with players!

Several stories have circulated about uncashed checks being found in lockers and training rooms for sums exceeding $100,000, and the players whose names followed "Pay to" never missing them. Years ago, before salaries ballooned, I know of one star who missed approximately half a season with injuries, yet he was given a half-million dollar raise just so he wouldn't feel bad! Granted, he was a star player, but what does that say about the mentality of ownership?

I was never in favor of reporting salaries. I don't know why or how the practice started, but its effect on the game has not been positive. The public has become involved in an area in which they do not belong. Fans will say they pay the athlete's salaries and have a right to verbalize their displeasure, and the First Amendment may arguably give them that right, but dollar signs have distorted the expected abilities of the athletes, something that seems misunderstood by far too many inside and outside of the game.

Contracts are no longer simple documents. The big ones are no doubt complex, in need of lawyers, financial planners, and tax consultants. It cannot be easy for an organization to maintain its sanity while remaining steadfast to the specific parameters of all forty contracts it must consider. Foremost is the monetary consideration, but attention must be paid to the length and terms of each contract as it relates to the age of the player, added incentives, the legality of its meaning and structure, the probability of deferring millions of dollars in compensation and, most important, the need for a particular talent that is never an absolute, but which affects everything else. Certainly not forgotten is the power of the agents who have a dominant role in the entire process, and too often have the owners running scared.

Athletes have always been bigger than life with the money they make magnifying and clouding their performances. Once the public knows what an athlete earns, they expect his performance to be commensurate and will ridicule anything less, seemingly never understanding that money is not the sole reason for a player's performance. Most players are motivated by having their pride hurt, and realizing they may lose their jobs. I can't say with any certainty that the prospect of a lucrative multiyear big-money deal might motivate someone to put forth a better effort in any particular year, but after being awarded untold millions, he simply doesn't want to be embarrassed. Professional athletes are too vain and proud to consider giving anything than their best. Even so, yearly performances do not come with guarantees. The game is too difficult.

Does ownership understand the potential of that volatility? I would like to believe they do, but it remains that year after year they are forced to spend and spend. Millions and millions of dollars sit idle as deferred payments to be paid to nonproductive players. You can argue the judiciousness of the owners giving away so much money, but their backs are too often against the wall. There is not much they can do except believe and remain optimistic. They are involved in a situation that is a total crapshoot.

Before the free agency system became a reality, players received little more than small advances in salary, usually through exhausting and frustrating negotiations. Because of the early efforts of Marvin Miller, the minimum salary increased, and it was nice to get five dollars more every day for meals, and single rooms on the road. But once the dam burst in 1975, the ship sharply turned course. What players like the late Curt Flood, Dave McNally, and Andy Messersmith courageously did when they challenged the reserve clause changed the game of baseball. It took great fortitude for them to fight the oppressive system in place, and all players in the game should forever be in their debt for what they sacrificed.

Curt Flood especially lost much for his bold and brave objection to the treatment he would no longer accept. A gifted, three-time All-Star with the St. Louis Cardinals, winner of seven Gold Gloves and a couple of World Championships, making nearly a $100,000 a year, in 1969 he refused to accept his trade to the Philadelphia Phillies. He felt that his life was established in St. Louis with one of the game's greatest organizations and cities, and though he'd accepted his first trade from Cincinnati to the Cardinals, he was not going to accept this second trade to what he considered a racist town with a dilapidated stadium.

Still fighting the taunts, name calling, and racial prejudice of his early baseball days because of his color, living through the radical protests and heated social unrest of the '60s over the Vietnam war, seeing the rise of Black Power and the enormous upheaval the country was experiencing on so many college campuses, he told major-league baseball that he would no longer be its slave; he was not going to accept his new assignment. Uneasy over the political and social climates of the times, and fighting for what he felt were his and America's values of freedom and self-determination, he sued major-league baseball and its 100-year-old reserve clause that had kept players anchored to one team. His argument was that his trade violated the antitrust laws and the Thirteenth Amendment, which barred slavery and involuntary servitude. He wanted a say in which city he would play, and it was not Philadelphia.

When I read my first professional contract, signed in 1960, I could not believe what I thought was the clarity of the traditional "reserve clause," and was more shocked at what I felt was its ambiguous and incorrect interpretation over the years. This was years before Flood. What I was reading said simply and straightforward that Kansas City owned me for the year of the contract, and for the next year only. Should I not agree to sign for that second year, accept the required pay cut, and play out the year, I would then be free to go to another club.

I remember reading it repeatedly, wondering what it was I was missing because it certainly didn't give Kansas City total control of me until they decided they'd had enough. Owner domination of players had been a naturally accepted phenomenon fueled by tradition. But should the clause have been interpreted the way it seemed to read, the decision to "play out my option," and take advantage of the freedom that offered, would not have been as easy as it may have sounded. What if no other club wanted me? The very best players who had the power could test the clause, but it might not go so well for the rest of us. Personal doubts and the ruthlessness of ownership in negotiations were important considerations against such a move. As they would in the '80s, they could have colluded to not sign anyone. It took years before some very courageous players challenged the legitimacy of their imprisonment.

Represented by Marvin Miller, the shrewd economist and battle-tested former labor leader chosen to head the players union, Flood took on America's pastime, and though the union voted to support his lawsuit, no player would testify for him during the ordeal. Miller retained the services of former Supreme Court Justice Arthur Goldberg to handle the case, and it went all the way to our highest court. Having heard this argument twice previously in 1922 and 1953—and stonewalling it both times—the Supreme Court would rule against Flood, and again in favor of the owners, simply following tradition, and not wanting to dirty its hands by altering a game so beloved by America.

Two later Acts of Congress, one in 1997 and particularly the other in 1998, repealed a portion of the antitrust exemption. The Curt Flood Act of 1998 gave the Players Association the same rights as the unions in professional football and basketball, but left intact the antitrust exemption regarding the reserve clause, relocation, the minor leagues, and broadcast rights. Furthermore, the Collective Bargaining Agreement Marvin Miller negotiated in 1968 between the owners and the union that has been continually upgraded has, for all practical purposes, made baseball's antitrust exemption irrelevant.

Losing his case, Flood was left dangling, and after sitting out the 1970 season, he played again briefly, but his career was effectively finished. He left baseball considered a pariah for having contested its will.

McNally and Messersmith, steadfast in their resolve despite the court battle lost by Flood, had a somewhat easier time gaining their own and everyone's freedom. Deciding to play out the one-year restriction imposed by the clause as I had interpreted it in the player contract, both put their fate in the hands of an arbitrator, Paul Seitz, who decided in their favor. McNally was considering retirement at the time, but nevertheless continued the legal battle. Messersmith became more incensed about winning his freedom because of some nasty negotiating tactics by then Dodger General Manager Al Campanis. The stalwart stance taken by both players opened the doors for others to follow.

Today's players know little of these pioneers that have given them their freedom and financial security, yet they reap the rewards of their sacrifices. Neither do they know much about the history of the game, or of the players who came before them, those who transformed the game that now gives them so much. That in itself is another telltale sign of what has taken place not only in the game, but also in society. It's all about what can you do for me: "Here is what I want...you owe me."

Baseball in the nineteenth century was not a very lucrative investment, but it was growing in popularity, and with that came problems. The game wasn't an easy sell, and though it wasn't floundering, it was definitely in need of professional organization of some kind to make it viable and sustaining. The players were tiring of their restrictive conditions, and with salaries not much better than those of the average workers of the day, they were lured by larger paychecks and would sign with anyone, going from one team to another year after year. This lack of loyalty did not sit well with ownership. Recognizing that the jumping of contracts and teams by the players was contributing to their financial dilemma because it allowed for no consistency or team cohesion, the owners got together in 1879 and unofficially decided that each club could "reserve," or exempt from being signed by another club, five of its players. They could do this every year. As the years passed, this reserve list was increased until in 1887 it reached fourteen, and with the smaller rosters of these early clubs, this was just about every player they had, and in some cases, the entire team. But, as were the times, the system didn't work especially well because owners, in their own inimitable fashion, started raiding the "reserved players" on other clubs.

Being "reserved" didn't sound that bad to the players at first because they felt honored to be retained, but as the years passed, that honor, coupled with other ownership constraints, lost much of its appeal. With clubs losing money, owners tightened their purse strings and explored every way they could to increase profits. Players were forced to pay for their uniforms and upkeep; had their meal money cut; were housed in shabby hotels for which they sometimes had to pay; had to clean the stadiums after games; work the turnstiles, and retrieve foul balls hit into the stands. Fines were imposed for missing games, no matter the reason. With salaries of less than $1500 a year for most players, and meal money reduced to fifty cents a day, it was understandable that something be done.

In 1885, hoping for the benefits of whatever their banding together might bring, the Brotherhood of Professional Base Ball Players was formed, the first union of its kind in professional sports, orchestrated through the efforts of John Montgomery Ward, himself a player and a lawyer. As the Brotherhood's first president, he was not allowed a seat at the negotiating table with the owners in an effort to get the union recognized until 1887 when the forces behind every National League club and Albert Spalding, the National League president, finally agreed to meet with player representatives at their winter gatherings. Ward proposed that a peaceful and congenial agreement, a cooperative between both sides, be worked out to halt the underhandedness and lack of fiscal responsibility of the owners. Rejecting his plea, the owners further strengthened their oligarchy by placing more restrictive financial restraints on the players.

During the winter meetings of 1888, a proposal by John Brush, owner of the Indianapolis National League club, was adopted and a classification system allowing no player to be paid more than $2500 a year was created. What that final figure would be took into account not only a player's on-field performance, but also his personal conduct. When told of this, the players needed nothing more to persuade them to follow through on the ongoing discussions they were having to go on strike.

They decided to walk out on July 4, 1889, a big day financially for the owners because of the doubleheaders scheduled, and the larger crowds that two games instead of one would bring. Never in favor of the strike in principal, Ward was able to stall it by talking the players into finding financial backing from each of their cities, and forming their own league. The players had been holding secret talks about doing something for themselves for some time, and Ward was personally provoked when he discovered that he had been sold to the Washington Nationals for $12,000 while his own salary had been frozen at $2,500. He was incensed, and his demand to receive a percentage of the sales price caused a serious impasse until the sale was eventually nullified.

The monopolistic arrangement between players and management had to end, and wanting freedom from the owners' grips and the reserve clause, the players union took Ward's radical suggestion, and with his guidance formed the Player's League in 1890. Because of his own powers of persuasion among the players, Ward secured the defection of more than half of the National League players, and the new league went head-to-head against the National League and the third active league, the American Association.

The Player's League attracted the best players, and was well received by spectators. It encountered no difficulty with players jumping from one league to another. The courts found nothing amiss with that because of the rights given players by the Fourteenth Amendment. But a problem surfaced when the players, who knew how to play the game, knew nothing about how to run it. Under constant pressure from the National League, and short of the necessary funding for expenses and the profit-sharing plan they had put in place for themselves, the players needed further backing and sought venture capitalists.

Without realizing what would happen by doing so, they found themselves back in the very position they had fought so hard to escape. The venture capitalists that became the new owners of the various clubs instantly assumed control of the finances, but, not realizing what they had gotten themselves into, were quickly drowning in red ink, and surreptitiously began selling their teams back to the National League. The fiscal strength of the National League prevailed, and the Player's League folded after only one season.

Ward had done all he could to propose compromise and cooperation between the owners and the players long before anyone saw the promise of its potential, but whether through a misunderstanding of its value, ownership greed, or the naïveté of both sides, it never materialized. Had it survived, quite possibly it would have transformed sports ownership, and the relationship between owners and players forever.

The formation of the Federal League in 1913 was the last of the serious attempts to change the game, and circumvent the reserve clause. The two major leagues, the American and National, were struggling, and many players jumped at the more lucrative offerings of the new league. With no restraint of trade, competition for talent flourished and player salaries skyrocketed, a historic harbinger of what havoc free agency would bring. But after two years of play, difficulties within their own operations, the constant pressure, disruptive measures, and eventual financial buyouts of their franchises by the American and National league owners, the Federal League folded.

Money had again won. The lone holdout in the surrender of the franchises was the club in Baltimore. Its owners refused to accept the cash payoff to go away as the other clubs had, and filed a separate antitrust lawsuit against all the Federal League traitors and the American League and National League owners. Once again, however, and after many years in abeyance, the Supreme Court in 1922 ruled that the Sherman Antitrust Act did not apply to baseball. The reserve clause remained alive and healthy.

In the late '60s and early '70s, a few players attempted to play out their second season unsigned as the reserve clause in their contracts allowed them to do. Though no legal precedents were established, the owners were nonetheless leery of having the clause tested should it go to court. The seriousness of the player's threat eventually died when the owners offered them considerably better contracts. Management wisely did not want to chance the "we don't know for sure if it's legal or not" deadline when the challenge to the reserve clause would have taken effect. These situations were nothing compared to what ownership would be forced to confront when Messrs. Dave McNally and Andy Messersmith held their contractual ground in 1975.

The owners had mistakenly argued before the Supreme Court during the Curt Flood fight in 1969 that the issue of free agency should remain a collective bargaining issue, and not one to be decided by the courts. This was a monumental proposal and one that would soon come back to crush them financially.

The Supreme Court, deciding in favor of baseball, not Flood, had based its decision more on the tradition of the game than on the issue of Flood's servitude. They threw the weight of a possible reversal of the antitrust exemption the game enjoyed back to Congress for a ruling. The reserve clause would continue to stand as it always had. It read as follows:

10. (a) On or before December 20 (or if a Sunday, then the next preceding business day) of the year next following the last playing season covered by this contract, the Club may tender to the Player a contract for the term of that year by mailing the same to the Player at his address following his signature hereto, or if none be given, then at his last address of record with the Club. If prior to the March 1 next succeeding said December 20, the Player and the Club have not agreed upon the terms of such contract, then on or before 10 days after said March 1, THE CLUB SHALL HAVE THE RIGHT BY WRITTEN NOTICE TO THE PLAYER AT SAID ADDRESS TO RENEW THIS CONTRACT FOR THE PERIOD OF ONE YEAR ON THE SAME TERMS, except that the amount payable to the Player shall be such as the Club shall fix in said notice; provided, however, that said amount, if fixed by a Major League Club, shall be an amount payable at a rate not less than 80 per cent of the rate stipulated for the next preceding year and at a rate not less than 70 per cent of the rate stipulated for the year immediately prior to the next preceding game.

Why the owners agreed during the Flood hearings to make the issue of free agency part of the collective bargaining agreement with the players remains a mystery. The answer would be astonishing, especially because historically the courts had been deciding in their favor. Therefore, in arbitration over the freedom of McNally and Messersmith, the arbitrator, Paul Seitz, reminded the owners of their concession, and gave the players their freedom. The owners promptly fired Mr. Seitz the next day. Several appeals were struck down, and free agency was instituted in 1976 through negotiations between the owners and the players union.

Players gained, and now have all the power. Their treatment is light years from the servitude of decades past. The owners made many surprising decisions when my teammates and I were at war with them. We won every battle, even in the courts, and as the tables continued to turn, ownership has more or less been resigned to their subservience, almost a reversal of roles. Instead of banding together, and standing up against us, their collective greed had them at each others throats. The rumors I heard during the times we struck, that some owners wanted to break the stalemate and settle the issues, must have been true. They continually complained they were broke, but always capitulated and paid higher salaries, which have become astronomical, and sometimes absurd. And in a strange twist of irony, it has been said that the chief agitator, and the one most responsible for ending the first player strike in 1972, was none other than my bombastic renegade owner, Charles O. Finley. The man may have been unpredictable, but he was smarter than given credit for.

Approximately thirty years ago, in an organizational staff meeting during spring training, all of us members of the player development staff were told that the most recent annual salary given one of the major-league players, $1.5 million, was all the organization could afford, and that we would need to develop new players to fill future holes because players reaching that level of pay would be moved or traded.

So what happened? The very next winter, salaries jumped to $3 million! Ownership couldn't stop their boat from leaking and cannot even today. The general manager who made that statement is still active today, doling out millions in another organization.

After I retired and the animosity between players and owners continued, the monies in the game kept increasing in phenomenal amounts. I thought surely both sides would eventually sit down and negotiate something to solidify the game for the sake of everyone for years to come, as Ward had attempted a century before. There was a lean in that direction, but the owners again missed maybe their greatest opportunity to regain some control when in 1994 they canceled the World Series. This was a monumental happening, the results of which cemented both the strength of the union, and the divide of ownership.

The owners inflicted more havoc on their own by accepting a luxury tax. In effect they fined one another! Only a few teams have ever paid this tax, but again they shot some of their own in the foot. And when they slyly, but quite obviously, and foolishly, stood their ground in the '80s, refusing to sign players in the off-season, the courts accused them of collusion, costing them nearly $300 million to be divided among the same affected athletes they did not want to pay in the first place. Even their attempts to not sign players went awry.

No matter what has or will take place, baseball will survive. Nothing can hurt the purity of the sport. Despite more than 100 years of servitude during which the public enjoyed and clamored for their heroes of the diamond, all the while criticizing the greed of some, the same adoration or more is accorded today's free spirits who make millions and are accepted with open arms. The battles that began behind closed doors and in dingy, dark offices, are carried on in the openness of today's society with unimaginable interest. The thrilling sound of "Play Ball" has not lost its magic. But, oh, how things have changed!

3

YESTERDAYS

In the late 1800s, the bleak and severe weather conditions during the first three months of the year north of the Mason-Dixon Line forced several major-league owners to look more seriously for southern locations where their clubs could train in the spring. Their hope was that the more desirable weather conditions and temperate climates would lead to their team being better prepared for the upcoming season. Albert Spalding, owner of the Chicago White Stockings, made an unprecedented move by finding what he thought was the perfect southern location in 1886.

Any city below the ill-defined line of demarcation between the free state of Pennsylvania and the slave state of Maryland was considered to be in the South, and therefore perceived to have the warmer and milder climate that seemed more suitable for these spring camps. The city that caught Spalding's attention was Hot Springs, Arkansas. It would come to be known as the first southern town in which clubs would train.

Besides the city's more pleasing temperatures that Spalding thought would inspire greater efforts from his players, was the added attraction of the city's therapeutic, and naturally bubbling, warm mineral baths. Spalding and his manager, Cap Anson, trusted that the heated waters would dissolve some of the extra poundage some of their athletes may have added over the winter while diluting some of the excessive amounts of alcohol they might have consumed. To round out what they believed a well-designed, and more than adequate conditioning program would be the opportunity for the team to climb and hike the nearby Hot Springs Mountain, and the many trails in the Ouachita National Forest.

It wasn't long before other major- and minor-league teams, numerous Negro League and House of David clubs, and individual players made Hot Springs their early season choice as well. Babe Ruth, who could have been the "poster child" for the city's heated pools, made it one of his favorite stops. If anyone needed the hot baths, it was the Bambino. He more than anyone knew the merits of flushing his system, and sweating away what off-season weight he always seemed to carry.

In the long run, selecting Hot Springs may not have been Spalding's wisest decision, not because it wasn't warm enough, but because of a number of other drawbacks the city offered the players. The mineral baths were only one of the attractions that drew thousands of tourists to the city every year. When Anson discovered how frequently his players were entertaining themselves at the local card clubs, pool rooms, dance halls, gambling houses, and brothels, he was not pleased. Even more annoying were the many unwanted requests for advances on their upcoming salaries because of the money being spent, lost, or wasted at those places.

Yet despite these negatives that must have similarly affected other clubs, the city remained a popular training spot.

From the first games played in the nineteenth century, and well into the twentieth, most players did little to stay in shape in the off-season. Many enjoyed their months off with little thought of the upcoming season. Financial obligations forced others to seek employment. Some prepared for the season by making regular visits to their local collegiate or high school gymnasiums to use whatever apparatus were available, i.e., pulley weights, dumbbells, Indian clubs, and medicine balls. A few boxed while others played basketball. For those who worked indoors, any throwing they did was done easily, or "softly," as some called it, not wanting to overwork their arm.

Hall of Fame pitcher Charles "Kid" Nichols had a different belief. A workhorse during a stellar career that culminated in 361 wins, and a couple of seasons throwing over 400 innings, his regimen was to throw indoors every day for about two months, and then move outside where he gradually increased his speed. Those who opposed his theory believed that moving from the warm indoor environment to the colder outdoor temperatures was not good for their arm.

One of the game's greatest pitchers, Cy Young, followed this same throwing "softly" regimen before cutting loose himself, and was proud of not once having a sore arm in piling up his incredible statistics of 511 victories, 749 complete games, and a lifetime ERA of 2.63. A firm believer in running to stay in good shape, Young was fanatical about his conditioning, and would shed any excess weight he carried by running up to eight miles each day in the spring. His Hall of Fame numbers more than attest to the veracity of his conditioning program.

With Spalding's move to Arkansas, other teams began to take advantage of what warmer climes they could. Florida became a popular training destination beginning in 1913. Other warm-weather states, such as Georgia, Louisiana, Texas, Kentucky, and Tennessee, offered certain of their cities that had facilities available. These were not strictly benevolent offers because hidden in their largesse was the anticipated revenue produced by the drawing power of the well-known professional teams and their star players.

Some owners considered spring training unnecessary. They were more concerned about their own financial situations, or other business interests they may have had. Whatever training they allowed their players was left to the discretion of their managers, many of whom had their own opinion as to the value of preseason work.

In the late 1800s, Arthur Irwin had his Washington Senators spend the first full week in camp working on their diet, doing nothing but running before he would let them throw or hit even one ball. In 1903, Jimmy McAleer, manager of the St. Louis Browns, had little concern about doing much of anything thinking that with the extra training his players would be worn out by midseason. Around the same time, Jimmie Collins believed his Boston Red Sox team required only a couple of weeks to be game ready. John McGraw, the very successful manager of the New York Giants, believed in working his players hard making them take infield practice and chase fly balls in the morning, then play a hustling, quick-paced intra-squad game in the afternoon.

When Clark Griffith took over the Washington Senators in 1912 and led them to a second-place finish—a jump from seventh place the previous season—he installed a no-nonsense policy that turned the club completely around. Hoping to curtail the free-time activities of his players, when the team was in training in Charlottesville, Virginia, he isolated them in a quiet, large, one-room dormitory outside of town. Not only did the discipline help, the proximity of Charlottesville to their home ballpark saved on the costs of any southern trip they may have taken.

Feisty Johnny Evers, in his brief years managing the Chicago Cubs, wanted his players up by 7:30 AM. If they weren't, he had them rudely awakened for breakfast, and worked them through two-a-day practice sessions. That early hour was an unwanted challenge for those who never saw that time of day during the off-season. Evers was much more in control of his players than John McGraw was of his who didn't mind his team having a bit of fun at their training site in Memphis.

But by far the most popular way for players to get into shape, and what most of them believed was the most productive was waiting for, and playing the scheduled games once the season began. It was commonly thought that the regular-season competition was sufficient, and more responsible for players getting into playing condition than anything else they might do.

My own personal training methods were not much more defined or complicated than those of these earliest competitors. In the early 1960s, living north of the Mason-Dixon Line, the unpleasant and sometimes harsh New Jersey winters prevented me from doing much of anything outdoors during the off-season to stay in shape. Going South was not an option, and with no suggestions from the Kansas City organization about what I should do, the traditional belief that spring training would condition a player for the season, seemed to make sense.

The one thing that was considered the best thing professional baseball players could do to condition themselves, was to run short wind sprints. So, during the winter, in the bitter and below-freezing New Jersey temperatures, I would drive to Donaldson.Park, and, more than once, shovel a path so I could run after a heavy snowfall. Anyone driving through the park may have wondered who the idiot was running in the snow, but they knew neither me nor my purpose. When the snow and ice melted enough to make running on the surface of the road possible, I would run up the hill leading from the park toward Second Avenue. An incline always increased the benefit of a sprint.

Once spring training began, the only conditioning that was somewhat of a requirement was to run these same wind sprints at the end of the day. It was not mandatory, we were not made to do it, nor did anyone monitor how many we ran. Ten was considered a suitable number, but because playing the game well was more important than what shape you were in, you did what you thought was necessary. At the end of each day's workout, as long as I went into the outfield and ran any number of sprints—how many was up to me—no one said a thing.

Pitchers had no choice, they had to run. It could be sprints, or a long distance run of about a mile—about six laps around the field. Pitching coaches loved a drill that had the pitchers flip them a ball as they ran by them which they would then return to them with a football type pass over their heads. The extra effort given to catch up to the "pass" gave the drill more purpose.

My spring training conditioning was a self-imposed demand. Nothing was more important than fielding grounds balls every day for as long I wanted. Missing a day made my day's work incomplete. I could feel the overall effect the work was having on me during these twenty to thirty minute periods, but the silent barometer of how much my legs were strengthening and my technique improving, was the increasing amount of ground I could cover.

To make these workouts more effective, I imagined myself playing in a game with the inherent pressure and tension that I expected to feel. I tried to execute every one of the fundamental fielding movements on which I worked perfectly. That increased my focus on what I thought was the stressful atmosphere I was after. Working on my mechanics in this manner made repeating them in a real game much easier, almost robotic. I never thought about making a mistake, only what I was supposed to do.

It was nothing for me to make the same play over and over again every day in practice, paying attention to what I did with my hands and head, trying a different lean of my upper body, changing an angle, or adjusting the length of my strides. Every detail got nitpicked until I felt satisfied that I was doing everything as best I could.

● ● ●

Highland Park, New Jersey, was a comfortable, friendly and quiet town, a wonderful place in which to grow up. Returning there as I have from time to time since my retirement, I've seen changes made to both homes in which I was raised. The second one has had the addition of some new exterior fencing and minor landscaping alterations while the first, the smaller of the two and the one in which I spent my youngest days, is now quite a bit larger having had the addition of much needed living space. Addressed as 204 Barnard Street, this house was a prefabricated, ready-to-assemble kit that cost my mother and father a whopping $2500 from, of all places, Sears, Roebuck and Co.

When Dad first told me he and Mom had purchased it from Sears, I thought he was kidding. I knew the Sears store in nearby New Brunswick to be nothing more than a department store popular for selling work clothes, tools and large kitchen appliances, but houses? What I didn't know was that the store originated as a mail order catalog company, and for about thirty years until 1940 it offered hundreds of designs of prefabricated homes that included indoor plumbing, heating, and electricity, all new and marvelous amenities at the time.

What was a small, but comfortable home, was assembled from a ready made kit, a kind of jigsaw puzzle, on a 5000-square-foot lot in a quiet, middle income neighborhood not far from Irving School where I attended kindergarten through the sixth grade. It could not have had more than 900 square feet of living space because an Internet search now says it totals 1200. There were two bedrooms upstairs—mine was no more than 10' x 10'— and one tiny bathroom. A second toilet was installed in a closet-type space in the basement. The dining room was just big enough for the table and chairs, and the living room, not much larger, had a sofa and the TV. The kitchen was such that I could stand in one spot, reach into the refrigerator, get a glass of water from the sink, and stir something on the stove without changing my position. Many nights were spent in this kitchen listening to the Jack Bunny Program, Amos and Andy, Burns and Allen, the Green Hornet, and other radio programs while Mom baked or ironed.

The finished rumpus room in the basement had a small corner bar that Dad built that was the focal point of the parties he and Mom had. Setting up my Lionel train set on a 4' x 8' piece of plywood every Christmas left little room to move around. A small adjacent room provided the space Mom needed to do the laundry, and for Dad to somehow fit a workbench around the bulky furnace and its ductwork. It wasn't a big house, but it was home, and an inviting gathering place for our relatives.

The newer—and roomier—second home was a block away at the corner of Harvard and Columbia Streets. Also having only two-bedrooms, it was a more modern, unique split-level design featuring a family room, an attached garage, and the added comfort of two bathrooms, one upstairs and one down that doubled as Mom's laundry room. When my paternal grandfather came to live with us, I was moved into the attic which Dad remodeled to make it a much more spacious bedroom for me.

What I was never aware of was how much Mom and Dad wanted one day to move to Florida, believing it would be a more pleasant place for them in their older years. Mom's sister, husband, and my cousin had been living there for years after their move from nearby Edison. When finally we did, I was twelve years old. It wasn't long, however, that missing family and friends, and realizing they were not as fond of the Sunshine State as they thought they would be, that we returned to Highland Park. It was then that our second home was built at 165 Columbia Street.

When I graduated from high school in 1960 and signed to play professionally, the fitness craze was years from being recognized as a lifestyle. Working out every day and taking one's health seriously had not yet captivated the country. Smoking cigarettes was advertised as enjoyable, and a large segment of the population were inhaling with no thought of the consequences. There were no exercise, fitness, or health clubs, no Gold's Gyms, 24-Hour Fitness Centers, or similar conditioning facilities. All anyone could resort to with any regularity, for what it was worth, was the Jack LaLanne Show on television. The exercises this fitness guru espoused were no more exhaustive than his directive that everyone "smile."

Despite the national lethargy that swept the nation at the time, I felt obligated to do something physical to prepare for my first professional spring training camp in 1961. But what? With no place else to consider where I might work out, I wondered if there was something I could do in the one-car attached garage that was part of our Columbia Street house. Though only ten feet wide, barely big enough to house the endless procession of sleek-looking '50s and '60s Pontiacs that Mom and Dad would own, it became my pocket-sized gymnasium.

Why I even considered making use of it I don't recall, but it dawned on me one day that the three-foot high cement walls lining each side of the garage's length might have more purpose than just structural support. Standing with my back to one wall crouched in a ready position as if to field a ground ball, I could throw a baseball across the width of the garage, bounce it off the opposite cement wall, field the rebound with two hands, and throw it back against the wall. Doing this "rebound drill" for fifteen or twenty minutes every day without moving my feet was murder on my legs, but it was an excellent way to learn how to manipulate my glove, coordinate my hands, build leg strength, stay low to the ground, and work on the accuracy of my return throw. As my legs strengthened, my hands got "softer," and I gained better control of myself. Unknown to me at the time was that this innocent little drill would be the foundation of the success I would have as a major-league player, and, eventually, an infield instructor.

Despite the cool reception the use of a wall received from just about every other infield coach I would eventually meet, using it was an important addition to the instructional program I established for my infielders when I began coaching. Only one other instructor saw its value, no doubt, because we were about the same age. Why the younger coaches did not puzzled me because it was so useful to improve footwork, eye/hand coordination, and was a welcomed change to the routine of fielding ground balls every day. So much could be accomplished just through the natural performance of the number of different drills the wall could be used for, and no coaching was needed because, like me in my garage, the players were forced to learn and make their own adjustments. One drill involved throwing two balls against the wall, one at a time, and keeping them both going. That required control, coordination, accuracy, and the same sense of spatial recognition that was required if you were to juggle three objects. If two players were side by side three or four yards apart, and threw balls at the correct angle and height, they could throw balls off the wall to each other. There was no end to what could be done, and by far, the greatest benefit was how the drills strengthened an infielder's legs.

The only reason I could come up with as to why the use of a wall was dismissed by other coaches, was because the drills were thought to be archaic, different, bizarre, and not up to the scientific training methods of the day that were more psychologically based, and devised through what was considered extensive and exhaustive research. Once weight rooms and what they afforded became popular, there was an eerie sense that those in charge believed what was accomplished in them was more important than what could be accomplished on the field.

There was also just enough room in my garage to run short "pickups." When done outdoors, this was an endurance drill that consisted of quick runs of maybe five yards, going back and forth in front of a coach who would roll a ball that you picked up and tossed back to him as you changed direction. Your legs would absolutely burn doing this ten, fifteen, or twenty times, but it was a great way to condition them and your back. In the garage, I would simulate picking up a ball with two hands as I changed direction.

These two drills—rebounding the ball off the wall and running the pick-ups—were the extent of my off-season conditioning program in the '60s when I was not playing winter ball. Simple, and maybe not considered much by many who feel they know better, both have stood the test of time and can be made to be as demanding as you might want them to be. Their benefits far outweigh many of the drills used today that are not position specific.

It was in this strangest of places—the room that housed the family Pontiacs—that I first gave a serious look at the intricacies of the mechanics that were necessary to properly field a ground ball. Never did I consider that the start of the meticulous scrutiny I would give my defensive play would begin in such a place. The longer I did the rebound drill, the more I realized its value. When I first assumed the proper triangular fielding position, my thighs burned and my back tightened, usually after only fifteen or twenty-seconds. As my legs and back strengthened, the number of repetitions I could withstand increased as did the coordination of my hands. The short, quick, snapping, over-hand throw I was making to the wall was what I thought was the best way to feed any second baseman I'd play with when turning double plays. It could be made more accurately, and would be easier for him to see than the typical throw made side-armed that had a chance of being partially hidden by my body.

One thing I specifically focused on each time I fielded a rebound off the wall, was that the ball hit the same spot in my glove every single time. That way I knew where it was, I didn't have to look or feel for it. This made it much easier to grab for whatever throw I had to make. When in the actual physical act of fielding ground balls, every movement I made was with the ultimate purpose of having the ball hit that specific spot. This was also my unique way of checking that I had done everything correctly prior to fielding the ball. In this case, the end did justify the means.

The garage provided just enough space for my fielding-related drills, but trying to do something about my hitting was another thing. There was certainly no room to hit baseballs, but I'd heard about a mental imaging technique that was considered effective for making changes called visualization. The process sounded interesting, and plausible. Supposedly, if you conceptualized yourself doing something correctly, imagining that you were doing it perfectly in your mind, you could extrapolate it into the real thing. In other words, if I could conjure up a picture of myself doing something well as I did it, maybe I really would. So with a scrap piece of wood on the floor as a home plate, I began swinging a weighted bat at imaginary pitches, mostly breaking balls, while visualizing myself making solid contact and hitting line drive after line drive.

What effect this visualization technique might have on my swings I wasn't sure, but when I realized I was using it when rebounding a ball off the wall, I had to rethink my position. There was, of course, the hundreds and hundreds of rebounds that, by themselves, were significantly helpful, but what I hadn't noticed as I fielded each rebound, was the mental image I was creating of how I wanted to look: how my hands should be positioned to work together, how far they were extended, how I held my head, how high or low my backside was, and how far apart my feet were. I was visualizing my positioning, and adjusted it until I considered it to be perfect. Using this imagery, my movements began to mesh, and eventually became so deeply ingrained into my psyche that I didn't need to think about what I wanted to do, everything became automatic. By doing physically what I wanted to do mentally, I would.

There was no chance of extrapolating this technique to my hitting, or so I thought, because there was no way to get the real swings at a ball that I needed in the garage. It did not dawn on me that if I at least continued swinging the bat, and visualizing hitting certain pitches, there might be some positive effect. Thinking I needed live batting practice, I stopped swinging the bat.

Spring training workouts in my era were quite different. What swings we got every day were minimal, not the hundreds players get today. On the other hand, it was easy to put what work was needed into achieving the right "feel" of a particular action or movement fielding a ground ball. I had plenty of time and repetitions to do that.

Batting practice during the season in the '50s and '60s didn't amount to anything close to what I needed to improve. With only one round of batting practice every day, it was difficult to work on anything. With the pitches that were required to be bunted, and five or ten to get comfortable, there were not many left, certainly not enough to benefit my approach at the plate in any realistic way, or utilize the visualization process. Had I recognized the mental value of what I was doing when fielding ground balls, I might have similarly improved my at-bats in a cage, or on the sidelines somehow. Something positive might have resulted even if it was to erase the psychological effect of the "no-hit" tag that scouts had pinned on me early in my career.

When I was hired by the Cleveland Indians organization to manage one of their minor-league teams and instruct their infielders, they had a dreaded spring training tradition called "The Warrior Run" that tested every player's physical condition. Indicative of what a player might have done to condition himself in the off-season, the run was scheduled soon after everyone arrived in camp. What it consisted of were several opposite directional runs of varying distances totaling approximately a half-mile on a football-field type of layout. Few players looked forward to it because of the difficulty of it having to be run in less than three minutes. For many players, their off-season workouts were dedicated to its successful completion because a poor first run—more than three minutes—required a dreaded second. This difficult sprint was one small part of the Cleveland conditioning program at the time that was as demanding as any I have witnessed. I was never accused of going lightly on my players, but this program had even me questioning its severity. It was put together by an ex-Marine, and included early- morning, before dawn, consequences for slackers. The result of the program was an organization that was very successful in the '90s. However, as greater minds gained control, the conditioning requirements retreated toward a more modern, player-friendly system, and the three-minute killer run was eliminated. It wasn't long before the entire conditioning program, considered to be too strenuous, was revised.

What replaced the "Warrior Run" were shorter runs which were nothing but the basic wind sprints of old. With the game on a path of trying to make itself look more involved in the training program, it appeared to be leaning toward new terminologies, studies, and scientific discoveries about the body that might improve its athletes. None of this was needed. Moving in this new enlightened direction, these wind sprints were given the title "gassers" to signify them as having some kind of fairy-tailed increased difficulty. They were nothing more than back-and-forth runs of maybe twenty yards as opposed to the one-way sprints I used to do of thirty to forty yards. Considered innovative and run only sporadically by position players, they were a spurious addition to the conditioning program, but with a requirement to be run under a certain number of seconds, there was at least a forced extra effort. But with the paranoia and constant caution against overworking the players, their use was limited. They were more like window dressing instead of indispensable supplements to a withering ideology. Their effectiveness was never capitalized.

Among the best cardiovascular drills for position players in my opinion, maybe the best, during any era, is one that is maybe as old as the game. It is a simple base running drill that I'd not seen used once I became a professional coach. It required players to run imaginary singles, doubles, triples, and home runs on the bases, the number and pace of each being set by the coach. The drill built leg strength, created endurance, and improved base-running skills in one fell swoop, and was much more effective than any wind sprint or gasser. As a player, I respected it for both its difficulty and its rewards, but hated having to do it.

With the affect it might have on my career, possibly even ending it, one of my greatest concerns was being injured. Everything I did, in and out-of-season, was with my safety in mind. The most troublesome injuries for active players prior to the onset of a new and scientific technology, pitchers excepted, were pulled muscles, hamstrings in particular. There were always other aches and pains from the stress of playing the game that could not be avoided, but muscular problems seemed to be the most prevalent. To avoid the possibility of having such a problem myself, I thought it a good idea to add simple yoga-type stretches to my every day running and ground ball routine, nothing of the difficult pretzel-like poses, but simple stretches focusing on the areas of my body taking the brunt of the daily punishment. With no scientific knowledge available, it seemed extremely logical, and to make perfect sense, that stretching my back and legs AFTER every workout, when my muscles were warm, would be the best way to avoid pulls of any kind. I adhered to this belief faithfully for sixteen seasons, and not once did I lose playing time because of a pull or cramp.

In twenty-five years of coaching, I never saw one player take a similar initiative to stretch in this same manner on his own.

What is now thought vitally essential, its execution mandatory, and implemented by every organization is that BEFORE any player does anything on the field, BEFORE he goes into the batting cages, BEFORE he throws in the bullpens, BEFORE he does anything physical, he must first be put through a short warm-up period of ten to fifteen minutes by the strength and conditioning coaches. A specific routine of stretches and short runs are believed to warm and prepare the body sufficiently for the day's activities. This ritual, thought to be crucial for alleviating the injuries about which baseball organizations are paranoid, does not, and has not come close to providing that safety, yet it is now ceremoniously embedded in every professional and amateur athletic program from the Little League on up. No matter where you look, every sports program follows this ritual. Its intended value cannot be denied, but I saw nothing effective in it, and it did nothing to alleviate an increasing problem.

Sometime in the early '70s, four or five years into my major-league career, the entire country began responding to the value of being physically fit. Long-distance running became an overnight phenomenon, a popular national compulsion. Lunch hours were no longer periods that interrupted a day's duties, but were instead an hour to add more miles to an individual's weekly running log. Runners were everywhere. The sedentary couch potato was becoming an addicted mileage "eater-upper." I began reading magazines like Runners World, Running, and Running Times to find out what it was I was missing. What was this craze all about? Several of my friends were runners, serious road runners, and a few were more-serious marathoners. Their physical condition amazed me. Thinly sculptured, not overly muscled, they just looked healthy.

The monthly magazines became my textbooks, explaining what I did not understand. Every month, someone's personal story extolled the benefits of what running was doing for them, how it had changed their lives, made them different people, enhanced their health, and that this was not just a fad, but a new and better way of living. Every story describing how thankful he or she was for having found this new life-changing event could not have been more inspiring. Article after article told of how to train, how to stay injury-free, and how to build energy and stamina through a more healthful diet. Every one of them fed my thirst for understanding what was transforming so many lives and providing such positives. Page after page of helpful hints covered every phase of running, training, eating, and sleeping.

Especially interesting and more intriguing were the articles about conditioning, more specifically, those about the benefits of the AFTER, or post-event stretch that I believed to be so necessary. I had reasoned it to be the correct thing to do decades prior to seeing the BEFORE or pre-event stretch that was solidly in place during my days as a minor-league manager and instructor. That it was made no sense to me, but the more knowledgeable determination of the times was that it was beneficial. With the stress that long-distance running has on the body—more than anything a baseball player would experience—the published findings came from studies specifically pointed at determining what would be more beneficial for the body being under exertion for so long.

Surprisingly, and to my astonishment, the PRE-event stretch, the PRE-workout stretch, and the PRE-game stretch about which I would eventually become suspect were all proven to be harmful—in every study. Research showed that stretching without being sufficiently warm made it possible for small muscle fibers to tear with the potential of that causing more serious problems. Medical practitioners, themselves runners, were advising that caution be taken doing anything prior to an event.

What was tested and found to be a far better way to warm up was to begin running or playing a sport slowly, moving into its required actions carefully. The POST-event stretch, on the other hand, was reported as essential and indispensable because it rid warm muscles of a lactic acid buildup and sped up the healing process. These findings validated my uneducated, but personal belief that being loose and somewhat exhausted at the end of a workday was the right time to further increase muscle elasticity, thus my yoga stretches. My unscientific, but commonsense conviction was corroborated some forty years before the supposedly intelligent stance taken by the modern management corps in charge of professional baseball to which I would one day return to work. I had never liked any type of structured warm-up; it went against what my body wanted to do. If we listen, I have always firmly believed that the body has an instinctive way of telling us what it needs. Anything done today must instead have some esoteric or analytical study behind it to validate and support its use. Commonsense seems to have no value any more.

The running craze in its infancy baffled me, but it was hard to dispute its popularity. What running I did as a kid on the playgrounds or in a game was one thing, but to go out and just run, supposedly for fun, uh-huh. I didn't even like to run wind sprints as a player, but they had a purpose, so I had to. With neighborhoods exploding with men and women running from the dinner table toward a healthy way of life, I had to find out for myself what this was all about.

In August of 1972 I succumbed to this national phenomenon. My sixth season in the major leagues was nearly complete, and my Oakland club would be playing the Cincinnati Reds in the World Series after beating the Detroit Tigers in the American League Championship Series. Thinking there was no time like the present, I awoke one morning, told my wife I was going out to run, and went to a nearby high school track. Completing only one lap around the quarter-mile oval, 440 measly yards, was the most dreadful couple of minutes I have ever experienced. Thankfully no one was around. I had been playing professional baseball every day for the past nine months—and for twelve years at the time—but felt so out of shape that I was stunned and embarrassed. I realized that what I had been doing, and believed so constructive, was, instead, cruelly insufficient.

That run remains seared in my memory, its futility an inspiration. From that day on I began running regularly, only a difficult quarter-mile at first, but consistently enough to erase having to recall that disastrous first one. I've run a couple of marathons in retirement that I consider among the greatest things I have ever accomplished. Those twenty-six miles on the road took more self-discipline than anything I had ever called upon myself to do. Running was something I had always dreaded, but as my stamina improved, I discovered something. I was gaining greater clarity about myself and life, which, according to the magazine articles, was something to look forward to, and which would occur. During the remaining four years of my playing career, I ran three miles almost every day and six during the off-season. I was better conditioned, healthier, and very proud of myself.

During the 1960s, our spring training workouts began with little preparation. We would throw on our own, as much as we felt necessary, to loosen our arms, maybe run a sprint or two, stretch a little, do some trunk-twists, try to touch our toes, and pretty much whatever we needed to be ready at the appointed starting time. Rarely did that routine vary. For many years there were no formal preparatory exercises except for the occasional manager who might have us do what are now nostalgic, antiquated movements, things like jumping jacks, arm circles, or simple torso stretches. They meant little other than for the joking around that took place during them.

Then came the spring of 1970. I was with a new club, the Seattle Pilots. I had been traded from Oakland during the winter, and my new manager's goal was to finish spring training in first place in Arizona's Cactus League, a ghostly title for sure. Who cared? Winning in the spring wasn't important. There were no trophies to be won or bonuses given, and where we finished meant nothing. It was a time to prepare for the long season ahead.

Seattle was an expansion club in 1969. I was a member of a hodgepodge group of players in the team's second year who had more than enough to do trying to gain respect more for ourselves individually than as a team. Our manager was a well-respected baseball man who believed that finishing in first place would give us momentum going into the season. His push for us to win the mythical spring-training title was a lofty, but unnecessary goal for a team hoping to simply avoid embarrassment. Besides tougher workouts, each day began with an even more demanding warm-up routine, and ended with some heavy sprinting, or the base-running drill I hated.

We were required to weigh in weekly, a mandate that continued throughout the summer, one that raised the hackles of many of my teammates. More than one player would arrive early every Wednesday, grumbling because they had to sit in the whirlpool, or don a rubber jacket to run off a few pounds just to meet their expected poundage lest they be fined. To me it was childlike punishment that further taxed a club having enough trouble just playing the game every day; it was an added pressure that helped no one.

As unexpected as it was, a fairy-tale ending had us finishing first. We were crowned pseudo-champions of the Cactus League, honored as such only by the final published newspaper standings. The manager looked like a genius. We, however, looked like anything but a top contender. The title fooled no one nor did we scare anyone. When the regular 1970 American League Western Division season ended, we finished next to last, just short of 100 losses. It was a year that saw us struggle mightily to not only win, but to score runs.

Physically pressured the way we were from day one in spring training was more than I was ready for. A few more stretches, some extra sprints, and a couple of agility drills weren't much to be added to our regularly scheduled workouts, but none of us had ever before been pushed that hard. Our individual leisurely preparations had been taken out of our hands. Add the additional weekly weigh-ins, the manager's incessant meetings after telling us in the spring he would hold none, and his occasional postgame in-season workouts all added undue tension to the natural stress of a major-league season. We weren't going to win the American League title, but if we hadn't been so unmercifully pressured, we might have finished the year with a few more wins.

The world of baseball in which I lived bears little resemblance to what it is today. The game's history and my connection to it seem not to matter anymore. I can only relive the wonderful memories I have of a different time, a time when the game put responsibility on my shoulders. I may not have known what was best, but I had a grinding commitment to find out.

Whatever my career was to be was up to me. There were authority figures, managers and coaches, who led with strict standards and rules, but how I and others performed was a solitary burden. We watched, listened, learned, and imitated. We looked for someone to follow, someone who might inspire us, and we worked. Not everything may have been helpful, but we sifted through it all for what was. I don't know that anyone does any such sifting today. Too many players seem oblivious to what's good for them, and what isn't. They seem content with themselves in a way that is frustrating. They have little drive and even less concern that maybe they should do more, that they could be better.

Much of what happens in the game of baseball today is missing the goodness of its history. I learned about winning from other players, and from an individual who was not a player, Charles O. Finley. This gentleman was more than an owner; he epitomized organizational leadership that I believe morphed into an individual governance that went unrecognized. Disrespected by many, his demands forced those he employed to search for more within themselves. He did not lord over them everyday with his presence, but everyone knew what was expected, and that he was somewhere watching, overseeing. No excuses accepted, no reprieves given. You either contributed, or you were out. Only your best was accepted. His program of inducement was surreptitious and misunderstood, but correct. He may not have been liked, but his efforts, and the success he and those of us he employed achieved, demanded respect. There is no greater satisfaction for an athlete than playing for someone with that passion.

That, and a good kick in the pants, is often all you need.

4

THE GENTLE TOUCH

The benchmark for success during the '50s and '60s was whether you could hit .300 for a season. Unable to do so, you were quickly branded with the tag "no-hit." At some point during the winter before every one of my six minor-league seasons, I was forced to read that demoralizing description of my offensive ability as it was brazenly, and unashamedly, printed iin several national magazines. Those two words read like my epitaph, and as unwanted and disheartening as that was, and unfair in the futility it suggested, it fostered an embarrassing legacy that, try as I might, was difficult to ignore. Pigeonholing me as it did, I was in an almost no-win situation from the start.

My four best averages in the minor leagues for a full season were .253 in Class D, .295 in Class B, .281 in AA, and .260 in AAA. Each was nothing outstanding, but much more than respectable when coupled with the four "Best Defensive Shortstop" awards I earned at each of those levels. For someone branded with the "no-hit" tag, I enjoyed a 10-year major-league career, and hit a respectable .252 for the one year I played every day.

Those of us given the chance fifty years ago to play the game of baseball for a living did the best we could with the limited facilities and resources available. Unlike today's comprehensive player development programs that include an ever ready stable of coaches who throw batting practice endlessly at a moment's notice, what hitting we got consisted only of our regularly scheduled daily sessions where the tosses of the manager, and any players who were on an "I can throw today" basis, were divided among those of us eager for our turn. Our one option, if a batting cage was even available, was to take a few extra swings off some rusty old mechanical "Iron Mike." That machine, in its early simplicity, was more dangerous than useful.

Every one of today's architecturally designed, professionally landscaped, and well-appointed baseball training complexes have an appointed batting cage or two equipped with the modern, small truck-sized versions of that early mechanical menace. The engineered precision of these present day behemoths, how well they are stabilized and meticulously positioned and adjusted, make it possible for players to swing at every pitch they deliver. They can be operated and used nonstop until a player's hands bleed.

My teammates and I were lucky if the old free-standing skeletal prototype available to us worked. If it did, our swings were at best intermittent because of its inconsistency. The noise it made as it cranked up enough tension to throw its pitch was scary. Balls got jammed or stuck in the feeding chute with more regularity than they were thrown meaning the "iron hand" never loaded consistently. If, and when a ball did fall properly into the machine's metal mitten, it was so precariously situated that it would either fall off as the arm came forward, or was thrown erratically. Phantom pitches were so common that waiting for one became a nuisance, and a waste of time. It was impossible to use the machine by yourself. Someone was needed to monitor, reposition, and readjust it after just about every pitch because as the arm snapped forward, the entire device bounced uncontrollably making strikes even more annoyingly rare. Tending to it was dangerous, a job that unfortunately got an unsuspecting player or two severely injured when, as a forgetful mechanic, they happened to drift in front of the machine, and were hit by the loaded arm as it sprang forward.

We were grateful not only when this scrawny metal robot threw a ball straight, but that it was close enough to the strike zone to justify swinging at it. With each of our turns limited to ten pitches, to gain something of value from its use we were forced to attempt contact with every one of its deliveries, including its errant ones, counterproductive as that was. And with a handful of players queued waiting their chance to swing at their own limited allotment, knowing full well that the greater majority of them would be thrown with little accuracy, standing around waiting for your turn was frustrating. It made our good intentions almost useless, and not worth the effort.

It would be years before the more consistent double-wheeled Atec machines would come off the drawing boards, and the stick-like, upright batting tee would prove itself useful. The Atecs—the modern tripod cannons that they are—have replaced the old Iron Mikes, and can spit out pitches for as long as electricity can spin their wheels. The "soft-toss" drill, now a main ingredient in every organization's practice schedules, wasn't even an afterthought, and not until someone suggested providing a protective screen for the tosser did this drill come into vogue. A coach could then feed soft pitches to a hitter from behind a safety barrier only ten feet away without fear of being maimed.

One of today's more interesting apparatuses is the Pro-Batter. Reminding me of Saturday afternoons at the RKO Park theater in Highland Park where I watched the latest adventure movies as a kid. This invention projects the image of a pitcher delivering a pitch onto a large movie screen that has a hole at the precise point the pitcher releases the ball. Coordinated with the pitcher's delivery, the Pro-Batter shoots a ball through the hole to the batter. The engineering miracle of this machine is that it can be programmed to throw any pitch, at any speed, to any location, yet, as incredibly helpful as that might seem it would be, it was not popular with every player.

No machine, apparatus, and certainly none of the modern gimmicky inventions I've seen tried in spring training has ever been as beneficial as hitting off a good batting-practice pitcher on the field. Nearly all of the live hitting we got during my playing days was provided by pitchers getting in their work, players throwing to each other, or a coach helping out. As a utility player in the major leagues, I threw to the pitchers who hit every day—this was before the birth of the designated hitter rule that eliminated their at-bats—to players not in the day's lineup, and often to those who were.

Throwing batting practice was not the easy assignment it is today where the thrower is only thirty-five or forty feet from the hitter and behind double-netted, padded, and geometrically designed safety screens. Those of us who could throw consistent strikes did so from the front part of the mound, on the dirt, about fifty feet away. I would throw almost as hard as I could for fifteen or twenty minutes, protected by a wobbly belt-high screen that provided protection when I was quick enough to duck. Only after being hit two or three times, sometimes pretty seriously by balls that left me with large black-and-blue ugly bruises, did I understand the danger of the line drives teammates hit back up the middle.

Trying to improve with the very limited batting practice we had left my, and many careers, in the hands of each player's inherent ability. The game's structure and its schedule, the limited facilities, and a lack of field staff members made it impossible to work as hard, or put in the same amount of time, to perfect my use of the bat as I could my glove. I got no where near the number of swings each day that I would have liked, and certainly needed, but it was what it was. On the other hand, no obstacles, constraints, or other reasons kept us from working at our defensive positions for as long as we might want. In my case, all I needed was an easy-to-find fungo hitter who could hit me ground balls. Blessed as I was with a relentless work ethic, and the belief that hard work would pay dividends, I fielded ground balls every day working on my mechanics until I was exhausted. Letting up was not my nature, and too many days ended with me worn out. That was maybe not the wisest thing to do, but a young mind does not always use good judgment, and, well, that was me. The results speak for themselves.

Unlike in the old days, when how we played was left completely up to the individual, today's players are given help that borders on overkill. And no organization would dare offend one of its athletes with anything rivaling the negative journalistic pronouncement that so matter-of-factly degraded my hitting ability. Today, every effort is made to avoid any reference, or mention, of anything negative about an individual, or his talent. Coaches are not only instructors, but interim psychologists, and surrogate parents, who coddle the players, and praise every move they make. A wealth of positives are delivered as gently as possible.

Compared to the verbal "Good luck!" wished upon my teammates and me that was a sly reference to the difficulty of what we were attempting while telling us that we were on our own, today's player development programs are meticulously detailed and friendly. Their design includes anything that could be thought of as useful, and it is all presented in a way that is more cordial than challenging. This begs the question of the degree of its impact. Since the game is obviously not being played to meet past standards, it remains unclear how effective or influential this approach is. Everything offered, required, or asked for, is with the understanding that it will not be too great a challenge, bruise the player's ego, or overwork him in any way. Nothing is forced, demanded, or considered mandatory; everything is gently requested, or better yet, suggested.

As commendable and as pervasive as the employment of this softer tone is, it is not an explicit directive. Staff members are not indoctrinated to its implementation in any specific way when hired, but that this more hospitable approach is the organizational protocol is quickly recognized. In the normal course of the administration of their responsibilities, no matter their questions, or even the disagreements they may have with the policy, field staff members—if they want to continue working—adhere to this genteel theory. But when after years most players are treading water with no significant change evident in their game as was predicted or expected, should not the value of this policy be reviewed?

Ignoring or dismissing the past is not always wise. The occasional wooden-spoon imprints that helped cure my youthful transgressions, and the strict discipline imposed on me are no longer considered curatives. Time has warped what used to be the path to excellence. Leadership today means that whatever positives this older style of counseling and guidance might have, it will never be recognized because it is considered unnecessary. There is no allowance for the "do it or else" tone of long ago. Much can be said for what moms and dads knew, what they taught us, and what came from those more rigid times. Given little credence, their punishments instilled commitment and perseverance, their demands dedication and responsibility, and their discipline virtue, honor, and integrity. What's unfortunate is that subsequent generations do not understand, or value such lessons, until they themselves become moms and dads.

Baseball has imposed its own leniencies. Couched flattery allows players to gradually drift through what should be a period of mandatory improvement. Extra effort is rarely requested, and unquestionable demands are never put on their skills. Lip service sometimes hints of them, but nothing really happens unless it comes from a lone individual who dares to enforce responsibility and compliance.

Being one to suffer the consequences of player prodding, I have lived with the indignity of a reprimand more than once. With winning never considered a priority in the lower minor leagues, when one of my teams was poised for a post-season championship run, their most recent lackadaisical play warranted a needed tongue-lashing to snap them out of their doldrums. In no way was I going to begin our playoff series with them playing as they had been for the previous two weeks, so I blistered their ears postgame one evening for about ten minutes.

The very next morning I was resoundingly criticized by my superior who had read the resulting published newspaper article about my pep talk. He told me that my "motivational" speech was a mistake, and shouldn't have been delivered in such tones. Why we won the championship he may still not understand.

Dealing with today's athletes does require a more reasoned and delicate approach, but to what degree has inspired questions and quizzical looks from those of us who remember what were the game's routine, and unrelenting requisites. Too much time is wasted tip-toeing around the discipline, structure, and stiffer approach that not only do today's athletes need, but from which the game in general would benefit. A softer tone may be fine, but it should be neither permissive nor accepting of anything less than what is expected simply because it might hurt egos. Players will respond when dealt with honestly and maturely.

When the pat on the back is not tempered with the truth, Junior is given a false sense of accomplishment and entitlement. Today, this begins before he is Little League eligible. What reason then is there for him to be better? Constantly told how good he is, and later instructed based on a similar philosophy, he plateaus, believing everything is fine. Granted this is not always the case, but it is now often the norm, and it has permeated professional baseball.

For those of us who knew what the game was, to see it change has not been easy.

Any advice now given that might improve a player's performance is done so delicately that the delivery sends no message of urgency. The game of baseball has been lured into a lesser performance at every level of play while doling an unwarranted amount of credit and adulation to its participants. That does not allow for the direction and discipline it so desperately needs.

Today's athletes are treated like none before. Coaching staffs have become custodians. It has become mandatory that today's athletes be handled gently. Is it possible that in years to come, coaches will be required to have degrees in psychology, or be professionally certified counselors?

What I've perceived of how the game is run may not be the absolute mindset of every organization, but there is a widespread softer, accepting type of leadership and instructional approach being condoned. The erosion of discipline, responsibility, and accountability has been a natural progression over the past few decades, and though supported by what is believed to be a greater intelligence, it has reached a point of comic acceptability among coaching staffs. Like it or not, some major-league staffs are infusing comical theatrics, costumed travel attire, and a more festive undercurrent into their programs as if their "men" will perform better in a child-like party atmosphere.

The answer to the game's woes is both simple and monolithic. Make a determination of what a player can't do, put him on the field, and make him work on it. Play has been diluted with its mediocrity accepted as being sufficient. No longer are historical references used to parallel performances. With no concept of what quality play looked like decades ago, baseball now has no reflection off which to work as guidance for whatever should, or could, be done today. Those now in charge are working devoid of such benefits. What, then, can realistically be expected? All you get is what you see.

What seems apparent, but may be pure supposition on my part, is that the executives in charge of the various major-league organizations may not recognize the similarity their personalities share with those of their players, and the bearing that resemblance has on why the programs they have implemented, and the development of their players, are falling short of expectations. When the new look baseball would began, its young bosses were only a decade or so older, if even that, from many of the athletes in their care. The discipline and structure they hoped to establish resembled what they experienced growing up, they knew nothing else. What they failed to recognize was that the same leniency they knew was now unproductive in getting what they wanted from their athletes in a profession that demanded excellence, and not just acceptance.

The men who manage the structure of the game today have, for the most part, been more privileged than the athletes they guide. But vying for what is essentially the same brass ring, both groups appear to misunderstand how to go after what they seek. The decision makers don't know what to do with the players they control, and too many players fail to recognize what it is they can do for themselves. In their own ways, both misunderstand what is expected from them.

Today's young executives grew up getting what they wanted, and being told how brilliant, smart, and wonderful they were. They were high academic achievers, no doubt parentally favored, and possibly in the upper echelon of society. They rightly believed what they were told, and yes, they had to work for it, but they found success easily attainable. In a similar fashion, they have reconfigured the game with policies and programs they feel are correct. Knowing only the ideology and principles that brought them success, they have instilled a more intelligently based method of development that is regimented and corporately toned, designed with the hope that it will siphon comparable achievements from the athletes they manage. Misunderstood is that the athletes in their care respond to, and require, a more regimented and physical approach than is given, and their growth demands it.

Today's players have likewise been similarly hugged, praised, applauded, given every accolade possible since childhood, and told how great they were. Maybe not as privileged, success has come relatively easy, not so much because of what they've done and earned, but because of the game's need for any degree of it. What they fail to recognize is what good fortune it is to have their lesser performances accepted as being major-league capable. Should this continue a similar, or maybe an even lesser level of competency will be perpetuated in succeeding generations. When there is no expectation of there being something better, there never is.

Both groups feel entitled, but both fail to recognize what is missing in their pursuit of what they want. Neither fully understands what they are not doing that contributes to them falling short of their individual goals. Both have had most everything go their way, but they don't see what they might do to be better. They listen to no one and feel everything is fine as it is. A lack of realism has the executives and players plodding along in their own morass, not understanding what more they can do to accomplish their goal.

The game has gone in a direction that has not produced better or smarter players. The decisions coming from the front offices, made in all sincerity and diligence, have not, and will not, produce the kind of athletes that are expected because, unrecognized, is how the naivety of this approach reinforces the coddling the players have experienced their entire lives. That today's athlete is not one of four or five decades ago increases the burden of what baseball's player development programs must provide. The evolution of society and the passage of time have combined to negatively affect the overall quality of play. There is no question that the game has changed, but it now demands reinvention, a reversal, a halt to the direction it is going. The core issue of why play is not as sound as it once was is because it is not being addressed as it should be.

Major-league baseball is all about winning, nothing else. Putting together a team with the talent to win is not easy, and, realistically, is probably more improbable than possible, but when talent is found, getting the most from it seems not to be very well understood. Mistakes, miscues, and obvious limitations are going unaddressed—not necessarily missed—just not responded to appropriately.

The corporate kingdom that baseball has become is clearly more intelligent than ever, but how much that knowledge translates into any player or team being better is inconclusive. It's difficult to say how much of an influence the infusion of this greater brain power has had on performances that appear to have worsened. There is no definitive answer one way or the other of the effect it has had, or that it should even be considered a reason. The direction baseball has taken is thought to be the more psychologically defined wiser path in contrast to the antiquated methods of old when players were chattel, isolated, and had so much expected from them. But is it? What has a more gentle maternal approach accomplished? Has it induced individual soul-searching and the development of a tenacious work ethic from the athletes? Or is it the athlete himself who is not shouldering his responsibility as he should? Both appear to be at fault.

With so many players incapable of sustaining a consistent day-to-day level of competency under the game's present guidelines, the answer to their inconsistencies is believed to be the implementation of an even softer solution, that being a day or two off from the grind and pressure of the game. There has also been a reinterpretation and revision of some of the game's rules—standards that molded its rich history—with no doubt more to come that accommodate and validate the lesser play seen. This engenders an overall sense of appeasement instead of a push for more. This puzzling concept fits well with many of today's athletes because they are either unable to physically handle the stress of day-to-day play, or their talent fails to respond. Instead of a dedicated emphasis and pursuit of correcting what the players cannot do being required, providing less chance for them not to do it is now the more appropriate response. Ways are continually being found to make things easier.

The game as it's being run is forcing itself to compensate for what can no longer be executed; i.e., the bunt and the hit-and-run are considered passé, and are rarely attempted; the knockdown pitch for all intents and purposes has been banned, and the hard slide is being regulated from the game to prevent collisions at second base and home plate. The MPH sign has reduced pitching to throwing; the intentional walk is a wave of the hand instead of four pitches being delivered with their possible misdirection. When the human condition could no longer be trusted, instant replay came to its rescue, and existing technology may soon be calling, or digitally signaling balls and strikes, giving the umpires their own days off. The game might not be that far from applying the Little League rules regarding substitutions.

Baseball will always have its fights because of the macho-male disposition, but the competition that was formerly fierce now finds players tipping their caps, hugging the opposition, and giving huzzahs for plays made against them. A bigger question is what affect this camaraderie has on the effort given by the players; some spillover is bound to affect how the game is played.

Many of the game's ills are being alleviated by removing or eliminating responsibility, patting everyone on the back, dumbing down its rules; all signs of the times. Wouldn't it be wonderful if reconfiguring the game and making every player happy actually had something to do with winning? It used to be that the only thing generating happiness was winning, but million-dollar salaries now make losing palatable.

Baseball today is comfortable on many fronts as a result of the financial freedom it has afforded owners and players. It has made the game less confrontational. In their largesse, the owners have never handled their wars with the players as they should have. Their giveaways have been historic, but as the coffers began to overflow, mutual capitulation made sense. Tensions have eased, and it is doubtful that a strike, a walkout, or a standoff of any kind will ever again need to be incurred by either side. Acceptance of anything is easily digestible when the bank account is full.

It was difficult enough for organizations to determine if a player was major-league-ready when no deadline had to be met. The passage of time was not restrictive. The advent of free agency changed that, accelerating the need for a more efficient way to ready what talent there was. With potentially less in some cases, but for sure six years to get the best they can from a player, teams either had to accelerate their programs, and make them more efficient, or live with what could be accomplished in that shortened period. All avenues were examined, and every possible resource tapped. Everything and anything that might expedite an individual's improvement was explored and studied. Major-league organizations were determined to do all they possibly could for their players, seeking what advantages they could from every resource they believed beneficial. At the same time, care was taken to not push the athletes too hard. How it was expected that they could force someone's development while taking it easy on them has yet to be explained. Even a demanding program cannot rush potential that develops in its own time. With the game in need of something for which it could no longer wait, this more gentle approach was thought to have merit. What has resulted is that players are promoted before they are ready, joining others who are likewise unprepared, validating the mediocrity that is now acceptable.

I understand the perceived psychological value of an overall positive instructional approach that is more a gentle persuasion, but veering off course now and then has its benefits. Treating players with respect, and as the men they are, doesn't mean they cannot be prodded, or that demands cannot be made. The gravity of any instruction may not necessarily be understood more easily if the tone of the message is increased, but it definitely gets emphasized. Unless someone is "forced" to do something, human nature will find a way to do it as easily, and with as little effort, as possible. And even though there will always be those who will run through a wall, they are getting harder to find.

Managing talent in a leisurely manner wastes the efforts of both player and staff. The most damning consequence is that a major-league talent is never completely developed. A player will not be ready when his opportunity arrives. This mismanagement increases the demand that the player share some responsibility, that he becomes capable of evaluating himself objectively and honestly, nudging his own improvement. Being personally introspective is extremely important for anyone's success, anyplace. It can profoundly affect a career, but just about every young player entering the professional game with whom I have worked has lacked this skill. When asked to expound on their capabilities and explain their actions, it was a rare player who could. Most needed direction.

The dedication and commitment every major-league franchise has for its success is unquestionable, but something is missing. A more cerebral probe may contradict what I've deduced from my many years of service that a weird kind of universal apathy exists in every franchise that blocks the achievement many hope for. Despite the breadth and scope of even the best of the player development programs, instead of combating the mediocrity into which everything is drifting, they condone the continuing malaise. When they continue to give and accept what is, setting no agenda that has expectations, requirements, or demands, nothing can change; the game's deficiencies will remain acceptable. What management is getting, and what it has to accept, is that it is producing players who feel more and more entitled, expecting to be rewarded, and they are.

So many of today's players have become tolerant of their own play and are satisfied as it is; they see nothing of what they might be capable. They take no personal initiative to do more or ask for help or extra work. But why should they? They don't have to. And with the organizations, in their own innocence, going to great lengths to augment their developmental programs intellectually, psychologically, medically, nutritionally, and physically while easing up on the work load, what else could be expected? No one seems to understand the amount of work that is needed to play the game properly; the only thing that gets in depth attention is hitting. So as good as all the supplementation is, what does it provide in benefits? Underlying everything is the truth that, no matter what is done, too little talent is available to take advantage of all that's offered. It is that reality that trumps everything.

5

THE WAY IT WAS

"Rub some dirt on it!"

When injuries were unlikely, and mostly undisclosed, these were the first words heard whenever someone got hurt. Why, was because even with a physical breakdown that left no doubt of its severity, there wasn't much that would, or could, be done about it. The terse rejoinder reminded you that you were okay, like it or not.

Being injured scared the hell out of me. I feared losing my job were I unable to play, and, as others did, suffered in silence many times. No one wanted to admit being hurt. If management or your teammates thought you were "jaking" it—not wanting to play because of some "silly" injury—not only would you get funny looks, your heart, toughness, and manhood would be questioned. It was also at a time when all management had to do was reach down into a pool of pretty good players for your replacement.

Baseball no longer holds to such a hard line with its players. It has become a doting parent. The ease and frequency with which the modern athlete breaks down necessitates that discipline. Injuries are no longer dismissed with the flippancy of the past. It may not be panic and alarm that has organizations asking more from their medical staffs, but a healthy precaution that has replaced the previous stonewalling given any ill. Because the bottom line is affected, injuries have woven their way into the board room discussions. Management is forced to live with them as best they can. The players have no fear of any down-time they may need because they lose nothing. Bloated bonuses and salaries see to that along with a thinning player pool, and the pampering and pandering that is now commonplace. Everyone remains confused by what has happened to the million dollar athlete despite everything being done to keep him invincible. He seems more in need of the Red Cross than anything else he is so unselfishly given.

No injury, ailment, ache, or pain is routinely dismissed today. Baseball organizations spend more time and resources on their injured players, and what can be done to keep the others free from harm, than they do on the game and how poorly it is being played. The slightest tweak or pain is given instant attention and compassion, and every injury has its own detailed restorative protocol designed to ensure that the player returns to the field without further repercussions.

Decades ago, the game's aches and pains were worn like a uniform. Time off the field was never considered a good thing. Today, the meticulous return-to-play processes for any injury can be cautiously long and drawn out, to the point that even the players see no rationale for their restrictive scheduling and protracted length. But, in a world where no one is pushed, where mediocrity is accepted, where coaxing, persuading, sweet-talk reigns, and money talks, the recuperative programs appear to work perfectly, and though weeks or months may be missed, the players willingly accept their highly lucrative mandatory respites—why wouldn't they—and usually return to form in full health.

The unsophisticated RX for injuries fifty years ago was a mix of ice, heat, massage, use of a whirlpool. and father-time. It was the player who was responsible for the better part of his recovery; he decided when he could run, throw, or perform again. Old-timers returned to play as soon as they could, and unless an injury was debilitating, the only days off were those that were scheduled.

The foundation of today's return-to-play process, and still effective, is the same hot and cold treatments used decades ago, but it is much more sophisticated because of the myriad of new medical technologies, scientific discoveries, diagnostic techniques, and innovative procedures. On-going research has provided organizations with more knowledge and a greater understanding of the body and its repair then ever before in our history. Recovery periods are all fact based, with a specifically planned etiquette including important off days lest the process becomes too burdensome for the athlete. He has no choice but to abide by its demands. With new breakthroughs every day, the care and feeding of today's athlete is very delicate. The question is, has this helped?

Our "older bodies" did not break down as frequently as do the modern day player's. Pitchers had shoulder, arm, and elbow problems, some career threatening, but they pitched. Whether that was wise or not, it was what guys did. Medical know-how was in its infancy. Position players had their own bumps and bruises, but developed a callousness to them. No one was ever pain-free. The game would not allow that. Those of us who played in the era of the '60s and '70s dodged the severity of most injuries with a work ethic that conditioned and protected us.

The increasing number of physical breakdowns today is startling despite a vastly improved medical umbrella and the ongoing search for answers. No one has found a way to control the growing lists of disabled bodies. Not only is there an increase in shoulder and arm ailments, core abdominal and calf injuries have become common, and it wasn't until I began coaching that I discovered there was something called an "oblique" to worry about.

The internal workings of the shoulder and elbow remained unresolved until Tommy John had his left elbow repaired with a never-before-heard-of procedure in 1974. In what is now common practice, doctors replaced his injured ulnar collateral ligament with a tendon taken from his other arm. Because John pitched successfully for years adding an incredible 164 victories to his total after the operation, the miraculous procedure has since been known as "Tommy John" surgery, instead of that of his surgical savior, Dr. Frank Jobe.

With few day to day crippling injuries about which to be concerned, the one lone trainer major-league organizations employed in the past was more a comforting ear than a medical aide. Our Oakland trainer's major responsibility was to get the pitchers ready for their assignments. The rest of us, as he so clearly made it known, were not to run to him unless it was an emergency. His personal mantra and firm edict was for us to enter his room only if we had a legitimate reason, otherwise, we were to "Stay out!" He wanted to hear no sniveling, whining, or belly-aching. Baseball from his point of view was not a difficult or dangerous sport, and not at all stressful.

The Oakland Coliseum's training room that was declared "off limits" could not have been larger than twelve feet square. There was a tiny whirlpool, two rub-down tables, and one smaller one that held the day's medical necessities: rolls of white adhesive tape—mostly used to hold up our stirrups (baseball stockings)— scissors, scalpels, aspirin, rolled gauze, Q-tips, Band-Aids, tongue depressors, a variety of cold and flu medications that were needed to survive the cold, winter-like summer nights in the Oakland Coliseum, a jar of Vaseline, one of the red magical elixir known as "hot stuff," and a canister of ethyl chloride that would instantly "freeze" any area hit by the ball, be it the hands, feet, ankles, or shins. Ball hitting bone was a horrible experience. The "hot stuff" that was applied to arms, shoulders, and elbows—it felt like you were on fire—was a petrolatum-based product used to either battle or mask some pain, or keep arms and backs warm and loose. Whether its benefits were more psychological than physically helpful was disputable.

Today's major-league training rooms are medical wonderlands the size of a small apartment. There are several rubbing tables, walls of health-related, first-aid, and pharmaceutically stocked cabinets; an assortment of exercise equipment; multiple muscle stimulation machines; and one or two of the newest exotic medical or therapeutic devices. Large ice-making machines provide the never-ending supply needed for all of the game's pains, and hydrocollators that supply the heat. A couple of offices off the main room are for the assistant trainer and medical doctors, and there may be an adjoining in-house "health club" with an exercise pool in which a player can run, and an underground whirlpool. And, of course, the necessary number of computers. The only thing missing is a nurse or two.

As early as I can remember, I could never throw anything with an easy, fluid, and natural motion; something was wrong with my shoulder. Be it baseballs, rocks, or snowballs, it didn't matter. There was no significant pain, just an annoying discomfort. Throwing a football was easier because the mechanics were different, my arm did not have to go back as far. What I was dealing with would be found decades later to be either a genetic abnormality, or the genesis of an injury that would require surgery.

Kansas City found a slot for me during the winter following my first major-league season in 1967 in the Dominican Republic playing for the Estrellas Orienetales, one of four teams in the league based in the city of San Pedro de Macoris. The brand of baseball played in the Dominican, Venezuelan, and Puerto Rican winter leagues in the '60s and '70s rivaled play in the major leagues. Each league had a tremendous reputation, and all were known to build rosters with the best players available. To be invited to play on any of the teams was an honor, and the experience invaluable. The makeup of every club included that particular country's home-grown major-league players, and a mix of talent from the United States who, if they didn't already have big league time, soon would.

Winning any game in any of the winter leagues was a major event, but a championship was as prestigious an achievement as anything there could be for the people of the winning city. The citizens of San Pedro de Macoris showed there excitement when, on my second go-round with the club in 1968, we were crowned champions of the Dominican Winter League. The people went nuts. We players were kings, and have remained so after fifty years because the Orientales have not won another title since. That drought has had the club jokingly referred to as the Chicago Cubs of the Dominican Winter League because of the similar futility the Windy City team suffered for so long.

Nothing had occurred during that Dominican championship winter league season that hinted of me having injured myself, but getting the ball across the infield the following spring was an absolute nightmare. My shoulder was killing me, and it wasn't just a case of "it needs more time." With 1969 being the start of only my third season in the major leagues, I was worried that something terrible had happened, but there was no way I was going to tell anyone.

When the season began, I was panicked. I didn't know what to do. For the first and only time in my career, I was thankful that I was on the bench. When I played, I hoped the ball would not be hit to me. Living and dealing with this for a couple of weeks, I finally had to surrender when I realized the importance of being able to play my best when asked. The team doctor who examined me believed a cortisone shot would calm down what he believed to be an inflammation. Needing to do something, I had to give it a try.

Several teammates cautioned me about the shot. The doctor was more to the point when before he injected me he said, "it might hurt a little." Today, the area to be injected would be numbed, but not in the '60s. As a needle I thought much too long was probing my shoulder, being manipulated to three or four different places, all I could think of was it snapping in two with the problems that would have caused. Told not to throw for three days to give the medication time to work, in a week or two, it actually did. Had I known this, months of suffering could have been avoided.

Two decades later, in 1989, when I began my coaching career, my arm was no better. It still took the same ridiculously long time to get it in shape, but now it was beginning to hurt, and not in a good way. It gradually worsened until late in the season in 1995 when, with my arm over my head ready to throw another batting practice pitch, it either wouldn't come forward, or I knew how much it was going to hurt if it did. I just walked off the field. Something had to be done, but X-rays, MRI examinations and evaluations by various team doctors had all corroborated that there was nothing wrong with my shoulder. I was emphatically told after one MRI exam, and its results read by specialists, that I did not have a tear. All of this made no sense to me, how could nothing be wrong?

When the season ended, I requested to be examined by the San Diego Padres' major-league physical therapist—I lived in San Diego—and it took only seconds for him to tell me that I most certainly had a major tear in my rotator cuff. I had no strength at all when asked to push against the resistance he was supplying.

On December 15, 1995, at 7:30 AM in Cleveland I was wheeled into surgery. Noticing that it was 12:30 PM when I awoke in a recovery room, five hours in the operating room seemed to be a long time. Just how bad was my arm? One of our trainers told me that a large tear had been found that had to be sutured. In his words "there was a big hole in my shoulder." A bone had to be shaved, and staples used to put me back together. So much for nothing being wrong.

But this was only the beginning of my body beginning to tell me it had had enough. With the thousands of ground balls and pop-ups I had been hitting over the years wearing on my left shoulder, it too had to be repaired. There was no doubt of it being torn this time, because I heard it. While working on an electrical outlet at home, it shorted and sparked. Reacting quickly I pulled my arm away only to hear something snap in my shoulder. The sound and the pain that lasted only a few seconds was a little frightening, I hadn't been able to lift my left arm well before this without feeling something, but it was now worse, and it hurt. The team surgeon who put me back together apologized for not being able to reattach the muscle saying it had retracted so far down my arm that even after twenty minutes of looking he could not find it. I wasn't sure why, but I was not very pleased when he added that I was also not going to be able to raise my arm normally. I've only lost a little mobility and overhead strength, but playing catch is a little tricky because I can't hold my glove up to receive a throw. I have to time the lifting of it so I can catch the ball before it hits me. That tends to be scary.

After fifty years of accepting the torque of every one of my throws and swings, my right knee eventually said "uncle" and had to be scoped. With this and my two shoulder surgeries, and being sutured, sewn, shaved, stapled, and put back together as best as good be done, I continued to hit ground balls and throw batting practice. What can I say? In retirement I have been told by a chiropractor that I have a stress fracture in my lower back. How that happened I have no idea. Despite it all, I wouldn't trade my baseball difficulties for anything; I loved being on the field and miss everything I used to do, wishing I could do it all again.

Decades would pass from the time I first realized there was something wrong with my arm until it was medically proven there was. Why it did not give out sooner than it did I don't know because as a young professional I practiced making every awkward throw I could. Wanting no surprises in a game, I wanted to know how much I could depend on my arm, so during my practice sessions I would make throw after throw overhand, underhand, or sidearm, from every conceivable, and inconceivable area of my shortstop position. Some were made flat-footed, others off-balance, and many with no stride. This was either strengthening my shoulder, or increasing the damage, but I knew no other way to improve or condition my arm.

Today, to strengthen, ward off, lessen, rehabilitate or eliminate potential shoulder injuries, professional baseball, high schools, colleges, and, I would guess, many of our youngest amateur teams have adopted a specific shoulder strengthening program designed_by Dr. Frank Jobe, the visionary surgeon who repaired Tommy John's elbow. It is known by some as Jobe's Program and by others as Jobe's Shoulder Exercises. Tommy John's name may have usurped Dr. Jobe's as it applies to the ingeniously imaginative operation, but it is the doctor's that remains linked to every pitcher in the game with the exercises he devised to keep their rotator cuffs strong. The exercises are nothing more than a variety of shoulder movements using very light weights. Despite the proliferation of their use, arm and shoulder problems are rampant. Why seems a fair question? The Jobe's Program and certain other recuperative methods designed for athletes have never impressed me. They must be of help to some athletes, but I do not find them universally beneficial, and though not privy to every organization's policies, the exercises seem to be the standard required protocol for all pitchers in most systems.

When my shoulder problem flared, the Jobe's program was the recommended panacea. It didn't seem the wise thing to do, and a hint that it wasn't was that I could not do the exercises correctly. I could not even lift the required three pound weights.

Dr. Jobe's program is considered the gold standard, the best preventive and maintenance prescription available to keep the shoulder healthy and to avoid problems. But do the exercises ward off a potential injury? Can they rehabilitate an arm that has been injured? Do they work for everyone? Yes, is assumed to be the answer to each of those questions, but is it possible that the program is tightening muscles that need to be free, loose, and flexible? Puzzled as I was by the acceleration of bodily injuries when the use of heavier weights became the foundation of the game's conditioning programs, why could I not apply the same quizzical concern when this venerated program was specifically applied to the shoulder? I am unconvinced of the program's efficacy. I cannot summarily dismiss its benefits, but there are far too many questions about a program that elicits subjective answers when the simple act of throwing more with caution and intelligence seems a more sensible solution to stall the list of disabled pitchers that continues to grow.

Players should be given more freedom to do what they feel is necessary. They are, instead, controlled by the trainers and strength coaches who, without sufficient expertise or personal history in the game, have devised the programs in place. Management would have to trust a change, but loosening the reins on the conditioning programs that have been so diligently devised might not be easy for them. It would be admitting to their erroneous design.

The belief that the increase in arm injuries stems from overuse, that kids beginning at a young age are throwing too much, that they play on too many different teams year round, and thereby get little or no rest, seems misguided. What were yesterday's playgrounds are today's paid-for, structured baseball programs that operate under precautionary guidelines that have restricted play, freedom, and fun. So often in these venues the clock sets the limits of time on the field. No one recognizes that the caution embedded in these programs, correct as it probably has to be, has become a formula for many of the unexpected breakdowns.

Without the solid underpinning of a long throwing history that would have developed through participation in a variety of playground activities, instead of punching numbers on a phone, IPad, or computer, a young arm cannot withstand even the little abuse it gets. Believing that arm problems result from playing too many games makes sense today if you are willing to interpret "too many" as too little. It's not the number of throws being made that is the problem, it's the number that have never been made. This is a catch 22 situation if there ever was one.

Consider how things used to be. My high school baseball team played twenty games with an additional three in a post-season tournament my senior year. Signed to play professionally one month after graduation, I finished the summer playing on a semi-pro team that was in three leagues. After spending all day on the playgrounds playing baseball with my friends, there was another game to play in one of those leagues almost every night. After a winter of doing what I could physically to keep myself in shape—which honestly was not much—the following spring, my first as a professional, I did more throwing than I had ever done at any one time in my life. Asked to make throw after throw from the deep shortstop position, at one point, I wasn't sure I could make another one. My shoulder ached, but I knew I wasn't hurt, it was only weak, unused to the demands being put on it. I went on to play one hundred and forty games that first summer in the Florida State League followed by another fifty in the Instructional League that fall. And with each of those games there was a pre-game practice early in the afternoon, and pre-game infield to take just prior to the game. Surviving the year's workload of well over 200 games, the practices, and thousands of throws healthy, was nothing heroic on my part. Many players did the same thing.

With a genetically sound arm, common sense says that its elasticity and strength can be increased by following a throwing program that begins easily, is wisely and cautiously monitored, includes rest, and is consistent. Consistency cannot be emphasized enough. The muscles of the body need to be worked if maximum performance is to be achieved. Because the arm does not naturally accept the motion it takes to throw a baseball, it has to be taught how. The shoulder muscles, like all others, take time to acquaint themselves with their tasks, but they will eventually strengthen. It is what the body does.

It could very well be wrong to increase the throwing programs for today's athletes simply because of the times in which we live. But something is not working with the current remedy of limitation, abstinence, and caution. The shoulder and elbow problems will never be resolved under the present restrictive guidelines. It makes no sense to think that cutting back on some physical activity will improve its results, but there is no simple solution to the dilemma the game has been facing

Consider this second scenario. The many professional coaches who throw batting practice do so almost every day of the week. Some are in their early twenties, others more than sixty years old. One coach usually throws to one group of three, four, maybe five hitters. Each player gets maybe twenty-five or more swings in a round of batting practice. With extra swings, bad pitches, and maybe an extra round, a coach will usually throw 100 to 150 pitches a day.

It is nothing for a coach to throw to two groups, running their total to well over 200 pitches per day. Granted they're not throwing hard, and it's from a distance of thirty to forty feet, but they do it every day of the season, year after year. Each group consumes maybe fifteen minutes and sometimes many coaches, including myself, have thrown for thirty, maybe forty-five minutes, or longer. The force of these throws is not much, and the conditioning these coaches need to throw this much occurs during the process of throwing. Some arms get sore, some tire, and once in a while someone experiences a breakdown, but they dutifully take their turns.

● ● ●

As the priorities of life have changed, as they will, players have not had the benefits of playing the amount of baseball during their childhood and teenage years that I and the rest of my generation did. They have not enjoyed summer days of playing the game all day with their friends, followed by an organized league game at night. Nor did they probably ever play stickball for hours on a hot afternoon, being pitcher, fielder, and hitter. When confronted with their own solitude, they may never have thrown a ball against a wall trying to hit a spot just because it was fun. How many passes do you think they've made with a football during that sport's active months? Even in basketball the arms are frequently used to make some kind of pass, to shoot, or to defend.

In how many snowball fights have today's computer wizards been involved? Have they ever thrown a rock across a lake or a pond to see how many times they could make it skip? How about just throwing rocks at a sign? The flat ones curved in flight. If the trajectory was correctly estimated, the reward was the sound of tin being hit. That success caused another to be immediately thrown. It was a lesson in physics. I still remember the joy I had hearing the hollow sound made when a rock I'd thrown hit a telephone poll twenty to thirty yards away. To do that took a good arm and some mathematical expertise to determine the flight path, but what a proud moment it was to have hit my target.

Every one of the traditional sports we used to play, or whatever game it was we may have imaginatively created, not only helped our arms but it taught us something about how to control the rest of our bodies to best use our athletic abilities. We didn't know it, but we were learning what we could and couldn't do, what we were good at and with what we struggled.

Because of limited space, specific obstacles or obstructions, the odd contour of various streets and corner lots, being required to adjust our playing area to a specific school's layout, not wanting to hit a ball too far, trying hard to make a play when the field conditions were so very, very bad, or any number of other impediments to our athleticism, we learned how to wisely and safely use our skills. Our abilities were being tested without even realizing what we were doing. Having more fun than kids do today, we were developing an understanding of what it took to avoid being injured while discovering so much about ourselves.

There are too many little Johnnies today who know little or nothing of what the freedom of a playground provides, or its inherent lessons. They instead get "on-the-job training" from membership on travel teams, or what practice time can be bought in some indoor building or facility that requires more than their allowance allows if they are to gain entry. Structured and regimented as little Johnny's play is, the physical activity he gets is limited. The everyday physical stress of the game, once it becomes a more serious endeavor, is a shock to his unsuspecting body.

Baseball is baseball; the game hasn't changed. Many of today's professional players are tremendously skilled. They are being given everything possible to help them succeed while being careful not to overload them in any way; they are protected. This same culture has filtered down to the youngest of our participants, but under the bravado of this largesse, the athletes have been pigeon-holed, stymied from learning anything on their own. Their freedom has been constrained, even worse, denied, to their detriment. There is a universal refusal to recognize how easy we have made it for players to not be as good as they could, and should, be. If someone is not made, or better, allowed, to do something, they will do nothing, and that is not good for the athlete or the game.

6

DOING IT MY WAY

During my tenure as a professional infield instructor, there came a time when I understood what Thomas Jefferson meant by his words written into the Declaration of Independence in 1776 that proclaimed: "We hold these truths to be self evident... ." One indisputable truth culled from my quarter-century of schooling infielders was that the good ones, those with more than a reasonable chance of playing in the major leagues, demonstrated that potential from the first day they stepped onto a professional diamond. What ability they had may have been crude, but it stood out; it was special. Another discovery was that although nothing could be done to completely alter an infielder's style of play, with a few suggestions, critical advice, constant monitoring, and a bit of a push, a good instructor, versed as he should be in his area of expertise, could make a significant impact on those entrusted to him.

Baseball's transformation and catapult-like leap in the past twenty-five years into a level of educational and technological brilliance never before seen in the game brings to mind another adage from the 18th century. In 1709, Alexander Pope wrote this in

"An Essay on Criticism:" "A little learning is a dangerous thing…" That statement aptly describes the slippery path America's pastime has taken since sabermetrics and a corporate intellect have invaded its hallowed hallways.

There is no doubt the infusion of a greater intelligence has been a benefit to baseball, but, as is the case when a new direction is taken, no matter its scope, it takes time for its true effect to be felt, and its value determined. If it was properly reasoned to have been the right thing to do, any change that renovates what once was, should be positive, but it is not unreasonable to assume that it may not be.

The degree of excellence of any infield instructor's attempt to teach the fundamentals of how to field a ground ball, are dependent on the depth of his knowledge of those fundamentals, and how well he can communicate and adapt that knowledge to the talent he sees in those he is teaching.

A good infield instructor has the unique ability to "embed" himself into the movements and actions of an infielder, and vicariously sense, or feel them. Somewhat similar to the technique known as visualization, it is an ability that allows him to more accurately determine what adjustments are needed to correct any difficulties the infielder might be having. Without this skill, any movements that might be considered "trigger" limitations—ones that affect others—typically go unaddressed. What then gets attention are the same basic movements and actions that have been getting all the attention ever since a ground ball was first fielded.

Timeworn suggestions such as watch the ball, keep your head down and your hands out front, stay low, and, the ever popular, charge the ball, are some of the normal, fundamental, and traditional directives that though correct, are only peripheral admonitions that do not address the crux of an infielder's problems, nor do they give any hope for real improvement.

The inability to be meticulously thorough in what he offers will make any instructor a self-indulgent, robotic, and inflexible teacher, able only to pass along the same lessons believed to be sufficient since the 1950s or before. His teachings are repetitive and trite. What I have witnessed in twenty-five professional seasons as an instructor has proven that almost all infield instruction is hackneyed, incomplete, and not as effective as it should be; its simplicity, however, is nevertheless readily accepted and considered adequate.

Despite the extreme confidence I had in what I taught, and a belief that certain absolutes had to be applied to everyone, I maintained a cautious and flexible approach that enabled me to adapt to an individual's athleticism, knowing that it was possible to maximize his unique abilities and minimize, circumvent, or eliminate his limitations all together.

Looking back at how my friends and I learned how to play the game, the best I can say is that we absorbed it, as if by osmosis. We watched the older kids, and, should we be so lucky, read the occasional instructional book. *Play Ball!* by Bert Dunne was a special birthday gift from an aunt and uncle when I was ten that covered everything about the game that any Little Leaguer needed to know. I still have it. And though they were not particularly instructional, articles in magazines such as *Sport* and *Sports Illustrated* hinted at the right things to do. They were fun reads as was what was considered "baseball's bible," *The Sporting News*. This newspaper was a revered encyclopedia of information about every minor league, and both major leagues. Its weekly publication was much anticipated by every one who loved the game.

How it was I learned to field ground balls as a Little Leaguer, I don't know. I had no idea what I was doing, but watched what others did. What I found most helpful was seeing how they moved around trying to get a good bounce to field. It wasn't that easy to do.

What a coincidence it was that the only thing I remember hearing was that the ball should always be fielded on a good hop. That's all any coach ever said, but there was never an explanation of how to do it. Even when I began teaching myself how to field as a professional, and recognized how involved the process was, I wasn't sure, but I quickly realized that getting a good hop was dependent on doing a number of things right. There was a mix of many movements that had to coordinate. Each one had a specific responsibility to the one that followed, and was affected by all that preceded it. There was a pecking or soldiering type of order to them that explained, in fact demanded, why one had to mesh with the next. If I was to ever field the ball consistently, and get that good hop, I would have to learn how to correctly execute and control each movement.

When I first became an infield instructor, I wondered which of the other instructors I encountered, and which of the players, had the same commitment I had to understand the smaller details of their efforts. In almost three decades of coaching professional infielders, only once did I encounter someone who was not relying on the banal and standard lessons of the past, but thought as I did. It was unfortunate that a language barrier, and a lack of time, did not allow me to get to know the scope of his method, or the breadth of his knowledge. Back in the '90s I was privileged to have been invited to work a few springs with the Yakult Swallows, one of Japan's Central League teams, when they trained for one month in Yuma, Arizona, prior to their own spring training sessions beginning back home. What a surprise it was when one morning I watched Shintaro Mizutani, the club's infield coach, work one of his rookie infielders for forty-five minutes on a single specific maneuver over and over, applying instruction that was identical to mine. How hard he made the young man work was impressive, guiding him as he did with each repetition. I could not have been more gratified to see that the unequaled Japanese work ethic validated my own.

Of the young players coming into the game, the greater majority were oblivious to what they were or could be doing better. Working with young infielders, attempting to change their mechanics, or making just one adjustment to movements that were part of their DNA for years took time, and not once did anyone take it upon themselves to work on something; they did nothing to help themselves. The hundreds of players I coached followed my instructions, never questioning my method, or what my reasons were for being so detailed and insistent. Unlike my rebuke of a demand by one of my major-league coaches who didn't like my pre-game preparation and stormed off in disgust—I was slowly working on a fielding technique—my students showed little self-awareness, and no ability to evaluate themselves. I could only wonder what the extent of their passion and commitment might be. It was extremely rare that someone would ask for help, and never was anything I suggested questioned.

Affecting and influencing someone's career is a great feeling, and very satisfying, but the greater percentage of infielders show only a minimal change in their play no matter how much time is spent with them. If there is improvement, a plateau is eventually reached that is the limit of their ability. More than a few show no change. And because ninety percent or more of draftees fail in no way means that those who survive have perfected their skills. Many long major-league careers have been fashioned by players with defensive shortcomings because of the totality of their skills.

When given the position of Minor League Defensive Coordinator for the Cleveland Indians, my intentions were to design and install a program of instruction that was thorough, and different, one that would develop a greater understanding of the importance of the defensive side of the game. After twenty years of managing in the minor leagues with Oakland and Cleveland, though not neglected, and so unlike the diligent attention given hitting, there was a blasé attitude toward defensive play, almost as if to say, it was what it was. I hoped my leadership would make a difference, mean something, have an impact, and give the organization a different look, one that I felt was needed if we were to become world champions.

With coordinators assigned to each of the specific fundamental areas of the game, my particular responsibility was to control and instruct the infielders. With that in mind, I spent months writing a completely unheard of 300-page infield manual with its centerpiece being a twenty-plus page detailed explanation of how to field a ground ball. This treatise covered every movement and action that I found to be necessary in my own search for answers when I was improving my own infield play early in my career.

Every infielder the organization signed received a copy. Its content included the basic and specific responsibilities for each infield position, an in-depth review of team fundamentals, explanations and reasons for every drill listed, and defensive alignments under certain scenarios. It covered not only the physical, but the necessary mental requirements of playing the infield. In addition to being given my manual, after spending sufficient time with each infielder to feel comfortable making an evaluation of his ability, he was given a one-or two-page assessment of what I saw as his strengths and limitations. This document emphasized what improvements he would have to make if he expected to progress. Copies of these assessments were also given to the minor-league managers because I needed their assistance developing the infielders assigned to their club.

To my chagrin, neither my manual nor my evaluations were well received. There was not one positive response from anyone in the front office and, in one meeting, there was a slight snide reference to the manual's length. Worse was being told rather coldly, and without explanation by my superior to stop distributing my "points of emphasis" documents. There was no discussion of their value, or their potential. A somewhat terse "don't do that anymore" was all that was said. I understood the obvious infringement these assessments had on the written plans the organization prepared for each player, but having my work ignored was upsetting and frustrating. Not telling the players all that was expected from them was unfair; they were the ones who suffered.

Being told that my efforts on behalf of our organizational infielders was unacceptable was disappointing especially in light of the ongoing organizational policy to always look for something better. Those running the player development program had no qualms about adding anything new they might have discovered no matter how it might lack in definitive value to player performances. That was hypocritical.

One thing being overlooked by the instructors in charge of the various defensive positions was that no one ever addressed the relationship one position had to another, or how the responsibilities of each overlapped. Most players performed in their own little bubble with no recognizable concern for how their play affected a teammate. That was selfish. Whether it was an infielder making a good throw to start a double play, or an outfielder being accurate with his throws, I wanted everyone to better understand how important it was for them to execute their defensive responsibilities with someone else in mind. I.e., a catcher's concern should not only be a quick release and strong throw, but a quick release and accurate throw that is low and over the base so the tag by the infielder can be made quickly. A pitcher with control gives his catcher a better chance of making that throw. The entire game would be played better if individual efforts were given with the mindset of not forcing the next player to have to do something special himself to complete a particular play. The instructor, to instill this, only needs to add to his instruction mention of what should be done to make this happen. When concern is focused on another player, the stress a player might have about his own play, is lessened. It allows him to work on his needs more freely. This became apparent to me in my own climb through the minor leagues. It was an invaluable addition to my own improvement.

My other concern was the lackadaisical consideration given team fundamentals. Rundowns, first-and-third situations, bunt plays, and the other team concepts had been approached, and practiced, in the same traditional ways for decades, often with little attention paid to the quality of their execution. What would it hurt to try something new? A little change could be beneficial. With the prevailing consensus that there was an overall deterioration of sound play, it seemed reasonable that if working on the whole of something was not producing the desired results, perhaps concentrating on its individual parts would be more efficient. It seemed to make sense that even the smallest amount of time spent on a specific maneuver would be more than worth the effort.

What that in mind, I broke each of the team fundamentals into its individual components, and had the players work on the segments that were specifically troublesome. For instance, the pitchers, who are not the most athletic players, were made to break as hard as they could off the mound to field bunts down the first and third base lines. They were only asked to get to the ball as quickly as possible and field, or pick it up, nothing else; they were not to make a throw. This was a problem area more than it should have been. There was a need for them to learn how to better control and balance themselves at a faster pace. When their throws were added, all they were required to do was stand, well-balanced, over the ball, and, as quickly as possible, field or pick it up, and make an accurate throw to the first base.

Outfielders were asked to do much the same thing; run hard to the outfield wall, pick up the ball, and make only a short throw to a relay man, all under control, being sure that the throw was made to the correct side of the relay infielder. They also worked on the accuracy of their throws to the bases—ideally on one-hop—by first beginning from the outfield edge of the infield dirt, then gradually backing up to their normal depth as they found the range. Their throws in a game improved significantly. Catchers were made to field bunts, running them down and making quick, accurate throws to every base while on the move, something they rarely had to do.

Catching a pop-up, traditionally one of the game's easiest plays, had turned into a nightmare. What a ball hit into the air was doing that it didn't do in my day was a mystery, but staff members were constantly entertained by the acrobatics performed in the futile attempts being made to catch what had always been "sure outs." Catching them was routinely practiced using a machine to shoot them to the infielders within the comfortable areas of their positions. What made more sense and more mimicked reality, was to shoot them into the problem areas because it was always the ball's height, trajectory, and location that was troublesome. The areas around the mound, near the dugouts and fences, behind second base in short center field, and anywhere that two fielders might converge were the danger zones. Increasing their familiarity with these more difficult areas could only help.

If all of this sounds childish and unnecessary, think back to the World Series in 2006 when the Detroit Tigers crippled their chance of winning because of the mistakes their pitchers made fielding bunts. Time and time again they threw the ball away, or did not make the play they should have. It wasn't pretty watching a major-league club perform the way they did.

Many clubs no longer attempt to use what were long-standing traditional plays because of how poorly they are executed. Moving a baserunner from second to third base with a ground ball hit to the right side of the infield seems an afterthought, as is asking someone to bunt. The historical hit-and-run play that required a ground ball be hit to the right side of second base is extinct. The hope now is that the ball will at least be hit.

Most major-league clubs rely on only one, maybe two bunt plays anymore. They've become content to get at least the out at first base. With a man on first base and a sacrifice bunt made, pitchers rarely make an attempt to throw the runner out at second base; they merely field the ball, and throw to first base, that's if they don't have the heebie-jeebies and can make the throw. Third base coaches no longer need to have much concern about having a runner thrown out at home plate because outfielders seem to have forgotten where it is located.

The game long ago abandoned "chalk talks." Thirty years ago I remember the intricacies of the game being taught in spring training, with the staff going over various situations and their solutions simply as reminders. What might be considered the right thing to do is now only mentioned in passing while everyone waits for the home run, or some blazing fastball to shut down the opposition and override the mistakes being made.

To avoid the late inning problems I frequently ran into as a manager, I forbade pick-off attempts because of the inevitable wild throws the pitchers made; and if it wasn't absolutely insane to do, I would have given any number of hitters the "take" sign on a full count of three and two because they would invariably swing at the next pitch thrown no matter where it was. Having the infield play "in" with a runner at third became useless. The infielders could not keep the runner from scoring; they were either too slow making the play, or their throws to the plate were erratic. Giving them the option of positioning themselves on the infield when the situation warranted it was out of the question. So few knew how to play the hitters, or understood what their defensive abilities would allow them to do. Try as I might to allow those who could steal bases the freedom to do so was also in vain, no one understood the game well enough to know when they should, or should not, run. And as for the strike zone, no player ever clearly explained his to me. When asked to map his particular hitting area, the most common response was a blank stare and a shrug.

In baseball's long history, the iconic team fundamental has been pre-game infield practice. This long-standing tradition has always been considered educational and preparatory. As a warm-up, it is no longer considered necessary in the major leagues, and though I don't see that as being monumentally detrimental at that level, its discard joins the decline of other regular disciplines. It has a definite purpose for young players in the minor leagues— especially if slightly altered. I believed its greater value came from separating the position players, and working them in their positions for a longer period of time than that consumed by the normal pre-game routine.

Instead of what had always been the standard way of hitting ground balls to the infielders that they threw to first, and then to second for double plays, I turned pre-game infield practice into a game-intense, shotgun-type, nonstop, taxing workout. Balls were randomly and rapidly hit—I would hit each one while the throw for the last one was in the air—to all areas of the infield at different speeds. The underlying premise of doing this was that it did not give the infielders time to think, they merely reacted and, in doing so, more naturally responded to what had to be done to field the ball. They didn't realize it, but they were teaching themselves by making their own adjustments. When they needed a breather—and they always did—I had the catchers make throws to each of the bases.

Running a pre-game infield practice this way had everyone on the move. Their confidence soared because of the game speed at which they were working, and the stamp of approval of its value, and the fun they were having, were the cheers that were heard when someone made a great play.

In neither of my intensive two-hour interviews for employment with the Oakland and Cleveland organizations, for positions that would have me responsible for many highly valued and expensive employees, were there any specific questions about how I might teach the game and its different aspects, what I believed did or didn't work with regard to motivating the players, how I might structure workouts, or what my methods were to build a successful team. In a business where subjectivity and unpredictability was understandable, I expected there to be more explicit questioning about how I might instruct infielders, the position that was peripheral to the managerial position I was seeking. Because I would be instructing and in charge of not only infield play, but every facet of the game, surely there had to be some interest in my methods or policies.

The hiring of employees to be field staff members for both major- and minor-league teams is an interesting process. The probing is detailed and comprehensive, but mistakes occur, human nature being what it is. It is not rare that surprises with regard to personality, intelligence, emotional responsibility and stability, psychological insight, and baseball knowledge have been known to emerge after someone has been chosen. Every field-staff position to be filled has specific responsibilities, and no matter what history or credentials the interviewee may have, or to what depth he is interrogated, only certain individuals are right for any specific role. Who that person is found to be cannot be completely known until he is on the job when even he may then be faced with, and surprised by, the requirements of the position that he had not considered.

Major-league selections should be more objective than are those for the minor leagues, but there really are no standards to go by for either. Sometimes it appears to be more of a crapshoot than it should be which is attested to by the number of changes that are made year to year in all organizations. Although every hire is made with good intentions, bull's-eyes are not always hit. Dismissals are also wrongly made. Very statured people, great baseball minds, and excellent coaches or managers get replaced quite regularly by others less qualified for any number of inexplicable reasons, most of them centering on some form of emotional attachment to the new-hire, unfortunate as that may be. Having a friend in high places goes a long way, and is one of baseball's longest standing and traditional qualifiers.

As time passed, I became more and more confident with how and what I taught. I dissected every infielder's actions as intricately as possible, always looking for perfection in them as I did myself. The struggles and emotions I lived through as my career progressed, were the same that every young infielder suffered. Understanding the difficulty of what they were attempting to do, made it easy to identify with the pressure they felt as they pursued their dream.

How my infielders performed was important; I felt a real responsibility. I pushed and prodded them, driving them to the limits of the talent few knew they had. My style was never questioned by management which I took as a sign of respect, but that silence was perplexing because I saw the same avoidance given others whose work I did not value. I therefore had to wonder if those in charge knew good instruction from bad, that which was beneficial from that which was not. Certainly not all instruction could be considered adequate? Was no one seeing the differences I saw? Everything being taught was accepted carte blanche as if there was no right or wrong way. What was difficult to come to terms with was when some instructors useless advice was thought to be responsible for the progress a player made when, instead, it was the passage of time, the experience gained, and the player's own inherent talent rather than anything he had been told.

Most who crossed my path, when asked to define me in a word, would probably say something like demanding or tough, maybe difficult. I do not apologize if that was my trademark. I expected a lot from my players, but it was for their own good. In all my years I had only two players confront me about my managerial and coaching style. Both eventually thanked me. I made my infielders work, but it was work they gravely needed that was too often overlooked by others. Drills recognized as important were a waste of time to me. The concern I had for what others taught had little to do with their style or method of instruction; it was that their instruction was of no consequence for the player. A good portion of it was busywork, offering little or nothing beneficial except the time it filled, and impressing the front office who didn't know any better.

There appeared to be an obvious lack of understanding of my analytical expertise when in conversation about an infielder's defensive play, the discussion would suddenly turn in another direction. No one would or could engage in any lengthy conversations with me. It was disheartening to find that only a few people were truly interested in my analyses. Being from past generations as I was, my obscure and anonymous career gave me no recognizable credibility with either staff members or front-office personnel which I understood. What bothered me was that so many who professed to care about the game knew so little about what mattered.

Something that puzzled me every spring were the one, two, maybe three, retired big-league players, some quite prominent and well-known with stellar playing credentials, who were invited to camp as advisers, and without sufficient vetting, allowed instructional freedom with impunity. Though they knew nothing about any of the players, or the organizational philosophies, their tutelage was permitted. To the impressionable players, their's was just another new and "never-to-be-heard-from-again" voice. The smarter visitors realized their greatest contribution was their celebrity while others did not see the value that came from them just wandering around the camp as figureheads from the past, imparting whatever positives their presence might spark, rather than interfering with the programs by interjecting their ideas. Their presence appeared to be idyllic to management.

Another unfortunate situation was the overlapping of instructional expertise because of the multiple hires for any one of the physical fundamental areas; hitting, pitching, base running, catching, etc. This was an industry-wide inevitability, and unavoidable. With the large number of staff members needed to police a minor-league developmental program, organizations could not help but have a number of experienced coaches for each of the fundamental areas. And, though they may have all agreed in principle on a line of instruction, they saw and did things differently, some better than others, some significantly better than others. Every infield instructor, for instance, could see the problems an infielder was having, but none recognized, could address, or even understood what the underlying causes of his difficulties were.

When the several instructors overseeing a specific fundamental area had differing opinions, and were not on the proverbial "same page," or the root cause of a fielding problem was missed, it was the infielders who suffered. This was a waste of everyone's time which was unfortunate. Multiple voices were sometimes beneficial because the same message worded differently might be more easily understood, but it became seriously divisive when divergent instructions frustrated players, causing confusion that was often difficult to untangle.

An illustration of how differing opinions could cause such confusion occurred one spring during a regular morning meeting of the Cleveland Indians major-league staff. Both the big-league infield instructor and one of these infield "special advisers" who was present, advocated a specific setup or starting position that was to be used throughout the minor-league system. It began with a little hop or jump. With both staffers contemporaries of the game and not far removed from their own playing days, it was surprising that they believed the maneuver had merit; I thought it was useless. The only reason for them even suggesting it might have been to show some weak evidence to management that they were earning their pay.

It's not odd that instructors, lacking the simple knowledge of what to teach and why, feel obligated to do something to justify their position. I spoke up and questioned the maneuver because I was shocked to hear it coming from a couple of supposedly good former major-league infielders, but whose play was unknown to me. What they recommended I had not seen done by any competent professional infielder. It was something that I never did, nor would I ever teach it.

My opposition about the maneuver raised some eyebrows, but as the Minor League Defensive Coordinator at the time, I needed clarity because I was expected to have it taught throughout the system. As I traveled from team to team trying to get our infielders to adopt the maneuver, the players were of the same opinion as me, not because they couldn't do it, but because they were uncomfortable with it, and recognized its futility. Almost to a man they complained that it was ineffective, that it served no purpose other than to satisfy the wishes of the "special adviser" who wanted it done his way. Stranger still—and a reasonable question—was why the same movement was never forced on any of the active major-league infielders?

When there was a clash of advice from the infield instructors, the confusion it caused the players was obvious. Should a suggested change have no effect, or an important limitation not be addressed, reversing, or at least limiting the damage this caused—which I felt obligated to do when I was in charge—required some sensitive psychological maneuvering on my part. Many times I held my tongue because if I were to say something that contradicted another's message, it would only further confuse the players. What I thought needed correcting had to be done with as little fanfare as possible, hoping also that the player would not notice what I was doing. Whether my under-the-table tactics were recognized I don't know, but the players were more important than some instructor's ego.

My evaluation of an infielder took into account not only his ability, but how he carried himself, how he spoke, what his mannerisms were on and off the field, in the dugout and the clubhouse, how he reacted with other players, how he responded to his own play and that of his teammates, and how he accepted criticism or instruction. Mechanically, I was first interested in the set-up or starting position he used to field a ground ball. I looked for it to have a freedom that would allow him to move easily and quickly for the ball, especially laterally. With his other actions and movements, I tried to mentally match what adjustments were needed with what ability I believed him to have to adopt them.

One thing I did not want to see was the little hop or jump used to get into his set-up or starting position that was so adamantly thought necessary in the major-league staff meeting previously mentioned. That little maneuver was an absolute no-no for me. To reinforce the uselessness of this maneuver, I held a few sessions when I showed my infielders video footage of one of the game's best second baseman ever, Hall of Fame member Roberto Alomar, who for twenty years set up the very same way I had been teaching. But even that wasn't enough to convince some who "knew better." To demonstrate the validity of my conviction to one of our unbelieving first-round picks who argued that he was quicker with his little hop, I videotaped him during a game. Only when he saw the video from the angle I had taken it did he understand the logic of my instruction. It clearly showed the ball being hit well before he was able to move for it because of his little jump.

Every young infielder coming into the professional game arrived with his own baggage in the form of the instruction he had received from his previous instructors. Some of what many told me of their former teachers was startling. One infielder from a prominent college program had a catcher as his head coach, which explained the strange squatting position he assumed when fielding the ball. More surprising was being almost unanimously told of no help being given them at all. Rarely, and I do mean rarely, did any new draftee come professionally ready. So little of what was being taught at the amateur levels, high school and college, translated into the play-for-pay game. What does this say for the quality of what is being taught in all of the clinics, classes, instructional schools in which Moms and Dads invest? Every once in a while a player would come along to whom there was nothing I could say, not because he was the epitome of sound fundamental techniques, but because he was highly efficient with his slightly unorthodox approach to the ball, had an uncanny ability to read it coming off the bat, and always found the "good hop" to field. Those abilities are the foundation, and the absolute requisites for anyone wanting to become a better-than-average infielder.

Are today's infielders better than those of years ago? Absolutely! Some of them do things that were never seen in the '60s and '70s. Most defensive plays made then were fundamentally sound, standardized by tradition, disciplined and scripted from years of use, rather than with the innovative and acrobatic style so often seen today, which, more than it's recognized, sometimes gets infielders into trouble. But it is what it is. ESPN displays the day's greatest plays, and yes, some of them live up to their exciting pronouncements, but most are lavishly, though undeservedly, praised.

So much of the mediocrity seen nearly every night on television in high definition does not warrant the accolades and applause it is given. The gratuitous hype that players receive is greatly exaggerated, making it difficult to watch for anyone old enough to compare generations. Relativity makes what they do acceptable.

Insiders agree that the game of baseball on all levels is not played as well today as it was twenty-five or more years ago. The home run and a growing media blitz add much to the joy the public finds in the game, but so also do the errors, bobbles, wild throws, unblocked pitches, missed-pitch locations, misreads, poor jumps, and base-running gaffs because of the excitement a dramatic comeback causes when a team overcomes such blunders to win the game. If it were not for the lenient scoring today, the number of player errors would be even greater. Mistakes and miscues cause many games to see-saw with the winner often determined to be the team committing the fewest bonehead plays.

So, after all of this ranting, and with all of my suppositions, can I say that my twenty-five years as a professional infield instructor were worth my second effort in the game? Absolutely. Were it possible, I would do it all over again! Knowing that someone made the major leagues in part because of my efforts will forever be a highlight of my career.

7

NEW KIDS ON THE BLOCK

Despite extraordinarily well-equipped weight rooms, and the introduction of conditioning programs judged to be of cutting-edge reliability, intended to not only enhance play, but reduce the burgeoning rash of injuries that were crippling rosters, baseball has seen neither occur. The physical problems and endless breakdowns of major-league players is an industrywide concern, and not even with everyone's collected efforts has a suitable answer been found for why this is happening. Keeping the training rooms even slightly less occupied would be considered successful, but how to do that remains a mystery.

When baseball morphed into the age of technology and corporate responsibility, a new mentality emerged that believed there had to be a more productive method to bring out the best in a player, one that was far better than what had been in place for the past 150 years, one that would keep players healthy and improve their on-field performances. With baseball a relatively passive sport, such thinking made sense. No consideration had ever been given to how play might be enhanced if the players were better conditioned. Logic seemed to indicate that a thorough probe and exhaustive research in this and related areas might prove useful with anything discovered more than welcomed.

The game may not have been ready for the renaissance that was coming, but its new leaders were determined to install new guidelines that revealed the scope of their degrees and diplomas. Their intentions were to infuse baseball with revolutionary scientific and technological ideas. Sitting in the games loftiest positions, the young guns in charge were resolute in thinking they were on the right path, and though it may not have been their intent with all they planned to do, they were about to reinvent the game.

In their conscientious resolve, baseball organizations now leave nothing to chance, either in their search for talent, or the need for its quick development. Any new concept that might accelerate that time-consuming process is given serious examination. Any resource thought to be of value to the athlete—his body, his mind, and even his life—will be studied and, if found even slightly advantageous, implemented. This approach is a radical change from history, and could be justified and determined worthwhile if it made a difference, but has it?

Players have their own inner clocks. They progress at a genetically calculated pace, talented or not. As welcomed as it would be to push their development, they are ready when they are ready, no earlier. This ill-defined and blurry truth cannot be denied. With the changes the game has inflicted upon itself from within by the new breed in charge, and those from the natural transformation of society, baseball is no longer what it was, and neither are its athletes. Today's player is oblivious to what the normal course of a player's development had historically been because his own has taken a different path. Outside influences and a modern psychology have joined to selfishly steal, alter, and redirect what used to be every player's laser-like focus on performance. Distractions abound. Any number of outside powers, including the histrionics of a media blitz never before seen, have transformed every process within the game into something old-timers have difficulty understanding. And no end seems to be in sight.

Workouts, practices, and "the old way" don't appear to carry the trusted value they once did. That can certainly be disputed, but like it or not, those of us who remember those old ways cringe at the new game and its array of different policies that have reshaped what we knew baseball to be.

Today there is a psychological state known as "mindfulness," and something called "deep practice" espoused by some of the game's mental doctors. They are two of the newest terms to creep into the clubhouse lexicon that define what is thought to be the esoteric and enlightened discovery that what the game needs from its participants is a more intense, committed focus for the task at hand. What seems to be misunderstood is that, for decades, this has been an old-school, never-questioned tenet. It is all the game was ever about. Couching the need for a greater effort as if it were some new-age awakening is nothing more than the twisted rediscovery of the past that is bought by those who are thrilled with all of the psychological abstractions that are present-day baseball.

It is hard to fault the effort being given the game, but a more-invincible athlete has not been created despite the implementation of state-of-the-art conditioning strategies, and the wealth of well-intentioned psychological, nutritional, and educational programs. Play has suffered, and injuries have surprisingly increased. Studies and analyses abound, all with a dedicated solicitude, but nothing in this unwavering commitment to find remedies for the decline in player performances, and the industry's growing health issues, has been found.

The physical breakdowns that many hoped would be controlled have instead escalated. Often just routine workouts, and the everyday ordinary physical requirements of the game become problematic. Injuries are increasing across-the-board at an alarming rate. For far too many young men entering the game, baseball's traditional skills that have been executed safely for decades are, instead, producing an unwanted uneasiness. With the direction the game has taken, and with a different kind of athlete in tow, the responsibilities of the men in charge have increased dramatically.

Words like "conditioning," "training," or anything with similar connotations may not have meant much to the game's earliest competitors, but beginning in the 1970s, in the 1980s for sure, the men who were gaining control of the game were about to transform and revolutionize it with an approach they believed would be of tremendous benefit on many fronts. Previously untapped territories would be explored, and many new visionary concepts never before seen in the game's history would be implemented.

There was no hesitation on their part in believing that with their new ideas and looming technology they could create more efficient athletes. That wasn't necessarily a wrong consideration, but to fully jump in headfirst without regard for the consequences could have been done with greater preparation. What they didn't realize was that drastic changes to tradition were not needed and, more to their surprise, would not bring about the success they had expected. Not all organizations have taken the same detailed path, but it seems to have permeated many of them in one way or another.

The game had survived for decades with the belief that nothing more than playing it would bring out the best in a player, that nothing else was needed, or had to be done to maximize his skills, that injuries were part of the game, and bound to happen. The new corporate leadership believed this to be antiquated thinking, no way for players to fully develop, and that a stagnant and less-than-complete athlete was the result. Thinking theirs to be a better way, the executives took the game in a more corporate direction.

With little knowledge of how the game had been played, and no baseball experience themselves from which to make a judgment, they felt that the game had been treading water; that it was ripe for a few scholarly and intellectual alterations. After years of study at some of the finest scholastic institutions in this country, these new, young managers hoped to inject a philosophy that would replace what they considered the stale thinking that had been guiding the game. They sought resources heretofore untapped and introduced innovative, radical, and bold proposals that broke from tradition. These new sheriffs were going to oversee a different future for their hirelings.

Conditioning programs were restructured, nutritional and supplementation protocols established, and the physical well-being of their athletes more strictly monitored. And to their credit—something from which I could have definitely benefited—they dove headlong into managing and alleviating the critical and pivotal emotional and psychological issues that were normal occupational stressors. They educated the players to everything they were seemingly unaware of about themselves and the game, hoping that a less-stressed athlete would be more productive.

The game was given a modern up-to-date identity, a new persona that would siphon away its old traditions. The results of this metamorphous may not have been easily recognizable on the field, but an unconventional master plan brilliantly devised and executed with a regimentation not seen before was being developed from within. Every potential alteration would be intensely scrutinized and implemented with what was thought to be sound and reasoned justification.

The rough, tough, jock mentality that was once baseball would have a more congenial, business-like persona indicative of the new executives themselves. What was misunderstood was that the players in their employ were no longer dyed-in-the-wool baseball junkies with no other interests; they cavorted in a new and different world. They had decades before railed against the subservient treatment they'd long endured, and with a staunch collective resolve that had been festering, wrestled the reins from the hands of the owners.

With players freed from the bondage of the reserve clause, management began to look at players differently, just as the players with their new perspective looked at the game differently. Changes were instituted that were expected to not only enhance a player's ability, and many tangential aspects of his character, but the game itself. It was a noble objective. The consensus was that each innovative program, thoroughly examined and diligently studied for its efficacy, would overhaul and modernize what was considered the unstructured and undisciplined lifestyle of the old baseball hero. Since the game's inception in the early 1800s, no one had given any serious thought to, or had any comprehension of the capabilities of the human body, but there had to be something, so it was thought, that could be done to improve a player's performance while keeping him free from harm.

The new moguls would recondition and remodel the athletes they inherited to better blend with the world in which they themselves lived. Some things, however, were missing in their planned modernization. They failed to recognize that all they needed to do was demand more from their players, and increase a workload that had lessened much as society had forsaken its own responsibilities in its own search for a lifestyle that was believed more deserved.

With no lengthy history in the game, the corporate heads could understandably be excused for this oversight, much as they could for not recognizing that they were dealing with a different athlete, someone no longer a student of the game, someone devoid of the expected sound baseball fundamentals who had neither learned nor been taught the game as those before him had. Committed to their vision, the leaders began to free the athlete from the traditional physical requirements of the game by generously and selflessly installing a solicitous program of standards that leaned more on his safety and well-being than his performance.

Their most strategic implementation was to march players as they might soldiers into well-equipped weight rooms on the assumption that stronger and healthier players would perform significantly better. With other resources to follow that were considered similar enhancements to maximize their athletes' skills, the transformation of baseball had begun. What went unrecognized with these new proposals was that the traditional and necessary fundamental field work, so vital and important for the expected improvement and consistency of play, would be commensurately diminished.

There was logic to the belief that a player who was stronger and better conditioned would be a better player. That sounded absolutely reasonable. What downside could there possibly be for any player to be more fit? But that rationale appears flimsy, and the question now is how flawed is this new philosophy? Or is it merely ineffective on a new breed of players who are less talented, not as fundamentally sound, and whose baseball background has been less complete than those of previous generations? No strong correlation between an increase in strength and an increase in performance has been proven except in those with talent, and even then there are limits. Strength cannot be discounted, but for those without sufficient skills, a buff mirrored reflection may be the best to hope for.

Of the hundreds of young infield draftees to whom I was introduced, few entered the game in the required physical condition that allowed them to realize their full potential. Moreover, of no help was the installed and inadequate method of development and conditioning. The amount of work done on the baseball field diminished under the new regime. The untold number of repetitions normally required that would merely just begin to affect the development of a particular skill was reduced, falling far short of what was needed. This workload should have been increased to at least offset the changes in effect, but the game was devoid of capable leaders able to determine, recognize, or understand where the apex of a particular player's development might be. The game was afloat, but sinking.

Whatever was being accomplished under the guise of baseball's new internal structure was not translating well. With no consistent, daily schedule of concentrated work on the actions and maneuvers that would produce the consistency of play required, even those players with talent would never deliver fast enough what was expected of them.

This constriction of on-field work naturally changed the game on display. Presumably played by better-conditioned athletes, the game was increasingly riddled with mistakes, miscues, and errors. Instead of incorporating strategy and skill with an understanding of the impact that defensive play had on the game, and for so long had been its persona, it relied on the air being filled with baseballs as the newly created athletes bombarded the fences with home runs. Unfortunately, the long ball was no magic elixir or cure for the continued sloppy play.

Precaution was a key word in this transformation of the players. Pampered as they were, lest they be overworked, they were more susceptible than ever to a variety of physical problems, injuries of major and minor varieties. What was happening? Were the players at fault? Did they lack a responsibility for their own well-being? Was it their lifestyle, a poor work ethic? There seemed to be no definitive reason.

Not to be ignored was the role played by the confusion and naiveté about the game and its needs, sports in general, and the athlete in particular by the "new-age" executives in charge. To say that both sides had a hand in sharing these problems to varying degrees would not be wrong.

Today's players are imposing physical specimens, but their indestructible look belies their anticipated performance. Appearance is not translating to sound fundamental play. The profound changes in the game regarding how its athletes are conditioned, and the significance of other programs meant to influence their physical and mental well-being raise many questions about their effectiveness seen from the results. The dots do not seem to be connected as intended. Unless fundamental work is increased, and accountability demanded, the game will continue to be played as it is. The path it is on will continue undeterred while the executives remain confounded and helpless.

No one is ready to accept even the slightest possibility that more time spent on the field working on specific needs would in any way be a fundamental and physical benefit. Baseball has somewhere forgotten that repetition is one solution if there is to be success, and for those with potential, it is the only way to maximize expectations. The work that should be taking place is not, and this paucity has done nothing but foster continued research, discussion, and a more intense move in the same misguided direction, with no better answers found. What were considered to be solutions are not solving the game's problems, They are, instead, feeding and condoning them.

Where is that athlete of yesteryear, that player who could endure the rigors of the game? Rosters are in a constant state of flux to accommodate the latest injuries. Has something happened to the human body, reducing its ability to throw, hit, and chase a ball day after day without a team of doctors nearby? Nothing is either strange or different about today's athlete except that his evolution has paralleled society's. Could that be what has triggered the supposedly new look the game is thought to require? Has this natural evolution been responsible for provoking a more erudite management of the old procedures and guidelines, once considered complete in their simplicity, and thought to be necessary to maximize a talent, that are no longer producing what was expected?

The contemporary player acts and reacts unlike his predecessors, and it wouldn't matter what is examined or questioned; he is simply different. Is the new curriculum drawing all it can from him? Are the imaginative programs as beneficial as they are perceived to be? Why hasn't the quality of play improved while all this is happening? Of greater interest, what is causing the rash of physical problems? Is it reasonable to have expected that the injected, supposedly superior training methods would have answered all of this? If they have not, what might there be to replace them?

Even if we were to disregard the effects of the physical conditioning methods under the new policies, there is no doubt why fundamental play is not what it was, or why players are so often found on the disabled list unable to perform. Players of my era and earlier grew up in a different world. Every minute we spent on a playground acclimated and conditioned us to whatever sport or game we were playing. The rules and nuances of each were learned through participation, thus building a storeroom full of athletic potential while simultaneously discovering the precautions and methods necessary to avoid injury.

The specific control of movements and techniques that kept us injury-free were unknowingly instilled while we threw, hit, ran, jumped, and chased a ball or each other. Being knocked down, tackled, or otherwise falling as much as we did, we learned we learned how to avoid or, otherwise, endure the mishaps. Our welfare was born from participation that conditioned our bodies to naturally tolerate specific actions and stresses.

So many of today's youngsters have no such history. A plethora of outside interests other than sports now occupy Junior's time, most that have him sitting in front of a monitor focused on a video game, or the newest application of some kind. When he does participate, safety is now more a factor than is his effort. Societal mores dictate that the youngest members of our households attend karate, dance, judo, or gymnastics lessons; enroll in a sewing, pottery, or art class; or learn to play a guitar, saxophone, trumpet, or piano, certainly at least one instrument. There seems to be no end to the extracurricular, time-consuming activities that are today's parenting responsibilities.

Even homework doesn't amount to much anymore. With little time at home for dinner and not much else before bedtime, educators seem to have given up on even asking that extra work be done. With a reduction in what used to be the old-fashioned "run around town playing as much as you could with your friends" playtime, our kids today don't know how to avoid the dangers inherent in any of the sports. They've not had enough of an embedded athletic past, or the much-needed fun time that would have improved their play, and kept them out of harm's way.

Consider baseball's "knockdown" pitch, if that action is even remembered. It was once common for hitters to "get decked," to be thrown at, and hit on purpose. It was part of the game. Certain situations made its occurrence mandatory. Pitchers routinely intimidated hitters by throwing at their heads. For any batter, "hitting the dirt" was a quickly learned response first understood as a youngster.

Today's hitters, with no such concern, cannot, and even worse, don't know how to avoid a fastball, whether errant or intended. They dig in armed for battle wearing specially designed protective gear, including face-guards, thinking only of how hard they want to hit the ball. They show no fear. Reinforcing their bravado are the many pitchers who express fear of hitting a batter! A ninety-five mile-an-hour fastball whistling inside to an innocent batter can quickly change his naiveté into a frightening situation with serious facial or head injuries the result. Less severe are the broken fingers, hands, wrists, and ensuing on-field fights and hostilities. The term "beanball" has all but been eliminated from our vocabulary because of the stricter enforcement of baseball's rules at every level, the enforced transformation of the game, and the specific changes in pitching philosophies. The only thing to provoke its use now is anger.

Injuries have occurred at an accelerated pace, and much too frequently to those who use the rooms filled with heavy balls, barbells, squat machines, and a mix of other equipment whose intended purpose was to mitigate them. Common problems that occur with backs, arms, and legs, now have company with bicep, calf, oblique, and abdominal issues. Too often something as harmless as infield practice sidelines a player.

Correctly diving for the baseball, running into an outfield wall, and stepping correctly on a base are now lessons to be taught. As a twelve-year-old, I learned very quickly to pay strict attention to what I was doing the day I ran into the pole of a playground swing set while chasing a fly ball without looking where I was going. The abrupt stop to my run and the ringing in my head was a sudden lesson to be alert to unexpected dangers. It was on-the-job training at its best.

The act of running the bases has presented its own precautions, and stopping at one by sliding remains one of the game's puzzling and greatest challenges. The feet-first slide is a lost art. New draftees and veterans do it with peril, but it receives little attention. Though outlawed by some organizations in their minor-league system, the headfirst slide is the slide of preference, and easily contributes to broken fingers and jammed shoulders.

Only playground time and the multiple situations encountered there can provide the understanding of how to safely navigate the game while learning how it should be played. Much of what was once naturally understood about the game by its players is no longer part of the genetic information the newest generations bring with them. This has added more baggage to the concerns and responsibilities of those in control.

Might there be a connection between the transformation of the game and the mounting number of injuries? Front-office personnel apparently believe not. Is it possible they believe that the plethora of injuries are simply an inevitability? I would hope not. That today's player is bigger and stronger is all the more reason to be cautious about making the body tighter and restricted with more muscle. But the strength programs continue unrestrained, and though cautiously watched and monitored as they are, there is no thought that any part of the entire program should be altered. With too much work done "inside" and not enough "outside," something somewhere in the body must give when called on to make the explosive movements and actions the game requires.

I have no doubt that the weight programs are more than partially to blame. They cause more problems than anyone is willing to admit, but the refusal to lay blame on them is easily understood. Should they be responsible, the organizations would look foolish. What a contradiction it would be were they to be the cause rather than the expected panacea.

The "pointy-headed pencil pushers," what my favorite former field coordinator called the front-office brass, have unconditionally handed over their athletes to educated, and carefully selected strength and conditioning coaches, whose efforts are to be commended. They do what they can to devise and incorporate programs that extrapolate the results of exhaustive studies, research, and critical findings into positives. It puzzles me how the athletes that cost franchises millions of dollars, and are the reasons for a team's success or failure, have been so trustingly placed in the hands of people who have no way to prove that what they're doing is foolproof, despite their degrees and certifications. As thoughtful and considerate as these conditioning programs might be, they have done nothing to end the regurgitation of the same perplexing question, "What is happening here?"

With weight training and its peripherals the most significant enhancement introduced to the game, nothing substantiates its validity to the entirety of the participants. Certainly it has value, but who knows what specific detrimental effects for someone might be hiding in this resource?

Whereas I preferred position-specific work, the strength coaches championed what they were taught. They pushed the protocol to what they had been indoctrinated as a requirement of their employment. They very responsibly wielded a carte blanche kind of power when it came to getting players ready to perform, much more than the on-field staff members who were schooled in the game's specific actions that were certainly more relevant. How the biggest portion of a conditioning program confined to a roomful of exercise equipment or an agility field benefits a player's performance was something I was unable to fully comprehend.

The one thing I questioned about any strength and conditioning program was the cogency of it to be universally instituted and demandingly implemented. It's improbable that any one program could fit the needs of every athlete. What is in place may be suitably generic and thought to be safe, but I have witnessed the negative effects that its singularity has had on some. A genuine and immense concern for the health of the athletes is evident, though it is so often hidden behind the shadow of hopeful probability.

One uncovered study perplexingly predicted the power potential of a hitter being dependent on his leg strength, which was determined by the amount of weight he could move on the leg-press machine. This was nothing definitive, but the connection raises questions. Leg strength is an important component of hitting, but no connection, or even mention of it in the study was made in regard to the more important fundamental hitting mechanics or overall ability of the player. The general finding of the study was not in dispute, but its application would require much more than what its simplistic conclusion offered.

How much greater would the current leg issues be, i.e., pulls, tears, cramps, if this study was believed and its policy implemented with impunity? An appropriate question might be: How often are similar studies and their similarly ambiguous results being injected into the present-day conditioning programs under the guise of accepted propriety to the detriment of the athletes?

Players have bounced around dots on the floor to supposedly make them lighter and quicker on their feet, been made to run with parachutes billowing behind for resistance, and have pulled each other along with large rubber bands to enhance their speed and strength. They've run around more rubber traffic cones than most of us have passed on the highways, raced full speed down ramps, tiptoed through ladders on the ground, and spent countless hours sprinting in different directions through an endless variety of agility drills, all with the intended expectation of improving their play.

Every activity spoke to an increase in athleticism, but when done sporadically with no consistency, of what benefit could they be? If excellence is expected, the execution of anything physical only once or twice a week will never affect an athletic performance. I've witnessed the use of a number of oddball devices, so-called "new-age" inventions, machines, and free try-it-for-a-while gimmicks that have provided little in the way of long-term benefits, mostly because their use was obviously unconvincing from the start. Each "bright idea" was nothing more than a time- and energy-consuming distraction from the more-important work that was required for the fundamental to which it was pointed.

Indoor work has value, but the extent to which it does is something for discussion. To consider it more valuable than extra field work more than tweaks my concerns. Gym time should be in addition to the very necessary work to refine and improve the skills that baseball requires. It should in no way replace it. With health issues as significant as they are, and such a huge financial hit to an organization, the weight and conditioning programs continue to escape blame. The idealities expected of them continue to be researched and studied, but no answers appear forthcoming. Furthermore, a refusal to go in any other direction is apparent. If the programs in place continue failing to produce significantly better players, and the injuries continue, maybe it is time to take a closer, and more critical look at them.

Exactly what is or has been the true value of any of weight and conditioning programs as devised? Have they contributed to more championships? That appears unlikely, but can that even be determined? I'm not sure that any analysis can conclusively say they have or have not. How about just more wins? That too appears doubtful, and indeterminate. More home runs? That would get a yes, but the mechanics of hitting and their tweaking is the only aspect of the game that truly gets attention.

So what does all this mean? If none of the new strategies provide recognizable improvement in how the game is played, and only a small percentage of major-league prospects within an organization reach their potential, which is usually what happens, can it be said that the real success of a franchise is only the result of having sufficient funds to buy the best players available once they reach the free-agent market?

If that is a reality, it is difficult to deny that the impact of the extra years of playing time have had a more profound affect on development than any innovative organizational program. The amount of time needed for any one player to master the difficulty of the game cannot be determined, but it is always longer than expected.

America's game is no longer the intriguing encounter of strategy, anticipation, and skill that it once was. It is now a media-hyped corporate contest that offers a lessening and disheartened style of play, a monotonous replication of itself from day to day. Nothing, however, deters the adoration heaped on it by an unsuspecting public.

What used to be two teams battling and combating each others tactics is now the tedium of waiting for the inevitable big hit in what are sterile home run hitting contests. What started as an unprecedented commitment to transform what was, has become a casual acceptance of what is, with the only reasonable consideration for its remedy being retreat.

Maybe the old way wasn't so bad after all.

8

BsR, VoRP, EqA, and xFIP

You may not have to remove your shoes, take off your belt, or empty your pockets, but gaining entry into the cyber-kingdom of any one of baseball's major-league front offices is tantamount to being inspected by the Transportation Security Administration. No one is permitted access without an official pass or escort, and identifying yourself falls just short of iris recognition, or being fingerprinted. The inner sanctums of our national pastime are considered hallowed ground.

Baseball is operated somewhat sanctimoniously with an intellect heretofore unknown. No longer is the general manager a crusty old baseball veteran, schooled on the game from decades of service as he was, who occupies a sparsely furnished office studying the day's sports pages to see how some young phenom he is hoping to acquire fared the night before. Information that was once gathered with eyes and ears, and sensibly and correctly extrapolated, now appears as lifeless numbers algorithmically calculated by computers. Mathematical assessments have become the life-blood of baseball.

Thirty or so years ago baseball began freeing itself from the judgments and opinions of the human "dinosaurs" who were running the game. The office personnel, of which there were few, worked under sparse conditions. The brilliant men and women who fill the cubicles and roam the corridors today cavort in plush, professionally designed and decorated surroundings. Every staff member is a pedigreed bookworm, a graduate from any one of the country's many prestigious universities. All are computer-literate and business-minded with an uncanny ability to scan technological data and Internet sites with the same interest the crusty, old general manager did the sports pages. You can't turn a corner now without bumping into someone. Back in the '60s, when I walked into the offices of the Oakland Coliseum and yelled, no one would have responded. I knew there were employees, the question was, where.

The title of general manager as applied to my Oakland A's could have been considered a fictitious position because it was the owner, Charles O. Finley, and his cousin Carl who ran the club in tandem. It was often the relative who had the upper hand. A comptroller, Finley's longtime secretary, the club's traveling secretary, and a few other essential employees were about all you'd find. This skeleton crew was kept in line by the owner's pecuniary idiosyncrasies, one being an unannounced phone call to be sure that everyone was accounted for, and another to be sure he was not being cheated out a full eight-hour day of work by someone.

Present-day organizations are not run in such a bleak or dictatorial fashion. They are well-staffed, well-structured, and corporately efficient. Management carefully goose-steps to a well-designed master plan with carefully thought-out principles. They know what they want, the direction in which they want to go, and they do so in wonderfully comfortable offices and board rooms. Marble floors, exquisite artwork, and statuary are common. Spacious waiting areas are beautifully decorated. Conference rooms seat dozens. The offices and cubicles that line every corridor are staffed with as many employees as there are computers, printers, and technological devices. The brilliance roaming the hallways is startling

Employees are outfitted with the latest cell phones contracted with ample amounts of minutes for the all-important messaging that takes place. There is no limit to the number that are sent during a day, and a single monthly personal phone bill topping $1500.00 has been known to occur. Why talk when you can text and avoid eye-to-eye contact? It is no longer important to be a people person to excel in business. The human element has given way to QWERTY, the coined word from a group of letters on a standard computer keyboard.

In place are Human Resources divisions. Whether my teammates and I were ever considered human was debatable. Seriously formulated mission statements on the walls describe the focus and intent of today's franchises. Conversations are educated, syntax perfect, and scholarly, and can easily intimidate the uninitiated. Baseball is in an era of intelligence it has never before experienced. Everything about the game has been given an erudite transformation.

Baseball organizations profited for decades because of the economic restraints of their owners. Today they are gigantic corporations making millions of dollars led by people who might very well be graduates from the Harvard School of Business. An executive of the past might have been a former player considered sufficiently competent for the position upon retiring, or some office worker who had learned every aspect of the game from decades of dedicated service for which he had received promotion after promotion. He might have even started out as a lowly "clubby" —a clubhouse worker—doing most of the club's grunt work, and running errands for the players; baseball was in his blood.

The game operates in a fiscal and legal discipline that requires lawyers, accountants, and financial planners to review and untangle the seven-, eight-, and nine-figure multiyear contracts that no longer have shock value. My world was characterized by the take-it-or-leave-it one-year proposals mailed through the US Post Office by either the owner himself, or his mouthpiece, that crusty old general manager. Negotiations, if our contract talks could have been so considered, might have been hours of contentious haggling just to finagle a few thousand dollars from a penny-pinching owner while hoping to survive the battle with as little emotional scarring as possible. For most of us, it was little cared, or not at all, how well we had played the previous season, we were not getting any more money. Decades earlier it had been even worse. Batting champions received nothing because their club didn't win. Should a World Series be won, the winning check was considered the following season's raise.

The increased wisdom and greater consciousness that have infiltrated baseball in recent decades are perfect alliances for every tangential aspect of the huge business it has become. But how that intellect benefits the players and the game on the field remains questionable. Somewhere in the future this new intelligence may prove to have influenced any single club's position in the pennant race, but we find no evidence of that happening. Today's pioneers have transformed the game according to their own steadfast reasoning. They avoid the past like a plague as if there is nothing of value to have come from the more than 150 years that the game has been played; the use of a bat and ball has not changed.

Technology and electronic thought have replaced the human element that at one time was the foundation of the game. Common sense, good judgment, and the experience of a lifetime in the game were at one time essential prognosticators, responsible for performances to come. That rationale has gone the way of the "been in the game as long as he can remember" general manager. Experience is no longer needed to run a ball club. Considered more important is to have matriculated at some Ivy League school.

Baseball evaluations long existed on "feel." Gut reactions, instincts, and decades of service fueled decisions. Today's player is computerized, molded, categorized, and slotted, his ability subdivided between positions. He is projected, and graded more than he is being developed. Much of what should be considered seems to go unnoticed, yet so much is expected.

Any algorithm, mathematical equation, or numerical finding that appears positive fuels an optimistic belief that is unconditionally accepted, yet this cerebral approach guarantees nothing. The way players are analyzed today would make Abner Doubleday and Alexander Cartwright sit upright in their graves were they able. There are pluses to what has been discovered, and the data to support all the statistical findings appear sound. The hope is that it will all provide an edge in finding that special player or two who will change the fate of an organization, and put a championship ring on everyone's finger. Unfortunately, nothing definitive indicates that all of this new intellect leads to the successes sought.

Decisions based on the definitions of conjured acronyms seem to hold more weight than reality. Old-timers know what RBI (runs batted in) and ERA (earned run average) mean, but they might confuse OPS (on base plus slugging percentage) with UPS (United Parcel Service) or WHIP (walks plus hits per inning pitched) with whip (a strap or belt or to beat or thrash somebody or something). They could explain HBP (hit by pitch) and GIDP (grounded into double play), but would have no clue what EqA (Equivalent Average), BsR (base runs), or xFIP (expected fielding independent pitching) refer to.

They would know much less about PFR (Power Finesse Ratio), LIPS (Late Inning Pressure Situation), and my favorite, PECOTA (Player Empirical Comparison and Optimization Test Algorithm). I won't begin to try and explain any of the more esoteric ones because first, it is unnecessary for my purpose; second, I'm unsure that I could; third, I would do none of them justice; and fourth, although many are considered to be an objective look at baseball by none other than the much-recognized historian Bill James and his colleagues, he and other sabermetricians agree on their subjective unreliability.

Each mysterious mix of letters categorizes, ranks, files, and purports to evaluate some aspect of an individual's play more cerebrally than could have ever been imagined, and in a way that can be understood only by an equally like-minded person. An easier category to understand is VoRP (Value Over Replacement Player) which, in simple terms, determines the contributing value a particular hitter or pitcher makes to his team in comparison to a replacement player with no more than average defensive ability, but who is a below-average hitter.

As if its definition is not difficult enough to interpret, who and what is an average player and how is "average" determined? Against what? Compared to what? And why must he be a below-average hitter? Every question provokes a subjective answer. Why would an average player even be playing if there were someone better? The better player should always be in the game. And why is "average" even used as the model against whom all others are judged? I am unable to understand all of this. More important, is there a need for it?

Any good baseball man could do the same with a quick thumbs up or thumbs down, avoiding the need to unravel the meaning of some confusing alphabetical abbreviation. The formulas for these evaluative categories result in abstract findings that have little practical use because, as with all of these suppositions, they are volatile when applied to but one game, just as all performances cannot be repeated from one game to the next.

A possible worthwhile study is something called Wins Above Replacement, or WAR. These initials are ironic considering what a battle it is to understand any of these alphabetical categories. Defined as Batting Runs + Base Running Runs + Fielding Runs + Positional Adjustment + League Adjustment + Replacement Runs/ Runs per Win, its final number tells which player does more for his team to win. That would seem to be important, but not once did I hear it or any of the other acronymic formulas ever mentioned in the clubhouse, or around a conference table when players were discussed. Their interpretations result in numerical calculations that mask the realities of the game while provoking meaningless discussions that appear to be informative, but are more appropriate fodder for the theatrics of ESPN, Baseball Tonight, and the cable networks. They are great sound bites, but predict nothing concrete in their pointed purpose. They can't because baseball is too unpredictable, and if it were to ever become predictable, what fun would that be?

What was it about baseball that brought such thinking and the computer into prominence? The better question might be this: what and how was it thought that the computer could contribute to baseball, or even influence it? Apparently some saw its possibilities.

With their never-ending search for athletic excellence, major-league organizations, some more than others, now use this cyber-sleuthing to what they think is their best advantage. Several have given the computer almost unfettered control, accepting its magical formulas with a form of religiosity. When the game's historical penchant for statistics is considered, we can better understand that it was only a matter of time before the young minds entering the game with PCs under their arms would gravitate to these in-depth analyses of the game believing the resulting computations to be beneficial. Would finding the best player be any easier? Could a ThinkPad discover some mysterious skill that was going unnoticed, or provide the answers that would quicken the road to a championship? The move to accepting statistical data as a determinant has significantly lessened the powers of observation that for so long were the backbone of evaluating talent. Numbers may not lie, but they also do not breathe. They are inanimate, incomplete prognosticators, black and white predictors lacking the shades of those colors that are so much the totality of a talent.

What opens the door for employment in the front offices of baseball today is a stellar intelligent quotient (IQ). The new executives have put their MBAs and other degrees to work examining the potentials of an array of mathematical equations and percentages that other scholars have put before them. They are faced with a columnar pad of categories, the number of which blurs the mind of baseball purists, each titled by some combination of letters of the alphabet, and providing a result that is intended to simplify, and more accurately, define the player-selection process. Most old-timers could argue from memory and personal experience the exploits of Ruth versus Cobb versus Mays versus Mantle versus DiMaggio, or any number of other players with clarity and conviction without such hieroglyphics. On the other hand, they would freeze open-mouthed trying to decipher and interpret the new statistical columns with their never-before-heard-of definitions.

The grizzled old GM, baseball junkie that he was, wouldn't know how to navigate a computer. He could, however, give you a similar, but more comprehensive answer to your queries about a player's talents than the computer could, and it would be contained in only a handful of words, such as "He can't play!" Furthermore, he wouldn't need a PC to tell you that so-and-so shouldn't be a leadoff hitter; player A might not be around for long; player B will never become a good outfielder no matter who thinks otherwise; and player C can really play, and should be given a chance.

Despite a relentless optimism within the game, the truth is that the sabermetric findings do nothing to solve the issues with someone who can't play. Finding, developing, and improving talent is the bottom line. The interesting and informative summations being mechanically calculated indicate where improvement is needed, but they provide no solutions. New technology, new analytics, new this, and new that are used as if the game was a science, and the search is continual for any psychological, physical, or emotional test or examination, program, theory, or study that might allow a step or two to be skipped in what is the normal development of a player. Unfortunately, there are no shortcuts.

Player evaluations have been traditionally made by the application of some number between two and eight, or twenty and eighty, that grade a particular ability or "tool," to use the baseball vernacular. Though made with as much objectivity as possible, they are always subjective, a guess, somewhat educated, but nevertheless a guess. Some clubs develop their own numbering system, hoping that some newer version will provide a greater and deeper clarification, but every projection of a player's performance is uncertain and ambiguous. No number, letter, grade, title, or name devised to make something appear better ever will. A skill is a skill; a tool is a tool. It will improve if worked on—maybe—but not by defining it differently, or giving it a different face.

Using numbers to make evaluations can confuse the issue of playability. No matter how great a specific tool is—it will be a constant only in the least number of players—it loses its significance when it doesn't blend or "play" with other player tools or skills. Someone might be considered a decent everyday player if certain of his statistics were considered, but he may have significant failings when his overall situational production is evaluated. A smarter approach would be to put more consideration into what a player can't do, and for that no number is needed. Knowing his limitations makes more sense, and eliminates becoming unnecessarily confident through any unpredictable calculated optimism.

Management surely recognizes this variable, they see a player's shortcomings, but changes in the game's structure have forced impatience and optimism, no matter how skewed they may be, and too often the positives are more heavily favored than they should be. Because of the loss to free agency in the '70s, the time needed for today's investments to materialize has been considerably shortened, and that does not bode well for the lesser talent that is available.

It's not unreasonable to think that just about every potential major-league player needs three or more years of weaning—five is optimally better—but even that apprenticeship can't guarantee that he will be ready and productive. Knowing this, and with the brief time organizations have control over their players, management needs answers quickly. Unfortunately, wishing something to happen generates hasty decisions. When a computer spews out what appears to be positive, enthusiasm for a player broadens, and had he been a high pick, and given a large bonus, what optimism there is balloons. With the return on a team's investment then thought to be on the brink of probability, an unwarranted and premature opportunity can easily be given. No decision is easy, but when statistical analysis is applied, it often tends to rationalize the selections organizations make.

The world of baseball is now too much a world of technological exploration. Many players use their Smart Phones, iPads, laptops, and tablets more efficiently than the bat and glove. The diversion in a locker room is not the game of baseball, but who tweeted whom and what did he tweet? Facebook and YouTube get more attention than strikeouts. Nights are never long enough for the video games played.

I'm lucky to put all my work on an E-drive correctly. I don't tweet. I don't know why anyone would be interested in what I do every minute because I'm certainly not interested in anything they've done. It took years before I was comfortable e-mailing people. I wanted real conversation, and avoided texting for as long as I could, but to stay relevant, and begrudgingly up-to-date, I was forced into navigating the tiny typewriter. It was the only way to elicit a response.

Baseball has become impersonal, as has the world. Scientific knowledge has diminished reasonable thought and creativity, eliminating the problem solving that occurs when people communicate, or find they need to think. Human contact will never reach a state of obsolescence, but verbal sparring may grow to be disappointing because the process will be unfamiliar or childish. We are already forgetting how to write. The only phone number I know is my own.

Communication and conversation among the responsible parties is vital if there is to be a full examination and complete analysis of something. The subjectivity of evaluations made of players requires nothing less, but because of technology, the free expression of thought and conviction is challenged. Opinions invite diversity and perspective with their vulnerability. Voiced expression is now often ignored, supplanted by computer analyses, sabermetrics, and scientific analytics. The man in the trenches, the common field-staff member, has become unwilling to speak because no one listens. Viewpoints, reasons, and explanations seem not to matter despite pronouncements to the contrary.

Discussions about why players aren't improving are meaningless. No one knows how to conduct or lead the inquisitions. The front-office personnel don't even broach such conversations. The serious issue of what it takes to win at the major-league level, which is all that should matter to an organization, is never given the attention it deserves. Instead of what should be done about a performance, the health and strength of a player gets more concern.

Meetings meant to establish productivity and consistency, fix guidelines, set precedents, and develop futures are nothing more than corporate tinsel for the owners and those who run them. They are inconsequential, except that everyone expresses their opinion. The depth of any one player's problems is never discussed, and with no understanding of how difficult it is to affect a change in someone, the caution that exists about overworking a player never gives even that possibility a chance.

Something has either been forgotten, ignored, or misunderstood in the instruction our potential professional players are receiving. This is not to say that today's major-league organizations ignore their responsibilities, but the change has been significant. Things are different because they've been allowed to be. Plays that were at one time fundamental to the game, for example, are now rarely attempted, because they cannot be executed with enough reliability.

- That no one can bunt goes without saying.
- Locating pitches is a lost art. Pitchers just throw.
- Contact by hitters is such that the strike-out is taking on home-run proportions.
- Inaccurate throws to home plate make it appear that it has somehow moved.
- Manipulating the bat now means swinging hard enough to hit a home run.
- And might we sometimes just catch the ball—please?

Did the mediocrity we are seeing today begin at some point with our youngsters? Is it they who have advanced it, or was it a lack of attention to detail by our professionals that has influenced the amateur?

I might have played more baseball during my years in the Little League than most of today's professionals have in all the years before they signed. It was nothing for me to spend eight hours a day during the summer on some ball field or empty lot. Kids these days miss the "on-the-job" training the playground provides. They instead must pay to play whether in a batting cage, or some indoor facility. They enroll in clinics and buy individualized instruction. To play on a travel team means that Mom and Dad must pay the asked-for ransom, or find Junior some other form of distraction. If participation is the only concern, this becomes an expensive playground.

I never attended a baseball clinic; there were none. I didn't visit a batting cage; again, there were none. I never received detailed advice about any singular phase of the game; again, none. What instruction I received was mostly inadvertent. Correct play was mystically handed down from generation to generation; there was no verbalization, only observation. I learned from watching others with skill and intelligence play the game, and used my own common sense and good judgment about what would be the correct thing to do in any situation. The execution of fundamentals that I considered "the game" now seem incidental and have become the larger and important moments that significantly affect the outcome of too many games. Because there is more than a good chance this haphazard approach may have started at the top level of professional play, is it not time to maybe change things?

Ever since Babe Ruth, the prolific pitcher that he was, left the mound to become the game's most feared power hitter, every club has paid more attention, and given more scrutiny, to a player's ability to hit the ball than to any other skill the game requires. Professional players receive more advice about hitting the ball than catching it. Their actions and approaches are evaluated, video-taped and monitored ad infinitum looking for the smallest of details that will improve their consistency.

Players see more videos of themselves, have their offensive approaches evaluated and tweaked more frequently, take more swings, and get more instruction on hitting in one year than I ever did in all my years as an active player. The home run, baseball's sexiest product, is now responsible for the huge financial gains made by clubs, players, and the game itself. And though performance-enhancing drugs and weight training share the responsibility for the barrage of long-distance wallops of recent decades—more than anyone cared to know while it was happening—what has resulted are greater numbers, bigger smiles, and larger egos, but not more wins.

To further emphasize the significance given player's offensive abilities, every major-league at bat can be analyzed minutes after its completion on a monitor somewhere near the dugout, or in the clubhouse. Adjustments can be made immediately, certainly before a player's next at bat. There are employees whose only responsibility is to record every move and swing a hitter makes. Video rooms are production compounds with stacks of tapes, screens, and nearly life-size monitors providing overlays and side-by-side comparisons. It is nothing to analyze a swing in slow motion, super slow motion, or frame by frame.

Computers extrapolate every offensive number. Anything attributed to scoring, any ball hit, the walk, the run batted in, the extra-base hit, and the stolen base is documented and entered into cyberspace to be later extracted when it might more correctly influence an organizational decision.

With the technological advances the game is experiencing, it may not be long before a computerized robotic batting stance designed by some well-meaning guru will be universally accepted making every player look just like the next. An electronic strike-zone surely is on the horizon.

Forty or more years ago the home run was somewhat of a surprise, unexpected, but hoped for, and though it had its effect, teams won with good pitching, great defense, and intelligent play, lessons that colored my managerial and coaching style. A defensive mistake held importance because just one could be critical.

The first serious look at how the game could be played differently was in 1964 when a gentleman named Earnshaw Cook published a book entitled Percentage Baseball. The Princeton-educated engineer believed there was a more intelligent way for managers to conduct their games than how they were being traditionally run. He believed that other strategies would provide a better outcome. Snubbing the sacrifice bunt, relief pitchers, the intentional base on balls, and even the traditional batting order, Cook formulated and equated the playing of the game into a puzzling and sometimes unfathomable reasonability.

Some say his formal analysis of the game was unreadable, either in its intellect, or its insanity. Its feasibility was questioned, and though skeptically received, his ingenuity inspired similar investigation by other statistically minded individuals who took their own off-kilter look at the game.

Bill James is the most prominent of them. And to further confuse the subjectivity of the issue of statistical paralysis, in his *Historical Abstract Books*, James was in disagreement with Cook as he was with another author with whom he collaborated, John Dewan.

Dewan leaped into an amusing dissection of the game by authoring a study of defensive play in *The Fielding Bible* in 2006, which laid out complicated theories that ranked baseball's defenders. In doing so, he gave their efforts much-needed credence, and pulled the defensive side of the game out of the shadows of baseball's explosive period of drug-induced invincibility.

Prior to Dewan's publication, Congressional hearings in 2005 turned up the heat on baseball's bashers, sentencing them to a lifetime of better nutrition. With a handful of the game's most powerful hitters fidgeting before a Congressional panel, the game was taken to task. Despite the deceptive, and flat-out denials by a couple of those interrogated whether they had used a stimulant of some kind to improve their play, baseball was reprimanded and accused of turning a blind eye to the situation. A quick agreement was struck between the Commissioner's Office and the Major League Baseball Players Association in 2006 that put in place policies and consequences—some might say with a wink or two—intended to end the use of banned and illegal substances. The governmental inquisition had done the job baseball refused to do.

In the meantime, Dewan had taken the lower road, or at least a new one, devising a method of evaluating defensive play by segmenting the baseball diamond into zones and applying more than 250 vectors, or directions, in which a ball could travel. By tracking every ball hit in the major leagues, and pinpointing on a computer screen the precise spot at which a play had been made on it, Dewan would then apply his unique plus or minus scoring system, and come up with a competency rating for every defensive player.

Dewan and James collaborated on the zoning and vectoring, but by their own admission could not agree on some issues. Neither could wholeheartedly accept even their own discoveries, or their accuracy. They recognized the potential subjectivity of the elements that affected their postulations.

Dewan's research and evaluations of baseball's defenders was simply another perspective, and though commendable and more than purposeful, his work exhibited an inherent confusion that affected its value. It was lacking some very critical and empirical details. The first consideration affecting its usefulness was the variance of what was thought to be the "precise" area to which a ball had been hit, and the spot at which a play was made. The accuracy of that must be questionable at best. Second, as with any of the sabermetric information being gathered about the game, it does not, and there seems no feasible way that it could account for the consistency or inconsistency of the actual physical movements made by any fielder that might have affected his play on any particular field, or any particular ball hit, the field conditions notwithstanding.

A case could easily be made for the findings and the conclusions showing efficiencies, but they lend themselves more to revealing deficiencies, as even the offensive studies do, simply because limitations are constant and clearly visible. They are a more salient use of the information gathered, and what I first consider before making any evaluation.

Because no precise answers resulted from the Dewan process, the real benefit of the science of his method is that it leaves its findings once again for the appropriate instructors to assess. It indicates failings, but even that is only an immediate timeline. The analysis has a semblance of reliability and probability. However, unless it is consistently accurate from field to field, and that the people doing the tracking have exactly the same subjective determinations, what's discovered merely states that something has occurred; it is a tactical emotional finding. For one determination to verify another when both are made by different people cannot possibly be considered solid or accurate corroboration. The zoning and vectoring can in no way be precise. More accurate information is obtained by observation that will inherently include the minute variables that affect any single play made by a particular talent.

In all my years in baseball, I attended only one meeting during which these detectives who did similar research explained their methods and findings. When questioned by the staff members in attendance—the professional coaches who worked day-to-day with the athletes—the investigators admitted to the weaknesses in their analyses, and willingly entertained comments that might have been proven helpful to their surveys, but nothing worthwhile was offered. Everyone in the room was somewhat dumbfounded by their discourse. No one bought that quadrants, zones, and territories needed to be defined to determine the defensive skill of a player. The authors readily agreed that no estimation can ever be concrete, and that no amount of categorizing or theorizing could ever correctly predict a projected performance. Their diligence, however, did feed appropriately into the intelligent course the game was pursuing, if nothing else. From the roomful of doubting Thomases, the dismayed researchers immediately headed for the executive offices where their information was more readily digested.

In this post-steroid era, it is gratifying that organizations are at least giving lip service to taking a closer look at their defensive play. Maybe it's just the thought that better play can make up for the loss of what the powerful performance-enhancing drugs provided, or maybe it's now being recognized how poorly the game is being played. Whatever the reason, it's about time!

No way exists to predict how a group of players will perform until they play together and show how well one complements the other, but baseball is now more mathematically and scientifically explored than defined by ordinary and common-sense observation. I know of no statistical computations or technology that could have helped assemble the '27 Yankees or the '76 Reds, two teams that steamrolled through their seasons with superb talent, and though put together with every intention of winning, that possibility was no doubt neither obviously seen nor accurately predicted in any way before their assemblage. Even my championship Oakland A's teams were almost ten years in the making, and we definitely demonstrated that talent included more than just numbers; too many things must coordinate. No matter what a machine may advise, there is no predictable formula for success, but as long as everyone is trying, what more can be asked?

9

THERE IS HOPE

The only obligations major-league players have in spring training, other than to show up every day, is to stay healthy. Hits and errors, though important, don't count at this time of year. With two months in the sun before every move made becomes a historical statistic, there is plenty of time for muscles to accept their responsibilities, arms to regain their elasticity, and legs to strengthen in preparation for the relentless grind of another season. Until the first official cry of "Play ball!" is heard, the only player concerns are what golf courses they will play, and at which restaurants they will dine.

Things, however, are different "down on the farm." In the minor-league camp, players know to report in season-ready form because everything they do counts immediately. The stress and pressure they feel won't match what they'll experience during the regular season, but until major-league status is achieved, these "wanna-bes" know that every spring day's play has to be better than yesterday's. Nothing they do can be done leisurely.

For many minor-league players, this is the time of year when their boyhood dream ends. Those not given special treatment, regular playing time, or consideration of any kind, realize their chance of having a baseball career is slim. For those being released, it comes as no surprise, most know when the ax is about to fall. Professional baseball is cruel, but with thirty to forty new draftees every year, the baseball merry-go-round never stops. Only the best survive.

No amount of passion, drive, or effort will save someone with marginal talent. On the day player releases are to be made, the clubhouse is solemn, and strangely quiet, with the pall encompassing even the player development staff. Players "on the bubble"—those whose baseball lives are in jeopardy—approach the ballpark that morning with trepidation. Knowing the helpless situation into which they may be walking, they do what they can to avoid an approaching coach who will request that they report to the farm director's office. They know not to ask why. Many will experience no greater hurt in their lives than what is felt on this day.

Witnessing dreams being shattered is never pleasant, and though the friendships that have been made will survive, the best that can be shared at this moment among teammates are hugs and good wishes, and a staff member reminding the unfortunate ones that they were not failures, that their chance at an opportunity thousands of young men would cherish is something for which they should be proud. Little else can be said. With the final dismissal, the clubhouse walls seem to sigh in relief, and the "thank you" from those who survive is an unusually energetic workout that day.

Prior to the start of the minor-league spring training practice games, there is a seven to ten day period of preparatory workouts. The time allotted for defensive work is never more than twenty to thirty minutes, rarely enough time to benefit anybody. With an unwieldy number of players, a period of forty-five minutes in length would be much better when you consider the time needed for the work, instruction, the collection of baseballs, and maybe a break given the players. Even better would be sixty minutes. None of what is to be accomplished then would have to be rushed, everything could be covered very easily, more specific work would get done, and the one hour would more psychologically underscore the value the organization placed on its defensive play.

Following this first period could be a second sixty minute period devoted to team fundamentals—bunt plays, first and third situations, cutoffs and relays, rundowns, etc.—or to cover other needs like base running, sliding, pitcher's fielding practice, (PFP), maybe a long infield practice, anything thought important. Being a kind of "catch all" period, no phase of the game would get overlooked.

Expanding the daily scheduled defensive work in this way would have no effect on the regular warm-up and throwing programs, the strength and conditioning programs that are run before and after the workouts, nor would it interfere with any rehab work to be done at the end of the day by the training staff. Whatever meetings were thought to be important by the player development department could also be easily accommodated; there would be time for everything.

Batting practice would not have to change, it would remain as traditionally scheduled. With the extra time spent in the batting cages early in the morning well before the regular workouts begin, what gets accomplished in the batting practice sessions during the workouts themselves, and with unrestricted cage time at the completion of the day, every player can easily get one to two hundred swings every day. Rarely is a limit set in a training camp on how long players can hit.

The only drawback to a work day of this length—which would be maybe an hour and a half longer than normal—would be the affect it had on everyone's afternoon tee times; they would have to be pushed back. The extra time on the field would fly in the face of today's concern with overworking the players, and there would be the inevitable moaning and groaning about being on the field too long from staff members, but it would be a very productive way to prepare not only for the schedule of upcoming games, but for the season. The aversion organizations seem to have about players putting in more time on the field is puzzling. Hitting is the only fundamental with an unlimited leniency.

The early morning batting practice sessions prior to the regularly scheduled workout for the day would not have to change under this extended scenario because with so many players in camp, time has to be found for everyone to get the number of swings they want or need. But what is gained from working the infielders with the sun peeking over the horizon was never clear to me. It seemed to be nothing more than an organizational "look-how-hard-we-work" facade; I never saw any long-term rewards. There was little gained from these early morning sessions as there was from the regularly scheduled, traditional work periods because of their time restraints.

The part of the day that should have been utilized with regularity never was. Few shared my feelings that the best time to get something specific accomplished was after the day's regular work was completed, or the spring games ended. Whether the work was with an individual or a group of three or four players, everyone was more attentive. Work done late in the day had a number of pluses. With everyone's muscles sufficiently warmed, injuries rarely occurred, time was not a factor, and, best of all, the focus given by the players increased tenfold, making instruction much more productive.

These schedule changes are suggested because the game I returned to a decade after my retirement was being governed by a new set of rules, and a vastly different kind of leadership. It did not take long for me to get frustrated watching mediocrity develop. Supervised as it was under never before seen corporate-type guidelines, every move a player made was planned, monitored, watched, and recorded. Anything that prolonged his daily prescribed regular work agenda raised eyebrows, a caution that rivaled insanity at times. With that, and the fear of injury overriding common sense, any needed defensive work that could have easily been accommodated at the end of the day, fell into an "irregularly scheduled work" category that was considered unnecessary. This was hypocritical because there was no limit to the time players could spend in the batting cages everyday with some having to be kicked out.

Baseball franchises are paranoid about injuries. Believing that an overworked player is more susceptible to breaking down, they are obsessed with making sure everyone's work load is monitored. There are days in the spring when major-league players are told not to report; they are given the day off, told not to show up. And during the season, though present, many pitchers can be considered unaccounted for. Believed to have merit, this policy is spreading to the position players. Concern for a player's health is laudable, and, yes, a solution must be found for the continued rash of injuries, but there is no indication that this restful policy sufficiently combats even the normal amount of work to be accomplished. Even if no significant gains were to be realized from demanding that a player be scheduled for extra work, and his performance plateaued, his improved physical condition would significantly lessen the chance of him being injured. One goes with the other, it is a win-win situation.

When my requests to work my infielders at the end of the day were repeatedly rebuffed, I quit asking. One refusal especially hard to swallow was when it was forbade by a trainer. Could anything else be more of an indication of what was going wrong with the game? How these particular medical aides—often young men and women just out of college, inexperienced as they are to know what it takes to handle the daily physical punishment of professional baseball—had gained the control they have over what players could, or could not, do was something I did not understand, yet, their every pronouncement went unquestioned. They were under no constraints and, though overseen by the team doctors, had full power to determine a particular player's work load, when and what he did, and how long.

It could have been behind closed doors that the expertise of these medical gurus was tested—there importance is not to be denied—but I saw no evidence of that during any meeting I attended; whatever they said was gospel. Field staff members like myself, those who were responsible for improving the players, had little say in the matter. I could only shake my head! The first item on the agenda in every early morning staff meeting was the head trainer's reading of that day's "obituary," the list of those wounded or injured, and what they were, or were not, allowed to do that day. The length of individual recovery periods became comical, but there was no questioning their determinations.

In a somewhat similar role, the strength coaches who were responsible for the present and future physical condition of every player had similar carte blanche. Entrusted as both of these departments were with the task of maintaining the health of the players, they never had any reasonable answers to explain why injuries continued to increase.

My role as Minor League Defensive Coordinator included the specific responsibility of the "care and feeding" of the organizational infielders. Despite being given the freedom to instruct in any way I saw fit, there were the occasional restraints and roadblocks put on the extra work I considered essential because it was thought to be excessive, unnecessary, too much. There was a definite neurosis about injuries, and the delusions about the negative effect extra work might have on an individual was hard to justify. It may have stemmed from how demanding I was during the day's morning workouts, but hearing "Your players have already done enough for the day," got old. To circumvent the negativity shown my late afternoon appeals, I devised a successful ploy. Once removed from the afternoon game in which he was playing, every infielder was to report to one of the half-fields—an area that was just an infield—to take extra ground balls, work on specific needs, or generally improve his conditioning. With two or three games played every day, infielders were coming over nonstop. While the games were still going on—and front office personnel preoccupied— a couple of other fungo hitters and I hit ground balls, and talked about or made adjustments for a fantastically constructive two hours. The players loved it, no one got injured, and I was able to avoid the paranoia about postgame extra work.

No one in any of the meetings I attended was aware that as a player I was at one time praised for my defense, considered one of the American League's best infielders. There was no defending myself having played long before everyone in the room was born. More frustrating was that my years in the game, and having played on one of histories greatest teams, didn't seem important enough for anyone in charge to even discuss with me the possibility that whatever I presented made sense, needed clarification, might work, or was of value. Not once was my advice sought. That was not only irritating but, I thought, no way to run an organization.

None of my ideas or suggestions were readily accepted. Despite no outright verbal rejection, the indifference to what I offered was obvious by a silence that showed either disbelief, resistance, or a lack of understanding. That had me wondering if we were trying to better ourselves or not. My proposals and explanations could not have been that confusing. If they were, why was I not asked to explain? Not only were my teaching methods given little credence, my player evaluations were likewise rebuffed or responded to in a way that was frustrating. It was only after the passage of time that I was proven correct.

During my tenure as the infield coordinator for the Cleveland Indians, I knew exactly where each of my infielders were in their development at any particular time. And to see that they were in peak physical condition for the season, my daily workout schedule was carefully and strategically planned with one day always set aside to put each of them through a workout that gave me a chance to evaluate both of those concerns.

On the day one of these individual workouts was scheduled, the staff members in charge of baseballs put two small bucketfuls on the field assigned to me. Both buckets together held the approximate 100 baseballs the drill required. One larger sunflower seed bucket would have been better because it could hold all the balls, but those larger containers were typically reserved for collecting the baseballs hit during batting practice on the various fields. Their greater capacity reduced the number of trips the unlucky pitcher "on the bucket" that day had to make to reload the basket that held the baseballs for the coaches who were throwing batting practice. The two small buckets worked just fine for what I needed.

The infielder being tested was required to field each ball hit to him with two hands. This demanded a fundamentally sound approach to the ball, and that he properly move into his triangular fielding position. Using two hands made it easier for me to accurately evaluate his technique. He was to make no throws, and he could neither backhand nor barehand the ball.

The success of this drill depended in large part on my ability to use a fungo, the long slender bat that is the lifeblood of every infield instructor. Each ball had to be hit in a way that tested the infielder's ability to field it correctly. The location to which each ball was hit, and its speed, was critical. It also had to be hit with "backspin" so it skimmed across the infield without any unwanted hops or bounces. Balls hit this way were much easier to field, and allowed the infielder to focus on what he was doing, and not on what the ball was doing.

Every ball would be hit to different, but calculated locations on the infield, often to the same spot three or four times in a row. This repetition obligated the player to duplicate his actions which magnified the consistency of his approach, and gave me a much better look at his technique. By hitting balls to the limits of his range without making them unplayable, it was possible for him and me to see how much more ground he was capable of covering while staying in control of his movements. The ultimate goal of the drill was to correct the infielder's actions, and make every one of them a habit.

With balls hit at a steady and somewhat rapid pace, the drill was a fabulous stamina builder. Each ball would be hit almost immediately after the infielder returned to his starting position. This kept him constantly in motion. Should he be able to work through both buckets, and field all 100 baseballs with no need to rest or catch his breath—itself an accomplishment—though I may not have been satisfied with his fielding techniques, I was with his physical condition.

What I looked for in this drill, besides the infielder's overall approach, were "trigger points," the specific movements that are the crux of whatever problems he might have fielding the ball. Many instructors see the big picture, but not these important brush strokes. Recognizing defensive shortcomings such as "bad hands," "not reading the ball well," "an erratic arm," "not very quick," "no range," or "booting too many balls" is not difficult. Knowing how to correct them, or at least suggest how, is. "Softening" someone's hands may mean strengthening his legs, correcting his strides and steps, altering his approach to the ball, controlling his aggressiveness, or getting him to use his upper body and head properly, getting both more into the play. If improvement was possible, it took time.

About once a week, to ensure that my infielders left camp in shape, the entire group was put through a conditioning drill something similar to how I tested them individually, but was a bit more taxing.

With eight to ten infielders, including the first basemen, divided into two groups, one at the shortstop position, and the other at the second base position, 200 baseballs would be rolled to each of the two positions from the edge of the infield grass. If the shortstop position was first to field the balls, after each one made his throw, or "feed," to the second baseman covering the bag—who was to merely catch the ball and toss it onto the infield grass—he rotated over to the second-base position. Those at second base who caught the throw rotated to the shortstop position. Everyone was constantly on the move throughout the entire drill from one position to the other.

One hundred baseballs were first rolled about five yards to the left of the shortstops, and then another hundred to their right at roughly the same distance. It took about five minutes to do this in each direction. Their action and their effort was controlled by how hard, and to what spot I rolled the ball. This was repeated with balls rolled first to the right of the players at second base and then to their left.

With one of the drill's purposes being to improve everyone's lateral movements there were several actions to be evaluated; the proper use of their head, the angle of their first move, their first few steps, the following longer strides, and what they did with their arms and hands. I was not interested in them just getting to the ball, I wanted them under control so they could ultimately field the ball in a good triangular fielding position, and make an accurate feed or throw to the bag. As with the drill I put them through individually, they were not allowed to backhand the ball, it had to be fielded with two hands.

This drill became known as the "figure-eight" drill because of how the players rotated from one position to the other. When done correctly it built leg strength, developed and improved quickness, and forced the players—with my prodding—to execute the proper lateral fundamental movements including the use of their head and upper body weight. It was simplistically efficient while making it possible for me to evaluate a number of infielders at the same time. With all of them in front of me, each player's fielding style was clearly visible, and any advice I might give to one could be heard by all, increasing the drill's impact. It was, without a doubt, the best conditioning drill in my repertoire.

The reason for running the drill at a quick pace, and keeping everyone moving, was because of my discovery that when an infielder got physically tired, two things happened. One, without realizing it, he reacted naturally and instinctively, usually in the way the I had been urging him to do. Fatigue untangled his thoughts, and he relaxed. And two, when exhausted, pushing him to stay fundamentally sound generated a greater chance of a movement being imprinted into his muscle memory. These were lessons I learned when first teaching myself to field. A few more repetitions done correctly when I was worn out went a long way to perfecting the specific action or technique on which I was working.

This figure-eight drill was best run with an even number of players with, ironically, eight being perfect. With ten or twelve, the pace at which the balls had to be rolled was so fast that the exercise became solely a conditioning drill—which was not necessarily bad—but its instructive purposes were diminished because I could not control their movements, and observe what they were doing at the same time.

With 200 baseballs rolled to the players at the shortstop position, and 200 rolled to them at second base, the drill's value was unmatched. The math shows that with eight infielders, they each got fifty repetitions; with ten, though the count dropped to forty, it was still an intense and worthy workout because of the constant movement. How difficult it could be was determined by how quickly I rolled one ball after the other. During the regularly scheduled defensive periods, in comparison, with so many infielders, and so little time available, each infielder would get to field no more than maybe twenty balls hit to them by a fungo hitter. Their effort would not be as good, and standing around doing nothing for too long was detrimental to their improvement.

● ● ●

My own ground ball workouts during each of my six years in the minor leagues could have been caste as being more robotic than athletic. They seldom varied. I was incredibly disciplined, and followed the same routine every day which would, if not completely, came very close to wearing me out. During my first two, maybe three professional minor-league seasons—what I considered my learning period—whenever I fielded ground balls I paid serious attention to every movement, tweaking them, doing this, trying that, experimenting with any action that I thought would improve a specific maneuver, or maximize my overall ability. What I discovered about fielding a ground ball was that every part of my body had its own responsibility, that one movement affected another, that they worked in concert, and in an orderly sequence.

Once I was satisfied there was nothing more I could learn, and that I understood what I was doing, it was just a matter of repeating and perfecting the movements until they became instinctive and habitual; that took a few years. The other aspects of infield play such as my responsibilities within each team fundamental, tag plays, working with the pitchers, were things that never concerned me. Nothing was as challenging or important as was being able to field ground balls consistently. Not being able to was, and is, the bane of every infielder.

Because I looked at my workouts as if they were games, I did not like being distracted. The mindset I developed served me well for sixteen season. Believing like everyone should, that how

I practiced was how I would play, I had tunnel vision during my workouts, and stressed myself to do everything correctly. This helped me deal with the pressure I might have felt during a real game because I never worried about doing anything wrong, but, instead, focused on doing everything right as I did in my practice sessions. There may not be a huge difference in the semantics of that statement, but there was when applying it to your play in a major-league game. I drove myself crazy with how fanatical I was about my workouts.

The two major objectives of my workouts were to improve my ability to field a ground ball consistently, and to increase the amount of ground I could cover. As a youngster on the Irving School playground, it was fun taking hits away from my buddies by getting a jump on where I thought they were going to hit the ball. All I had to do was pay attention to where the ball was pitched, and watch their swings; it was easy. No one asked me to do it, told me to do it, taught me how to do it, or even mentioned its possibility, but even as a Little Leaguer, it seemed to be common sense that "reading" a hitters swing could only improve my defensive play. It became a huge contributor, and a major factor, in my range increasing.

Two things irritated me during my workouts; one, was having someone wanting to take ground balls with me; and two, having my workouts interrupted once they began. Working alone was not much of a problem because I could pick one or another of the batting practice periods during which I could do my work. It wasn't hard to find time to be by myself. I would never join someone else who was taking ground balls. My bigger concern was that whomever was hitting the fungos could do it for the twenty or thirty minutes I needed, non-stop. Whether it was a coach or a player—it was usually one of the pitchers—he had to be able to control where he was hitting the ball. At some point, I wanted it hit to the farthest edges of my position so I could work on the movements that increased my range.

Each of my workouts began slowly, and built in intensity until I reached what I thought was game speed. With a sense of how long I should work every day, when I felt that a particular ground ball would be the last I would need, I was satisfied with that day's effort.

Twelve years after retiring as an active player, I returned to professional baseball as a manager and infield instructor in the minor leagues. Expecting that the game had changed, I was anxious to see how infield play was being taught, and what may have been discovered about the mechanics of how to field a ground ball that I thought so important. Surely, there was something different, something that would help me because, soon to be instructing infielders, but never having done so, what I might teach, what my approach or style might be, I had no idea.

Some organizations had hired the psychologists in my absence that I had longed for decades before, but, instructionally, the only significant difference I noticed was the way hitting was being taught. Not that their importance had been abandoned, but where once the game's emphasis was on pitching and defense, it had become focused on power and the long ball. The instruction hitters were being given was comprehensive and analytical; there were a number of new and fascinating theories. Instead of the "swing and hit the ball hard" edict of my era, terms such as "bat path," "staying inside the ball," and "clearing the hips" were part of the game's new offensive lexicon. There was a much more theoretical approach to hitting.

What instruction there was on how to field ground ball remained simple, elementary, and cliched. No one had apparently taken the time to analyze the movements that were involved. Suggestions such as "watch the ball, keep your head down, follow the ball into your glove," were the same banal instructions that had been given to infielders for decades, and merely hitting them ground balls, and leaving it up them to figure out what they needed to do was helping no one.

There was so much that I believed could be taught that affected how a ground ball should be fielded that wasn't. This seemed a disservice to every young player. Every instructor knew the basics, but players were snowflakes—no two were alike—meaning that every infielder had his own mannerisms and actions that required their own specific individual adjustments. This was not being recognized.

What and how I wanted to teach would be radically different, my approach more critical, definitive, and emphatic. The players would be made to do what I thought would benefit them individually, and every adjustment suggested would be made with an explanation. For a while I just observed the other instructors, trying to get a feel for the procedures that were in place, wondering how, and if, my approach would be accepted. It wasn't long before it was hard to watch the perfunctory way things were being done; I had to address the limitations our young infielders were demonstrating that were being summarily dismissed; they deserved better.

Always looking to improve my teaching methods, I was hoping the other instructors, many who themselves had a long history in the game, had programs that might supplement mine, but it was the infielders I was teaching that were much more enlightening. I loved to talk to them during our workouts. Their responses were insightful; their feedback important. I was curious and wanted to know what they were thinking, what they were feeling about what I was having them do. Were they comfortable with my adjustments? Did they like the changes being made or suggested? So may times their actions and comments highlighted something I was missing, or had no answer for. Our give-and-take was important to the process.

There was, however, something in my absence that had been instituted, that I considered unproductive. Why it had become popular was puzzling. I understood its intended purpose, but it never got the focus, attention, or time that might have given it some value. Calling it a drill was maybe incorrect because it was more a request. Every infielder, when not hitting with his batting practice group, was to be at his position to field any balls hit his way. In baseball terms, this was called "taking balls live off the bat." Meant to simulate a game-type situation, during the fifteen or twenty minutes it took, the number of balls hit to any of the infielders was unpredictable. It might be none, or more than he could possibly handle because of how quickly the batting practice rounds went. The number varied from position to position because it was also dependent on what the hitters were required to do in each of their turns at-bat. Few defenders took the drill seriously—it could not be monitored by an instructor—and except for maybe one or two dedicated individuals who put some effort into it, I thought it mostly a waste of time.

If the regularly scheduled defensive work period for infielders was as productive as it should have been, spending time during batting practice doing what I thought a time-filler was unnecessary. The infielders were better off fielding the ground balls hit to them by one of the coaches. Repetitions were more important for young players even should they be unmonitored.

My personal aversion to this exercise was because I had no use for it when I taught myself how to field. I worked myself so hard with a fungo hitter that for me to get emotionally motivated for what would be only one or two random ground balls during a batting practice round—when I didn't have to—didn't make sense. In a game you have to be ready for every pitch, your focus is intense. In practice, that's hard to duplicate. This "live off the bat" drill did nothing to improve an infielder's focus. It did, however, have another value, one that I believed was extremely important. Had the infielders been asked to "read" the swings of the hitters instead of just taking the live ground balls, something worthwhile could have been accomplished.

This aspect of the fielding process was one that I absolutely expected to see being taught when I returned to the game, but not only was it not, neither was it addressed, mentioned, or referenced in any way. It was never part of any other instructor's program as it was in mine. More surprising was the number of times I heard a player being faulted in a meeting or conversation for the ground he couldn't cover, which this skill addressed.

The value of being able to read the swings of opposing hitters seems to not be understood. Knowing how, and learning how to correctly move laterally, improves and increases an infielder's range dramatically. For five years as the Cleveland Indians Minor League Defensive Coordinator, I attempted to teach this skill—it was one of my priorities. Coordinating both of these actions that I considered easy, gave many young infielders trouble. I could understand the inability to learn how to read a swing, but not the difficulty there was executing the proper steps to be made when moving left or right.

Not once in my twenty-five years as in infield instructor, did an infielder ask to be taught how to read a hitter's swing, increase his range, have questions about, or just show interest in either. And when it became evident that neither did the other coaches or the higher-ups, I figured, why should I? No infielder's career has ever been detrimentally affected by his lack of range. Not that it should be because fielding the ball is the priority, but why not enhance what ability someone might have? The status quo was considered more than acceptable. This was not the winning philosophy of little things meaning a lot that I was taught. One AAA player registered complete surprise to my helping him execute the correct lean and takeoff on a swing that improved his lateral movement. More than gratified, he said he'd never been told of the possibility.

Proof of the frustration that I had trying to teach this technique were the times I sat my young infielders in front of a monitor to watch videos of some of the best hitters in the major leagues. I reasoned that the consistent approaches of major-league hitters would make it easier for my lesson to be understood. This was maybe not fair because the process does take time to understand, plus it was harder to do from a video than on the field. As each hitter swung at a pitch, I stopped the video at their point of contact with the ball and went around the room asking every infielder where he thought the ball might go. I did not expect even a minimal number of right answers from the group—I was hoping the exercise would at the least make them think—but not one guess was ever even close to being correct. The range of the determinations caught me completely by surprise; they covered the entire playing field. When seeing the true direction in which each ball was hit, the room filled with laughter. Though a fun session, I was lost as how to move forward. Despite my use of other charts and diagrams, and my constant harping on how much effect greater range could have on their careers, I could only hope that something was sinking in. Their lack of desire to practice something that might prolong their baseball life was frustrating, an all too surprising revelation of what had happened to the game and its different players in my twelve year absence.

Correctly reading the swing of a hitter, and recognizing accurately where the ball will be hit, results in the infielder being able to get a "jump" on fielding it seconds BEFORE it is hit. This ability requires the infielder to be observant, focusing, and paying attention to everything the hitter does in the batter's box.

Batting orders are put together for a reason. Each spot demands specific abilities. The position in which someone is hitting will reveal a lot about the kind of hitter he is. Just one at-bat can substantiate what was thought to be his tendencies. What you know about a player's reputation, what you have been told, or heard others say, may be all you need to know. For someone unknown, you look for several things. Analyze his stance. How big is he? What is his body type: is he heavy, thin, short, tall? Does he look to have strong legs? Is his stance open, closed, upright? Does he set-up deep in the box, or up front? Does he choke up, swing the bat from the end, or off the knob. Does he look to be aggressive, a slap-hitter, a free swinger. Does he swing for the fences? How short or long is his swing? What path does his bat take through the strike zone? Is he balanced? Can he be fooled? How often does he get jammed? Does he bunt?

The infielder must know the strengths and weaknesses of the pitchers on his team. On what pitches do they rely? What is their best pitch? Are they aggressive? What kind of command do they have? What pitches can they control? Is their ball heavy or light? Does it sink? How do the hitters react to, or hit each of their pitches? How do they react when in trouble?

Some of the best information comes from watching the catcher who calls the pitch and sets up where he expects it to be thrown. He tries to counteract what the hitter does best, and though not always successful, what he calls gives the middle infielders, with a fair amount of certainty, a good idea in what direction the ball should be hit. The corner infielders, who cannot see the catcher's signs, should at least be able to tell if he sets up inside or outside. They can also be helped by their infield counterparts—the shortstop for the third baseman and the second baseman for the first baseman—giving them a verbal sign of some kind that tips them off as to when an off-speed pitch is to be thrown.

By far, the most informative data comes from the defensive charts that every team in an organization maintains. These "spray" charts, as they are called, are encyclopedic, and provide the details about what areas of the field should be defended for the different pitches thrown to every opposing hitter by every pitcher.

Armed with this information, and aware of the game situation, it is possible for an infielder to move in the direction the ball is hit BEFORE it actually is.

● ● ●

The goal of every major-league organization is to win, and because the measure of how well it's players perform is somewhat reflective of the quality of the instruction their minor-league players receive, should their instructor's methods not be challenged?

One thing I questioned during my time as a minor-league instructor was why the quality of any particular player's performance never sparked any in-depth discussions about what course of action should be taken to alleviate his problems. What specific limitations an individual had with any phase of the game were never addressed with the seriousness they should have been. They were not overlooked, but were given passing attention, and flippantly accepted, as if nothing could be done. And because nothing was, the same concern would later resurface in similar evaluative conversations.

In much the same fashion that no one in a position of authority seemed concerned about increasing the range of their infielders, neither did anyone see the value of looking into the details of any of the organizational instruction being offered. The instructional system in place—the organizational player development program—seemed always subjective, dependent on and controlled by the coordinators employed at the time. And with a fairly active change of personnel from year to year, the programs of instruction that were introduced for the various fundamentals were rarely if ever reviewed for their efficiency or consistency. The coordinators who were hired were considered competent. Whether their programs were new, old, trite, innovative, sketchy, elementary, or shocking, as some were, they were accepted at face value, their quality not scrutinized as they should have been.

Today's player development departments bear little resemblance to those operating twenty or thirty years ago when there was no instruction. Improvement was an individual responsibility. As the game moved forward, it was believed that it had stagnated, that it needed renovation, that the players had been locked into staid, and less than productive developmental procedures. An overhaul of the system was thought to be needed. To improve what was believed lacking, instead of delving into, and concentrating on the physical performance of the players, a theory of production began to emerge that put greater emphasis on the overall fitness, health and well-being of the player.

A new methodology was installed that affectively praised the player, made him more comfortable, lessened his work load, and catered to his ego. That the game has been "modernized" with a bevy of internal changes, and a new-found dependence on scientific technology cannot be denied, but should not this renaissance be challenged for its effectiveness? Should it not be asked whether it was necessary? That the quality of play has eroded is a fact that has surprisingly gone uncontested. Strike outs are up, and rising as are the number of physical mistakes and miscues. Something is obviously not working.

The coordinators—those considered to be an expert in one of the specific fundamental areas such as hitting, pitching, outfield play, base running, etc..—present their particular philosophies each spring for the assembled staff. But even with the best attempts at dispensing their guidelines, expecting them to be precisely followed by the field staff is asking a lot, if not an impossibility. There will always be subtle differences when the message is delivered to the players because of a staff member's personal interpretation. A practical solution would be a roundtable discussion with every staff member infusing his own thoughts and ideas, respectful of the coordinator's ideology, not to dispute, but to clarify, solidify, and possibly embellish, the instructional tone of every fundamental area being taught throughout the organization. Surely this would bring positives to the developmental program, but should it result in only an increase in staff camaraderie, that in itself would be a plus. Making it easier for staff members to communicate among themselves would be tremendously beneficial, and, it would have to have some affect in alleviating any confusion that might occur as players moved from instructor to instructor, and level to level. There is always too much expertise not to make use of it.

Under the present system, the higher-ups, in their desire to better the organization, have given carte-balance to those hired to instill their individual beliefs. Instructional methods are never questioned. This policy produces an unnecessary subjectivity about what is taught. When the quality of the instruction is left up to the luck of hiring the right people, it is always a hit-and-miss proposition. The importance of being "on the same page" should be as strictly applied to those responsible for the on-field instruction as it is for those in the boardroom establishing the organizational policies. There should be a stricter bottom-line strategy, and tighter standards. I saw no one take charge of an organizational program to see that the consistency that was sought actually was. Everyone was afraid of stepping on everyone's toes.

Implementing any program and expecting it to be administered with finite accuracy is an impossibility, but just the attempt was jeopardized because no one in authority had any understanding of what the organizational policy should be regarding the specific areas of instruction. More important, was the vague understanding there appeared to be about those being employed, and their expertise to properly disseminate the organizational policies. Having but only a smattering of baseball experience, today's management does not understand the intricacies of the game's requirements. The long, useless meetings in spring training that only regurgitated known abilities would have been more wisely used had the leaders and coordinators met with the field staff and constructively dissected each player with feedback from all concerned.

It is uncontested that defensive play in the major leagues has taken a hit. There are many reasons why that has occurred, all legitimate, but one that may not get the attention it deserves, though a long shot, is the acceptance of the subjective decisions that baseball's scorekeepers make. Is there a connection, dubious as it might be, between their verdicts and the quality of the defensive play seen today? When you consider how the game has changed, there is some merit to this theory. The old standards of defensive play have been eroded to the point that should any defender be given an "error" for not making a play on a ball that had just the slightest semblance of difficulty, instead of it being scored a "hit," the scorekeeper might be considered to have committed a felony. The professional defender's feet are no longer held to the fire as they once were which, if we stretch the premise, begs the question of whether the decisions made by these press box officials is further perpetuating the thought that good defensive play is no longer considered possible. Has the game become more difficult to play? Certainly it has its exceptional fielders, but the decisions made on whether something is a hit has grown to be extremely lenient. It may be irreverent to consider this being possible, but it fits the pattern of giving the players everything they want, making things easier, and "dumbing down" the game. Do the scorers believe there are legitimate reasons why so many balls are missed, dropped, misplayed, booted, or thrown away, instead of them being caught as they were in the past?

Obviously, these arbiters are not responsible for the poor play of the game's defenders, but when they rule a bobble, boot, miscue, or mistake to be a hit as often as they do, such altruism masks and adds fuel to the fire of those watching that lessens any thought that maybe play can and should be improved. Watching the slide of defensive play that has been trending for decades, and the mislabeling of the efforts given by the game's defenders might have any number of people concluding that maybe there are many plays that are just too hard to be made. Is it possible that these rulings have something to do with management believing that corralling a baseball has become so difficult that nothing can be done about it? If you have ever been on the field to experience what it is like to field a baseball hit as hard as they are, you too might see how easy it would be to justify everything being ruled a hit, but major-league infielders are there for a reason.

If it is believed that the game has become too difficult, that the players are not good defenders, and their many miscues are being properly ruled in the positive, a case can and should still be made for trying to improve; we are dealing with top-level talent. Do you then have to look at the instructors who are working with these players? Is the quality of their work not what it should be? And what responsibility do those in charge of the instructors have to be sure that what is taught is the best it can be? If the leaders are lax in their expectations, indifferent on the subject, or ignorant as to what should be done, what is there then to do? This whole scenario becomes somewhat of a vicious cycle, a catch-22 situation. Making players more accountable would be great, but that no longer seems feasible.

Defensive play appears adequate because it has been buttressed by the generosity and leniency given the standard practice of catching the ball. It has been frustrating to watch the game transition from one of relatively sound and reasonable play to one that now, more than frequently, has its misplays and errors cloaked as hits with the excuses that the ball was hit too hard, the play was too hard to make, the ball did something odd, and on and on. There is really no excuse for any major-league player not fielding or catching a ball if he can get his glove on it.

Scorekeepers are not the only ones who may be contributing to, and condoning, the slide of defensive play. It has become hard to listen to play-by-play announcers too often extolling the ability of a player as exceptional when it is unwarranted. The mishandling of a routine play which was made difficult by an infielder's actions is not reported as such, but instead has his bungling attempt couched in a way that skirts the truth of his clumsiness.

All of these observations and suggestions are nothing more than my way of trying to hang on to and, yes, save, or, at least, resurrect the game I see fading that has been my life; a game that I've seen change in ways that are hard to reconcile. I don't want to forget what was. I do not expect my opinions to make any difference other than to have others know what used to be. Whatever conclusions will be drawn are personal, but should my thoughts make a difference, or change someone's thinking, great. The game seems to be on a never-ending path of transformation and discovery. Those rewriting its script are doing what they think is correct. I, and many others, hope they know what they are doing.

THE PLAYGROUNDS

Little League baseball would not have the world-wide appeal it does today were it not for the commitment Carl Sotz, of Williamsport, Pennsylvania, made to his two nephews. He loved playing catch with the boys, and thought how great it would be if they some day had uniforms, equipment, and a place to play the game they loved. In 1938, while chasing one of their errant throws in his backyard, he twisted his ankle tripping over a lilac bush, and while nursing his injury he thought about what he might do to form a league of some kind for them and their friends. With no organized baseball at the time for boys their age, he felt there wouldn't be the constant bickering during their games as there was if they had adult supervision.

Looking for help and what financial support he could get from relatives and friends, he was unable to raise the money he needed to get his idea up and running, but when his efforts to find individual donors failed, he sought sponsorships from the local business owners. Turned down by fifty-six of them, he finally found two who were willing to contribute thirty dollars each to the cause. Still short of his goal, he sweet-talked his boss at Lundy Lumber into becoming the third. He then had enough money to buy a couple of bats, four balls, a catcher's mitt, shin guards, and a few uniforms, just enough equipment to launch the first structured baseball league for boys with three teams named for their big-hearted sponsors, Lycoming Dairy, Jumbo Pretzel, and Lundy Lumber.

It was 1939.

Forced to come up with what little money he had from time to time he was able to keep his dream alive. His passion for his new little baseball league was so strong that he traveled from town to town hoping to interest others. Promoting it became a lifelong obsession. He experimented with designs for a playing field whose size would accommodate the boy's abilities, eventually determining that one with a pitching mound thirty-eight feet from home plate, and base paths of sixty feet, were just about right. Today the base paths remain at sixty feet while the mound is now forty-six feet from home plate.

Sotz believed the standard home plate of seventeen inches was too big for the boys, so he made one that was fourteen. He also made the game's first bases, drew sketches for the uniforms, and after discussions with a local sports editor over what to call his new creation, decided "Little League" to be a perfect title. He even managed the team named for the very first sponsor he secured, Lycoming Dairy. From his initial dream that began with only three teams, his idea became a phenomenon, and by the 1950s thousands of teams had been formed throughout the country.

For the next sixteen years, as his Little League exploded across the country, Stotz fought to keep it from becoming commercialized. It was a battle he would lose to the US Rubber Co., the very company he first secured to support his idea of a Little League World Series, and the one he persuaded to develop the first rubber-cleated baseball shoes for boys. As the game's popularity grew, US Rubber saw the potential for its own growth through a stronger connection with this new and exciting enterprise, and bankrolled the burgeoning Little League organization. In the early 1950s, with their own interests at heart, they chose one of their own executives to be on the Little League board, and made Stotz the first full-time commissioner.

The relationship between Stotz and the US Rubber Company eventually soured, becoming strained when the corporation recognized the increasing national passion for this novel baseball venture, and wanted to capitalize on it. Stotz, however, remained adamant that the game remain fun for boys, and not exploited in any way for financial gain. He would not bend to the board's desire to expand play and make the game more competitive. When he realized what he was up against, and that the original spirit of his idea was being abandoned, he sued the organization to protect his rights. After an ugly legal battle, he was unceremoniously ousted from his position as commissioner, and not allowed entry into the very offices he had created.

The man, who with his wife and a few relatives had helped shape the future for millions of children around the world with his unselfish devotion to a simple idea, was no longer recognized, or given any credit for what he had done. Though he did not once visit the new fields, or the Little League Museum in Williamsport for the remainder of his life, he never wavered in his dedication to what he had started. He stood firmly behind his principles and philosophies, continued to promote the game to any who would listen, and formed a similar league, the Original Little League, on his own in Williamsport. He was not going to let his idea die. The bitterness he felt about what had happened to his dream even tore apart his marriage.

Despite the unfortunate ugliness of the early beginnings of the Little League, the legacy of Carl Stotz lives; he has not been forgotten. Though it took far too long, after an out-of-court settlement in 1956 forced him to sever ties with the organization he had so lovingly founded, and well after he passed away in 1992, through the efforts of several people and his family, he is finally honored for having established what is now an American institution.

The home plate he carved out of an old piece of rubber, as well as the pesky lilac bush that may have been more responsible for the creation of the Little League than anything else, are now on display at the Little League Museum in Williamsport on loan from his family. The little game of baseball he so cherished now has an estimated 7,000 leagues worldwide, and is played by untold millions of young people every year.

My own introduction to organized baseball occurred one summer afternoon in 1949 on Amherst Street when, while playing in the driveway at a friend's house, one of the older boys I knew stopped as he delivered his newspapers, and asked if I would be interested in playing for the team in town on which he was the catcher, the Blackhawks.

I was honored and surprised to have been asked—I was only seven. What sealed the deal for me was knowing was knowing the league had uniforms. The fact that they consisted of just a hat and T-shirt made no difference, I was never prouder than having "Blackhawks" emblazoned in iridescent red letters across my chest.

This was two years before Highland Park would become an official member of Carl Stotz' nationally organized Little League. The Blackhawks, Rinky Dinks, Scooters, and Cobras were the four teams that comprised Highland Park's Midget Recreational League that played its afternoon games at the high school field.

The only difference between this Midget Recreational League and our playground games was that it had some structure. There was a schedule of games, definitive rosters, and an umpire. The teams were made up of many boys who were five years my senior.

We kids ran the games. Bats and balls were supplied by the high school, but we made the lineups, put them into a scorebook, found someone to keep score, recruited someone from the playground to umpire, and prepared the field which meant nothing more than strapping their bases to their stakes on the same beat up field on which we played every day. Whether a ball was fair or foul was a judgement call because there were no chalked foul lines. The games were not much different from those we played ever day when we just chose sides except that the line scores got printed in the Daily Home News the next day. My name would occasionally be mentioned as having done something to help my team win; that was pretty neat.

Two years later when it found local businesses willing to fund the costs for a team just as Carl Stotz had first done in 1938, Highland Park became an officially recognized member of the national organization known as Little League Baseball. Five teams were formed that were named for their sponsors: Hub Motors, the MacKinney Oilers, the Exchange Club, and the Fire and Police departments. The original rules established by Stotz prohibited girls from playing, but with laxity to that edict, and to build the rosters for our funding sponsors, every interested boy in town and one girl—a daughter of the MacKinney Oil sponsor —submitted their names to a selection committee. From that list of entrics, a "draft" was held by the organizers, and the very first sanctioned Highland Park Little League teams were formed. In a bizarre, and fascinating historical anomaly, the American and National Leagues of professional baseball did not hold their first draft of players until 1965, more than a decade later.

The team to which I and one of my best friends, Ron Schmitt, were drafted was sponsored by a local car dealership, Hub Motors. Ron's father, who was one of the better softball players in town, was our coach. Each of us were given a brand new uniform, and as proud as I had been wearing my Blackhawks T-shirt, a soft flannel uniform with black and red piping and "Hub Motors" across my chest, matching stockings and hat, trumped that simple outfit. Mom and Dad completed what I thought was my "professional" look by buying me a pair of sneaker-type shoes with small rubber cleats on the soles, the same kind U.S. Rubber had designed for Stotz's boys in the '40s.

Every one of Highland Park's playground and recreational league games were played on the same, much-abused, high school baseball field. The outfield distances were not defined by fences, but by the configuration of the land. Its base paths and pitcher's mound were the normal major-league distances of ninety feet, and sixty feet, six inches. These distances were shortened to the more appropriate distances required for our Little League and Junior League games. Used all day as this field was for either our pick-up games, or one league game or another, and then those at night, the field was battered, never watered, never dragged, rarely even raked, was sloppily lined when it was, had crater-like holes in front of the pitching rubber and in the batter's boxes, and was as dusty and bumpy as a country road. In other words, it was absolutely fantastic, the greatest place in town, and golden as far as we kids were concerned. I couldn't wait to step onto it every day.

The newly organized Highland Park Little League functioned under the same rules that defined a major-league game, with two exceptions. Leads on the bases were not allowed, and stealing could occur only after the pitched ball had crossed the plate. That last restriction has since been amended to "after the ball reaches the hitter," which seemed more a semantic change because "what's the difference?" Under the rules originally coded by Stotz, stealing was prohibited. He believed it was too hard for a young catcher to throw out a would-be base stealer.

Little League baseball in the '40s and '50s was baseball as it was meant to be, three strikes and you were out, four balls you walked. There were no "pings" heard when the ball was hit; we swung wood bats. Our head protection was a large earmuff-type of helmet worn over our baseball caps, nothing like today's face-guarded football helmet-looking headgear. Not every one on the team got to hit in an inning, and not everyone had to play. There were no age-categorized Tee Ball or PeeWee Leagues—eight year olds played against those nearing thirteen—or one that had a coach or parent pitching. Anyone who could throw strikes pitched, for as long as he could.

Teams were either winners or losers; not every player received a trophy; only the winning teams won awards. There were no expressive forms of group praise, no congratulatory or exuberant yelling for a performance by a mom or dad to boost moral, and no post-game conga lines to slap high fives, or caravans for ice cream or pizza. When the games ended, we went home. A game was recognized for what it was, good or bad. We learned to compete. Should we be defeated, we accepted the fact that we had lost. We'd do better next time.

We learned the game by paying attention. The opposition became our instructors. The hard-and-fast golden rule, preached by every coach, was to watch how others played. At some point in baseball's early history, the rules of correct play, what to do in various situations, where to throw the ball, how and when to run the bases, what to do as a hitter, and so on, became rituals passed down from generation to generation. Television eventually provided useful visuals while radio induced mental images that forced us to think. We learned to play the game based on what was best for the team, and what we needed to do to help the team win.

The only other thing our coaches told us was to always know where the outfielders were positioned when we were on base. We could then make the right decision about whether to take an extra base on a ball hit into the outfield. That bit of advice would come into play in a situation in 1973 that is now part of major-league history.

In Game 3 of the World Series between my Oakland A's and the New York Mets, we were tied at two when I walked to lead off the eleventh inning, and went to second on a passed ball. Having checked the positioning of the Mets left, center, and right fielders as I'd been taught decades prior, our shortstop, Bert Campaneris, hit a line drive over the head of their shortstop, Bud Harrelson. My read of the trajectory of the ball told me it had no chance of being caught by either the greatest of Harrelson's leaps, or by the left or center fielder. Trusting my instincts, I broke for home. Had my judgement of the outfielder's positioning been wrong and the ball caught, I would have easily been doubled off second base ending the inning, making me look foolish nationally, and a much repeated "goat" in the annals of baseball history.

Ignoring the third base coach's sign—which I do not remember seeing— the game situation required that I had to try and score. The outfielder's throw home was on line, but, with maybe not the greatest hook slide, I scored the game's winning run. We went on to beat the New York Mets in seven games for the second of our three consecutive World Championships.

Who could have predicted twenty years earlier that in my thirteenth year as a professional, on the biggest stage the game could present, the World Series, that I would use what I'd learned as a little leaguer to help the A's win a World Series game? Our three World Championships, a rare "three-peat," is forever etched into the annals of baseball history. The decisions I made that day in Shea Stadium were reminders that little things mean a lot, and often make a big difference in winning or losing.

Highland Park's recreational baseball season ended, and the playgrounds closed in mid-August. The only baseball left to be played was the Middlesex County Freeholder's Little League Tournament. This event was highly publicized, much anticipated, and was well-attended that featured the very best players from teams throughout Middlesex County. Highland Park always had enough good players to enter two teams. With only fourteen teams participating in the tournament's inaugural season, we won the championship. Two years later, with forty-four entries, we won again. Dad told me that if the money could have been raised after our second win, we might have gone to the Little League World Series in Williamsport, Pennsylvania. How awesome would that have been? In my final year of eligibility, I was asked to pitch, and threw what was reported to be the first no-hitter ever in the tournament's history.

The condition of a baseball field was always important to me, especially the infield, and those in this Freeholder's Tournament were incredible. They were fantastically groomed, nothing like the washboards of our playgrounds. Immaculate and stone and pebble-free, they had thick, white chalk lines outlining the catcher's and batter's boxes, and those setting the foul boundaries were so straight and precise that it seemed both unfair and punishable to step on them. The pitching rubber was actually usable because it was without the little crater in front of it as was common on most playground fields, and there were no holes from which you had to hit, the batter's boxes were level.

Lush green grass blanketed an outfield that was without ruts, divots, clumps, bare spots, or dandelions. Home runs were not determined by the ball being hit some unretrievable distance, but by clearing fencing that was a symmetrical arc 200 feet from home plate. More commonly known as a "snow" fence, it was a flimsy distance marker made of thin slats of wood intertwined through wire that would in no way prevent an outfielder from running over or through it should he not be paying attention. This fence alone "professionalized" the field.

Not long after school started again in the fall, an awards banquet was held at the Pines Restaurant in Edison. This was a night of celebration when trophies and medals were handed out to the individual winners of the various summer baseball, basketball, and tennis leagues, the playground contests such as horseshoes, ping pong, and shuffleboard, and, best of all, when we received our individual trophies for our wins in the Freeholder's Little League Tornament. Attendance was not mandatory, but with an overflow crowd every year, there was never enough room to seat all the families and relatives who attended.

The program for the evening was agonizingly long. The boring obligatory speeches by the mayor, the city councilmen, and other dignitaries that praised and paid tribute to certain individuals and their civic accomplishments, had to begin before everyone received their meal. If they didn't, we'd have been there until midnight— and it was a school night. The baseball trophies were always the last awards to be distributed, so sitting through the introductions, the speeches, and the other medal ceremonies for the various "miscellaneous" playground winners was frustrating, but how nice it is now to have the many awards that I won.

At thirteen, and too old for the Little League, I moved up a level to play in the Junior League. In a draft similar to how Highland Park formed its Little League teams, I was selected by the Lions Club, a local service organization. Having played shortstop and left field in the Little League, for reasons unknown to me, my Junior League coach, Ben Steiner, put me at third base. Ben had a three-year major-league career himself playing for the Boston Red Sox and the Detroit Tigers, so he may have recognized something about me that I didn't. What I did know was that I was not fond of the "hot corner."

Playing on a major-league size baseball diamond for the first time in this older league, was a challenge. I wouldn't be six feet tall with enough weight to matter for another year or two, so it was a bit of a struggle for me to make the longer throw across the infield to first base. My greater concern, however, was that third base was largely dependent on instincts and quickness. Unlike shortstop where, even as a member of the recreational league Blackhawks years before, I had learned to read the hitter's swings so that I could be on the move for the ball a split second before it was hit. This was a skill that was easily employed playing the middle of the field, but practically useless playing third where my shins and body may have stopped more ground balls than my glove.

From the Junior League, I had one option, the town's Senior League. Giving the league a title was generous because of how unstructured it was. Our playground games were better organized. Eligibility to play was restricted to anyone who was sixteen and not yet drawing Social Security. There were no uniforms or hats that identified to which team you belonged, but were a pair of khakis or jeans, and a T-shirt. Though my team had a sponsor, Frederick Paint, a local paint store, you wouldn't know that unless you were to read the line scores in the paper the next day. Each team's roster was filled through invitation by its manager, forsaking the draft process of the previous leagues. With no upper age limit and most of the players much older than I was—some by more than a handful of years—I was a bit uncomfortable, but this was the only local league in which I could play.

With many of the older players having jobs, getting off work so they could play presented a problem. Losing even just one game by forfeit from a schedule of only fifteen drove me crazy. Finding out that a game had to be forfeited simply because a player or two just didn't feel like playing was even worse. Why join the team? The league was disappointing, but was special because of the one person who had maybe the most influence on my young baseball life. For the first time in all the years I had been playing baseball in Highland Park, my time in the Senior League gave me the chance to play on a team organized and managed by Tom Lempfert.

Tom was seven years my senior, a baseball junkie who lived and died with every New York Yankee win or loss. We first met when I was in the Little League and, because of our mutual love of baseball, his relationship with me and my parents grew over the years to the point that he began addressing them as Mom and Pop.

211

If anyone was responsible for my professional career, it was Tom. He made me feel that I was a pretty good player.

Tom was a rare and special individual to everyone who knew him. At one time he owned the Fifth Avenue Sweet Shop, our high school hangout, drove a cab to make ends meet, and operated a lawn-care business, offering me some grass cutting hours now and then to make some money of my own, money I knew he needed.

He was the only one in town who I could ask to throw batting practice to me. And though my constant nagging him to do so must have driven him nuts, he never once complained. I was a nuisance, but my desire to hit was stronger than whatever guilt I felt about pestering him. It was because of this willingness on his part to put up with me that I remember the emptiness that overwhelmed me when he told me he was leaving town for two years to fulfill his military obligation. When he returned, he earned a college degree at Baltimore State University, and became the Athletic Director at St. Peters High School in New Brunswick.

Something we laughed about for years, long after it happened, was when I would literally knock him off the mound with line drives. Insolent, inconsiderate, and selfish as I was, I would tell him to shake it off and get back on the rubber. "You'll be all right!" His only response to my brashness was his usual silly grin and the brief, smiling kind of laugh that was so much him. I don't think he knew how to get angry.

Whether he was bothered by my arrogance, or just didn't show it, I don't know, but he put up with me. He was similarly kindhearted to everyone that knew him, asking for nothing, but giving so much of himself. Spending every evening with my father as he did for the last couple of years of Dad's life while I was away with my baseball obligations says more about him than I ever could. It was easy to consider Tom the brother I never had, and his passing at the age of eighty left me, and those he touched, with a legacy of gentleness, compassion, and generosity that was unequaled.

Today the Borough of Highland Park is not much different from the days I roamed its streets and playgrounds. The neighborhoods, no matter their economic standing, quiet and mostly tree-lined, are still as inviting and relaxing as ever, each one reminding me of some early adventure. Over the years, the town has remained proud, more than holding its own among the larger surrounding communities, if for nothing else than the athletic successes of its teams and some individual players.

Whether it was the success we had in the Middlesex County Freeholder's Little League Tournament, or that of the high school teams, the "Owls," the borough of Highland Park has had more than its share of sports honors and awards over the years. The baseball team had one good group of athletes following another, and won one Group 2 title after another, more than maybe such a small school had a right to. During its seventy-five-year history, the football teams have won more than twenty sectional titles, had seven undefeated seasons, and seen several individuals capture New Jersey State honors. One of my best friends, Joe Policastro, was named All-State Quarterback when the team went undefeated in our junior year, and then went on to play for Holy Cross.

Three young men after me also signed professional baseball contracts, only to have their careers curtailed by injuries. Rickey Earle signed with the New York Yankees and Ed Cipot with the New York Mets. And one high school football star, John Smith III, went on to a long NFL career with the Philadelphia Eagles and Baltimore Ravens. That's not a bad professional representation from a high school with a modest annual enrollment.

Hoping to preserve some of the memories of my early days on Highland Park's playgrounds, on visits decades after last being there, I sought whatever old photos or newspaper clippings I could finagle from Tom, Joe, and Ronnie. The old write-ups I was able to acquire of our Little League days, the championship games we played in the Freeholder's Tournament, and my days as an HPHS "Owl," were wonderful reminders of events and games that I had forgotten. With the extensive scrapbooks I have for each of my sixteen professional seasons, I now have a wonderful detailed history of my entire baseball life to pass on to my children and grandchildren.

But of everything I have achieved, every award received—including three incredible World Series trophies—every accolade and all the notoriety, the one thing that holds as much importance to me as anything else is the 1960 Most Valuable Player baseball trophy from Highland Park High School with my name engraved on it. It was graciously given to me by the high school's athletic director.

The day I was announced as its recipient in our assembly hall, I could not have been more surprised. Stunned would be more accurate. Daydreaming and not paying attention to the ceremonies that were dragging on and on, and fully expecting another teammate to be chosen, I was snapped out of my trance when it was my name instead that was announced. More startling was the resounding applause from my classmates. Completely caught off guard, my reaction was so typical of how I have viewed many of my successes. I never thought much of what the results might be, but more of what I was doing, the fun I was having, wanting nothing more than to do the best I could.

An appropriate psychological explanation for my response that day might be that I've never given myself sufficient credit for my accomplishments. That MVP trophy now sits proudly alongside my three championship trophies and several plaques from our Oakland World Series wins in 1972, 1973, and 1974, a large Midwest League minor-league championship trophy from my managing days with the Cleveland Indian organization, miscellaneous other awards, and all my Little League honors. Every one of them is important and cherished, but the Highland Park Owl baseball team MVP trophy for 1960 means more to me because it was an individually achieved accomplishment recognized by my peers. There is no denying its sentimental value, and the reminder it is of the wonderful times, good days, years, and friendships for which no amount of awards or trophies could justifiably honor.

Few have the wonderful array of memorabilia and memories from a life in baseball that I do, but as proud as I am of all I have accomplished and of all my awards, nothing gave me more joy than just their pursuit. I loved being on a baseball field, even the beat and battered one behind the high school.

11

MANTLE, THE YANKEES, AND NYC

The suburbs were booming, housing was in demand, the economy was strong, and millions of babies were being born. Our future was looking bright. But while President Dwight D. Eisenhower was moving the nation forward on a conservative and prosperous path, there was war in Korea, a crisis in Egypt over the Suez Canal, Castro's overthrow of President Batista in Cuba, the battle against the spread of communism in Southeast Asia, the continuance of the "cold" relations between the United States and Russia, and a beginning restlessness with the inequality and injustice African-Americans were suffering here in the United States.

It was the decade of the '50s.

Television entertained us with shows that delivered spiritual-like messages of family love and togetherness portrayed by an idealistic household where everyday problems were easily solved by perfect parents. Kids like Beaver and Wally on *Leave it to Beaver*, Betty, Kathy, and Bud on *Father Knows Best*, and David and Ricky on *The Adventures of Ozzie and Harriet* had no more excitement in their lives than I had in mine. These shows mimicked real life, and though there may have been conflicts around the globe, things at home were rather peaceful.

The portrayal of family life on television was no parody. I went to school, Dad went to work, and Mom took care of the house. At dinner time I'd watch *The Howdy Doody Show* every night, and we'd all watch *The Honeymooners, The Ed Sullivan Show, You Bet Your Life, The Jack Benny Program* and *The Milton Berle Show* in their time slots every week on our black and white TV. Life was simple.

Sports were a pleasant distraction to the world's ills, and our country's growing restlessness. New York had half a dozen professional teams with the New York Yankees not only dominating them, but the sports world in general. I can't say it wasn't warranted because they were good. Many nights I'd lie in bed listening to Mel Allen's play-by-play on the radio, imagining what it might be like to be playing in iconic Yankee Stadium some day. The Yankee players, everyone a superstar to me, could be seen live and in action at their playground in the Bronx, an hour's ride from Highland Park. My other heroes, Superman and Batman, were fictitious, and only spuriously came to life on the pages of my comic books.

From the group of sixteen major-league baseball teams at the time, I had no favorite, nor did I idolize any particular player, but I admired the Yankees more than either of New York's other tenants, the Brooklyn Dodgers and the New York Giants. Both of those clubs had their own limited success, but neither won as consistently as the Yankees, nor did they receive anything close to the same amount of media coverage. It was reasonable to assume that every

September the Yankees would again triumph over the Dodgers in the World Series.

All three New York teams had great players, but there was no one to compare with Mickey Mantle. Not only was he the best in the city, and the league, he was one of the game's greatest, ever. Bigger than life, he got more attention from the media than anyone else because of his ability to do on the field what few others could. Two other center fielders in the city were establishing their own Hall of Fame careers at the same time, but I held neither the Giant's Willie Mays, who played in the Polo Grounds just across the Harlem River from Yankee Stadium, nor the Dodgers' Duke Snider, doing his thing south of the Bronx in Brooklyn's Ebbets Field, in the same esteem I did the great Yankee slugger.

Mays staunchest supporter among my friends was Tom Lempfert. An absolute die-hard fan of the "Say Hey Kid," he never wavered in his belief that Mays was the best player in the game, better even than Mantle which, naturally, riled me. If it were not for Tom's passionate support of the Giants' star center fielder, I might have never known much about him. In a strange twist of hero worship, his obsession with Mays belied his rabid support of Mantle and the Yankees, a dichotomy for sure. Say anything derogatory about the "pin-stripers," and he hastened to defend "his boys."

As for Duke Snider, the third member of this All-Star triumvirate, my maternal grandparents idolized him as they did Jackie Robinson, Roy Campanella, Pee Wee Reese, Gil Hodges, and all the Dodger players known in Brooklyn as "Dem Bums."

You couldn't go wrong rooting for any one of the these teams, and to have three Hall of Fame center fielders in one city was something very special if you were a baseball fan.

● ● ●

Mickey Charles Mantle, often referred to as the "Commerce Comet" in reference to his home town, was the fair-haired, good-looking, powerful slugger from Oklahoma. Stepping into almost the same footprints of Yankee greats Babe Ruth and Joe DiMaggio, his tenure kept alive the tradition of great Yankee outfielders. And because his off-the-field antics somewhat paralleled the spirited, party-going, carefree path of the Babe's, his popularity took on Ruthian dimensions.

Taking over DiMaggio's reign almost to the inning, Mantle made the conversion from one super-talent to the next easy for Yankee faithfuls who were used to an illustrious chain of superstars supplanting one another. A day didn't go by during a season without some news about something "the Mick" had done. Everything he did was better than anything anyone else could despite a pair of legs that did their best to keep him from doing so. If he had been healthy, many thought he might have been the best to ever play the game.

During my 1967 rookie season with the Kansas City Athletics, our first meeting with the Yankees had me more on edge than usual because I was going to see Mantle live and up close for the first time, not just his image or some photograph, but the real guy. I wasn't sure what to expect, but figured him to be somehow different, something out of the ordinary; overwhelming, big, powerful and larger than life.

What I saw was certainly not a disappointment, but not at all what I'd expected. That he was smaller than I imagined only magnified his accomplishments. About as tall as I was, what he didn't have in height was made up for in width. His back was bodybuilder thick, his arms like sledgehammers, and he seemed to be wrapped in muscle. He was built as well as an athlete could be. It was hard not to stare at him.

How it was that fans could idolize a player, almost to the point of worshipping him, I never quite understood, but respecting as I did everyone against whom I competed, especially someone of Mantle's stature, I could relate to the off-the-wall fascination certain athletes generated. No matter how many times I saw, talked to, interacted with, or competed against the biggest names in the game, I felt honored. For ten major-league seasons I was a fan, awed to have been privileged to be among such talented athletes.

Whenever my Athletics played the Yankees, I wanted nothing more than to see Mantle hit one of his monstrous, tape-measure home runs, but that had become an impossibility. He was only two years away from retirement in my first major-league season, and his knees were so bad it was hard for him to generate the power he once had. He was no longer the slugger whose hunched-over swing from both sides of the plate I tried to emulate on the playgrounds as a kid. It was heartbreaking to watch him try to maintain his balance on legs that were bandaged from ankle to thigh.

What I was grateful to have witnessed was his signature head-bobbing, arm-pumping, piston-type jog that at one time produced his incredible speed. His time of 3.1 seconds on a drag bunt from the left-side of the plate to first base could easily have been thought to have been the result of a quick finger on the stopwatch. There was no indication of how fast he might be from watching him casually saunter to home plate, and settle into the batter's box. His "aw-shucks" Oklahoma manner and casual approach in no way hinted of what he could do with either his legs or his bat.

Sadly, for those who admired his awesome power from either side of the plate, he had a penchant for striking out. Not that I ever wanted him to, but whenever he did, it gave me another opportunity to watch him grab the back of his helmet and toss it aside in disgust. That silent gesture was a Mantle signature, a trademark of the frustration and anger he had with himself. It was the only demonstrative act I ever remember seeing him exhibit. No flamboyant showboat, he just hit, ran, and played the game as well as anyone ever had. Some would say even better.

Mantle was one of those players who comes along every decade or so who captivates the public with his every move. The few times Dad took me to see the Yankees play, my fingers were always crossed hoping he'd be in the lineup. His bad legs made that a toss-up. The power he had from both sides of the plate was unmatched. This he proved on one of our visits by hitting a ball left-handed that on one bounce landed in the left-center field bleachers. Why that was so prodigious a feat was because this happened in what was the old, old Yankee Stadium at a distance that was out of reach for most right-handed batters.

More impressive was the display he put on during a Labor Day weekend doubleheader in 1961 against the Detroit Tigers. My first professional season had just ended, and Tom Lempfert and I went into New York to watch eighteen innings of Yankee baseball. This was the golden year of the home-run battle between Mickey and Roger Maris. Both sluggers were chasing the immortal Babe Ruth's long-standing record of sixty. Mickey did not disappoint during the doubleheader, hitting two home runs, one a line drive to right field that hit the back wall of the mezzanine section.

To understand the enormity of that at-bat, you need to know that the original House that Ruth Built had three tiers of seating in right field, with the mezzanine section being the second of the three and set back some under the third tier. To hit a ball under that upper tier that would hit the back wall of the mezzanine section, meant it had to be a hit like a bullet.

His other homer was his typical long, high fly ball into the right field bleachers. He played two great games, and finished the day still in contention with Maris for the home-run title, but a serious hip abscess later in the month forced him to drop out of the race. He finished the season with fifty-four round-trippers. Maris, of course, went on to break Ruth's longtime record, hitting number sixty-one on the last day of the regular season.

It was impossible not to marvel at the power Mantle had, but until I stood in right field under the corner of the Yankee Stadium facade off which he hit a ball, I could not imagine the extent of it. Had the facade not been there towering over the right-field bullpen, and had Mantle hit the ball years earlier before that architectural mural was extended from the Stadium's original design in the right-field corner, many say it would have been the first ball hit out of the stadium.

There have been claims that Josh Gibson of the old Negro Leagues had once hit one out beyond the bullpen in left field, and though he is recognized by many as having more power than anyone ever, there is no evidence of him having done so. Some say he hit the roof's facade in left field just as Mantle had in right, but there is no corroboration of that feat either.

It was unthinkable that any normal player could have hit the ball to where Mantle did. In a futile comparison, one of our relief pitchers, Paul Lindblad, hit a home run into the first couple of rows of the upper deck in right-field one Sunday afternoon. Paul was powerfully built with long arms and strong hands, and though we all thought that had been a prodigious clout, and pounded him with congratulations, it was not even close to Mantle's feat. The facade wasn't that far in linear distance from the plate, but the height at the point of impact, estimated at approximately 117 feet, stretched the distance the ball would have traveled to an estimated 700 feet by some, well over 600 feet for sure.

Mantle compiled a career of awesome statistics despite two gimpy legs. Injuring a knee stepping on a sprinkler-head in right field during the '51 World Series kept his exploits to what they were, or there was no telling what he might have accomplished.

● ● ●

New York City presented a panoply of entertaining events for its visitors, more than any other city. Whether it was a sporting event at one of its three major-league ballparks, Madison Square Garden, any of a long list of Broadway theaters, sights such as the Statue of Liberty, the Empire State Building, and Radio City Music Hall, one of its museums, Central Park, its many famous buildings and ethnic neighborhoods, you could not be disappointed, certainly not bored, or left with nothing to do on any visit. The Naked City with its eight million stories was twenty-four hours of constant activity. It well earned being known as "The City that Never Sleeps." I looked forward to every visit, not only because I got to see my mom and dad, other family members and friends, but because the city was so alive with so much to offer, and so much of it unexpected.

The City was energizing, its din without comparison. Every car, truck, bus, and pedestrian was in a race to wherever. With the constant bleating of horns, the whine of truck and bus engines, people yelling for taxis, and the shrill of police whistles as the men in blue kept things moving and under control, it was a world of commotion with a cacophony of sounds that only New York City could produce.

Nearly all of New York City's distractions were more than welcomed, and the many bus rides that my Oakland A's teammates and I had from the Americana Hotel at 52nd Street and 7th Avenue to either Yankee or Shea Stadiums were uproariously fun times. Any number of strange occurrences or sights on the sidewalks of the Big Apple, or any of the internal conflicts or personal irritations between certain members of the team were sure to provide a hilarious moment or two during the forty-five minute rides.

Most of the hooting and hollering was inspired by the city's female population, or those we suspected were females, but so might any police action by the officers keeping the peace on horseback. People-watching was its own reward, a show unto itself. Should someone point out something weird as we barreled up the avenues, and it happened to be on the opposite side of the bus from where you were sitting, you had to be quick to see it because the bus drivers had our trips so well-timed, and their speed calculated so precisely, that they flew through every intersection as each light flashed yellow. They could run up any of the avenues, and not hit one red light for fifty blocks.

Whether we were going to or from an airport, hotel, or ballpark, something would happen on the bus that had everyone hysterical. We were a loose and close-knit group of pressured ballplayers, some of whom had no qualms about criticizing or making fun of one another. Whether the instigators were Bando, Blue, Fingers, Hunter, Holtzman, or Tenace, broaching the stupid play someone had made the night before, the bad swing someone had taken at a pitch, someone's ethnicity, or a simple personality quirk that rubbed someone the wrong way, everything and anything was up for grabs. The amount of money being paid an ex-wife or wives, and just about every extracurricular off-field antic, or postgame activity, received its share of what was thought to be good-natured ridicule. It might have pushed the limits of decency and respect, but never enough to silence the instigators.

During the years when a coat and tie were the travel attire, one of the pranksters began judging the sartorial selections of the neck garments being worn, and instituted a voice vote on their acceptability. Should it be voted down by a shouting consensus, which it always was, out the bus window it went. The more we won, the looser we got, and the more fun it was. When the voting moved to shirts and jackets, Catfish Hunter's sport coat was unanimously turned down on one trip, and the whole bus went nuts as it fluttered curbside.

On one early morning arrival at our Minneapolis hotel, while waiting for my room key at the front desk, I found myself standing next to a shirtless Jim Pagliaroni, one of our catchers. His coat and tie looked great but I had somehow missed the thumbs down consensus on his shirt, and didn't know that he had thrown it from the bus on the trip in from the airport. Sometimes there was too much going on to catch it all. Comments, mockery, derision, and the resulting indignant attitude of the teammate who was the brunt of the good-natured scorn usually had the rest of us in stitches. The clowning around may sometimes have been crude and didn't always go over well, causing tempers to flair, but it was what twenty-to-thirty-year-olds did to relieve the stress and pressure of major-league baseball. We could not have said or done the things we did unless we shared great mutual respect for one another. We grew to be pretty secure in who we were. Every member of the team played his heart out night after night, and any win might have been because of the efforts of the player who had recently suffered the cruelty of our laughter.

With a long list of historical points of interest and fascinating stops for its visitors, it was impossible to miss the visual and more expressive way the social and fiscal diversities of New York's residents were displayed. The apartment buildings were blatant signatures of the city's economic conditions. Ranging from the elite structures patrolled by uniformed doormen to the abandoned boarded-up retreats farther up the avenues that were home to more of the poor than they should have been, each one represented a fascinating picture of the diverse human environment among the city's smorgasbord of ethnicities while flaunting their varied lifestyles unashamedly.

The city was a mobile parking lot with every vehicle in a frenzied race to its destination incessantly honking individual warnings to pedestrians who didn't need to be told to step lively. Whether jaywalking was legal or not, do it and you became a target for the vehicles who played "chicken" with you. Anyone caught between curbs was forced to scurry for cover like mice in the Junior Frolics cartoons I watched on TV as a youngster. Those little creatures scampered frantically to escape the clutches of the big bad cat.

On a visit to the city with my children years after I retired, we stood dumbfounded on a corner as a well-dressed Manhattan businessman in a dapper overcoat and tie, attaché in hand, attempted to cross the street, only to be spun around, and knocked to the pavement when his heel was clipped by a speeding taxi—who rightfully had the green light. Nobody, including us, because we were in shock, ever stopped what they were doing to help the poor guy who was on his feet immediately. He matter of factly brushed himself off, retrieved his case, straightened his clothing, and continued on his way, undeterred. He made not a sound nor a gesture at the cabby, but took the incident in stride. How could you not love the city!

And not to be forgotten were Manhattan's panhandlers, individuals who rummaged around the city trying to survive. Those with ingenuity preyed on newbies like us ballplayers, picking us out as if we were comic book characters with a flashing lightbulb over our heads. It was nothing to be approached by someone offering some "today only" unbelievably low, special purchase price on a Rolex watch that we would never find again at such a ridiculous discount. Admonished with "You won't find a better deal anywhere." might have been believed until closer inspection of the timepiece revealed it to be a "Polex," not the acclaimed Rolex. With the uncovering of that deception, the peddler, sometimes indignantly, would turn and walk away, determined to find another pigeon.

With all that New York had to offer, attending a game at Yankee Stadium was at the top of any baseball fan's wish list. To see its interior was an honor, and I had the privilege to see the deep inner recesses of its original historic construction. It was a mysterious, magical kingdom to anyone who loved baseball. I was more than honored to have experienced its heart beat.

We were not a good club in my rookie season. The Athletics of 1967 were a maturing bunch, just beginning to show potential. My first bus ride that season from Manhattan to the Stadium was a quiet contrast to the frolicking trips to be made with the A's in later years. I sat in silent anticipation as I thought my rookie status required. Arriving at the player's entrance hours before game time, the fabled ballpark that greeted us stood silent. There was no traffic, no milling crowds, none of the pregame hustle and bustle I had come to know as a kid when there as a fan. Manny's Baseball Land, the fabled souvenir store across the street, had no lines yet with fans clamoring for a pennant, pin, or pictures of their beloved Bronx Bombers.

The Longines digital clock above the ticket kiosks outside the front of the Stadium told us of our arrival time, and "Yankee Stadium" emblazoned boldly above it suggested the Stadium's importance. It was a sleeping giant this early in the afternoon, a big, tall, white, monolith, exuding its magisterial but quiet presence, in no way indicating the decades of celebrated events that had taken place within. In its silence, it projected a dignity that was a bit eerie.

A small contingent of fans greeted us—as they would on every visit—as we pulled up to the player's entrance, many with pens in hand seeking autographs, others simply gawking and greeting their favorites as we got off the bus. This enthusiastic gathering was part of what was Yankee Stadium.

New Yorkers loved their baseball, every one of them a student of the game, a history buff well versed about every player who had ever thrown a ball or swung a bat inside the Stadium. No player, whether a Yankee, or a member of the opposition, escaped their scrutiny. Brash at times, they were never hostile or bothersome. I found them friendly and entertaining, pushy at times, but having grown up off Exit 9 of the New Jersey Turnpike, I understood the tenor and passion of the East Coast personality, a New Yorker's in particular, and admitted to some of the same rough and sarcastic edge in myself.

Moving quickly into the building through the security provided by the sawhorses and the policemen, we wound our way past what seemed to be too many tiny offices for such a magnificent place. Following a hallway of twists and turns, lined overhead with exposed vents and pipes, we came to a dark, catacomb-like area, seemingly below ground, where we found the locker room. Had "VISITORS" not been stenciled on the door, I would have walked right by mistaking it for a workroom.

This fabled locker room had a surprising dinginess to it that was made more dreary by the dark blue it was painted. It was lifeless, not very spacious, had a weird right-and-left angled entrance, and was somewhat cramped with a low ceiling. Each cubicle had one stool. It may have been too much to have expected anything better from a ballpark built in 1923, but Yankee Stadium was supposed to be the crown jewel of the major leagues, baseball's official palace, the home of more World Championships than any other ballpark in the country. Though a bit shabby and disappointing, the storied history of the room elevated the atmosphere to an elegance that was unforgettable.

Just off the heart of the locker room was the manager's office. Not very big, it had only a desk and a few chairs. The training tables, showers, and bathroom facilities shared a cramped space farthest from the entrance at the opposite end of the room.

Who might have sat on the stool that was now mine? Who had first used this particular locker on opening day in 1923 when Babe Ruth hit the Stadium's first home run that drove in three runs to beat Boston 4-1? Had other greats over the years, such as Ted Williams, Hank Greenberg, Bob Feller, and Walter Johnson, hung their clothes where mine now hung? So many stars and so much history had graced the room. I was humbled.

When the ballpark opened in 1923, the average height of a player was maybe 5'9" so the original entry into the dugout—a short walk from the locker room—though ample at the time, now had its lintel heavily padded to protect the head of the athletes as they grew. The small dugout comfortably accommodated the smaller players, but for me and my teammates, it was tiny and narrow with not much room to move around. Had we jumped up quickly during a game for one reason or another, we could easily be injured, maybe knocked out, by hitting our heads on the very low concrete dugout roof.

Two steep wooden steps put me on the playing field. It was impossible not to be overwhelmed by not only the massiveness of the place, but by the legendary and historical frieze that rimmed three-quarters of the stadium's interior. Seeing this architectural mural in person was more impressive than expected. Originally constructed of shiny copper, no doubt to add an elegant Romanesque effect to the place, each section was now painted white. It was so much the Stadium's insignia that it has been included in the construction of the new Yankee Stadium that opened in 2009. Looking up and following it as it wrapped around the upper level of the ballpark, it capped the magnificence of the ballpark's enormity with its almost 70,000 seats.

Neither its infield or outfield surfaces were very good, and the place was out of date, yet, so much of it is unforgettable. The three monuments immortalizing Babe Ruth, Lou Gehrig, and Miller Huggins stood guard in their deep center-field location, completely in play, just in front of the 461-foot sign on the wall. There was the famous waist-high right-field wall to the right of the bullpen that Roger Maris's 61st home run cleared on the last day of the 1961 season, and the grand bleacher sections in the outfield that ran from bullpen to bullpen. In left field to the right of the Yankee bullpen, and to the left of the visitor's bullpen in right field were the two iconic field-level scoreboards that told of nothing but the inning by inning score and the hits, runs, and errors for each team. They were as much what Yankee Stadium was for me as anything else; I loved their simplicity and their locations.

In right center above the bleachers was the huge Ballantine Beer & Ale scoreboard that on the left side displayed the game's line score and lineups, and on the right side were the on-going activities of both leagues. In between was a large vertical message board that once displayed the greatest message ever, the announcement of the birth of my daughter, Kristi, in August during my second big-league season. It was an unexpected and wonderful gesture by our traveling secretary at the time, Ed Hurley, long an American League umpire who, in retirement, was accepting some of Charlie Finley's money to arrange our road accommodations.

Yankee Stadium had more than served its purpose and boasted of more moments to be remembered than any other ballpark in the country, but after fifty years its original design was in need of repair. Chunks of concrete were falling and putting patrons in danger, so for the 1974 and 1975 seasons all the Yankee home games were moved to Shea Stadium, home of the New York Mets of the National League, while the aged Yankee home was renovated.

During the ballpark's demolition, seats that had been removed were for sale, and had been dumped in large piles in several nearby locales. Luckily for me, many were dumped in the parking lot at the E.J. Korvette store in neighboring New Brunswick. Anyone could buy an original Yankee Stadium seat from 1923 for $7.50 and five empty boxes of Winston cigarettes. My son and I now have a wonderful piece of baseball history, a souvenir from the original, legendary Bronx arena that Jacob Ruppert built.

New York City and Yankee Stadium had an influence on my life like no other city or ballpark could, but every ballpark created an excitement for me that can't be explained. They were all special, and no matter how many times I might walk into any of them, or get to play on fields I had only read or heard about, I felt proud to have had the opportunity. It's difficult to explain the feeling of being in places where so many great athletes in history had performed, and in which I had earned the right to play.

Nothing I might say could express the awe of playing alongside or competing against so many of my contemporaries who are now considered some of the game's greatest. Being teammates with Hall of Fame members Reggie Jackson, Catfish Hunter, Rollie Fingers, Bob Gibson, Joe Torre, Lou Brock, Willie McCovey, and Dave Winfield; to have defended against the talents of Brooks and Frank Robinson, Harmon Killebrew, Roberto Clemente, Eddie Matthews, Al Kaline, Luis Aparicio, Johnny Bench, Joe Morgan, Pete Rose, and Rod Carew, to have swung at the pitches of Steve Carlton, Jim Palmer, Tom Seaver, Gaylord Perry, and Nolan Ryan, to name a few, to have been managed by, or able to watch the managerial skills of other Hall members such as Dick and Ted Williams, Red Schoendienst, Luke Appling, Yogi Berra, Earl Weaver, Sparky Anderson, and Tom LaSorda, and associated in some small way with so many others who have plaques in Cooperstown's Hall of Fame has been a very special part of my life.

When I take time to remember all that took place during my career, the teams and teammates, losses and victories, and in my case, championships, I don't know what to say other than that deep down I have a calm acceptance of it all, a thankfulness, a lot of pride, and a peacefulness for what I've accomplished; a satisfaction that may have no other worry explanation other than to say that, yes, I was a major-league player.

12

HIGHLAND PARK

The county seat of Middlesex County, the city of New Brunswick, lies on the southern banks of the Raritan River in Central New Jersey. It was my birthplace, and home to Rutgers University. Across the Albany Street bridge, on the other side of the river, high on its banks, to the east of New Brunswick, is Highland Park, the two square mile, quiet, diverse community in which I grew up almost eighty years ago. Since its inception in 1905, the borough has catered to a variety of ethnicities while offering its citizens everything needed to feel safe and comfortable. Growing up in a sports-oriented atmosphere, and raised by parents who made me the center of their world, I don't know how my childhood could have been improved. I had all I wanted, and a life that was uncomplicated. With Mom in charge of everything, my upbringing wasn't perfect, but the love she and Dad gave me was unconditional. Their doting spoiled me while softening the blow of being an only child. We weren't wealthy, but I never felt deprived, nor did I need more than I had.

Our family was small. All of my aunts, uncles, and cousins were loving, kind, and friendly. My cousins, like me, were sibling-free, so there were no nieces or nephews. As it was with most families, its titular head were the grandparents, and, in my case, that honor belonged to my mother's mother and father, my maternal grandparents. They were the heart and soul of the entire clan, the glue that held everything and everyone together. It was at their home that everyone would gather to celebrate the major holidays of Thanksgiving, Christmas, and Easter, to talk, reminisce, and cap a wonderful day together with a dinner of all the typical Polish foods: pierogis, kielbasa sausages, stuffed cabbage, a horseradish I loved, and for dessert, doughnut-like prune-filled paczkis, and powdered, twisted chrusciki angel wings pastries. After dinner the men commandeered the dining room table for their hours long, boisterous pinochle card games while the women retreated to the kitchen to talk about whatever it was they talked about.

Inquisitive as kids would be, my cousins and I liked to eavesdrop on the adult conversations, so we'd hang around the card game until we could no longer stand the smoke-filled room, and then wander into the kitchen under the pretense of wanting more to eat. What the women talked about was of no interest to us until they began speaking Polish. Changing languages was their intended ploy to keep us from knowing what they were saying, but as often as our families got together, I'd learned enough of the oddly sounding words that I knew when they were talking about me, and some idea of what was being said.

These gatherings were some of my happiest childhood memories; I looked forward to every one. What puzzled me, and what I never could understand was how on Christmas Eve every year, Santa Claus always found my grandparent's house at around the same time after dinner. It was as if he had a certain route to follow that was precisely timed year after year. It was years before I made the connection between the brief disappearance of one of my uncles, and Santa's visit.

My father's parents emigrated from Poland and retained their family surname of Kubiak. My mother's parents, who also emigrated, changed their alphabetical maze, Podboroczynski, to a more easily pronounceable Pochinski. Being strong Polish Catholics my maternal grandparents enjoyed the occasional Sunday when Mom, Dad, and I would take them to mass at the Polish church in New Brunswick. It was primarily for them that we did this because sitting through both the Polish and English versions was excruciatingly long. When only Mom, Dad, and I attended nearby St. Paul's Catholic Church in Highland Park, we would visit them after the mass just as we did every Thursday night after shopping for groceries at the local A&P food store. On most of our visits during the week we found them engrossed in the wrestling matches on their black-and-white TV. They completely bought into the choreographed shtick they were watching.

The small, overweight, and flabby grapplers that excited them were nothing like the muscular, athletic giants that enthrall today's fanatics with their dramatic, theatrical, acrobatic, and sometimes violent performances. But Grammy and Dziadziu—which I believed to be the Polish counterpart for grandfather—thoroughly enjoyed the bogus grunting and groaning of these staged events. I never understood everything they yelled at the TV, but I knew enough Polish to know when they were calling one of the "bad guys" a devil. One of their "good guy" favorites was an Italian named Antonino Rocca. His performances were renowned because he wrestled barefoot. He was a showman, an instigator, and the architect of every one of his matches. Extremely nimble and agile, he would tease and outrage his opponents by tauntingly putting one bare foot or the other in their face as he bounced around the ring. Knowing the end of a match was near, the crowd got frenzied in anticipation of what was to come. The scripted end to every one of Rocca's bouts, and his coup de grâce, was an athletic leap onto the shoulders of his stunned opponent from behind to straddle his neck, and then somehow somersault him to the mat where, to the raucous cheers of the crowd, and my grandparents clapping, he would pin his man to the referee's three count slap of the mat. I do have to admit that he was entertaining and fun to watch!

Although my grandparents liked and watched wrestling whenever they could, their first love was baseball and the Brooklyn Dodgers. Their heroes were Duke Snider, Pee Wee Reese, Gil Hodges, Jackie Robinson, the rest of "Dem Bums" and me; they never missed any of my Little League games. Regrettably, they and my father's parents passed away before I reached the major leagues, but they all got to see me play during my second professional season in the Eastern League at nearby Binghamton, New York. I know they were proud of me.

Fifty years removed from those memories, with moderate changes, Highland Park remains two miles square and retains its old familiarity. Businesses have come and gone along Woodbridge and Raritan avenues, but the same houses I remember as a child still define the neighborhoods. The two homes in which I grew up, one on Barnard Street and the other on Columbia Street just a block away, despite renovations, look much the same today as they did then. The most noteworthy change to the town was the renovation of Donaldson Park. Several Little League fields were added, as was a walking path around the park's perimeter, and with new tennis courts, a bigger boat launch, a fenced-in dog run, and larger picnic areas, the park's ninety acres is so much nicer.

My old high school, having for decades been a traditional ninth through twelfth grade campus, now has students being schooled from grades six through twelve. The expansive wooded area behind the high school baseball field that was a shady retreat from the summer's sweltering temperatures, and a wonderful place for us to see how fast we could ride our bikes on its winding pathways, was bulldozed and replaced with a newly resurfaced synthetic turf football/soccer field, a rubberized track, and a much nicer baseball field. These renovations were to have accommodated an expected expanding athletic program that never materialized. The other schools in Highland Park have gone through major transformations of their own. Irving, my grammar school with grades K through six, is now K-two, and includes a generous outdoor playground for the youngsters. A new grammar school, Bartle, now educates third-to-sixth grade students. Lafayette and Hamilton schools, where I attended grades seven and eight, are now office buildings.

Some things that haven't changed are the high school's distinctive tall white dome, which gave birth to our yearbook being called the Albadome, its magnificent Doric-pillared main entrance, and the entry steps on which we teenagers loved to sit and flirt. The impressive structure has always seemed too architecturally sophisticated for little old Highland Park. The original footprint of the classrooms remain, but gone is the small second-floor library. It now has its own singular location only a short walk across the street from the school. Not far up the block from the library is what used to be the Fifth Avenue Sweet Shop. For decades the emotional oasis for the town's teen-agers who regularly filled its booths enjoying hamburgers and cherry cokes, playing the pinball machine, or just "hanging out," it is no longer that fun corner, but is, instead, offices for a couple of medical professionals.

The Irving School baseball field that I remember is now the new playground with swings, slides, and climbing equipment for the school's toddlers. Calling it a baseball field was never correct because there was no right field to speak of. Running through what should have been the right fielder's position, and not far behind the second baseman's, into center field, was Merilind Avenue. Beyond the street, and covering what ground there was up to a nearby house with its exposed windows in what was right field, was a growth of unruly, knee-high weeds. To avoid the problems presented by the street, the weeds that gobbled up our baseballs, and the windows of the house that were close enough for even our ten and twelve year old power to reach, we made a rule that you were called "out" should you hit the ball to the right of a telephone pole that was across Meriliind Avenue in center field.

No matter where we played—and we had a number of choices—there was always an obstruction of some kind that caused us to have to slightly alter our games. Donaldson Park had the only pure baseball field, but it was too far away to trek all the way there and back. I always had the feeling that it was out of bounds anyway because of its seemingly official status as a recreational and picnic spot for the townspeople.

The local street traffic occasionally caused an intermittent delay or two in whatever games we were playing, but that was no big deal. Parked cars became hiding places for our games of hide-and-seek, served as goal lines for our football games, or were used as bases for our baseball games. And though they were dangerously in the way when we hit fly balls to each other, we were forced to control the direction we hit the ball to avoid breaking any windshields. Unfortunately, one day I did.

The Irving School baseball diamond—the one with no right field—often had other kids playing somewhere in our left and center fields. Everyone just played around each other. At the high school, we did our best not to hit the ball into the woods in right-center field because there was no finding it, and with baseballs hard to come by, that was a no-no. The few bushes in left-center at least gave us a better chance for their recovery or, if we were lucky, finding one we'd previously lost.

We turned the empty lot at the corner of Harvard and Columbia Streets into a baseball field. Unlike Irving's diamond, this one had a right field though it was limited. The house across the street not far from where we positioned home plate had five or six windows facing the field, all excellent targets for our foul balls, but they were the least of our worries. The major problem was the huge, neatly stacked pile of what looked like wooden pallets in left field that we had to avoid running into. What it was doing there no one knew, and we made no special rules because of it except to caution everyone. When we weren't playing baseball it served as something fun to climb on. This lot would eventually be surveyed and subdivided for the construction of four new homes, one that became the second home in which Mom, Dad, and I lived. Every night I fell asleep in what used to be our center field.

● ● ●

The world of professional baseball was mysterious and surreal to me and my friends. Our fantasies about it and the players were best fueled by radio or television broadcasts, newspaper or magazine articles, or being lucky enough to attend a game of one of the three New York teams. The closest we came to establishing contact with a major-league player was through the colorful baseball cards the Topps Chewing Gum Co. first produced in the '50s. These little pieces of cardboard with their vividly colored player portraits were pretty neat, each card a personal introduction to one major-league player or another. We'd play games with the few we had, or attached them with clothespins to the spokes of our bikes to make a really cool flapping-kind of sound as we rode around town. Neither me nor my friends collected them.

Baseball cards were first produced in 1951 when the Topps Chewing Gum Company came out with a fifty-two card set that had both red and blue-backs. In 1952 they introduced what would be their most important set ever, one that totaled 407 cards, with each card featuring a player, and a good-sized logo of his team. Matching those logos became a popular game. A small pile of cards would quickly build as each of us, in succession, turned over a card to reveal that team's insignia. If yours matched the previous logo discarded, the accumulated pile was yours. That might happen right away, or not until there were ten, twenty, maybe thirty cards discarded. The greater the number, the greater the chances the game would be over because someone surely would have lost most of what he had.

The toughest, and maybe the most fun game, was flipping the cards one-by-one against a wall maybe six feet away, trying to make it stand up or "lean" against it. When one did, you won all the cards after every other player had one last chance to flip another card at it in an attempt to knock it over. Should someone be so lucky as to do that, they won the pile, and it was usually quite a pile because it was not easy to throw a "leaner."

Baseball cards were hard to find. They were not popular when first introduced, few stores had them. The only place that did, from time to time, was the small neighborhood ice cream and candy shop across the street from our Irving School baseball field. We knew the store as "Helen's," but whether that was the store's legally incorporated name, no one knew. It was what we called it because Helen was the pleasant little lady behind the counter who owned it. She lived behind the store, and would come out once she heard the bells ringing that she had hanging on the front door. Stocked primarily with canned goods and household staples, she always had her ice cream freezer stocked with a handful of flavors, and her counter full of candy for us kids. A ten cent ice cream cone was a great way to end a full day of baseball in the hot sun.

When they were originally produced, a single pack of Topps baseball cards contained six of the little cardboard pictures, and one rectangular piece of pink bubble gum, colorfully wrapped in wax-coated paper. Calling it gum was generous because it didn't take long for it to feel like you were chewing rubber. Years later, when the cards became valued collectables, Topps was forced to do away with the bonbon because its sugary residue defaced the player portraits, thereby diminishing their value for what was a growing cadre of collectors.

The only card I ever wanted was one of Mickey Mantle, but all I ever unwrapped were those of players from the Washington Senators, Philadelphia Athletics, Detroit Tigers, or any other team that I could not have cared less about. Why there were so many Bob Porterfields, Jim Busbys, Johnny Groths, Eddie Joosts, and Gus Zernials, but rarely any stars from the Yankees, Giants, or Dodgers, our local New York teams, was puzzling.

A Mantle card was as elusive then as it is expensive now. The "Mick" was the best player in the game at the time, and his card was at the top of my want list for no other reason because it wasn't worth anything in the '50s. Who would believe that one day one, in mint condition, and graded a ten, would have the value of $100,000 or more. As with the Mantle, neither did I run across a Willie Mays, Jackie Robinson, or a Duke Snider. It made you wonder if there was some diabolical Topp's scheme to deliberately short the insertion of popular players from the nearby teams into our neighborhood packs hoping that we would be encouraged to buy more.

What I did not know at the time, and maybe the reason why I never found a Mantle card, was that Topps was struggling with their new enterprise; they could not give the cards away. Few stores sold them as Helen did. They would not become popular, and then valuable, for years. Until then, discouraged and finding few takers, the company was forced to dump pallet after pallet with hundreds of cases into the waters off New York City. Collectors grimace thinking of how many were drowned that included the now very expensive first 1952 Topps complete set, which, of course, contained the also now very expensive Mantle rookie card.

● ● ●

New York City, with the Brooklyn Dodgers, the New York Giants, and the New York Yankees, was home to more professional baseball teams than any other city in the country. It was also the mecca for entertainment in the '50s. Dad's boss at Gerber Plumbing in Woodbridge had tickets to just about every sporting event and theatrical production in the City which is how I got to see Yankee Stadium at an early age. Walking up the serpentine ramps of the ballpark's underbelly to our seats, knowing that in moments I would be seeing major-league players for the first time, was as anxious and as exciting a few moments as I've ever had. Bursting from the walkway into the open expanse of this venerated ballpark, and seeing the field for the first time, there was not a better place I could have been. The Stadium was massive, the field so much bigger than I expected. It was not yet dark enough yet for the lights to be on, but with the usual East Coast haze from the heat, and rain expected, the place had a somewhat dreary feel. Batting practice was still in progress, and the balls being hit seemed to float in never-ending high lazy arcs in the gloomy atmosphere deep into the twilight of the outfield. The scene was ghostly, made even more so because we could not hear the ball being hit from where we were.

One of New York's other landmarks was Madison Square Garden. An endless variety of events were held in what I thought a weird, though historical, arena. My first visit was when Dad was again given complimentary tickets, and also use of the company limousine, so he, Mom, and I could see a New York Rangers hockey game. Dropped off curbside at the entrance, the Garden looked like every other large building in New York. Its lone distinguishing feature was the huge, impressive marque that hung over the sidewalk announcing that night's and upcoming events. Nothing about the place gave any indication that it could seat 18,000 people, or that it held some of the first football games, hockey and basketball games, prize fights, circuses, dog shows, and even political conventions and party rallies.

When we entered the seating area, except for a beam of light filled with swirling cigarette smoke shining down onto the ice like a huge flashlight, it was dark, and hard to see anything. Once my eyes adjusted, I realized there were two upper levels of seating. They seemed so steeply angled that it looked like everyone would slide down onto the ice at any minute. Our own seats could not have been better; right behind the Ranger's bench, practically in the player's laps, only a couple of feet from the ice. I had never been this close to real professional athletes, and though much of the game's action was blocked by the players jumping on and off the ice changing lines, I spent more time watching them than I did the game.

Something I never thought to question was why I was so good at most sports. How did I come to have more athletic ability than most of my friends? As I got older, it was apparent that it was definitely a "hand-me-down" not only from my father, but also, surprisingly, my mother. Dad told me about how he played baseball and hockey when he was young, and I had seen the rhythm to his cast when fishing. When I learned he had joined the Gerber

Plumbing bowling team, I was anxious to go with him to one of his Friday night matches because, never having seen a bowling match, I was curious. And was I ever impressed by how good he was. Bowling may not be the greatest test of athletic ability, as I'd figured fishing would not be, but any physical activity requires a certain amount of coordination, and there was an ease and grace to how Dad attacked the pins. Never did I expect to see the control and agility, or the finesse, with which he rolled the ball down the alley. His approach and balance were amazing, and more than responsible for him scoring in the high 100s and low 200s the few times I was with him.

My greater surprise was finding out how nimble and athletic Mom was. When she and Dad danced at a wedding, they were by far the best looking couple. Both were extremely light on their feet and could spin and stomp to a Polish polka better than any other couple. Mom easily followed Dad's lead as they circled the dance floor lapping everyone. And, she could play a little baseball herself. During a Mother-Son Little League charity game one summer, not only did she play a great second base, she ran out a well-stroked double. Unknown at the time was how secure my inheritance was.

Mom was Mom: mother, wife, disciplinarian, and guardian of the household. All I really knew about her childhood was that when she was maybe ten, her sister accidentally poked a finger in her left eye as they were jumping on a bed, leaving her with serious damage to her sight. After revealing how it happened, she said nothing more about it again. I have to admit to not understanding the effect it may have had on her, but the disability was never a crutch, never an excuse, and never a reason for her not to do something. She knitted and crocheted her entire life making sweaters and blankets for anyone she thought might want one. When macular degeneration further darkened her vision, she would tell me how hard it was for to see, but still somehow made a few small blankets for her great-grandchildren.

How did her handicap affect her, and what did it do to her psychologically? Was it responsible for the sometimes harsh personality Dad and I knew? She was as congenial with friends and those outside of the family as Dad was; the two of them at those times equal, one and the same, but just how deep was her hurt? I wish I knew. The strength she had to cope with her disability had to have been immense. I was as blind as maybe she really was as to why she was who she was. Maybe someday I can apologize.

In contrast to Mom, Dad had a calm, quiet demeanor. Nothing rattled him. He never talked about himself, bragged about anything, or judged anyone. He told me of his love for hockey, playing sandlot baseball, and bumping into Babe Ruth and Lou Gehrig once at an exhibition game in Tennessee when the Yankees had stopped there heading north after a spring training session in Florida. Ruth's personality did not impress him, but he said Gehrig was a true gentleman, and very patient with the fans. Was that bit of information maybe a furtive lesson for me?

Dad was also the stalwart member of his and my mother's entire family, and the one everyone turned to when they found themselves in financial difficulties. I would sometimes hear him and Mom disagreeing about whether to bail out certain relatives from another of their problems because, from what I could tell, they were not often repaid whatever monies they had loaned. The emotional control Dad maintained over that slight was impressive.

It emphasized the concern and passion he had for others, and the love he had for my mother because it was her side of the family that always seemed to be the needy ones.

Not afraid of work, his industrious nature masked a somewhat mischievous streak. At nineteen during Prohibition, with money tight, he ran a small speakeasy that he set up in his garage, selling shots of liquor for what was big money at the time, one dollar. Where the liquor came from I never asked, but I wouldn't doubt he had his own still someplace. More interesting was his apparent "friendship" with the local police. Whatever connections he had kept him alerted to the neighborhood shakedowns intended to ferret out such illegal operations. A warning phone call gave him time to move his little operation across the street into a neighbor's garage to escape detection.

During the depression with money and jobs scarce, he joined the Civilian Conservation Corps established under President Franklin Delano Roosevelt. This public work relief program was for unmarried, unemployed young men up to twenty-eight years of age that required a minimum commitment of six months with a maximum stay of two years. Dad's responsibility was to take a truckload of twenty to thirty men, every day, some thirty miles or more into the wilderness areas of Wyoming and Idaho to clear the forests and build roads and trails. He was paid thirty dollars a month with a governmental mandate that twenty-five of it be sent back home to family and relatives to help them make ends meet. With his own food and lodging taken care of, he said the five dollars he had left was more than enough for him to enjoy himself, and maybe see a movie every Saturday night. It was very possible he had a hand in the development of a few of our national parks, Yellowstone being one.

If pressed to define him, I'd say my father was a gentle soul, clearly his own man, assured, confident, and comfortable with who he was. He had a quiet strength and a deeply hidden sense of humor. Mom would get upset when he and I would be cracking up with laughter over something she didn't consider funny. Always friendly, he was well liked by everyone who knew him and was, without question, the congenial host and center of every party or get-together at our house.

Of the few times he did tell me something about himself, that he had met Fidel Castro was the most surprising. Dad was the trusted foreman in charge of the day to day operation of Gerber Plumbing, a plant that manufactured toilets, sinks, and bathtubs that outfitted many of the apartments and housing units built in and around New York City, and other areas of the country. Every once in a while I went to work with him which I loved to do. I'd watch him do whatever it was he did in his office for a while, and then wander around the plant and its dusty aisles fascinated by the manufacturing process.

One day, as he told it, a small group of visitors, headed by the fatigue-clad Castro himself, was escorted into the plant, and he was asked to give the dictator and his entourage a tour of the facility. Castro was so impressed with what he saw that he asked Dad if he would consider being the foreman for a similar factory in Havana, and wanted to know what salary he might need to run the place.

Believing it to be an outrageous amount, and hoping it would be a polite way to say no, Dad said he would need $30,000.00 a year, an utterly exorbitant amount at the time. Castro called his bluff by responding "No problemo!" Even though he talked it over with my mother and the Gerber employee he would have taken with him, he had no intentions of going, and turned down the offer. I can't imagine my life had he accepted.

It didn't dawn on me for some time that the reason Fidel Castro was in Woodbridge, New Jersey, visiting this seemingly innocuous plumbing manufacturer, was because Gerber Plumbing must have been supplying Cuba with its products. That made sense because my Dad's bosses were very well off financially.

Highland Park, small as it was, had a reputation for fielding some impressive sports teams in the '50s and '60s. With a population that has held steady at around 15,000, whether it was baseball, basketball, football, tennis, or track and field, the high school teams took a back seat to no city or school no matter their size or division. Even our recreational teams were dotted with great athletes. Much of the credit for all of this success had to be given to Highland Park's Recreation Department, and its dedication to keeping its kids active, and out of trouble. Not only were the high school and the town's other schools, Irving, Lafayette and Hamilton, open from nine to four every day during the summer making other recreational activities available, the department organized a number of leagues for the different age groups, and the various sports. There was a match or game of some sort scheduled to be played daily at the high school. One followed another, morning, afternoon, and night, and with no other distractions at the time disrupting our free time, there was ample opportunity for anyone with athletic talent to improve.

Finding a playground full of kids today is virtually impossible, unlike my friends and I who were never at a loss of what to do, or a place to play. One of games I loved best was the one we played within the confines of the fenced-in tennis and basketball courts behind the high school. It was challenging, fast, and a test of your quickness.

The four courts—two tennis and two basketball—occupied the same area perpendicular to one another. Each tennis court was two half-basketball courts, and each basketball court was two half-tennis courts. This entire field of play was pretty much a square making one side of one of the tennis courts, or one-half of one of the basketball courts, depending on how you looked at it, our "infield." Because hitting the ball over the fencing that enclosed the courts was so easy, we ruled that a batter was automatically out if he did. This forced everyone to hit line drives, or hard ground balls. With the layout of the concrete infield being smaller than that of a Little League infield, the infielders were almost on top of the hitters making it so often wiser to be careful and safe, than to try and field the softball we used. Had it been a hardball someone would surely would have been hurt, but even a softball could be hit so hard in such tight quarters that you had little time to move for it.

My favorite game, however, was stickball. Needing only a tennis ball, and a wall at one of the schools on which we chalked a strike zone, we were good to go. We didn't run any bases, but made up distances that determined singles, doubles, triples, and home runs. I threw a knuckle-type, nasty, straight-down, "drop curve" that impressed even me, and was, for all intents and purposes, un-hittable. No one could hit it, not even the the older kids who constantly complained the pitches were never strikes—the pitcher was always the umpire—but they had no chance to hit the ball anyway, so I let them bellyache all they wanted.

Playing marbles and mumbly peg was occasionally fun, but because my hands were so small, it was hard for me to "shoot" the marbles so it didn't take long to lose what "nibs," "aggies," or "purees" I had; and I had to be careful not to inadvertently stab myself attempting the acrobatic tosses with a pen knife that mumbly peg required.

Other games like "kick the can," "steal the flag," and "hide-and-seek" were much the same where someone who was "it" tried to find everyone who was hiding before they could rush in and kick the can, grab the flag, or touch what was home base. These games were usually played after dinner with the neighbor's houses, cars, or bushes our hiding places until either the streetlights came on, or the fireflies began flashing their tiny yellow lightbulbs. Both were recognized parental demands to go home. One of the neighborhood mothers watched for them like a hawk, and no sooner did she see one or the other, she would be on her front porch yelling as loud as she could for her son Rudy to "Get in this house…now!"

It startled me to hear one day that someone I knew had been sent to "reform" school. I never knew what that meant or where this "school" might be, but it sounded like prison, and was a little scary.

With there being so few ways to get in trouble, I didn't know if he had broken some law, or was just unruly. I was scared to death to just be given "detention" for disrespecting a teacher. My mother would have killed me had I ever had to stay late after school for any reason; teachers were authority figures to be respected.

There were not a lot of things to do that would get us in trouble. About the most mischievous thing we did was finding a way to sneak into the new high school gymnasium that was under construction during my sophomore year. When a large addition was being made to the school, this new gym was in close proximity to the baseball diamond making it easy for a bunch of "inquisitive" kids to snoop around the construction site looking for an entrance. When my buddies and I found an opening, we'd sneak in and play on the beautiful new basketball court for an hour or two every Sunday when there were no workers around, and no one ever knew. This new gym looked to be three times the size of the old bandbox that was only a couple of feet larger than what seemed to be a smaller than a regulation-sized basketball court. The new court was lacquered to a glimmering sheen, meticulously lined, had glass backboards, ample out of bounds room, and pull-out seating on either side. It was almost too nice to walk on, but a very welcomed change.

Summers were special. I couldn't wait for school to end each year. Mom never had to worry where I was; she knew I was on some baseball field. I'd be out of the house by 9:00 AM, come home for a quick lunch—I hated this interruption—and didn't return until around 5:00 PM. And then there might be a game at night to play or watch.

A typical East Coast lazy summer day was hot, humid, muggy and uncomfortable. A warning of how sweltering the day was going to be was the early morning chirping of cicadas. With their singing, and a hazy heat drifting through my open bedroom window waking me up, I knew the day would be a sizzler. It was nothing to come home soaked with perspiration from playing baseball all day.

Mom and Dad owned a small 700 square foot bungalow at the Jersey shore where there was, at least, some relief from the relentless summer heat. Even though you could find comfort under a beach umbrella, there were many times when you had to go back into the water to cool off. Body surfing, riding the waves on my raft, and chasing little sand crabs that washed ashore was fun, but there was nothing better than crabbing in the nearby bay. Attempting to lure the blue shelled crustaceans to the surface with a fish head on a string from a dock, and netting them was a challenge. They were worthy adversaries, apparently able to see the danger of their impending capture with their protruding eyes because many of them would let go just before being scooped up. Once in a while, after a dinner of having boiled the unlucky ones, we would spend a couple of hours enjoying all of the amusements, rides, and games on the boardwalk at Seaside Heights.

Summer, of course, had to end, and with the shorter days and cooler nights signaling the impending closing of the playgrounds, another school year beginning was not far off. This did not keep the borough of Highland Park from doing what it could to keep us kids occupied throughout the winter months. It readjusted the recreational programs, and opened the school gyms every Monday, Wednesday, and Friday evenings for a couple of hours. A group of us would play basketball for two hours at Irving School on these nights. Roundball was far from being my best sport, and though a member of the high school team, I was one of the last to get in a game. Being small, unable to handle the ball very well, and not being a good shot, was no resume to indicate that I should be on the court.

But I was a different player, physically and mentally, almost the go-to guy, during these after dinner recreational games. I was relaxed, confident, and controlled the ball much better, and surprised even myself with how well I played. Unlike the scheduled games for our high school team where we each had specific positions and assignments, these games were unstructured. This allowed me the freedom to use my skills as I saw fit which I reasoned was why I did so well in professional baseball. In that similar singular atmosphere, I could concentrate on what it was I had to improve without worrying about pleasing someone or following a prescribed plan of action.

One of my best friends, Joe Policastro, and I almost broke our necks putting up our own basketball hoop on the street behind his house. Why we didn't while trying to nail a clumsy, heavy, and hard-to-lift makeshift backboard to a telephone pole while balancing on a couple of rickety ladders, I still don't know. The street wasn't the greatest place to play, potholed and crowned as it was, but it was the best spot in the neighborhood. Joe was a good basketball player—clearly better than me—but good at all the sports. He was a starter on all of our high school teams, was an All-State football selection, and then went on to play for Holy Cross. Trying to guard him while navigating the street's uneven surface, the occasional rain puddles, and often ice and snow— nothing stopped us—was not easy, but we had a good time.

There would always be one or two winter snowstorms that brought with them the chance of missing a day of school. Knowing that it would be snowing all night, I'd be up early listening to WCTC, the local New Brunswick radio station Mom always had on downstairs in the kitchen, hoping to hear that Highland Park schools would be on the list of closings. Why we never seemed to make the first list I don't know—Highland Park seemed reluctant to give us the day off—but because every other school was closed, we always made the second. Free for the day, we roamed the streets and neighborhoods, built a snowman or two, maybe a fort, or had snowball fights. A very heavy snowfall made for hours of fun sledding down the big hill at Fox's farm where not even having to drag our sleds back up the hill dampened the joy of the ride down.

And no matter how cold or how snowy, Sunday morning was reserved for a "touch" or "flag" football game. Fifteen or twenty of us would gather at Donaldson Park ready to play at the appointed 10:00 AM starting time. In the heavier snowfalls, we kicked things up a notch and played tackle, never minding being wet and cold from falling time and time again in the white stuff for a couple of hours.

Growing up in Highland Park has given me much to remember. What first comes to mind are its baseball fields and playgrounds… the funky right-field starved Irving School baseball diamond…the baseball field my friends and I laid out at the corner of Harvard Avenue and Columbia Street where the woodpile in left-field interfered with way too many attempts to catch fly balls…the always dusty, well-used, and worn high-school field where whoever played right field had to do his best to keep the ball from getting by him because should it, and then go down an embankment onto the lower running track, the batter could circle the bases twice before it was retrieved...any wall at any one of the schools that was a substitute backstop on which a strike zone could be drawn for a stick ball game...the open area directly in back of Irving School that we configured into a cone-shaped baseball diamond because of the interference of the playground equipment and swing set in what would have been left-field, and the fencing along the sidewalk on Eleventh Avenue that severely limited any right-field their might have been...the makeshift baseball field we made out of the high school's basketball and tennis courts where hitting the ball over the surrounding fence meant you were out...the one real baseball diamond in Donaldson Park with its limitless outfield distances, and the mound from which Tom Lempfert often threw me batting practice...and any street in town on which we played some form of football, baseball, or on which we roller skated, and, during one really cold winter, ice skated.

Not to be overlooked is the too elegant looking Highland Park High School that still stands proudly with its stately columns, capped with its still perfect white dome, or the two homes in which I lived, the first on Barnard street, and the second on nearby Columbia Street from where I would run to the First Aid Squad a few blocks away as a volunteer in response to the siren atop Irving School that went off to signal that help was needed somewhere in town. It wasn't but maybe five minutes before an ambulance was on its way.

Saturday afternoons were always fun, usually spent at the RKO Reade movie theater that was across the street from where the World War II "Doughboy" statue still stands at the convergence of Raritan and Woodbridge Avenues. For a quarter, after walking up the red carpeted ramp to a small concession area where only popcorn and a couple of different candy bars could be bought, we got to see a cowboy and Indian movie, a Disney cartoon, a newsreel, and, if we were lucky, a Superman serial. And heaven help us if we made noise, or had our feet on the seat in front of us. The usher who was on a constant patrol with his flashlight might ask us to leave.

Pedaling my bike home from Lafayette School against the searing winter winds and the freezing temperatures was a horrible experience, as was the many times my fingertips would split from playing outside in the cold. More pleasant were the school dances except for being afraid to ask the girls to dance. There was changing classrooms for the first time in seventh grade at Lafayette School that I thought was so cool….the old, tiny cramped high school gym, and its smelly locker room…the Senior Prom…presiding over our class meetings as Senior Class President…the great teams the Owls had…the overflow crowds at every Saturday afternoon football game, and the very much anticipated Thanksgiving Day morning game versus our neighboring town rival, Metuchen…the hours spent on homework in high school, and the various classrooms beginning with Mrs. Compton's kindergarten room in Irving School where I was knocked unconscious when I fell off the big slide in the room.

Not to be forgotten is being laid up with the mumps, lying on the couch in the Barnard Street house with my head wrapped in a poultice of hot mashed potatoes that was some magical Polish remedy… doing what I could to remain calm at age seven while Dr. Hamburg, without numbing my chin, put three stitches in it to close a gash so big that by looking into a mirror I could see the bone. I split it open trying to balance myself walking around the edge of a neighbor's U-Haul trailer.

And, of course, there were all the teachers, especially the dedicated persistence and frustrations of Mr. Gromelski in high school, sweating profusely no matter the freezing temperatures, stripping off his suit coat, loosening his tie, and opening the windows while trying desperately to teach us how to conjugate verbs, and remember him saying when he got overly frustrated with us—a sign of the discipline meted out at the time—"I will bounce you off the wall like peas!" He was hilarious. There was Mr. Garth, the only male teacher at Irving School who actually did pin a student against the blackboard who had gotten out of hand.

What fun it was making a large cardboard grocery store out of a big box in Mrs. Underwood's second grade class…there was pretty Mrs. Dye, my third grade teacher…making candles and peanut butter filled dates as Xmas gifts for Mom and Dad in Mrs. Monroe's fourth grade…Mrs. Boehmer's unique ability in fifth grade to lift her one eyebrow to show her muted disgust at something or someone.

And not to be forgotten is Mrs, Lynch, the roving music teacher who made sure we hit the musical notes properly when we sang the Star Spangled Banner…saying the Pledge of Allegiance to the flag every morning and the Lord's prayer…my high school graduation speech as class valedictorian…the good times I had at neighbors' homes…the high school coaches, Maude, Jay, and Bus… good friends like Jo-Jo, Ronnie, Tommy, Larry, and Snob Bicky…and, well, you get the picture.

Highland Park was quite a place

13

THE FORK IN MY ROAD

The face in the mirror staring back at me says, yes, time has passed, but, if that means I am supposed to be different, why do I continue to struggle to make sense of the same childish and immature behaviors that so confused me a half-century ago? What has time and experience done for me? I'm the same guy who, as a puzzled teenager walking to high school one day, thought how great it would be when, at age fifty, my life would be in order, and the world's ills settled. What was I ever thinking?

Life used to be simple. I don't remember my friends and I ever having any great problems. When teams had to be chosen for our playground baseball games, it didn't take long to decide who the two captains should be. With no complaining or whining from anyone, the unwritten playground "rule" was that either by default or reputation, the best players always received the honor. They then either decided between themselves who would have first pick, or settled the issue with a quick game of "paper-scissors-rock."

The selections they made for the two teams may not have made everyone happy, but they were what they were. An occasional trade or two might keep one club from being much stronger than the other, but by the captains alternating their picks, the talent on both sides was relatively equal. It was hard to keep two or three of the very good players from being on the same team, but with the two best players made the captains, and therefore on opposite teams, it was difficult for one team to have a significant advantage.

There was another way for the captains to decide which one of them would get first pick that was more fun, and a little challenging. It was a little "game" that made use of the bat. Who first thought of doing it no one knows, but pictures have been found of kids, and even professional players, picking teams with this method since the early twentieth century.

It began with one of the appointed captains tossing the bat vertically, knob up, to the other, who would catch it with one hand a foot or more below the knob. They then made alternating grabs climbing strategically up the bat's length until either a winning grab completely covered the knob, or one more tenuous grab would. The one who had last grab of the bat had to then twirl it around his head three times. Should he drop it, he was an immediate loser, and would pick second. He would also pick second if, after the twirls, he could not hold onto the bat when it was given the one kick allowed the other captain. Should he survive that seemingly unfair tactic, he, deservedly, picked first. Everyone knew to calculate their grabs, and hang on to the bat!

When there were not enough players to make two full, nine player teams, the two captains might be picked by having everyone form a circle and hold their fists in front of them. Someone would be appointed to go counterclockwise from one player to another, touching each extended fist with his while reciting the shortened version of an old childhood rhyme, "One potato, two potato, three potato, four," and so on to the end, "...seven potato, more."

Each numbered segment of this timeless rhyme would coincide with a touch of one of the extended fists, and every time the word "more" landed on a fist, that fist was eliminated, and placed behind the player's back. Repeating the verse over and over, the last remaining fist in the circle belonged to the player who became one of the captains. Repeating the process found the second captain.

The most lopsided way for teams to be chosen, one that always sparked an argument, was for the appointed captains to assign individuals to the teams; "You and you are with Joe, and you and you are on Bill's team," or "I'll take these guys, and you can have the rest." Because buddies wanted to be with buddies, or the best players banded together, these teams were always uneven, and a swap or two would have to be made. Anytime the teams could be kept equal in talent, they were more competitive, and the games a lot more fun.

Until my senior year in high school began, I paid little attention to what I wanted to do with my life. As a freshman, I had enrolled in the college curriculum course; there was no question I would be going on to some higher level of education. High school was no walk in the park, but with my mother demanding the same good grades I received in grammar school, I worked hard to not let her down. But as important as my education appeared to be, she and my father never sat down with me to discuss what my interests might be, or what I would like to do after graduation.

My senior year was not as nonchalant and carefree as were my freshman, sophomore, and junior years. The real world and adulthood was just around the corner, and with no idea of what to do about either one, I began to panic a little. Still there was no discussions with Mom or Dad about my future. With no direction at this point, taking a liberal arts course my first year in college seemed to be the right thing to do, but, sooner or later, I had to hone in on something. To be honest, going to college felt like an obligation. The one talent I had that could have been considered somewhat special was an ability to draw. I wasn't great, but had enough artistic know-how to do a crude portrait or two, and, from time to time, simple cartoon figures. I doodled a lot, and enjoyed the mechanical drawing class I elected to take my senior year. With this as the unstable foundation it was for my future, and worrying what I was going to do with my life, three or four months before graduation, almost by default, I decided to become an architect.

My decision to pursue an architectural career was both sensible and pragmatic. Anything that connected me to the earth was always comforting, and I loved nature. So without guidance or discussion with my parents, and with skills I considered sufficient, my decision seemed to be a good one. When Pratt Institute in Brooklyn, New York, offered me a scholarship, my life was settled, my future decided, or so I thought. In the meantime, for no other reason than my love for the game, I continued to play every day for the high school baseball team.

As if the complications of just being a teen-ager weren't enough, when the chance to play professional baseball materialized, what to do about my future suddenly became a very serious situation. It wasn't that I had no interest at all in becoming an architect, but neither did I fear that I might not make a living had I chosen to play baseball. Conflicted over my options, my instincts were telling me that both paths had merit, but, still fighting my way through adolescence, I did not know which way to turn. And there was still no advice, or even questions, coming from my parents. It didn't help that I was more concerned about what they might have wanted me to do than what I did. Given a scholarship to attend Pratt Institute was more than I'd hoped for, and as an architect I would not have to change horses in midstream as baseball would require me to do in my mid-thirties when I'd be forced into retirement. But neither would it be wrong to say yes to baseball. How many young men were even given that opportunity?

My decision to design buildings for a living—unique homes more specifically—may have been made with a bit of hesitation, but not in desperation. It satisfied a mysterious need I had to see how far my limited artistic talents would take me, and was intellectually based. Could I breathe life into my designs? I would love to have pioneered some phase of the vocation, but had no feel for how imaginative or innovative I was.

A decision to play baseball, on the other hand, would be strictly an emotional response because of my love for the game, the challenges it presented, its intoxicating competitiveness, and the possibility of achieving some level of notoriety. I also can't deny there being some faulty optimism on my part about everything concerning my future falling neatly into place because of the money I would make. What problems could there possibly be? Talk about being naive!

What I did not give enough consideration, or serious thought, was what the long-term effects of my decision to play baseball might be. What kind of a future would the game provide me and an eventual family? The only thing that registered with me when the opportunity to sign presented itself was that I would be a professional baseball player, someone special as far as most people were concerned. I let the celebrity of a life in baseball cloud my judgement.

With life being confusing, and making no sense to me as a teenager, I was doing my best to control emotions that I did not understand. Having to make a decision about what I wanted to do for the rest of my life did not seem fair, I wasn't ready for it; I didn't know what I was ready for. When I was asked if I would be interested in playing professional baseball, it came at a time when just living every day was hard. The angst caused by the fact that classes at Pratt Institute were starting in a couple of months was enough to deal with, but now, all of a sudden, out of the blue, I hear, "Would you like to attend a tryout camp?"

In fairness to the times, college was not the positive stabilizing factor that it would eventually become. It was, of course, important, but it wasn't something I'd seen any of my family members take advantage of. My parents were "old school," as were every one of my aunts, uncles, and cousins. No relative had ever pursued any type of formal education, so there was no familial understanding of its value that would have influenced me; I had no role models. My parents may have looked at college as the best thing for me, but for what? In my mind it was nothing more than an option even though I didn't have any others. Considering the effort I had to put into achieving what I did in high school, I had serious concerns about what I thought might be the difficulty of college, and failing scholastically.

I had no such reservations about baseball, and no fear of failing.

My astrological sign is Taurus, the second sign of the zodiac, one of the three earth signs. If my life was truly determined by the stars, it was only natural that I would decide on a career that was real estate related. My decision to study architecture was made before I had become the believer in astrology that I one day would, but there was definitely an esoteric celestial-based validity behind it. From a more reality-based perspective, being a Taurean, I seriously wondered what it would feel like to one day be able to incorporate the elements of nature and the environment into my future designs as Frank Lloyd Wright did so creatively with his masterful and marvelous renderings.

Wright's genius came to my attention in Mrs. Boehmer's fifth grade class in Irving School when, for a class project, I constructed a large one-story, ranch-type plywood house. In my research for this first architectural attempt, I stumbled upon Wright and his philosophies. The variety and scope of his work, and his artistry, was enormous. His ingenuity and vision, the breadth of his imagination, his minute attention to detail, and the artistic functionality of his designs that were so naturally compatible with their purpose, was remarkable and unmatched. His belief that no design was bad because more important was the wise use of space to match its function, was an extraordinary insight. He was well ahead of his contemporaries with creations that exalted life.

Fundamental to the dreams of what I hoped to do with my own designs, as Wright did, was to integrate and have nature's beauty justify the structure, softening and blending the transition between its interior and exterior creating a peaceful and totally utilitarian atmosphere. Whether I could fulfill these ideals would eventually be discovered, but as with baseball, just their possibilities were intriguing, challenging, and intoxicating.

When I first saw Wright's drawings, each was more impressive than the last, but one aroused special attention. It was the extraordinary home he had built over a waterfall, appropriately called Fallingwater, in Mill Run, Pennsylvania. It is now a National Historical Landmark. Another work so honored was the winter home he built outside of Scottsdale, Arizona, called Taliesen West; it housed his studio, and is now home to The Frank Lloyd Wright School of Architecture. This desert creation was complementary to his summer home in Wisconsin, which he called Taliesen East. To blend the low design of Taliesen West into the natural appeal of the Sonoran desert that he dearly loved, he used what organic materials were available in the region in its construction. Wright was an architectural genius with his work made all the more incredible because he was self-taught; he had no real formal education.

Unaware of what to expect when I first visited and saw the décor and construction of his Southwestern landmark, for the first time I realized how it, and the innovative style of his other buildings, brought life and nature together. No doubt they invoked the same looks of disbelief as my own when they were first seen by his contemporaries in the late nineteenth and early twentieth centuries. Voted America's greatest architect in 1991, Wright's structures are truly unique and vastly different from those of others because he compelled the occupants to live with his designs, not just in them.

Baseball was the one sport I could never get enough of, and though there was never any thought that it would consume my life as it has, it is foolish of me to even think that another profession could have been as fulfilling, provide more joy, or been as satisfying. But what the game has given me is not what many might expect.

What I consider its rewards have nothing to do with anything financial, nothing about what trophies I have gloriously displayed, and certainly not any of the accolades adoringly bestowed on me in sixteen professional seasons. Those things, of course, matter, but what I consider the true gift is what I feel when just the word baseball is mentioned. I feel linked to the sport in the same mystifying way that I am lovingly linked to my son and daughter and my grandchildren. That bond has no physicality, no substance, it cannot be seen or touched. It defies explanation, but it is definitely what has to be love.

Though the game tested every ounce of my physical and mental toughness, and frustrated me more times than I care to admit, it was never tiresome or menial, never just a job. Real work was the eighty hours I would spend every week in retirement simultaneously juggling the ownership of a laundromat and dry-cleaning business, a fitness studio, and a real-estate company, along with the stress of making monthly payrolls, paying tax after tax, fending off competitors, and being at the mercy of a fickle public. Withstanding the aggravation of the business world was work enough.

My ultimate decision to trust that baseball would be the best thing for me carried none of the hesitancy and trepidation that my decision to study architecture did. Why, was because of the comfort and familiarity I had with the game. I may not have understood the potential difficulties I might run into, but neither did they scare me. Maybe they should have.

Though the game could be physically frustrating, playing it never overwhelmed me. What did, however, was not knowing how to deal with the emotions that were triggered by my play. As wonderful as the game can be, it is nothing but negatives and disappointments. Overcoming them is what gives the game its life, and makes it so much fun, but accepting failure was the most difficult thing I think I've ever had to do. I had no understanding, knowledge, or ability to handle the emotional side of the game. Plus I had no outlet; no one to talk to. Worse was isolating myself from anyone or anything that might have helped. Trying to keep a sensible perspective of everyday life through it all thoroughly blindsided me.

Raised to be the "perfect little boy," I never doubted that Mom wanted only the very best for me. Being taught to distinguish right from wrong and to be respectful of others, well-mannered, and polite were wonderful character traits to have instilled, but her disciplinary methods often made me nervous and anxious; I never knew when I might do something she didn't like. With that in mind, the psychology behind how I developed a dogged determination to succeed is something I don't understand. The same desire I must have had to please her may have been what allowed me to not let the physical and mental challenges of baseball get the best of me no matter how bad things got. I was used to the punishment.

My feelings of inadequacy, a lack of self-confidence and the fear I had of not pleasing others was a cruel penance to live with. It was only when I was able to accept who I was, and become vulnerable, that I realized the complexity of what I was doing to myself.

My parents doted over me. I never questioned their love, but what I needed was a more demonstrative expression of it. Always reminded to be "the good boy" I sought recognition and acceptance from wherever when, out of the blue, like a lightening bolt, here comes professional baseball. What could possibly be better than to be recognized as a baseball hero, idolized as athletes were. I knew it was not a good thing to be looking for approval from others, but the game presented a comfort that I had never felt.

When my career began I wasn't even close to being mature. I was living and behaving with an obstinacy that verged on childishness. I was idealistic, believing that everything would turn out OK simply because I was a professional. During my six minor league seasons, I was single with no one else to care for or worry about. Getting married just prior to my first year in the major-leagues, what should have then been "us," remained "I." The game continued to receive the bulk of my attention. As noble and as important as that was, and maybe had to be, I should have more wisely divided my priorities between the game and my wife and, in time, our children, but I didn't know any better.

Professional baseball is a unique occupation. It is nothing like those that provide a more normal existence. It required a greater commitment and a deeper kind of focus that, because of my average talent, required my full attention; or so I thought. It wasn't that I ignored or shirked my familial responsibilities, but to survive, and have the kind of career that would take care of the important people in my life, baseball deserved the time I gave it, physically and emotionally. It may be strictly semantics to say that while I was doing all I could to master the game, it was pushing back at me in a way that said if I refused to commit to it, I was not going to last long, that if I did not remain on an emotional high, I would lose the edge that was needed to play it as best I could. And always in mind was the possibility of never performing good enough, and losing the livelihood my family needed.

The family unit was of little concern to baseball organizations in the '70s. Too many events occurred when Dad was at the ballpark whether he was at home or on the road. There was no recognition of the impact the family unit had on the player's performance, an insensitivity, no doubt, that contributed to me isolating myself more than I should have. Baseball took precedence. Today there is a psychological understanding of the family being an integral part of a team, and the damage that can occur because of either a physical or emotional event that affects that unit is more seriously responded to. Not to dismiss the effect that any such incident would have on the family itself, it is how it affects the husband's performance that triggers this consideration.

Too many of my children's day-to-day activities, birthdays, holidays, and school recitals, along with so many breakfasts and dinners together were lost, forever. I regret not being with my wife when my daughter, Kristi Lynn, was born in 1968, but births fell into that insignificant category. My A's were in New York playing the Yankees when my wife called at four o'clock one morning with the news that I was a father. As excited as I was, I felt terrible not to have been there with her. As much as I was hoping Kristi could wait until I got home, that was just not her. She was going to do what she wanted to do, when she wanted to do it.

After a too-long flight back to California, and about to see the little girl I had fathered, I could not believe how nervous I was walking into our Alameda apartment. Knowing I had a child was a little scary, but what an experience to see her that first time. I will never forget seeing this beautiful little girl curled up into a little ball on all fours, stomach down and asleep in her crib. I could not imagine her being comfortable. She looked so small and fragile crunched-up the way she was. For a minute or two I could only stare at her until my wife told me it was OK to pick her up. I wasn't sure I was doing it right, but it is impossible to explain the feeling of first having Kristi in my arms.

Another equally incredible experience was three years later when I actually witnessed the birth of Justin Rodger Kubiak. He was born in Waukesha, Wisconsin, in February, 1972. Seeing him at that fantastic moment, I remember shouting, "He looks just like Kristi!" What did I know; I thought he did.

Without question, the two greatest rewards of my career are the births of my children.

● ● ●

For far too long I looked at life and its challenges with a selfish and arrogant matter-of-fact attitude that sheltered me from reality, but that was my coping mechanism. It caused me to do, and not do, certain things. The most crucial mistake was not giving enough consideration to my wife's and my relationship, our love, our life together, and what our future would be after baseball. Although I realize it "takes two to tango," that had to contribute to our marriage failing. I shirked what I saw too late as my responsibilities by naively believing everything was fine.

Baseball consumed my waking hours. As a profession it is unlike any other because it's not an eight-hour-a-day job where when five o'clock comes everyone goes home and the day is over. A baseball day never ends. The pressure to perform is unrelenting. Staying emotionally strong every day to cope with the stress could not be ignored or taken lightly. Had I been a more natural talent, one of the game's more elite players, my commitment to excel might not have had to be so driven and focused. I could have given greater consideration to the other things in my life.

The emotional high I was on became evident on days off when my body would literally shut down from exhaustion. In those twenty-four hours of freedom from the stress of the game, the uniqueness of life as a professional athlete became very apparent. I needed to better understand how to live day to day in this exciting, and uncommon world of baseball, instead of behaving as if I was its prisoner, but I could not ignore the fact that I loved being captive.

● ● ●

Mom controlled my life with her fastidious edicts. Her discipline was loving and well-intended, and though I was not to speak unless spoken to, a demand that was not as literally applied as it sounds, its intent was clearly understood. It would be years before many of my neurotic fears would be understood to be imagined or exaggerated, but until then they controlled everything I said or did, and kept me from doing much of what I wanted to do. Any decisions I might have to make were what I felt to be my duty.

My decision to pursue a baseball career was no mistake, but it was made ambiguously because of the need to untangle the confluence of the different paths my life could take. Choosing baseball over college had the potential of great rewards with the odds of receiving them not so great, but it was an opportunity few received. College was not to be abandoned, just delayed. Had everything transpired properly, the years it would have taken to become an architect would have withstood whatever baseball career I might have had; both careers could have been accommodated. It did not turn out that way, but any blame I might want to attach to the game for how my life has turned out is now an empty excuse.

As shy and restrained as I was, devoid of expression, self-direction, and individuality, choosing a path that would feed me much-needed confirmation and approval was a decision not difficult to make. What better way to get personal affirmation than to be one of a select group of individuals adored by perhaps millions? A baseball career would fulfill that need in an instant. The doubts I've expressed about it being a correct choice come only from having lived through its consequences.

It didn't take long to realize the time and effort the game required, and my commitment to make it my future was further strengthened by the fact that from day one, I was thought to be a good player. The early positives coming my way made it easy to overlook my education, and I rolled over very easily on what should have been a more serious attempt to accommodate both careers.

What I've accomplished cannot be denied. Few have experienced the incredible things I have. The pangs of conscience I have about my decision to play baseball result only from living with its aftermath, and being unprepared as I was for a second life. The effect that had on my family is something that has been hard to accept. It took a long time to accept my life as it was, and it hurts to say that I only feel OK about it.

High school was not easy. Homework was monotonous. Pages and their words blurred because my mind wandered. Rereading something for the second or third time drove me crazy. I never did understand the purpose of word problems in math. Who cared how long it took two trains to meet racing toward each other at different speeds? And what use were algebraic equations and mathematical formulas? Trying to decipher the intended meanings conveyed in the literary works of very famous authors was impossible; how could I figure them out when I didn't understand myself? And worse was that I was expected to have all the right answers.

What compounded the struggle I had with my schoolwork, and so many other things, was that I was never satisfied with just an answer. I wanted to know how it was derived. I wanted to understand the hows and the whys of a problem, the mechanism of the conclusions and solutions. My perfectionist nature did not allow me to be comfortable memorizing what I had to, but being able to was responsible for me being a four-year member of the National Honor Society, Junior Class Vice-President, Senior Class President, Senior Class Valedictorian, ninth academically in my graduation class of just over 100, and accepted to study architecture at one of the better architectural schools in the country.

Scholastic honors have lost their glow; they've become irrelevant with the passage of time, while those from baseball are continually revived by the one or two pieces of mail I receive every day from fans asking for my autograph. Their letters, comments, and reminiscences of the old days are welcome reminders, but each comes with a bit of self-condemnation about not having taken proper charge of my life as I should have.

As a player, all I ever wanted to do was play the game, leave the field a winner, know that I had done my best, and was a little better than the day before. Nothing mattered more to me than being with my teammates. Even as a manager and coach, I could have done without the extracurricular responsibilities. They were a distraction and, in my view, often unnecessary.

One of the characteristics of my astrological sign, Taurus, is a keen intuition. I am no clairvoyant, fortune teller, palmist, or mystic, nor can I see the future or predict it, but I believe in this sixth sense. I now live by my gut feelings, and have used information received from psychics to better understand who I am, who others are, why my life is what it is.

Woven into my introverted personality, lack of self-confidence, hang-ups, and other neuroses, is the unique ability to understand and unravel things immediately. I've always been intuitive. My first impression of people and their personalities, and life's predicaments and problems are usually correct. Though I will analytically dissect everything to the nth degree, I will more than likely return to my first inclinations. For a long time I never accepted or acted on these instincts, I refused to listen to myself. Had I taken them more to heart, my decisions would not have been so influenced by others.

Had I been aware of this intuitive sense, my life might have been very different. It may have softened somewhat the tenor of how I was raised. I now believe we all have our own answers; the trick is to listen to what we are telling ourselves. This is not a special gift or miraculous skill, but an ability that simply needs to be given attention. Life now seems little more than common sense. I am mostly free of the baggage that once dominated me.

As a Taurus, my "bullish"—the bull is the symbol of Taurus—personality was responsible for many of my actions and decisions, many not the best. Taureans are born under one of the best signs of the zodiac. They have tremendous skills and insights, but also an analytical personality that is headstrong, unyielding and serious, what many would call dull. And I agree. I had to learn to accept my goodness, open up, be more vulnerable, laugh some, and learn to listen a bit more before reacting.

Not everything always goes well, but I am now much more in charge of myself because I listen to and trust the voice in my head. Do I make mistakes? Of course. I needn't delve more deeply into the psychological issues I have had to deal with, nor into the years of therapy that have allowed me to better understand myself, but I am so very, very glad to have found the answers I have.

My life hasn't been easy because of the wrong decisions I've made. The contingent issues from being without my children for too long because of my breakup with their mother are things I will never live down. My relationship with them is now better than I could have ever expected, and I could not be prouder of who they have become as adults and parents, and wonder how that came to be. They have taught me more in how they live their lives than what I may have given them.

Writing a book such as this is more like who I really am than my playing sixteen years of professional baseball. I like cerebral confrontations and writing this absolutely was. It forced me to think, tested my intellect, and educated me. I love talking to brilliant people. I love learning. As a youngster I could not stand to read. Now I'd like to read every book I see, and will usually have two, three, or four going at one time. I'll stay with one as long as it holds my interest, then move to another. Someday I would like to say that I have read Moby Dick, Crime and Punishment, War and Peace, and all the classics. I have hundreds of books with more than a few of our early presidents—Washington, Jefferson, and Lincoln—among them, and well represented in my library. And my literary collection would not be complete without the more than 500 baseball titles I have.

Certain books have been instrumental in my self-discovery. They drove me deeper into peeling away my layers to better understand myself and life. One of my favorites is *Zen and the Art of Motorcycle Maintenance*. It was as intriguing and thought provoking as are the many I have on Zen, Taoism, Buddhism, and East Indian philosophies. I find the history of our Native Americans inspiring, and one book, *Where White Men Fear to Tread*, an autobiography by Indian leader and activist Russell Means, gave me the clearest explanation of what religion really should be in contrast to the confusion I felt with my own.

The inner turmoil that I survived and the emotional immaturity that took too long for me to realize, stymied my growth longer than maybe they should have, but I have met and resolved life's challenges as best I could. And there is no doubt that, whether right or wrong, good or bad, baseball was, and is, who I am. The comfort it alone provides in my solitude is perhaps the best evidence that it was what I was destined to do with my life.

14

THE TRYOUT

One of baseball's most significant and historic changes occurred in 1965 when the first major-league draft of high school and college players was held. Once this process was implemented, though there were certain restrictions to who was, and wasn't, eligible it effectively ended the bidding wars that had been waged for decades, prohibiting wealthy organizations such as the Yankees, Dodgers, and Cardinals from stockpiling young talent, and overwhelming the less financially secure franchises. It leveled the playing field.

When I graduated from high school in 1960, five years prior to the draft, I was a free agent, one of those amateur players able to sign with any interested club. Not only was I a free agent, as far as I knew, I was an unknown free agent. I liked baseball, and though considered by everyone to be a pretty good player, there were others I thought much better. Never did I picture myself playing the game anywhere than on the local baseball diamonds.

What I didn't know was that there were some in the world of professional baseball who were watching me; a couple of different organizations had been following my progress. That one of them was the Kansas City Athletics, one of those less financially secure or successful franchises, did not matter. In July of 1960, on their way to finishing last in the American League, thirty-nine games behind the first-place Yankees, the Athletics made their interest known by offering me a contract to play professional baseball.

Not that I was any judge of talent, but why any baseball scout would be looking for someone in my little hometown of Highland Park was beyond me. The one player in the area who had been drawing attention for years was a hard-throwing left-handed pitcher from nearby New Brunswick who would eventually sign with the Boston Red Sox for a reported $25,000.00. I had been facing him since our Little League days and getting my hits. Other than him, no one else in the vicinity had any special talent.

Just days away from graduation in 1960, my high school team, the Highland Park Owls, was participating in the oldest and most prestigious high school baseball tournament in the state, The Greater Newark Tournament of New Jersey. With us ahead by a run late in the game, and trying to hold onto our lead, we were at-bat. I was sitting at the end of the bench engrossed in the action on the field when someone tapped me on the shoulder. Turning around I was looking into the face of a gentleman whom I had never seen before. As if in a hurry, he got right to the point. Introducing himself as Ray Sanders, that he was a scout for the Kansas City Athletics, he asked if I would be interested in attending a tryout camp that his organization was conducting in a few weeks. What? Was he kidding? Did I just hear what I thought I did? Whatever else he might have said, I didn't hear, and the game we were playing no longer had any relevance.

For a while I wasn't sure what I was going to do with my life, and though it did not have any overwhelming appeal, beginning the study of architecture at Pratt Institute in Brooklyn, New York, seemed the best, and only thing to do at the time. Since making that decision, I had been growing anxious about attending college, experiencing campus life, and being away from home for the first time. My insecurities were doing a number on me. Was I doing the right thing, or was I again just trying to please others, doing what others thought I should do, and not at all what I wanted to do. It was in this state of uncertainty that, suddenly and unexpectedly, baseball entered the picture. It had never, ever been considered to be one of my options, yet, almost immediately, I felt that though I would be doing something with my life that might have had a greater and riskier downside, it would be a much more comfortable undertaking.

Realizing the gentleman standing behind me was waiting for my answer, I choked out "Aaaah, sure." With that, saying he would be in touch with me, he was gone. I was stunned, but experienced something that to this day defies explanation. Obviously sky-high by what this stranger had just asked me, I immediately felt that I was a major-league player. Not that I hoped to be, or would be, but was. That was a ridiculous assumption to make by just being asked a question, but there was no doubt in my mind that I would one day play in the major leagues. Professional baseball was never anything I considered as a livelihood. but I now instantly felt validated as the type of player I believed myself to always be. Somewhere within me, hidden, frightened to reveal itself like so many other of my skills that were suppressed by my lack of confidence, and what I thought would be the difficulty of their accomplishment, was a baseball ability, just judged by those who should know, that was better than all other players in our local area. Someone was telling me, yes, that a life in professional baseball might very well be something quite real. More important was that I had just been given permission to say "Yes, I am that good." This was a bizarre and eerie experience.

Though my life had just been turned upside-down, it was at a time when I was so in need of a lift from the confusion of being a teen-ager. I was shy and insecure, entangled in a morass of adolescent curiosity, most of which I did not understood. But now, in a matter of a few seconds, I felt better about myself than I had ever thought possible; my self-esteem could not have been any higher.

But I had to be careful. My tendency to jump to optimistic conclusions too often got me in trouble. It was my way of avoiding reality. At the same time I also had the good fortune to live with an uncanny intuitive nature; my first impressions of anything were mostly correct, and this seemed one of those times. A calm understanding that I would one day play in the major leagues seemed very appropriate. Rarely did my first judgements feel so right.

As Ray walked away, there was nothing I could say that could have more succinctly summed up my feelings than what were the trademarks of a couple of great New York Yankee broadcasters. Phil Rizzuto's "Holy cow!" and Mel Allen's "How about that!" said it better than I ever could.

● ● ●

Ray Sanders was what was considered a "bird dog", one of baseball's pedestrian scouts, the super-snoopers for the major-league scout in charge of a specific area of the country. In Ray's case, he reported his findings to Tom Giordano, the territorial scout. Tom had a brief major-league career with the Philadelphia Athletics, but was now in the initial stages of his new position as a territorial scout with a handful of states to cover in the Northeast. Needing more eyes, he had men like Ray search the more remote out of the way areas—like Highland Park— hoping to find players he felt had the talent to play professionally.

The tryout I was invited to was held at a ball park in Bayonne, New Jersey. On that morning, after Dad dropped me off on his way to work, I mixed in with about thirty other hopefuls. Expecting an extensive, special kind of "professional" workout, we were instead rushed through what seemed a few useless drills. Fielding a couple of ground balls, making a couple of throws, taking a few swings, and running a forty-yard dash for time didn't seem like any of us had much of a chance to show what we could do. That was disappointing, and, I thought, almost a waste of time.

When rain forced us off the field after about an hour, it was hard to imagine that any of us had made an impression. Ray, who was running things, rescheduled everything for the next day, but only about half of the group was asked to return. I was one of them. Confused about what was going on, I now know that these tryouts were where scouts gathered all the players from a particular area that they thought had potential to more easily determine who were the real stand outs.

The second day's workout went exactly like the first, including another rainstorm, but well before the rains came, I was taken off the field and asked to sit in the dugout. Now what? Why? With my need to always please everyone, my first thoughts were "What had I done wrong?" My father told me years later that the area scout, Tom Giordano, who was there this second day, removed me from the drills so that no other scouts who might be there would see me. He was hiding me. Once the workout ended and the other players had gone, Tom asked me to sit with him and Ray for a few minutes. The most distinguishing quality about Tom that I would come to know was his straight-forward honesty, so he was not out of character when he wasted no time getting right to the point as we sat there staring at each other: "We would like to sign you to a contract to play for the Kansas City Athletics."

Oh my God! Being invited to attend the camp was praise enough, that I was now being told that something better might be possible was incredible. This was unbelievable. Here I was, sitting in the dugout of a strange ballpark, on a dreary, wet, rainy day, with no one else around, staring back at two men whom I had known for only hours, being asked if I wanted to do something that was maybe the one thing I wanted to do with my life, but never expecting there would be even the slightest chance of just the opportunity to try when now, all of a sudden, there was.

Since first becoming fascinated with the work of Frank Lloyd Wright, it appeared I would be headed toward a lifetime of design and ingenuity as an architect, and though a solid career choice, that decision was marred with uncertainties and a little trepidation. Now, this new possibility was making that even more tenuous. What do I say? I just sat there trying to look like I had control of myself, but my insides were doing cartwheels. I'd never felt so alone and adult in my life hoping that whatever I said would come out intelligently.

Tom and Ray sat their patiently waiting for my answer. It may have been only seconds, but the gap between Tom's question and whatever I was going to say seemed interminable. None of what I was thinking was making any sense. This was new territory for me; I had never been in the position of being asked what I wanted to do, let alone something of this magnitude. Had I responded according to how I'd been raised, the way someone else wanted me to, my parents in this case, I would have said no, that college was the more sensible choice. But I couldn't do that, not just then anyway

When my senior year in high school started, I had no idea what I wanted to do after graduation. When I decided to study architecture, I never felt more than reasonably comfortable that it was what I wanted to do. Was it possible that what was now confronting me was the life truly meant for me? Was there a way to make both professions work? There was so much to sort through and no time to do that at the moment. As I sat there, still somewhat awestruck that this was even taking place, an unexpected peaceful excitement enveloped me. I felt myself relax. It was as if my intuition was telling me that this was the right thing for me to do.

Because it was only right that I gave my parents their say, I dutifully told Tom of my plans to go to college, and that I'd have to discuss all of this with them.

Sometime during my sophomore year in high school, Dad had been given a heads-up by my high school coach that a baseball career might be something I might have to consider, so he began to do a little snooping. Despite hearing nothing encouraging, it wasn't until long after I had retired from the game that he admitted that he and Mom had hoped I would go to college, that they thought that best for me.

Highland Park had a resident who was not only a prominent business man, but one of baseball's "bird dogs." When Dad asked him what life in professional baseball might be like, he did not sugar-coat anything. He held nothing back in detailing the rigors of life in the minor-leagues, how difficult the game was, how many long, late-night road trips there would be in cars and buses, the lack of money, and how very low the odds were of making it a career were; not exactly a glowing report. Dad never told me any of this. Whether he should have or not, whether it would have made a difference in my decision to play the game, I don't know, but more startling was when he confided that it was my mother who persuaded him to let me make my own decision about what I wanted to do. That was something I never expected from her, but for both of them to allow me the freedom to turn down college—for a while anyway—revealed more about the kind of parenting I'd had than everything else they had done for me. I may have needed more guidance at this time, but the trust and love they had for me could not have been expressed any more deeply than leaving such a monstrous decision in my hands.

● ● ●

About a week after the tryout camp, Giordano met with Mom, Dad and me in our living room on Columbia Street to discuss everything, explain what could be happening down the road, and to see what I may have decided. After the initial polite and obligatory exchanges between everyone, and getting the normal pleasantries and small talk as would be expected under the circumstances out of the way, Tom got serious and began telling us exactly how he felt about my ability, and what my future chances might be. Should I say yes, he was prepared to offer me a monthly salary of $325.00, and he could sign me to a contract right then and there.

That someone was willing to pay me to play baseball blew my mind. I still remember how shocked I was when I heard how much which really didn't matter. What all was finally said, I don't remember, but when a silence stalled the discussion, in order to give my parents a chance to collect their own thoughts, I mentioned the scholarship I'd be giving up. Tom, without hesitation, jumped right in and said he'd throw in $500.00 to defray some of what I would be giving up.

Signing with the Kansas City Athletics on July 4, 1960, with Mom and Dad and Ray Sanders, the Kansas City scout.

The four of us sat there for a brief moment, saying nothing, just looking at one another. I think it was Mom who spoke first by asking me what I wanted to do. Knowing it would probably hurt her and Dad, it was not easy to say that I wanted to give baseball a try, but they calmly accepted my decision. There was no fanfare, no wild celebration, just the quiet agreement to play for the Kansas City Athletics of the American League, one of the worst teams in the major leagues. Tom made that fact a selling point in our conversation, meaning that there was a greater chance that I would get to the major leagues quicker with them than with any other team.

And with that I was a professional baseball player.

Talking with Dad many years after I had retired, he said that Tom had told him that I was the best-fielding high school shortstop he had ever seen. Had that little bit of information been known the the day I signed, our negotiations might have gone a little differently, but Tom, working for Kansas City and not me, had done his job by keeping quiet. He has since supported those assertions, and even admitted to the congratulations he's received for signing me.

Until Kansas City came along, there had been no interest in me at all, or so I thought. Now, other clubs wanted me. Not that teams were falling all over me, but a couple did make offers. The local Detroit Tigers' "bird dog" who had told Dad what I could look forward to in the minor leagues offered a small bonus and $250.00 a month, and the Cincinnati Reds were willing to part with $1500.00 and a similar salary.

With the baseball season more than half over when Kansas City signed me in July of 1960, and so little left of the playing schedule, it made no sense nor was there an opening for me to join any of their minor-league clubs. But not wanting me to sit idle for what was left of the summer, they had Tom Giordano convince a friend of his who managed a semi-pro team of twenty-and-thirty year olds called the Elizabeth Colonials in nearby Elizabeth, New Jersey, to let me play shortstop. The Colonials were entered in three leagues so I would get to play three and four times a week against this older competition. Had I not done well, Kansas City could have released me before spring training saving themselves my monthly salary.

As it turned out there was a third life path that I might have been able to follow. An architectural career was one, baseball was two, and the Army a possible third. What I did not know until Dad told me well after my playing days, was that my high school baseball coach, Austin "Bus" Lepine, who believed I might one day play in the major leagues if I could hit enough, was also of the opinion that I might qualify for an appointment to the West Point Military Academy, and that with his Congressional connections, a recommendation might have been possible.

Having an Army career was not as far reaching a consideration as was that of me playing baseball. Because of how I was disciplined by my mother, I could have easily handled the regimen of life in the military. If I was to one day be addressed as General Kubiak, the only thing that would have sounded better was when Bob Sheppard, the long time New York Yankee public address announcer said in his sophisticated, mellow voice, "Your attention please, ladies and gentlemen. Now batting, at shortstop, number 14, Ted Kubiak, number 14." I don't know how many times Sheppard announced my at-bats to thousands and thousands of fans over the years, but to those of us lucky enough to have been so eloquently introduced by him, it is a cherished memory. The everyday spectator may not have paid much attention to what he was saying, his tone, or his significance to Yankee Stadium and its history, but his articulate pronunciation was as unmatched as it was unforgettable. I marveled at it the first time I heard it in the '50s as a spectator.

Sheppard was as much a fixture in Yankee Stadium as were the center field monuments, its short right field fence, and its illustrious frieze. He taught speech at St. John's University and was an iconic part of "The House that Ruth Built" for 56 years. Players such as Reggie Jackson, Carl Yastrzemski, and Mickey Mantle thought it an honor to be announced by him, and Derek Jeter has a copy on tape of the last time Sheppard announced his name.

With Bus Lepine believing that I might have a chance at a professional baseball career, he tried to convince Dad that playing high school football might not be wise. His opinion warranted consideration because, unknown to me, was that he had played professional baseball for Scranton in the class A Eastern League, meaning that with his background he was probably the one who "bird dogged" me to Tom Giordano.

Despite Bus's concerns, I did try out for our high school football team, but the equipment that I had to wear was more responsible for me not enjoying the sport than anything else. I was not very big in high school, and once outfitted with all the necessary protective gear that was too heavy, too cumbersome, and too restricting, I could hardly move. The football shoes I was given were too big, too uncomfortable and useless. Not only was it hard to run in them, I didn't weigh enough to have the cleats penetrate the ground. Raising my arms enough to catch a pass was a problem because of the shoulder pads, and the helmet forced me to have tunnel vision; I couldn't see what was going on around me. With as much as I have always wanted to control what I was doing, the equipment alone had a lot to do with me not enjoying the experience. The contact didn't excite me, but worse was that once tackled or knocked down, it was a struggle to get up off the ground with everything I had to wear.

But the nail in the coffin, and what really turned me off, was that I was made a halfback by the football coach. I was hoping to play an end position so that my best friend, Joe Policastro, who was the quarterback, would be throwing passes to me. There was no doubt we would have made a great combination. It was largely because of that snub that I gave up the game after about a week.

In 1961, Kansas City held their spring training camp in Fort Walton Beach, a small town near Pensacola in Florida's panhandle. It was my first camp, and also my first time away from home for an extended period. Though homesick for a while, I could not have been happier than being on a baseball field every day. The workouts were long, but professional baseball—getting paid to play—was better than I could have ever imagined. What turned out to be a lucky break for me was that Kansas City invited Tom Giordano to be one of the coaches in camp. He may have thought I had tremendous potential as a shortstop, but something wasn't right. I felt awkward fielding the ball, and not all as coordinated as I thought I should have been. Seeing the problem almost immediately, Tom changed the sequence of my steps, and straightened me out in a matter of seconds. It was so simple a solution that I could not believe I did not see it myself.

When camp broke, I was assigned to Kansas City's Class D team in the Florida State League, the Sarasota Sun Sox. The team was a mix of teens and first year players managed by a fiery little Texan by the name of William "Robbie" Robertson who spent his winters overseeing a peanut farm. How he had lasted in the game as a catcher, slight as he was at 160 pounds and standing 5' 9" was remarkable, but he did not hesitate to put on the tools of ignorance when our club needed his help. As a manager, he was the perfect fit for our young group, being more of a father than manager. Easy to play for, friendly and outgoing, he made the year fun, and he put no pressure on any of us. Many years later when I was into my own minor-league managerial career, I recognized that one of my biggest responsibilities was to make players comfortable, and lessen as much as possible the stress under which they performed. Not everyone was good at it; Robbie was.

He took a liking to me, and because I was quiet and shy and didn't say much, he began calling me "Mumbles." The nickname was not embarrassing, nor did I take it critically, and he meant nothing derogatory by it. It was his good-natured attempt to get me to loosen up, and relax my uptight personality a little. I have to admit to liking it because I understood what he was trying to do. Often times, not only in sports, something that may appear to be ridicule is a sign of acceptance by your peers, indications that you are well liked, and that's how Robbie made me feel. The name stuck; I was always "Mumbles" to him even after I made the major leagues.

Nicknames can produce a variety of responses for a variety of reasons, and though I liked "Mumbles," I was even prouder when answering to the nickname "Smooth," another descriptive term that Catfish Hunter tagged me with to describe my defensive abilities when we were teammates at Oakland. Coming from him, it could not have held more significance to me or my Oakland teammates. Several of them followed Cat's lead and addressed me in the same way.

The Florida State League in 1961 was the lowest classification at which anyone could start in the professional system. Each level of play was designated by a letter. In ascending order, they were E-a rare and early designation-D, C, B, A, AA, and AAA. The use of letters for the different classifications had begun in 1912, and for the most part the levels remained similarly alphabetized for the next fifty summers. In 1963 only the letter A, and multiples of it, would be used to differentiate one classification from another.

One explanation for this alphabetical diminution might have been that it eliminated any negative reference implied by the other letters, in contrast to just the A which, of course, was the superlative grade used on old school report cards that assessed a student's progress. Use of the letter may have given an innocuous psychological lift to the entire minor-league system at a time when it was needed. If that was the thinking, with this system formalized decades before implementation of the present ideology that rules the game, which is to "make the baseball environment as positive as possible for the players and never infer anything negative," it was an early sign of the mentality that the game would eventually embrace.

What the reason was for the leagues being pooled using only the letter A, even for the subclassifications of some levels, has never been clear, other than that it appears to have been an easier method of defining the minor leagues. With the periods of volatility and attrition that took place among the various teams and leagues in the '40 and '50s, there was a need to reorganize and balance the system. Some leagues were eliminated, some upgraded, others downgraded. A few changed names and locations, were combined, or reorganized for their greater financial viability.

This was all triggered by two events. First, there was the loss of players to the Korean War in the '50s that significantly reduced the number of leagues and teams. Second, was the loss of revenue experienced by several minor leagues—causing their demise—as the major leagues began to reap greater benefits from their contractual television rights—many American homes now had television sets—and, accordingly, increased their broadcasts just as the other major sports had been doing.

As they stand now in ascending order, a Rookie level is the lowest level of play, and includes teams commonly called academies, which all organizations have in the Dominican Republic. Venezuela has a few. These clubs are for the very youngest and most inexperienced players from the island; young hopefuls flock to them for tryouts every day. There are Rookie Leagues in the United States in Arizona and Florida that run from June to September after spring training breaks where a significantly less number of games are scheduled.

The first big step for young professional players is to advance to the Short-Season A level where seventy-six games are played. This is slightly more than half the number of games played in a regular season by every upper-level minor-league team. Short-Season A has replaced the former Class D, and the infrequently needed Class E levels. Next up the ladder is the Low A level, which can be considered to have replaced the earlier Class C and B levels, followed by the High A level, also known as the Advanced A level, and then the AA and AAA levels.

To be advanced one level of play during the six years I spent in the minor-leagues, a player had to successfully handle the competition at the level to which he was assigned. Even if he had been playing well, the chances were more than likely that the move would not be made until the following season. An injury might force a change, but even if a player was far exceeding expectations at his level, the parent club was under no demands to push him through its system. The reserve clause saw to that. Organizations owned their players in perpetuity, and with only sixteen major-league teams, competition was stiff. Players were not moved until they were considered absolutely ready.

Up until about about thirty years ago, players were more concerned about being sent down a level rather than being promoted. We all lived in a state of anxiety, fearing that our play was never good enough. It is doubtful that similar thoughts run through the minds of today's young athletes. Should one of them have a decent month, or show just minimal success, he expects to be advanced a level, immediately— and more than likely is. With the present dearth of talent available, players have sometimes been advanced a couple of levels during a season, including the rare jump from the A level to the major leagues.

The size of any bonus given a drafted player is thought to be correctly based upon his expected talent and potential, but whether that talent blossoms is never assured. However, the player receiving a high six-or seven-figure sum—not the $500.00 I received—gets every chance to see his name above a major-league locker. It may not be for long, or with the organization that first signed him, but the "bonus baby" always has an advantage. He will be given the longest look and afforded every possible chance to succeed. Major-league organizations want something in return for what they have paid a young man, and exhaust every effort to get it. With the available talent thinning as it is, the luck of most early round picks is that they will be given looks by two, three, maybe four other organizations.

Large bonuses, contractual and monetary promises, the prospect of impending arbitration, the upcoming winter drafts, "free agency," and very often the overall financial health of a franchise influence the agonizing decisions that must be made by every organization during the winter when the forty-man rosters are put together. More than talent must be considered in the legal world that consumes so much of today's game. Building a major-league roster unerringly, and within an organization's financial capabilities puts added emphasis on the correctness of these decisions.

Only a handful of clubs needn't be concerned about the amount of money they spend.

Belt-tightening backs many organizations into a corner causing high salaries to be pared, and although play may suffer, lower-salaried and less-experienced players will fill the rosters. Financial considerations can often easily outweigh physical ability, and push a talent undeservedly upward, with the possibility of the move stagnating a club.

More than twenty years ago I recognized the beginning of a decline in talent, and believed it would continue until the quality of play at the major-league level looked to be the equal of that of our colleges and universities. One day the skill levels of one would look like those of the other, and this melding would accelerate. When the natural attrition of good major-league players collided with the need for wiser and more frugal organizational structures, it was inevitable that, sooner than later, high-salaried major-league players would be jettisoned, leaving only an already waning pool of amateur talent from which to choose. As revenues increased for both the clubs and players in the ensuing decades, the convergence of both levels of play, as I had imagined, remained on course; the best of the amateur players began to be looked at as the best the major leagues had to offer.

This was not peculiar to the game. Within the structure of society, quality people needed to fill top positions in every vocation were getting harder to find. Day-to-day living was experiencing a downturn in its standards. Character, respect, integrity, and responsibility were eroding, no longer holding their significance among a certain segment of the citizenry. Society was much too easily settling for a mediocrity that was alarming.

The face of the game changed dramatically two or three decades ago as it took on the patterns of a growing "feel-good" society. The electronic age took kids off the streets and into a world of fantasies. They began to play more games on a screen in their house than on a field in the neighborhood. The joystick replaced a bat and ball. Mom and Dad both had to work. The kids were sent off to a variety of structured activities. Children's safety became an issue, and their outdoor freedom and activities were curtailed.

Confined to the indoors and their electronic gadgets, any "on-the-job" training they might have experienced was limited. Less and less time was spent on a playground. Most of whatever baseball instruction they were to receive would come from the camps and clinics they attended, or the teams on which they paid to join. Whatever playground leagues there were for youngsters had their seasons shortened, and as conscientious as coaches and instructors might be at any of the structured venues, their efforts too often come up short.

Fewer and fewer groups of children were seen on corner lots and school fields, and the time and effort needed to perfect their athletic skills diminished accordingly. The natural improvement they would have developed by daily participation in a sport on a field, diamond, court, even a local street, ebbed. Skillful and knowledgeable play, though on a downtrend, had to be accepted because there was no way to counter the new culture of the younger generation's athleticism that was developing, which was that it wasn't.

Everyone was considered a hero, a star, no matter his ability. You did not have to be exceptional to be rewarded. Moms, Dads, and society made sure that Junior felt good about himself. As any brand of play was accepted and validated, the pool of athletic talent declined.

A special individual, that exceptional player, will still emerge now and then, but not with the consistency of years past. Today's major-league rosters change continuously. More and more they consist of players who are younger and younger. At some point there has to be an end to what is happening because it can go only so far, but we don't seem to be there yet, and I'm not sure when we will be. It is disturbing to think that we have begun to settle for nothing better than mediocrity.

15

BEATING THE BUSHES

If someone had told me that less than one year after graduating from high school that I would be in a professional baseball spring training camp, I would have told them they were crazy. There was no questioning the circumstances that had earned me the right to be there, but I wasn't completely sure why or whether it was wise that I was.

My first professional season with the Sarasota Sun Sox.

The camp was a mix of approximately 150 players from the United States, the Dominican Republic, Cuba, Venezuela, and Mexico. It wouldn't be until 1965 that the first player draft of free agents would go into effect which meant that everyone in camp had been scouted as I had been, were likewise free-agents, and able to sign with any club that was interested. But, unlike me, everyone seemed to have been selected as the best in their city, county, or state, and being thusly honored, had some accolade attached to their name as a reward for their accomplishments. This, of course, meant that many teams had engaged in bidding wars for their talents, and who they eventually signed with was only a matter of which organization offered the most money. None had to survive a tryout camp like I did.

It would be decades before I would be proficient at evaluating talent, so after this initial season of professional baseball I had no idea how well I might have done, or how good the competition was. Though impressed by more than a few of the opposition, and some on my own team, the fact that only a few ever saw the major leagues validated my lack of expertise. The overall talent easily out-classed what I faced as a Highland Park Owl, but it was not intimidating, and I absolutely loved playing every day. Nothing about the baseball life dampened my spirits, or minimized the fun I was having. And, it was still hard to believe that someone was paying me to do this.

Baseball offered no guarantees, but I knew I had made the right decision; my instincts that I had to give it a try were correct. There was much to be proud of after this first season, but raised not to feel or act on anything, I was unable to cherish what I'd accomplished. It was as if the season never happened. Whether

I was experiencing something called alexithymia which is an inability to understand, process, or describe emotions, or was just in the apathetic little world in which I had grown up, I had no idea. Things that should have been important remembrances meant little. I was always more concerned about what I should be doing next, and whatever that might be, that it would not be the wrong thing to do. Lovingly silenced and protected as I'd been for eighteen years, I had no opinion on a lot of things, and believed my feelings were inconsequential. Being very critical of myself as I was, experiencing the joy of anything was irrelevant, and summarily dismissed. So many games, situations, even at-bats that I would like to have remembered are, even today, blurred in my memory. Not one to live in the past, or off my accomplishments, at the end of my first season when asked what kind of year I'd had, I didn't really know. As far as I was concerned, it was neither good nor bad, just a start to what I hoped would be a long career.

As a member of the Sarasota Sun Sox of the Florida State League in 1961, stats show that I missed only one of our 140 scheduled games. With one game postponed by rain, and never made up, I played in every one. The twenty-or-so games on my high school schedule were a far cry from the nearly 200 I would play during this first season, but I could have been doing nothing I enjoyed more. My Sun Sox team turned out to be a scrappy group of young hopefuls like myself who lost the league championship series, but finished the year with a very respectable 79-60 record. Of the thirty-three players on the roster during the season, I would be the only one to enjoy a major-league career of significance.

Hitting .253 for the season was nothing to get excited about, but neither was it terrible; at least not for my first year out of high school facing pitchers bigger than I'd every seen. And although I was not particularly thrilled with how I had played defensively, it was considered good enough for me to be named to the Florida State League All-Star team. Instincts and raw talent earned me that honor because I had no idea what I was doing. Figuring there was more to know about how to correctly field a ground ball, with no knowledge of what to even consider, I began to study and dissect every movement and action I made. Surely there was an easier way than how I was doing it.

My biggest challenge was surprisingly not the pitchers, but the mental toughness that was needed to cope with the never-ending assortment of negatives that were so much a part of the profession. I did not respond well to them. When something went wrong in one of our playground games, or even those in high school, though disappointed, it was easily forgotten. Having a bad day now and then when it did not matter was nothing compared to having one when your professional life was on the line.

With teen years that were confusing and emotional, trying to grow up and succeed in a stress-filled profession that allowed little time for that to occur was not easy. Until I understood that being perfect was impossible, both quests were troublesome. The confidence I had that I could play the game ran smack into the lack of confidence I was living with, and this was on top of what self-esteem I normally lacked. But beneath this blanket of inferiority was the notion that I was something special, a feeling that I harbored, thankfully I thought, in large part because of how I was raised. Although Mom made sure I toed the line, she also doted on me. The juxtaposition of those disciplines made me feel like a caged prince. Having lived for as long as I had under her proverbial, and powerful, thumb, I had grown accustomed to the emotional baggage I carried.

As an only child, I was my mother's whole world. She made me the center of attention which was responsible for, as far as I could tell, the deeply rooted, lofty opinion I secretly held of myself. Her devotion to me, however, was counter to how she made me feel that I was always doing something wrong, or that nothing I did was good enough. Expected to do everything right left me straddling the fence with regard to my self-respect. I waffled between feeling like royalty, and an ordinary commoner. I existed in a state of emotional chaos, hesitant and inadequate, not exactly sound footing on which to begin any professional career. Handicapped as I was, I had nevertheless been groomed to endure not only my own insecurities, but also the game's punishment.

What I thought to be so much fun about our road trips that first summer in the Florida State League, absurd as it might seem, was finding enough room for eight or nine major-league wanna-bees, our baseball equipment, and everyone's luggage in three used station wagons for what was always a hot, muggy, couple of hours ride to the next city on our schedule. With little room to move around, or even readjust our positions, the trips were sometimes grueling tests of our patience, but being imprisoned as we were, it was a great way to get to know your teammates. With three of us in the front seat, three, sometimes four, behind them, two or three sprawled across the bags in the back of the wagons, and most of our luggage tied onto the roof, our miniature convoy had to be quite a sight for other travelers.

Finding relief from the incessant heat and humidity that was summer in Florida was a useless battle. To escape at least some of the sun's rays blasting through the car windows, I made sure to be early for our road trips so I could finagle a window seat on what I thought would be the shady side according to the direction we'd be traveling. Unfortunately, that never helped, but it was easier to sleep resting against the window than when you were sitting between two teammates trying to sleep sitting upright. Just trying to get comfortable was difficult with what little space there was. Catnapping for a few minutes was about the best we could do before either the heat, a cramp, or our sweat-soaked clothing that required repositioning woke us up.

What I would discover about professional baseball was that the owners of a ball club, whether in the minor or major leagues, were always looking for ways to save money. My guess was that was why we traveled in station wagons around Florida rather than a bus. Rationalizing that it was a smart decision was hard because of all the problems the vehicles had. If one thing or another did not delay our departures, something was sure to happen somewhere on the road. If it wasn't engine trouble, a transmission failure, perhaps a radiator leak, it was to change a tire. At least one of the cheap retreads the owners tried to get by with blew out on every trip. There weren't many that could withstand either the heat of the highways, the miles we traveled, or the load they we're asked to carry. Having to fix a flat tire got us into most of the towns so late we barely had enough time to eat before heading to the ballpark, and as annoying as that became, the real problem was sitting on the side of the road for a half an hour or more in the sun while the tire got changed.

Life in the minor-leagues was exactly what Dad had been told, nothing had been exaggerated. But whether it was the packed station wagons, a lousy bus, the tough times trying to find someplace to eat after our games, the crowded and challenging motel/hotel accommodations—sleeping four or more to a room was nothing—the constancy of bad infields, the absolutely horrendous lighting in every ballpark, having to wash our own uniforms and underwear, the heat, the grind of the schedule—we played every day for five months—or not getting to sleep until 2:00 or 3:00 AM every night, I loved every minute of it. Getting paid $325.00 every month covered my expenses, and with an extra $1.50 a day for meals on commuter trips—those to Tampa and St. Petersburg from which we returned home that same night—and $2.00 a day on overnight stays, I was more than well compensated.

Most minor-league stadiums in the '50s, and '60s were nothing more that just places to play. They tried your patience and love for the game, and seemed to be more like testing grounds than baseball fields. Unable to afford putting any money into something so trivial as their condition, management usually paid only one lone caretaker to keep them playable. And try as he might to prepare the field for the game after hours of pre-game work on them in the afternoon, what little he would do could only camouflage their problems. Rarely watered, the infields were either rock hard or dust bowls, and should they be "dragged" or "raked" smooth, all that did was move the incessantly annoying stones and pebbles to new locations.

It was a rare night that I did not spend nine innings manicuring my shortstop position. There'd be too much dirt in one spot, not enough in another, too many stones and pebbles to avoid, and always too much loose topsoil. Dealing with the topographical hazards became a nightly ritual. The grass part of many infields had unruly growths, the occasional dandelion and/or mushroom, ruts, worn spots, random hard and soft areas, and the difficult to avoid little curbs or "lips" where the grass met the infield dirt. Trying to teach myself how to field on these washboards was more treacherous than it should have been. Instead of playing the hitters according to their tendencies, it was often the topography of the field that dictated where I positioned myself.

Thirty-five years later, managing in Modesto, California, looking down the third base line while meeting with the umpires at home plate, I noticed that the squiggly, white chalk foul line was one foot outside of the base, well into "foul" territory. Believing I had that mistake corrected by the conversation I had with the fifteen year-old who was responsible for the field maintenance, the next night he had the chalk line going directly across the middle of the base; he was getting closer.

Any serious attempts to fill the customary deep hole in front of a pitching rubber and those in the batter's boxes before a game were a waste of time because as soon as the first pitch was thrown, they instantly reappeared. None of the fields had any clay which could be used to properly pack and fix these craters, so they were merely "refilled" with the same loose dirt that had been dug out of them. I can't imagine how the holes affected the pitchers, but knew first hand the problems associated with standing in a batter's box in the hollows made by other hitters that never matched where I wanted to stand. Unable to get a solid toehold made hitting more of a test of how well you could hold your balance.

To protect the field when it rained, most ballparks had only a couple of small tarps available, one to cover the mound and another for the home plate area. The mad scramble to put them in place during some of the more severe thunderstorms often required one or two members of the front office, or a couple of us players, to rush onto the field to help. I watched many fields flood cancelling not only that night's game, but the next day's because of the still standing water—there were no drainage systems. Should a field be wet, but thought to be playable, what was typically done was to pour gasoline or diesel fuel on the wet areas, and set it on fire. Watching an infield go up in flames for the first time was something not to be forgotten. As unhealthy as the air became, more and more fuel would be added until the field became usable, not good, just usable. The barometer of whether it was or not was usually the condition of the first base line. It had to be fairly safe for us to run on. Setting the fields ablaze, or having the occasional helicopter flown in to "blow them dry," were the only ways to save a night's attendance from the downpours. There were many games played in mud until we could no longer stand up.

Payne Park, in Sarasota, Florida, the spring training site for the American League Chicago White Sox, and the home field for my Sarasota Sun Sox, was huge by anyone's standards. The first professional ballpark I played in, it was the biggest I would ever see. Both the left- and right-field fences down each line were an equal distance of 375 feet from home plate. Left- and right-center field had no markers but had to be at least 400 feet away because the center-field wall was measured at the incredible distance of 500 feet. The footage of that straight-away barrier far outdistanced the ones I thought unbeatable, one in Yankee Stadium in the Bronx that stopped Mickey Mantle at its three historical monuments 461 feet from home plate, and the other in the old Polo Grounds in New York that had Willie Mays patrolling an area that was 455 feet deep. For me to think I could reach any of Payne Park's fences was ludicrous, and that I did not expect to hit a home run was proven correct in the year's final tally of my statistics.

Two other cities in the league with major-league tenants were Orlando where the Minnesota Twins trained, and St. Petersburg, spring home of both the St. Louis Cardinals and New York Yankees. St. Pete's infield was by far the best in the league, and better, I'd find, than most I would see in my six minor-league seasons. It was a carbon copy of the state's hard-packed Daytona Beach on which cars could drive. Ground balls rolled across it with no unwanted bounces, and, better yet, it was pebble and stone free. Why the other Florida ballparks were not similarly landscaped was something I did not understand; there was certainly no shortage of sand in the Sunshine State.

The only city in the league with a major-league affiliation and a ballpark with the legitimate right to be called a stadium was in Tampa, where the Cincinnati Reds trained. Al Lopez Field had a full grandstand that wrapped around the infield from first base to third base, and locker rooms that emptied directly into the dugouts. This meant we could dress and shower at the ballpark instead of at our motel like we did in all the other cities. It was in this Tampa ballpark that Pete Rose, playing for the Tampa Tarpons, in this my first season, hit most of his thirty triples.

This was Pete's second professional season. As a switch-hitter he had the unique knack of routinely hitting the ball to the opposite field. Driving the ball into the large left-and right-center field gaps in his home field and the other ballparks throughout the league as he did, all he had to do was run, thus the triples. When I first saw him sprint to first base after drawing a walk, I couldn't help but wonder who this guy was. No one else did it then or since. It became his trademark, his signature, and something for which he is, of course, well known.

Every ballpark excites me, not only because of their size and idiosyncrasies, but because there is something magical about the competitiveness they invite. Of all I've seen, there was only one that should never have been considered to be a professional venue. Rose Stadium in Palatka, Florida, a small city in the northeast portion of the state, was a deceiving and inappropriate name for this rickety structure. The classic Western song *"Home on the Range"* made popular by Bing Crosby had a line describing a place where the "buffalo roam," a refrain that could have easily been inspired by this arena's playing field that was more suitable for livestock. Infielders routinely refused to take pregame ground balls; pregame infield was never taken; and outfielders feared having to climb a small hill trying to catch fly balls near the wall. The contour of the field was such that if you stood at home plate and looked for the center fielder, you saw him only from his knees up. The poor guy had to play out of a sink-hole.

Old, wooden, rundown, and seemingly deteriorating by the minute, how its press box and grandstand remained upright was a mystery, and why any fan would trust the support of the bleachers was puzzling. The clubhouse was home to an ungodly number of spiders, some as big as the palm of my hand, hard at work laying down their labyrinth of lacy trails that were as thick as the Spanish moss on the state's trees. There were no cubicles or lockers, just a nail in the wall every few feet on which each player could hang his clothes. Two rusted shower heads trickled drops of water.

The lighting in most minor-league ballparks was never great, but here it was dangerous. The unit of measure for the intensity of light affecting a specific area is usually referred to as candle power, and how appropriate that was for Rose Stadium because it seemed its lighting was supplied by only a few candelabras. What lighting it had was wisely focused on home plate giving the hitters at least some chance of seeing the ball. How outfielders saw and tracked fly balls while navigating the goofy hill was miraculous. And even from my shortstop position, which was half as close as they were, seeing the ball was a challenge. If I took my eye off it, I might not pick it up again right away.

About a month after this first season ended, I read in *The Sporting News* that I had been named to the Florida State League's All-Star team. It wasn't long after learning of that honor, that Kansas City added me to the forty-man major-league roster for 1962. This was an unbelievable achievement for anyone after only one season, but I did not place as much importance on it as I should have. The fact that the organization was protecting me from being drafted by another club over the winter never phased me. For one, I had yet to understand how the business end of the professional game worked, and two, the honor was more appropriate than surprising because of my belief that one day I was going to be a major-league shortstop. It just seemed the right thing for the organization to do. I may have been withdrawn, but I was quietly egotistical.

To further emphasize how well Kansas City thought I had played, they promoted me to their Class A Eastern League club in Binghamton, New York, the Triplets, for the 1962 season. This jump of three levels from the Class D Florida State League was an unprecedented advancement, but, blind again to reality, I figured, OK, so I've been moved up three levels, now what? Baseball is baseball, or so I thought.

Baseball, however, wasn't baseball in the Eastern League, at least not how I knew the game. The league had a notorious history of seeing many of its pitchers and position players move on to have long careers in the major leagues. It was a level of play that thinned the herd. I could only trust that Kansas City knew what they were doing by assigning me to this higher level. It was a flattering move, but one that would have dire consequences for me.

Neither Kansas City nor I knew at the time what a mistake the move was going to be. Their intent was to speed my development, hoping I could handle the promotion. Believing I had hit enough in Class D, they gave me more credit than they should have. The year turned out to be one to forget.

Some of the pitchers who were honing their skills in one or another of the Eastern League cities, awaiting their turn in the major leagues were Luis Tiant, Tommy John, Wilber Wood, Dave McNally, Sonny Siebert, Bill Hands, and Herm Starrette. From my own Binghamton club, Lew Krausse, Ken Sanders, Ray Blemker, Ron Tompkins, Rupe Toppin, and Aurelio Monteagudo would have various lengths of service on one big league club or another. And there was no shortage of quality position players. Richie Allen, Billy Sorrell, Jim Ray Hart, Andy Etchebarren, Pat Corrales, Dalton Jones, Bob Chance, and Duke Sims were all on their way to either the American League or National League. My own teammates, Ozzie Chavarria and Ken Harrelson, would likewise see themselves promoted.

"Hawk," as Harrelson was nicknamed because of his rather pronounced facial feature, would be a central figure years later in 1967 when he would be inexplicably released by our owner, Charles O. Finley. Hawk's abrupt dismissal occurred because of an incident on one of our return commercial flights to Kansas City from New York. A few players were accused of drinking too much and harassing the stewardesses, and though neither accusation was ever corroborated by anyone, the whole thing blew up into a battle of wills between Finley and certain individuals.

Finley first fired Manager Alvin Dark, alleging that he had lost control of the team. With tempers flaring, Harrelson was attributed to have said the owner was a menace to baseball. The accusation may have been correct in its intent, but not how it was reported. No matter, Finley promptly disciplined Harrelson by releasing him, a short-sighted, rash, and petulant move that backfired on him, and rewarded Harrelson. The Boston Red Sox wasted no time and signed the first baseman to a very lucrative contract. He went on to help them win a league championship that season, and gained All-Star status in 1968.

Struggling as I was against the pitching I was facing had me wondering if professional baseball was going to be too difficult for me. What I didn't realize was how mentally strong I was to put up with one lousy night after another. I should have given myself credit for just showing up every day.

Expecting that I might be helped, there was none to be had. And believing that I might get some advice from our Binghamton manager, veteran major-league infielder Granny Hamner, himself a former shortstop for the Philadelphia Phillies' Whiz Kids, was a mistake. He was more interested in reviving his own career. When his active playing days were winding down, he had a few brief pitching stints for a couple of big-league clubs, and because of how badly our Triplets team was struggling, and short on pitching, Kansas City inserted him into our starting rotation.

Hamner's weapon was a knuckleball, a very good knuckleball. It danced all over the strike zone. As the season wore on and we struggled toward a lackluster 60-80 won-lost record, he became our most reliable pitcher. Kansas City was so impressed with his 10-4 record at one point that they promoted him to the major-league club, hoping he could bolster a mediocre big league staff, but the flutter ball that dazzled Eastern League hitters did not miss many major-league bats, and after a few unimpressive outings, Kansas City let him go.

When Hamner was released outright from the major-league club, he did not return to manage in Binghamton. Instead, an organizational scout by the name of Dan Carnevale was brought in to manage the club for the rest of the season, and with his interim assignment came a glimmer of hope for me. Dan recognized the difficulties I was having, and suggested that maybe switch-hitting would be something to consider. Neither he nor I knew at the time how important his suggestion was. Hitting left-handed was nothing new to me because I fooled around with it on the playgrounds when I was young. Doing it with my friends was one thing, attempting to do it in a high A league was another, but there was nothing to lose by trying. Though my at-bats during the last couple of weeks of the 1962 season were no better, I did hit the ball from the left side. Unbeknownst to me or the organization at the time, was that the change would save my career.

Despite feeling some positives from hitting on both sides of the plate, my year in the Eastern League shredded my confidence. Nothing went particularly well, and with it being only my second year, I wondered how poor play so earlier in a career might have affected it. Whatever it was I was learning I wasn't sure. I couldn't help but be a little frightened about my future.

What kept me somewhat sane during the summer was that Nick Curtis, one of our pitchers, and I played golf every day it didn't rain at the Binghamton Country Club. Whether the amount of golf we played had any bearing on our collective team performance, I can't say, but it was probably no help to me personally that we sometimes played thirty-six holes before heading to the ballpark,

The year in Binghamton drained me physically and mentally, I was exhausted. It was impossible not to rehash the decision I'd made, and that it may have been wiser for me to go to college and become an architect. Had I made a mistake? And should I not have accepted Kansas City's invitation to attend the Florida Instructional League during the previous off-season, but instead, begun classes at Pratt? Turning down their invite would not have been easy, or smart, especially because of the good first season I'd had that impressed them. It was something I could not refuse.

When this second season ended, I was depressed, and couldn't help but wonder if I would even have a baseball career. Confused, frustrated, and unhappy, and with where my head was, there was no way I could even think about enrolling at Pratt Institute, so, for the second winter in a row, I put it off. Actually, enrolling was out of the question because I could not coordinate with Pratt the necessary semesters of work with the beginning or end of the baseball season. Even with an allowance from Pratt for registering late, starting classes in the fall was impossible because the season ended well beyond the time classes were to begin, and, not that it mattered, they would end well after I had to report to spring training. There was little I could do.

So, it was the game or nothing, and it seemed to be slipping away from me. For two years I'd been working toward what was an expected career in the major leagues, but I had to now stop and think. It was still early, but had my assumptions of stardom been wrong? Was the game telling me I should quit? Not having those thoughts was hard, but there was no way I was going to give up. Doing so would have been admitting defeat, and failure scared me more than how poorly I was playing. Life may have had me stymied, and I wasn't doing much better with the game, but somewhere from within me, deep inside my psyche, keeping me going, and helping me through the agony and torture of the season, was still the belief that I was going to one day play in the major leagues. I was not going to surrender.

Players were often demoted when they couldn't compete at the level to which they were assigned, so it was puzzling why I was left to struggle in Binghamton. With my weak bat, what was Kansas City thinking? Unlike the precaution and concern given today's players, careful that they are not placed at a level of play in which they cannot compete, did Kansas City not consider that maybe I was a bit too young to play in a very good Eastern League? I had just turned nineteen, was one year out of high school, had signed out of a tryout camp, and was not some highly touted amateur player. What reason was there to push me?

It never entered my mind why Kansas City promoted me, why they shouldn't have, or that I was not at the level I should have been. My focus was trying to compete. I never had any reason to complain or bemoan my situation, never did not want to play, never considered my age to be a factor, or had any similar thinking. The only thing on my mind was that I was not playing well. Every night was just another bad night with another game to be played the next day. There was never enough time to recover mentally.

To add to my woes, when the season ended, I was humiliated by not being invited back to that fall's Florida Instructional League. There was no reason for me to even think I should be because of the season I'd had, but I sulked about what I thought was a snub. I was feeling sorry for myself. Why didn't someone from Kansas City come to my rescue, put their arm around me, and tell me that everything would be fine, that I'd be fine? I spent a good part of the winter wallowing in my own self-pity. My first season accomplishments in the Florida State League were now history, my post-season All-Star selection, the invite to the Instructional League, and a spot on the forty-man major-league roster no longer meant anything. My career had gone in an entirely different direction in just one year. Everything was falling apart. Not only was my future in doubt, I had to wonder how the season I'd had affected how Kansas City felt about me now; might they have lost interest in me?

The off-season was going to test my fortitude and resilience. Regaining my confidence was not going to be easy because I was now paranoid about my future. I had little talks with myself every day trying to lift my spirits. Erasing the doubts that were constantly running through my mind was not easy. How good was I? Was I as bad as I had played? I was in no frame of mind to do anything but think about my baseball career, the coming season, and what I had to do turn things around and get myself back on track.

Not wanting to repeat my 1962 season, that it might became a possibility when Kansas City again sent me back to Binghamton in 1963.

In the words of that great master of the fractured thought, Yogi Berra, going back to Binghamton a second time was "déjà-vu all over again." It was like a bad dream. Spring training started positively as they all do, but it wasn't long before the Eastern League was once again doing its number on me, only now my troubles had doubled because I was an undisciplined hitter both left-and right-handed. And there was the same nagging question: "What was I doing here; why was I again in Binghamton?"

That question was answered one night in York, Pennsylvania, while attempting to field a slowly hit ground ball that had skipped past an effort to field it by our pitcher. The ball was not hit hard, but it hit something as I reached down for it only to have it bounce up and hit me just below my left eye breaking a blood vessel, swelling and closing my eye.

X-rays showed no facial fractures, but I was going to be sidelined until my eye opened. My parents, who were in town at the time, told me that John McNamara, our manager, wanted me back on the field the minute I could see because of how much my defense meant to the team. And that answered the question of why I was still in Binghamton. That it was felt I was doing something to help the team actually surprised me. Unfortunately, the fact that Kansas City was willing to put up with what I couldn't do offensively because of what I could do defensively was crippling me.

McNamara and Kansas City may have liked my defensive play, but, personally, I was unimpressed. Ever the perfectionist, I was consistently inconsistent having committed forty-two errors my first season in 1961, forty-one in 1962, and a yet to be committed forty-nine during this 1963 season. Research shows numbers that high were common for some of the game's best in their first seasons, but that was no consolation. I had not yet gained control of myself defensively nor learned what I would, but forty errors was an atrocious amount.

What never registered with me during this difficult summer was just how much growing up I had to do. All I knew was that no matter how bad things were, or how badly I might have played, come hell or high water, I was not going to let the game get the best of me.

I needed help. How much and exactly what kind I was not sure, but I needed it fast. Unknown to me was that it was on its way.

16

A SECOND CHANCE

The Binghamton Triplets of the Eastern League played their games in Johnson Field. The ballpark was not in Binghamton, New York, as you might expect, but in nearby Johnson City, and was therefore aptly named. The team's nickname was not to honor the multiple deliveries attributed to one of the local ladies, but to appropriately reward, and recognize, the unselfish regional support given the club by the cluster of three towns, Binghamton, Johnson City, and Endicott. Built in 1913 and well-dated when I first saw it in 1962, Johnson Field was one of those weirdly configured early neighborhood sites that nestled itself in what available square-footage there was between houses and streets. Its dimensions stretched from an odd triangular point in left-center field 450 feet from home plate, sharply across the outfield to the right-field corner in a way that made the straightaway center-field wall a short 375 feet from that same base. That was 125 feet less than the center-field wall I never could reach in Sarasota's Payne Park in the Florida State League.

When I first saw Johnson Field, it was a fifty year old, weary, tired stadium speeding toward extinction. With not much more life to it than my game at the time, its old wooden construction would be relieved of its own decay by being demolished in 1968.

By sending me back to Binghamton for the 1963 season, Kansas City apparently expected a better performance from me than I had given them in 1962, thinking surely the experience of that season would have had some lasting and beneficial side effects. But when one month of trying to switch-hit was proving to be no help, after another poor nightly performance, I was called into the tiny corner Johnson Field clubhouse office by Hank Peters, the Kansas City farm director, who was in town watching his young farmhands. With a reputation among his peers as one of the game's finest gentleman, Mr. Peters calmly, and compassionately, informed me that he thought it best for my future to go down a classification to Lewiston, Idaho, the organizations Class B affiliate, that the Eastern League was a bit too difficult for me.

Being demoted hurt, and though embarrassed and ashamed to have failed, I was not shocked. The move was deserved and, more important, welcomed by the fact that no sooner had the words come out of Mr. Peters' mouth, every part of me relaxed. I never realized how uptight I was from the stress and pressure I had been under for more than a year. Our conversation only lasted about five minutes with me listening more than talking—I don't think I said anything—but in that brief time, Mr. Peters convinced me that the move would prove to be good for my career. It would also mean that I would no longer have to endure the gloomy atmosphere of Johnson Field, the sullen mood of a losing ball club, and my own poor play. A change of scenery might be just what I needed.

It was not to lift my spirits after the poor year I'd had in 1962, but because of the money I saved from my first year's monthly salary of $325, and the previous season's raise to $500, that I purchased a brand new 1963 Pontiac Tempest convertible during the off-season. It was my first car, and it was sitting in the parking lot outside the clubhouse not far from where Mr. Peters and I were meeting. Sensing that I needed time to digest and adjust to his suggested move, Mr. Peters said that if I wanted, I could drive to Lewiston. It would take three days to cover the 2500 miles, plenty of time for me to think about the game, my future, my life, and college which still loomed as an alternative to baseball. Allowing me to drive was a thoughtful concession by Mr. Peters at a time when I was so in need of compassion from someone.

The Interstate Highway System, the brainchild of President Dwight D. Eisenhower in 1956, was strategically mapped for its users. When traveling east and west across the United States, you followed the even numbered routes, north and south, the odd numbered ones. To get to Lewiston from Binghamton, I followed I-80, I-90, and some of I-95. Seeing parts of our country I thought I'd never see made the thirty hours on the road bearable, and everything was fine until I hit Missoula, Montana. Then, according to the map I was following, if I stayed on I-90 until I hit I-95 South, the drive on the interstate would be easier, but it looked like it would take me miles out of the way. I wasn't sure it would be the best way to go. The other option was to chance a "short cut" on unknown US 12 that seemed more direct into Lewiston though a windy road. Figuring how bad could a shorter route be, I wound up twisting and turning on US 12 through the Clearwater, Bitterroot, and Nez Perce National Forests, in the dark, on a road with no lights, going no faster than twenty-five miles an hour for more than two hours, going uphill and downhill around one hairpin turn after another before finally dropping down a long, steep grade into Lewiston. I could not believe I had made such a mistake.

The final downhill into Lewiston was a gradual grade with a drop of 3000 feet, and is famously known as, what else, the Lewiston Hill. It wasn't the only way out of town, but it was the best way to reach Interstate Highway 1-95 and then I-90 from which you could travel east or west, a fact I wish I'd known before driving through the rugged forest terrain. We were stranded more than a few times on the hill because the yellow school bus that was our transportation could not make the climb. A new bus was called to rescue us.

It was my assumption that because Lewiston was close to the state of Washington, its climate would be temperate and rainy, very similar to what it was like in the Northwestern corner of the country, in particular, Seattle. That was not, however, correct. Lewiston was as close to the western edge of the Idaho state line as it could be, separated from Clarkson, Washington, on that state's eastern border, by only the Snake River, and though it would get a little rain during the summer, its heat index more closely rivaled some of the country's hottest zones. Certain cities in the Northwest League such as Eugene and Salem, Oregon, were cooler being near the coast, but Yakima and Wenatchee, Washington, along with Lewiston, were places in which I spent some of my most sweltering minor-league days with the unbearable humidity making the 90 to 100 degree temperatures much worse.

Lewiston, where I would spend the rest of the 1963 season, was the smallest town to ever have a professional baseball franchise.

Primarily an agriculture and manufacturing community, the town was a snapshot out of the old west, a true, real-life Western community with cowboys, cowgirls and saloons. One of those saloons featured a long, intricately designed backbar with its traditional brass rail, and a number of snooker tables in a back room that amused and entertained most of my teammates and me after our games.

The three days it took me to drive to Lewiston gave me time to come to terms with the humiliation of my demotion. Though Mr. Peter's decision was absolutely warranted, it was, nonetheless, embarrassing, but, much more relaxed, and with teammates more my age, I hoped this Class A level—Lewiston went from a level B to a level A in 1963 because of a reclassification of the minor league system—would prove him right. The move reunited me with my 1961 Sarasota manager, Robbie Robertson, who I enjoyed playing for, and with a good friend, a young pitcher from Long Island, Gary Sanossian, whom I'd met in the Florida Instructional League in 1961.

With no intention of commiserating with him about my demotion, but rather to save what little money I could, Gary and I decided to room together and split the rent. But there were no apartments available anywhere in town, absolutely nothing for just the few short months until the season ended. Concerned about what to do, we were given a heads up about a rundown, vacant house on the outskirts of town that was, maybe, for rent. Both suppositions were correct, but there was no mention of how bad a place it was. The entire house was surrounded by overgrown weeds, and was totally boarded up; it looked abandoned. That it was even available to rent was one thing, whether it was habitable another. We tracked down the owner who obviously couldn't wait to have us look at the place. From the outside, we debated about going in; from the inside, we couldn't wait to get out. It was filthy. Surprisingly, the electricity was on, but whether the water was potable, and the plumbing in working order, we didn't care because we had no intentions of using either one. What furnishings it had included a bed in its one bedroom, a dusty fold-out sofa in the living room, and a couple of kitchen chairs that I refused to sit on. It was not a place you could call home, but with no other choice, we could not refuse the ninety dollars a month rent that was being asked.

Chancing a look in the basement hoping more to find nothing dead or alive than something useful, we came across an old mattress with big, black tire tracks that ran up and down its length. It had apparently lost a battle with a truck somewhere. Because it was otherwise in decent condition, and because I let Gary have the bedroom and needed a bed, we laid it across the foldout sofa for me. Keys to the place were useless; there were too many ways to get in.

To lessen as much as we could the effects of the hot, humid, sticky, and very uncomfortable summer, and to make our living conditions somewhat more bearable, we left what windows we could open hoping cross ventilation would cool the place. That, however, was an open invitation giving unrestricted entry to a menagerie of flying mosquitoes, moths, and insects who had no trouble congregating and using our place as a rendezvous point. Because some of the bigger ones dove at us tauntingly, and without fear, we started calling the place "the airport." Answering with that retort when asked by our teammates where we had found a place to live drew some weird looks.

The 1963 Lewiston Broncs were pretty good; we had a good season. Finishing third in the Northwest League with a record of 77 and 63 was a huge turnaround for me after my two previous losing Binghamton seasons. Switch-hitting was proving to be effective, and using a thirty-six inch, thirty-six ounce bat, I hit a more than respectable .295, including five home runs, all from my newly established position on the left-side of the plate. In time, I would hit better left-handed than I would right-handed which was my natural side.

This abbreviated season in Lewiston had a significant and positive impact on my career at a time when it was in desperate need of a lift. In 1962, when Kansas City moved me from the Class D Florida State League up to the Class A Eastern League, a jump of three levels, I was way over my head. Lewiston would have been the more appropriate destination that year. Thankfully, Mr. Peters decision had me where I should have been then, and the year turned out to be just what he had promised.

With my career seemingly righted and back on track, I returned home after the season rejuvenated. But after only a few days to savor the season, I was off to Fort Leonard Wood in the Missouri Ozarks to fulfill my military obligation. Though I knew of the scheduling problem of enrolling at Pratt, attending maybe another college had to again be put on hold.

The prospect of a military life was not something I had ever given any thought to, much like I never thought about baseball becoming a career, and though at first taken by surprise at the structure and organized discipline, the strict adherence to authority for which it was known was no more than an extension of how I was raised, and, all in all, it turned to be an educational experience.

After being home for just about enough time to unpack, I flew into Kansas City where I was officially sworn into the U. S. Army at a local downtown recruitment center. Thirty other recruits and I were then silently and unceremoniously shepherded onto a bus for the four-hour ride to Fort Leonard Wood, Missouri. As we rolled through the entry gate passing the stiff salutes and frozen postures of the military guards, I couldn't help but wonder what I was in for. It was not long before I found out. No sooner had we reached our company area, and before anyone could make a move to get off the bus, an irate little drill sergeant, impeccably uniformed, and sporting the standard flat-brimmed drill sergeant's campaign hat, climbed onto the bus and started yelling at us to "GET YOUR GEAR AND GET OFF THIS BUS RIGHT NOW. MOVE IT! MOVE IT!" We fell all over each other like fools trying to accommodate him, but it was hard to do much of anything quickly because of the bags and luggage we had with us. Still, he continued yelling, telling us to get our "a....s into formation."

Responding to his frenzied orders, we scrambled frantically to get into what was my very first military formation. Lining up as best we could, an arms length apart, with our belongings underfoot, whether our lines were as straight as he wanted didn't matter, he was still yelling. Standing at attention as best we knew how, the veins in his neck were now bulging as he berated us in not so friendly terms, informing us that (1) he was in charge of us from that moment on; (2) how we were going to be treated; and (3) what was expected of us. Then, he walked through our ranks, angrily calling us a sorry looking bunch of girls. Looking us over, and not liking what he was seeing, he randomly selected one and then another of us with a stern order to report someplace immediately for some unknown military duty.

When he stopped in front of me I thought, uh-oh, this is not going to be good. Looking me up and down, he ordered me to report to the mess hall for "KP," or kitchen police duty as it is more commonly known. This was an assignment with which I was familiar because of the Phil Silvers Show, a 1950s TV comedy about a bungling Army sergeant and his shenanigans. Real KP, however, would turn out not to be that funny.

Pulled from our hurried and sloppy formation at 3:00 PM for my assignment, I threw my luggage onto my assigned bunk in the barracks, and was hustled to the kitchen in the company mess hall where I worked non-stop until midnight, washing, cleaning, and scrubbing the food trays, tables, and floors. After three hours of the quickest sleep ever, I was awakened by the same little sergeant, still impeccably dressed that early in the morning—had he not slept—who barged into the barracks and rattled my bunk, telling me how late it was, and that I should have been up already. I was back in the kitchen by 3:30 AM to begin my regularly scheduled eighteen-hour day of KP.

To make matters worse, during the eighteen hours while I and five other recruits were scrubbing what seemed to be hundreds of pots, pans, and trays, and then the dining hall floors and walls, the drill sergeant would come storming in every couple of hours, and, incensed by the "sloppy" job we were doing, turn over onto the floor the neatly stacked racks of dozens and dozens of food trays that we had feverishly scrubbed clean of fat, grease, and leftovers screaming how poorly they had been cleaned. The day could not end quickly enough. I just wanted to get back to what I thought would be the safety of my bunk, lie down, and put this kitchen duty behind me. If this first day was an indication of what Army life was to be, it was going to be a long six months. I doubt that no one sleeps so soundly, for as short a time, as recruits do in basic training.

When eventually assigned to be a platoon leader, one of the perks of the appointment was never having to face another greasy tray, mop another dirty floor, or scrub another pot or pan proving how moving up in the ranks was a good thing.

Fort Leonard Wood was rumored to be an unfriendly, and not very well liked combat training facility. Why, I wasn't exactly sure. Winters in Missouri could be bad which might have been one of the strikes against it, but I found it to be no worse than New Jersey's, so, at least as far as I was concerned, it was not the weather that gave the place its black eye. However cold it got, it had little effect on our training which was all outdoors. What was a problem, and maybe why the post's reputation was looked down upon, was that coal was used to heat the barracks and every building. The soot— the residue of it being burned—was everywhere, there was no escaping it. Not only could you smell it, you had to cover your nose and mouth with your hand to keep from tasting and breathing it.

Overall, the post was not that bad, nor was military life. The potential appointment to West Point as was suggested by my high school coach might have not been something to scoff at. Never getting enough sleep, the long marches, the soot, and the constant psychological beatings were hard to endure at times, but were quickly accepted as standard treatment. The compliance and respect for authority that was expected had its pluses. Responding to it was easy because of what my mother required from me every day. She more than prepared me for a life that would have been strict and orderly. Not that I needed it, but I appreciated the discipline that kept others in line. This was in much the same way that I liked playing for a demanding manager.

The one thing about which I was slightly nervous and apprehensive was firing an M-16 rifle. Though not a gun person, as a teenager I had shot a BB gun and a .22 rifle owned by one of my cousins. The M-16, in contrast, was nothing recreational, but a serious military weapon. Leery of what to expect from it, learning how to use it turned out to be an unforgettable experience. Knocking down a target I could barely see 600 yards away was not only impressive, there was an excitement to it that made it fun. Without going into detail about the mechanics and the psychology involved, military service indoctrinated you in such a way that I could see how it would be easy to defend your life and the lives of others. It was a simple doctrine to accept under the circumstances.

My time at Fort Leonard Wood was unfortunately punctuated by the shocking and tragically sad assassination of President John F. Kennedy. Why he had been killed, who was responsible, or what the consequences might be for the United States, no one knew. With no immediate answers, the entire camp went into lockdown.

The rumor was that some country was threatening to overthrow our government.

On the day it happened, my platoon had completed our morning exercises and were at noon chow when we were abruptly ordered from the mess hall, told to get into formation, and stand at-ease until further notice. When, after fifteen minutes or so, it was our company commander who came out to address us instead of our drill sergeant, we knew that something serious was either going to, or had happened. Told that President Kennedy had been killed was the last thing we expected to hear. We were dumbfounded. The news from Washington was that the assassination was thought to be a conspiratorial act by some foreign entity, presumably Russia, and that it was highly probable that the United States was going to be attacked. Investigations were underway, and we were to sit tight until further notice.

The captain, who had long since become a military lifer indoctrinated into defending our country, was irate. Doing his best to keep his emotions in check as he explained what might be taking place, the longer he talked, the more enraged he became. Looking for someway to vent his anger, he grabbed a nearby garbage can, and when he lifted it over his head intending to throw it somewhere, he emptied the soot that was in the can all over himself. Though funny, no one laughed or so much as snickered.

All duties were suspended and everyone was confined to their barracks to await whatever information could be ascertained as to exactly how serious the situation was. When it was determined two days later that no one was going to invade the United States, Washington ordered everything to return to normal. This was an extremely emotional time for our nation, a tragedy of the greatest proportions, and a scary time for a group of raw recruits.

With the post up and running again, it wasn't long after this depressing news that Uncle Sam surprisingly informed us that we would have two weeks off for Christmas. My parents were visiting an aunt and uncle in Florida so I flew there for the holiday. Just prior to the break, my unit had spent three days bivouacking in below freezing weather, and much of the time I wore nothing but a T-shirt. I felt no ill affects, but by the time I landed in the Sunshine State, my body was aching, I had chills, a sore throat, a headache, and felt awful. After a once over by a doctor, I spent one whole week in bed, and the rest of the time recuperating.

After the Christmas break, my orders were to report to Fort Carson near Colorado Springs in Colorado. My MOS (Military Occupational Specialty) for my last three months of my military obligation was to be an orderly in the post hospital delivering and emptying bed pans, changing bedding, giving sponge baths, and running little errands while taking care of patients; I was a male nurse. With literally no physical activity during my time there except for walking up and down the halls of the hospital, the good physical condition I had been in after the first three months of basic training with its ten mile marches, and three measured meals a day, slowly eroded.

Discharged in March, in no condition to play baseball, I flew straight to spring training in Florida hoping to get what I could out of the few days that were left of the camp. Overweight and out of shape, I was going to need two, maybe three weeks to not only lose the weight I'd gained, but to come close to what could be considered playing condition, and that was if I was playing every day. I was not at all happy about the situation I was facing.

After the turn-around season I'd had in Lewiston, I was looking forward to continuing my progress, but my military obligation had replaced the winter of workouts I'd become accustomed to. Because of that duty, the upcoming 1964 season, which would have been my fourth, was not getting off to a very promising start.

By the time I showed up to camp in Daytona Beach, Florida, the season's rosters had been set, and with there being no regular spot for me, Kansas City assigned me to their AAA affiliate in Dallas, Texas, as an extra player. It was just a place for me to be. This assignment was another jump of three levels that brought up the unpleasant memories of the terrible year I had in Binghamton in 1962 when I had also been moved up three classifications from the Florida State League the year before. The move then, however wrong it was, was predicated on the good year I'd had in in 1961; it was merit based. The rationale for Kansas City assigning me now to Dallas in 1964 was because there was not much else they could do with me. Under normal circumstances, and a full spring training, my guess was that I would have been ticketed to be the starting shortstop for our AA club in Birmingham, Alabama, but with no one with experience to replace me, Kansas City decided to assign Bert Campaneris to the position, leaving me with no place to go.

Campy had originally been signed as a small, slim catcher from Cuba with a bushel of speed and ability. Without a real position for him, Kansas City made him a shortstop and and sent him to Birmingham where he proved to be more than adequate. Not only did he hit well, he had exceptional base-stealing potential, an asset that would benefit any big-league club. Because of his overall play, he was promoted to the major-league team midway through the 1964 season where he would be the teams's spark plug for years.

Finley had to put Campy on the major-league club. The team was not very good, but it would soon be infused with much of the young talent he had been signing, and Campy would be an integral part of the rebuilding process. He became a respectable defender, and the perfect lead-off man. Always a better defensive player, I could not complete with his bat or his speed.

Many believed I was the better shortstop, and during our early years together in Oakland, Bob Kennedy, during his brief stint as one of a revolving stable of managers during Charlie Finley's reign, moved Campy to left field and opted for me to start at the position, but that experiment was short lived. In a few days, whether it was Finley, Campy or someone else who did not like the switch, Campy returned to the infield, and I returned to the bench.

So with Campaneris entrenched at the shortstop position in Birmingham for the 1964 season, the only place I could have been sent was to our AAA club in Dallas. When I played, which wasn't often, I struggled. I was sluggish, heavy, and completely out of sync. Getting back into shape playing as sporadically as I was, was not happening.

With no regular playing time available for me in Dallas—they had an older veteran at the shortstop position—and not wanting to waste whatever talent I had, after about a month I was optioned to Fort Worth, Texas, home of the Chicago Cubs AA club, the Fort

Worth Cats. The team's manager, Alex Grammas, like Granny Hamner, my manager in Binghamton, was a former major-league shortstop who, unlike Hamner, was very personable but, like Hamner, taught me nothing, though admittedly my stay with him wasn't long. When the Cubs signed their future shortstop, Don Kessinger when he graduated from the University of Mississippi, they had him report to Fort Worth. The Cubs then optioned me to Austin, Texas, home of the Milwaukee Braves AA affiliate, the Austin Senators.

My fourth professional season was spent criss-crossing the states of Texas, Oklahoma, and New Mexico where I had more success dealing with another blisteringly hot summer than I did playing baseball. Batting less than .200 at both stops in Dallas and Fort Worth, and .221 at Austin, had me finishing another season I wanted to forget at a combined .209. The winter leading into the 1965 season would be another one during which I would again have to claw my way back to respectability.

My career had been see-sawing back and forth; I'd had a decent year, a not so decent year, another decent year, and then another not so decent. What that meant I don't know, but it was certainly odd how it fluctuated so consistently. Kansas City had assigned me in two of those four years to levels of play they probably should not have. Valuable time, time I didn't have, was wasted. Of course neither they nor I knew that. Whether another winter of work in my garage instead of fulfilling my military commitment would have changed anything for 1964, I can't say, but being shuttled from town to town around the Lone Star State did me no good.

Having previously battled through a depressing 1962 winter rebuilding my confidence after my disastrous Binghamton experience, I knew how to deal with what once again lay ahead. But there was now the possibility that I might have lost my ranking and status within the organization. At an age at which I was expected to produce, if I didn't, the baseball career I'd so believed I'd have, would, instead, be over.

Searching for answers, and doing all I could to look at the brighter side of things. I tried to be as optimistic and confident as possible during the winter preparing for 1965. With still a belief in myself, I rationalized that because I'd had a good year in 1963, and was still only 22, Kansas City would give me at least one more year to prove myself, that I had at least one more bullet to fire. Time would tell if my suppositions would again be correct.

Returning to the safety and familiarity of our garage, I was once again determined to clear my head of what was an almost useless 1964 season, and regain my confidence. By how my seasons had been flip-flopping, if the pattern remained on track, 1965 was going to be another decent year.

17

THE WORD

As my fifth professional season was about to begin, my life in baseball was hanging in the balance. Two of my previous four seasons had not been very good. Another bad one would be my third strike, so to speak, and more than likely, my last. Having been given a bonus of only $500.00, it was unlikely that I would be given more time to produce. The thought of having to return home a failure devastated me. Knowing that something had to change, I had no idea what to do. My play had been seesawing from one year to the next, so-so in some years, and not even that good in others, all while dealing with the quagmire that was my life.

After a poor 1964 season, not only did I have to, once again, rebuild and regain my confidence during the off-season, a process with which I was familiar, it hadn't yet dawned on me that I had not taken the game as seriously as I should have. I mistakenly thought I was. No one had to tell me that my baseball career was in jeopardy. After being forced, in as meaningful a way as the Kansas City organization could, to hopscotch the Lone Star State in 1964 with no success, I returned home depressed, but, knowing what had to be done, wasted no time getting back into my daily winter workout routine of rebounding a ball off the side wall of our garage, and running the short side-to-side pickups. Staying positive during the off-season after the disastrous season I'd had was more difficult than the drills.

It hadn't taken long during my first year in 1961 to realize the importance of the relationship between having strong legs and good infield play, and how important it was that my hands were coordinated fielding the ball. With that in mind, I had devised these two "garage" drills, and was doing them faithfully every winter since. Wondering what more I could do, having heard so often how important strong hands were to a hitter, I decided to add a couple of hand strengthening exercises to my workouts.

The two additions were squeezing a rubber ball, and using a wrist roller. Neither required any unusual apparatus. A rubber ball was not hard to find, and a wrist roller was easily made using a short dowel with a knotted piece of rope threaded through a hole in its middle. With a weight of some poundage tied to the other end, by holding the dowel in front of you and turning it in one direction, and then the other, you wound the rope around the dowel lifting the weight up and down. The consensus at the time was that doing this faithfully to strengthen your hands, along with running sprints, was just about all a ballplayer needed to do to stay fit. I could neither agree nor disagree.

Had I given these hand-strengthening exercises half-a-chance, especially the wrist roller, I might have become a better hitter. With the skewed belief that it was doing more harm than good when my forearms tightened and burned from rolling the weight up and down, I stopped using it. Not realizing that the discomfort was an indication of its need, I whittled my conditioning routine back to only the rebound drill off the garage wall, and the little side-to-side sprints.

Feeling the effect these two little drills had on my fielding was easily recognized, but there was no way to evaluate what effect the wrist roller might be having on my swing; there was no benchmark from which to make a judgement of the progress I might have been making swinging the bat.

After maybe two months of workouts, and daily talks with myself to bolster and rebuild my confidence, an ad in a sports magazine touting the benefits of an "Exer-genie," caught my attention. This was an isometric device used to increase strength, endurance, and flexibility.

With the Cold War in progress at the time between the United States and Russia, the two adversaries were jockeying for position to see who would be the first to conquer the new frontier known as outer space. Both countries were intensely engaged in a race to land a man on the moon. The astronauts who had been selected to participate in our program to make the trip were preparing for the stress of the mission using an "Exer-genie" and, from what the article said, they were committed to its merits. From the explanation of how it was to be used, it appeared to be easily adaptable to certain exercises that might benefit my swing. The more I thought about it, the more logical its use sounded so, with nothing to lose, I ordered one. If it was good enough for NASA, it had to have some legitimacy.

What arrived was a cylindrical mechanism with a rope threaded through it—in my opinion, a sophisticated NASA designed wrist roller—that you attached to a wall. By turning a dial, you could increase or decrease the tension on the rope as it was pulled one way, and then another, through the cylinder. This produced the isometric resistance that led to greater strength and fitness. Today's players use surgical tubing and giant rubber bands for the same effect.

With spring training three months away, there was ample time to see what magic the Exer-genie might have. Using it the best way I could to replicate my swing, I pulled and tugged on it every day. Just how much it contributed to the productive season I had the next summer in a very good AA Southern League, I couldn't say. I didn't consider my .281 batting average a suitable barometer of its value because I had hit for a higher average in Lewiston the year before having done nothing but my two indoor drills during the previous off-season. From what I could tell, the Exer-genie had no discernible affect on my swing. With nothing to convince me otherwise, as I did with the rubber ball and wrist roller, I put the Exer-genie away and never used it again.

There was no good reason for me to abandon its use except for the traditional hackneyed belief that tugging, pulling, or lifting anything would do little to improve a player's physical condition, or his play. No one had proven or substantiated the benefits of such efforts, the astronauts notwithstanding, and I more or less remained steadfast to that same theory. Other theories postulated that being muscled-bound in any way was detrimental to the agility and flexibility the game of baseball required. I loosely interpreted that to include my hands and forearms.

Up to this point in my career, I was not turning many heads, and there wasn't much to draw from that indicated better things were to come. I may have believed that I would one day play in the major leagues, but I was not convincing anyone that I could.

My career had begun with a relatively solid first season in Class D. At this lowest level of the professional game, and so far from the major leagues, it was hard to determine what the future might hold from anyone's performance. My second season saw a precipitous slide in my play. The third was a redemptive summer that may have opened some eyes, but the wasted fourth that had me shipped to other organizations dampened that effort, and any belief that anything better would be forthcoming. I had been exhibiting tiny flashes of potential that promised nothing. Something, however, not of my doing, was about to happen that would be volcanic to my career; it would change my thinking and turn me and my game around.

With a workout completed in spring training in 1965, Tom Giordano, the scout who had originally believed he had seen something that warranted him to take a chance on signing me, said he wanted to talk to me, so we sat down on the McKechnie Field bleachers outside of the clubhouse in Bradenton, Florida. Tom was a very caring, easy to like individual from the time I first met him at my tryout in Bayonne, New Jersey, and in the few years I had known him, he had become a comfortable and trusted friend.

He was one of those people, if you are lucky, that you meet during your lifetime. Always friendly, he was a gregarious Italian who loved to cook, and whose passion for the game was such that he scouted until he passed away at 93. What he said to me that day on the bleachers was not the pep talk I had expected. Instead, in the fatherly way only he could, he told me how close I had come to being released the night before. In the organizational meetings, the overall feeling among the staff was that I was not having any fun, and should be let go, but that he had stood up for me, and requested that I be given more time.

Tom may have had little idea how what he said affected me, but thank God for adrenaline, it kept me coherent as I sat there stunned and panicked by what I'd just heard. My heart was pounding, and I may have stopped breathing for a while. I didn't know what to say, what could I say. Tom was giving me a warning, letting me know—in the best way he knew how—that I had to turn things around, and quickly, that time was running out,

My thoughts leapfrogged from one thing to another faster than I could keep up with them, jumping from what Tom had just told me, to how I was playing, to how I was not playing, to how I should have been playing, back to what Tom said, to what I looked like when I was playing, again back to Tom's warning, to what I should do, to what I had to do, again to what I'd just been told, to what I would do if I was released, and finally back to us sitting on the bleachers, and what I was feeling. I was numb, shocked and scared. My heart starting pounding, and I began to panic.

Tom was asking me, again, as he did in 1960 on that rainy afternoon in Bayonne, New Jersey, if I wanted to play professional baseball. This time, however, it was not did I want to, but how much did I want to. Because of his tone and the compassionate way in which he gently broached the issue, I realized he was not so much talking about me the ballplayer, but, me, the person. His inference was clear.

Always quiet, shy, and confident in my ability, or so I thought, I wasn't, not in the way I should have been. I believed in myself, but never thought I was good enough, never believed or trusted, to my core, in my goodness, not just in baseball, but many things. I lived with a neurotic fear of making a mistake; wondering if others were happy with me; were they pleased with what I was doing; was I doing the right thing? I was so worried about disappointing them that I was.

Having grown up with this emotional burden was bad enough, but sitting with Tom, I was finding out that it was killing the career I wanted. What was sad was that I knew what I was doing, what I was projecting, what my game probably looked like, but I refused to believe that anyone else could. I was living in my own little fantasy world, disillusioned into thinking that everything was fine, allowing an emotional insecurity to control so much of what I was doing, both on and off the field. Saying that I was naive was no longer good enough, it was no excuse.

The fear of not pleasing people was a horrible way to live, and it was now affecting something that I wanted so badly, and truly thought I could achieve. Thinking how smart I was, that I was fooling people, I was only fooling myself.

There was no way that I could have been taken care of any better, or provided more, by my mother and father. I had everything I wanted or needed, but I was not raised to feel good about myself. There was never a doubt about how much I was loved—fawned over may be more accurate—but it was shown silently within certain old-school behavioral boundaries, as if it was something I should have known and never questioned. I was never demonstrably praised or applauded, never told that whatever I did was good, wonderful, great, or anything I would have loved to hear. Though I knew how my parents felt, I was left to carve my own plaudits from my accomplishments.

It's astonishing how significant it is to your psyche that it be fed verbal affirmation, to be told that you had done something well, that you are special. Nothing I did ever seemed sufficient; I had to do more, be better. I grew up unsure whether anything I ever did was correct or enough to please others. To survive, I retreated, walled myself from people, put myself into a shell of sorts looking for any comfort I could find. Whether misguided or not for doing that, I didn't know any better.

The human condition can often be our greatest obstacle, and much was coming to light as Tom and I sat on the bleachers. He continued to talk, but after the word "release," I heard nothing. Yes, I had had a couple of bad seasons, but baseball was not my problem. I didn't want to face reality, and worse was that I wasn't sure I knew how. What Tom was telling me as a surrogate parent was: "Snap out of it. Grow up and be a man." He told me I had to become more vocal, more aggressive, and that others in the meeting had thought I'd gone as far as I could.

Other people often see us for who are better than we see ourselves. Those baseball staffers critical of me were correct in their assumption that I was not having any fun. I had no idea others could sense that. Tom was now telling me that it was not only a few, too many did. Everything he said was so difficult to accept, but so absolutely right, and I knew it.

Although it hurt, hearing that I might be released was the best thing I could have been told. Thankfully, it came as a warning, not a final determination.

In 1964, the year prior to Tom's warning, while my career wallowed in three Texas towns, Dagoberto Campaneris began playing shortstop for the first time with the Birmingham Barons in the Southern League. This was a new position for him. With him now in the big leagues, the Barons' shortstop position was handed to me in 1965. I was hoping that Kansas City recognized the circumstances of my topsy-turvy summer in 1964, and were giving me a chance to possible recover the momentum I'd had after my good year in Lewiston in 1963. I wanted to get back on their radar. Not only did I owe that to myself, I owed it to Tom. With a different frame of mind, I was determined to do all I could to look positively at my skills instead of crying over what I wasn't doing. Something had to change.

I had done nothing to help myself up to this point in my career. How lucky was I that Tom did.

● ● ●

Charles Oscar Finley was born in Ensley, Alabama, a small neighborhood community on the outskirts of Birmingham. Five years into his ownership of the Kansas City Athletics franchise, he chose Birmingham to become home to his AA minor-league club as a member of the Southern League. To kick off the 1965 season, a "Meet the A's" luncheon in a downtown Birmingham hotel honored him, and introduced us Barons players. Also present was Finley's famous Missouri mule, Charlie O, who was cordoned off in a corner of the ballroom eating from a huge silver bowl.

Charlie O. Finley and Charlie O.

The mule was inside the ballroom! I hadn't yet come to fully understand my enigmatic owner, but he was definitely making baseball more fun. This animal, a cross between a female horse and male donkey, was beautiful, one of Finley's prized drawing cards, and a tremendous advertising gimmick. A mule was the official mascot of the state of Missouri, and since being given the animal by the governor of the "Show-Me-State," Charles O. Finley made it the symbolic figure for his Kansas City franchise. The mule replaced the elephant that had been the long-standing insignia of the Athletics franchise since the early 1900s.

A mule is not normally a large animal, but Finley's prize was as big as a horse. He was treated royally and lived in luxury, hauled around the country to such events as our Birmingham luncheon in his own air-conditioned green-and-gold trailer, and attended to by his own personal handler. His treatment far overshadowed ours. With a custom green-and-gold blanket over his back emblazoned with his name, he became a pregame favorite of kids and fans who enjoyed watching him parade around the field before the cry of "Play ball."

**Ken Harrelson trying to tame Charlie O
during pre-game activities in 1965.**

Charles O. Finley was an anomaly among his contemporaries, an upstart, an owner who dominated his organization, and as much of the game that he could. He made just about every decision concerning anything on and off the field that affected his team. He personally negotiated with and signed his own players, made the trades, designed the uniforms, devised the press-room menu for the World Series, limited complimentary tickets to those of his choosing, offered game strategies to his managers, and kept his office workers on a short leash, those few he had.

Carl Finley, his cousin, did most of the administrative work early on, and the team got by with a comptroller, a handful of employees, and Finley's personal secretary. Many wondered how someone running a multimillion-dollar operation with the few people he employed could build a championship team, but he worked hard. It's ironic that men with much more money could not equal his success.

With free agency not yet born in the early '70s, I twice took him to arbitration. He bested me the first time, but the score was evened when we next clashed, despite the position he presented to the arbitrator. What I was forced to listen to made me want to jump across the table that separated us. The stance he took against me was incredible. Without once looking at me, he calmly told the arbitrator that I didn't belong in the big leagues, that I couldn't field or hit, and that if it weren't for him I wouldn't even be in the game; I would be doing something else, exactly what, he didn't know.

I was livid, literally shaking in my chair, wanting to do or say something, but with the decorum the situation required, wasn't sure what to do. How could he say such things? Did he really believe them? When his bloodbath ended and we finally left the room, I was fuming, speechless, absolutely irate, but before I could say a word, he wasted no time coming over to me, put an arm around me, and said not to believe a word of what he told the arbitrator. "It's only business!" Only business! Are you kidding me?!! Then, as if nothing had happened, he handed me a new watch and a gift for my wife, saying: "Here's a little something for you and your wife. I'll see you in spring training in a couple of weeks." I was speechless.

The man was controversial and unique. He controlled everyone and everything, or was going to die trying. Some in the game thought he was crazy, others that he was as colorful as the "wedding gown white, kelly green, and Fort Knox gold" uniforms he outfitted us with to go with the equally bizarre, first-time-ever-worn white baseball spikes.

Every owner had his idiosyncrasies, but Finley was a maverick among even them. A business warrior, he backed down from no one and battled everybody. I don't believe he knew what "no" meant, and neither did he ever want to hear it.

This was a man desperate to own a major-league baseball team while knowing nothing about the game. When he finally cajoled his way into the American League, he was relentless in learning what he could, and was successful at outmaneuvering and manipulating everybody. It was he who turned my Oakland A's into a world championship team while constantly confronting Bowie Kuhn, the Commissioner of Baseball, over whatever issues he disagreed with. He never wavered from what he thought were good ideas, many of which are now mainstays of the game, such as the colorful uniforms worn by today's players, and the night games now common during every season's World Series. For decades they had been afternoon contests.

Some of his ideas stuck, others didn't. The orange baseball he touted, used in a spring training game in 1973, was unsuccessful, as was giving a hitter first base on three balls instead of four. Thinking that the use of a designated runner would be a brilliant innovation, it wasted one of our roster spots for a couple of years as he forced his manager to use it. When our designated runner, Herb Washington, who never played a position in one game, was picked off first base in the '74 World Series almost before he left the bench, he finally saw its futility.

The mule that might turn up anywhere in the country wasn't the only thing that drew attention to the A's. He had sheep grazing beyond the right-field fence in Kansas City; a zoo down the left-field line that had a monkey or two who would be given ex-lax, and who knows what else, by a couple of my fun-loving teammates; a mechanical "Harvey the Rabbit" that popped out of the ground with baseballs for the umpires, and "Little Blowhard," a button the umpires could step on that blew dirt off home plate. All of those attractions made him the ringmaster of the circus other owners thought he was making of the game.

He was a challenge, but easy to talk to. Every spring was a battle to get just a few thousand dollars more in salary, and though our conversations were contentious, they were congenial. He lived by no normal schedule. It was nothing for him to call at any hour. One late-night phone call around 11:00 PM had us arguing over my salary for the upcoming season. Realizing at one point that my argument may have been justified, he excused himself for a few minutes—he obviously had to regroup and change his strategy—only to return with new ammunition to throw at me. When I again gained the advantage, he feigned laryngitis, and said he would have to call me back another time.

Despite the brutally intense contractual negotiations he had with many of my teammates, Vida Blue and Reggie Jackson at the fore, he did some wonderful things for many of us. Rumors that he had done extremely well in the stock market prompted me and others to invest a large sum of money with him that he matched, and guaranteed us no loss. He took care of several personal problems, and quietly handled player issues that would have caused unnecessary and unwanted publicity. Despite those and other generosities, several of my teammates bristle to this day just hearing his name.

He was tightfisted, an individualist who, whether you believed he was mistaken or not, thought he could beat the system. When he stubbornly refused to honor an insurance payment to Catfish Hunter, he lost control of the Hall of Fame pitcher. And when he realized that salaries were going to get crazy the moment players were given the freedom the new free-agency system promised, he attempted to sell pitcher Vida Blue and left-fielder Joe Rudi, and trade away other high-priced pieces of the club, only to have most of his attempts thwarted by his archenemy, Bowie Kuhn. The two were in constant disagreement with each other during their reigns, and Finley did all he could to keep Kuhn's contract from being renewed.

He was a businessman, and a sports entrepreneur with supreme confidence in what he wanted to do. He did not live vicariously through his players, but made them play the way he wanted them to, successfully. He had an ego as did most owners, loved the notoriety and the limelight, but what he wanted most was to win. When free agency fractured the salary structure of the game, he stood up against it because he saw how detrimental it was going to be to his bottom line. The other owners lacked his vision. They failed to see how the newly negotiated settlement with us players would affect them, and would not listen to whom they thought a renegade.

Finley was smarter than he was given credit for. He realized that higher salaries could well be the beginning of the end for him. Able to hang on for a few more years despite personal financial problems and a divorce, he finally succumbed to what was probably more animosity than he wanted to admit to from other owners, and had to sell the team.

One day in his Chicago office, we were talking about his other franchises, the American Basketball Association Memphis Tams and the Oakland Golden Seals hockey team. He ran the Seals with the same exuberance he did the A's, causing internal disagreement, player disenchantment, and defection. When a proposed sale found no buyers, he was offered $6 million by the National Hockey League just to go away, to leave, to get out. Knowing the extent of their desire to be rid of him, he told me with a smirk that he intended to wait them out just a bit longer believing he could probably get another half-million. When the sale was finalized, he received almost $6.6 million dollars. The team had cost him about $3 million a few years earlier. If that's a crazy man, how could you not admire his style?

Operating his Memphis Tams from a distance for only a couple of years with the same typical unproductive ferocity, and promises of financial support, he once locked the doors, stopped paying the bills, and forced The American Basketball Association to take over the franchise much like the NHL had his hockey team.

The man owned three professional franchises at the same time, snowballing people and cities into thinking he was looking out for them. Like him or not, he was the consummate salesman. I played under his rule, oops!, his ownership, for thirteen years, and lived through, or heard of his many confrontations with one or another of my teammates. He frustrated me as he did so many others, but you could not deny his success; the man was a winner.

When our Oakland club was in its championship runs, he would show up during the tough times—he had rented an apartment on Lake Merritt in downtown Oakland—to give us his usual vitriolic, inspirational pep talk. His tirades worked when we were young, but in time they lost their magic and were ineffective. For as long as we had been together, his bluster no longer mattered. Everyone on the team had probably had their own run-ins with him, or knew of incidents that others had endured, so his histrionics meant little; he had come to understand us, and we him. His attempts to motivate us became simple rhetoric with a few good laughs.

Despite all the frustrations of dealing with Charles O. Finley, once under his wing on the big-league club I looked at him objectively, and began to cautiously respect him. Because of the undertone of the volcanic message I'd been given by Tom Giordano, I began to look at people differently. Instead of looking for ways to denigrate the success of others to bolster my own insecurities,—criticizing someone made me feel better—I began looking for the positives in people, events, life in general, and, more important, myself.

Finley's personal motto was "Sweat plus Sacrifice equals Success." It's emblazoned as "S + S = S" on all three of my championship rings. He was proof of its worth, having survived almost a two-year battle with tuberculosis as a young man to become a millionaire selling disability insurance to doctors.

Because of how he owned, operated, and shuffled his time among three professional sports franchises at the same time, it dawned on me that his sometimes arrogant, gruff manner may not have been his personality, but a personal philosophy that to be successful you had to drive yourself and others. Working for the man as long as I did, certain of his traits revealed why he acted the way he did with us. His actions were shrewdly calculated; he knew what he wanted from himself and everyone he employed. I came to believe that he liked you to fight, to stand up for yourself, to not quit. Had he hired you, he had faith in you, but you'd better produce, do your job, or you would be quickly replaced. His ability to find and mold players who grew to have a fiery hatred of him, is something not many could comprehend.

I believe the man was intuitive. How else could he assemble a championship team from scratch, signing future Hall of Fame members and other star players when they were unknowns, while others floundered with their so-called expertise? Because he kept me as a member of his organization for so long, I must have been doing some of the very things he was looking for in players and people. I would like to think he respected me.

The Boss.

There were those in our ranks and others with whom he dealt who would stand in line against him, but he knew the power of a feisty personality. Being assailed by his players through the media did not seem to affect him. Allowing and accepting retaliation as he did told of the resolve he had for what he was doing. He did things his way, and made it all work, fighting the establishment, and coming out on top. Was it all planned? Did he know exactly what he was doing all along?.

Though no saint, Charles O. Finley should be remembered and honored more than he is. Along with men like George Steinbrenner, Marvin Miller, certain umpires of long standing, and other baseball dignitaries and notables who left their footprints on the game during my playing days, Charles O. Finley deserves to be in the Hall of Fame for his contributions to the game. Like it or not, he made a difference, a big difference. I very much respect him as much as anyone I have met in the world of baseball.

It is inevitable that men of his magnitude will always have enemies.

Birmingham, Alabama, has had a connection with baseball since the late 1800s. The city's ballpark, Rickwood Field, constructed in 1910, is generally regarded as the country's oldest. Recent renovations have brought it back to life, making it usable for a Classic game each summer between certain Southern League teams. Concrete, underground dugouts had replaced the original wooden structures by the time I arrived in 1965 to play for the Birmingham Barons, but its renowned huge, tall, left-field scoreboard that had seen only one or two balls ever hit over it, primarily because it was 400 or more feet away, remained, as did the tire mounted on top of the fence in right-center field that rewarded anyone who hit a ball through its bulls-eye center with four brand new tires. To do so was almost an impossibility, but history has reported it to have been done one time.

Despite a disappointing 51-88 team record in 1965, I had a much-needed turn-around year hitting .281 with seven home runs and stealing eighteen bases. Maybe not an outstanding season by the day's standards, but a huge improvement over the disaster I'd experienced in Texas the year before. There was no denying the effect Tom Giordano's message had on me. He, more than anyone, was responsible for my about-face.

Rickwood Field was showing obvious signs of its fifty-plus year existence in 1965. It was much in need of renovation. More room would have been welcomed for its shabby, cramped, and tiny clubhouses, along with being better located and not squeezed as they were underneath the stands; both of the claustrophobically small concrete dugouts, the underground-like shelters they were, definitely had to be bulldozed, and rebuilt; and a playing surface that could, in the kindest way, best be called challenging was in need of being totally re-landscaped, specifically to be rid of an infield that was not cut deep enough, had "lips" more like curbs, and a dirt portion that was more a combination of pebbles and stones, some almost big enough to be called rocks, than dirt. Field conditions were not good anywhere during the '60s, but what Rickwood Field offered should not have had Birmingham considered the highly touted AA level stop that it was.

When the season ended, I'd committed twenty-eight errors, all in all not too bad considering the difficult surface I had to navigate. My defensive play was finally becoming consistent. My movements and actions, angles, rhythm, timing, and balance were all beginning to coordinate, and I was again honored with a post-season All-star team selection, my third, at a good AA level.

What resulted from my year in Birmingham, and more important than my All-Star selection, was realizing how anger had been controlling my life. I hadn't seen it, but it was quite possibly to what the staff members were referring when they recommended I be released the previous winter. And it may have been what Tom Giordano was attempting to point out that day on the bleachers when he said it was felt that I was not enjoying myself. I was angry, about a lot of things. The perfection I was seeking, impossible as

357

that was to achieve, and my emotional insecurities were a deadly combination; I was never going to be who I thought I should be. And worse, I wrongly believed that if I changed, my game would be affected.

Thinking it was just my sensitivity, I had not been handling life's difficulties, or the game, with any kind of assuredness. Every strikeout, error, or simply not playing well was a personal reminder of not doing what was expected of me. As critical as I was of myself, it was impossible to think that something might go right. I blamed everyone and everything; nothing was my fault. This was frustrating baggage to be carrying, but it would all come to an end that was a rude awakening.

In the short stretch of a few games, for maybe twenty-five or thirty at-bats, I went hitless. Not getting a hit in one game is bad enough, but when it becomes two, then three, you start talking to yourself. My average was plummeting, and I was angry. I was in the throws of a slump. No one knew how I was feeling because I didn't throw things, hit walls, or show any emotion, but with each at-bat, with every out, my anger was building. One night after another futile at-bat, I came back into Rickwood's bunker-like dugout and sat, by myself, on the small ledge that was at the far end. I was absolutely furious, madder than I'd ever been, and just wanted to scream. With little time before I had to return to the field, I wasn't sure I could. For maybe ten or fifteen seconds I was frozen with an anger I'd never experienced, absolutely livid, unable to do anything, unable to move, unable to focus. I don't even remember seeing anything during those few seconds. Whatever was happening to me was not good, and it scared the hell out of me. I felt as if I'd lost control of myself, that I was having a nervous breakdown, and feared how that would look should it happen in the dugout.

They say you have to hit bottom before you can make any changes, and I'd hit it hard sitting on that ledge in the Barons' dugout. I could not live this way anymore. As miserable as the slump was it was as valuable an experience as any I'd had, or would ever have. It awakened me to the fact of just how much anger had been ruling my life. The feelings that everyone was against me, that I was being treated unfairly, and that nobody liked me had to stop. Instead of doing something about all of this, my reaction was to get mad. It was my destructive response to almost everything. Not only was my life a neurotic whirlpool of emotions from which I was drowning, it was full of excuses. It was poor me, poor me. Were it not for this slump, who knows how long it might have been before something else rescued me. A week of going without a hit was the psychological trigger that unleashed the understanding I needed of the detrimental and destructive hold that my temper had on me.

There were reasons why I wasn't hitting, it wasn't a lack of ability, and it wasn't all bad luck. I was doing nothing to help myself. The shame of this situation was that I was not oblivious to the direction I was allowing my game to go, I was more afraid of what I thought the consequences would be if I changed, all while having no idea what those consequences might even be. After five long years I began to understand so much of what I hadn't. Whether this revelation would save my baseball life, I didn't know, but it saved the one I was living.

● ● ●

My self-confidence might not have yet been completely restored, but my Birmingham experience in 1965, and the awakening I had, changed my outlook on life completely. It wasn't easy, not easy at all, but finally understanding what I hadn't for so long, made me capable of confronting whatever might happen at the AAA level in 1966 with a much delayed maturity. Could I play well enough at this highest minor-league level to ensure that I would be in Kansas City in 1967?

Vancouver, British Columbia, Canada, must be one of the world's prettiest cities. Framed by beautiful mountains, inlets and bays, the overall beauty of the region, and the Canadian culture made my 1966 AAA season one to remember.

As much as I loved our home ballpark, Capilano Stadium, there was either a light mist, a slow drizzle, or just enough rain every night to make the field sloppy, and the atmosphere a little dreary and gloomy. And because Canadian summers were short, a month, maybe two, most nights were cool. That and the heavy air cut down the distance a ball could travel, no matter how well it was hit. Home runs were rare.

The infield, to my surprise, was absolutely incredible, better even than what I had thought was the best at Al Lang Field, in St. Petersburg, Florida, during my first season. Stepping onto it the night we arrived from spring training, I could not have been more pleased. Had someone had a fungo, I'd have taken ground balls in my street clothes.

My confidence soared just seeing how smooth, level, and pebble and stone free it was. Many major-league surfaces, as I would find out, would not be this good. The heavy consistency of the dirt, the short, thick carpet of infield grass, and the wet Canadian nights would keep just about every ground ball from reaching the outfield, to the delight of our pitching staff. The "lips," edges, or what were little curbs where the grass transitioned to the dirt that were common on other infields, were non-existent, and with the infield cut as deep as it was, and the topography of the surface being what it was, I had no worries about where I might position myself, or that my range would be impeded.

My Vancouver Mounties battled the Seattle Rainiers, a California Angel franchise, for first place all year, but had to settle for a second place finish with a 77-71 record.

As the season progressed, the games between our two clubs turned into heated rivalries. Certain players on both clubs exacerbated the situation, which was typical in tight competition, until one game got especially ugly. One of the Seattle pitchers, Jim Coates, was known to intentionally throw at people. That was really nothing to be overly concerned about, it was part of the game, plus, his reputation was well-known.

Coates was, however, considered to be a notorious headhunter. It did not take much for him to intimidate a hitter by knocking him down. More than any other, his targets, from what was rumored, were players of color, no matter their ethnicity. And as often occurs when someone is intentionally thrown at, players retaliate, and in one particular game, things deteriorated quickly.

One of my teammates, Ricardo Joseph, was a dark-skinned Latin player from the Dominican Republic. Whether it was his color, or because he was one of our better hitters, or perhaps it was just an errant wild pitch, who knows, but that he was hit by a Coates pitch precipitated some posturing, harsh words, and the beginnings of what looked like trouble. Seattle's catcher, Merritt Ranew, quieted the situation by restraining Joseph as he headed toward the mound and Coates and, for a while, tempers settled.

A couple of innings later another of our hitters, Tommie Reynolds, bunted down the first-base line, forcing Coates to field the ball. I immediately knew what was going to happen. It looked to be a harmless play, one that should have had Coates tagging Reynolds for the easy out, but instead of avoiding the tag, Reynolds just flat out ran him over, and the two of them wrestled to the ground as all hell broke loose and the dugouts emptied.

When something like this happens, you never know where to look. Everyone is swinging wildly and you're doing what you can to protect yourself. Players were jumping into different piles, there were individual skirmishes, and at one point I watched our second baseman dance around the infield dirt in a kind of "you-swing-first fight" with one of their infielders when I heard someone shout, "Get the guy with the bat!"

With that everything stopped! Fists, stomping, kicking, and maybe even biting could be tolerated in one of these free-for-alls, but bringing a bat into it was an absolute no-no. In an incident reminiscent of Juan Marichal of the Giants hitting John Roseboro of the Dodgers with a bat in a similar way just a year earlier in 1965, our first baseman, Santiago Rosario, another Latin and the batter after Reynolds, had run from the on-deck circle with his bat and hit Ranew over the head, knocking him to the ground seriously injured. The fracas quickly went from a multiplayer brawl to the entire Raniers team chasing Rosario, who ran for his life into our clubhouse.

The fighting stopped immediately, but with emotions high, everyone's attention went to their catcher. Ranew was badly hurt. He almost died from the incident, but with surgery for a blood clot and a three-week hospital stay, he recovered and continued to play for a few more years. The whole scene was horrific, eerie, unfortunate, uncalled for, and scary; there was no excuse for it.

But it didn't end that night. From what I understand, the following morning, Ricardo Joseph was up early, waiting in the lobby of the Seattle team's hotel for Coates to come downstairs. When he did, Joseph, swinging at him again, but this time with his fists, applied a few cuts to the pitcher's face and chipped one of his teeth, somewhat settling the score. I don't recall if Joseph got any hits off Coates the night of the brawl, but he went two for two, maybe three for three, versus Coates that morning.

For the next few days, a pall hung over the ballpark as league officials investigated the situation, trying to determine the next course of action. Ultimately, our first baseman was suspended for the balance of the season. Throwing at hitters was a common practice in the game so what punishment Coates received I don't know, but it couldn't have been much. A dental bill might have been the harshest thing. Legal issues, of course, ensued. Ranew sued Rosario, Reynolds, the Kansas City organization, the Mounties, and Mickey Vernon, our manager, and though he won the lawsuit it was little compensation for what he suffered.

This incident was, unfortunately, the highlight of what was otherwise a good AAA season for me.

When the best players at each position were chosen after the season ended, I was named the best shortstop in the league, the fourth time I'd been so honored. I hit a respectable .260, played in all of our 148 games, was involved in 125 of our team's 186 double plays, and fell just short of 800 total fielding chances, numbers that were more than lofty when compared to some of the game's best.

Fulfilling my potential may have been stalled for more years than it should have been because of my insecurities, inhibitions, and a crippling self-doubt, but what had begun in Birmingham, when I first realized the destructiveness of my anger, continued in Vancouver. With a more mature outlook, personality changes, an up-tick in self-esteem, and improved confidence, I saw much more clearly what I had been doing to myself. It had been a good year.

My intuition was telling me that Kansas City would again put me on the major-league roster over the winter, and they did. That put me in a strong position to become a member of the Kansas City A's in 1967.

18

THE SEATTLE BREWERS

For approximately fifty years, the major leagues consisted of sixteen teams. There was an equal split of eight in the American League and eight in the National League. Boston, St Louis, and Philadelphia, and Philadelphia, each hosted two teams for a short period; New York had three. It was expected that the emotional rivalries that would develop in the multi-teamed cities would spark an increased interest in the game, but that never occurred. Fiscal difficulties, or the inevitable obsolescence of a ballpark proved fatal for many clubs, and one after another they began to look elsewhere for more lucrative locations.

It had been customary that when one team left a city, especially if it was its lone resident, another would take its place to either keep an increasing populace happy, or forestall legislative action. Baseball knew that should it fail to redeem the loss a city experienced when its team moved, the threat by Congress to reconsider its antitrust exemption, and its player restrictive reserve clause, might be seriously challenged.

What could have been tenuous organizational shifts, and financial boondoggles for the Brooklyn Dodgers and the New York Giants when they respectively vacated Ebbets Field and the Polo Grounds in 1958, were instead venturesome transitions that secured the future for both franchises. Gaining confidence through the success of those two moves, baseball's waters were stirred, and with other clubs getting restless, major-league expansion was triggered.

Three years later, in 1961, the American League added the Los Angeles Angels and, in our capital, the Washington Senators. The Senators replaced the same-name team that had moved to Minneapolis and became the Twins that same season. In 1962, to soothe a disgruntled New York after the loss of the Dodgers and the Giants, the New York Metropolitans (aka Mets) were born.

For several years prior to these additions, there had been rumblings that several cities–Houston for one—were vying for membership in a proposed new Continental League. This rival league would have threatened the traditional structure of the game, and had it found support, the raid on players from the existing major-league teams would have been devastating. To thwart that possibility, major-league baseball wisely awarded Houston a National League franchise to begin play along with the Mets in 1962—they would be called the Houston Colt 45s. This was an early and savvy political maneuver by baseball's executives that effectively killed any possibility of the new league being established.

Prior to expansion, it was newsworthy when a new player was added to any of the major-league rosters. The careers of some very good players stalled at the AAA level. When teams began to relocate and new franchises were added, players previously destined to become minor-league lifers found renewed hope in the many new openings. From the eight rosters that had been each league's total for decades, the number jumped to ten in 1962, then to twelve, then fourteen, and now both leagues each have fifteen with more being discussed. Only 640 major-league roster spots were available in the '50s; that total is now 1200.

Being honored as the best shortstop, and named to the AAA Pacific Coast League All-Star team in 1966 put the Kansas City organization in the difficult position of having to decide whether to keep me, or risk losing me to another club in 1967. I had hit enough at a tough AAA level, and my defensive ability was such that there was expected to be a lot of interest in me from other major-league teams during the ritual hunt for players in the off-season.

Had Kansas City left me on the AAA roster over the winter, I would surely have been drafted by another major-league club. That was something I knew they would not allow to happen. On the other hand, had they added me to the major-league roster for a third time—which I believed they would—and later in the spring wanted to again send me back to Vancouver for the 1967 season, I would have been out of options, and would have had to clear waivers. Every other organization in reverse order of how they finished the year before would then have the opportunity to claim me, and it was obvious someone would because there were rumors for years of clubs wanting to trade for me. The third scenario was for them to keep me on the big club for the season. No matter what was to happen, I was in a strong position with a lot of leverage to be in the major leagues in 1967.

Talent at the AAA level in the '60s was more than formidable. My concern was how much better would I find the players in the major leagues to be. What I would discover was though there was more consistent position-player talent, only a few were head and shoulders above what I had seen in AAA; the big-league clubs just had no holes. A pitching staff at the AAA level might have had three, four, maybe five quality pitchers; on a major-league team, they all were. The big-league level simply had more of the best of everything.

As spring training inched toward its final days, I felt more and more confident that I would stay with the big club for the 1967 season, and I did, but it was a long and frustrating first year. We fell one game shy of the century mark in losses, and hit .242 as a team which was better than the entire American League that hit a combined .233. I played sparingly.

Hoping for a better 1968, neither we nor the league were any better. Transplanted in Oakland from Kansas City by owner, Charles O. Finley, we hit .240 as a team while the league averaged .237, not a significant change. It was another difficult season. Both the American and National League ERAs—earned run average— were under 3.00. Pitchers dominated the hitters. Carl Yastrzemski led the American League as its lone .300 hitter with an average of .301. Pete Rose topped only four National League batters who hit over .300 with his average of .335. Denny McClain won 31 games for the Detroit Tigers, and Bob Gibson fashioned a minuscule 1.12 ERA for the St. Louis Cardinals. Luis Tiant led the Cleveland Indians staff and the American League with an ERA of 1.60.

The dearth of hitting in both leagues in 1968 caused the Commissioner to reduce the strike zone strike zone for the following season, and lower the mound from fifteen to ten inches, considerably lessening the leverage pitchers had working off the higher slope. Even so, there were more twenty-game winners in the first five years of the 1970s—ninety-six total for the decade—than any other similar period. Consider the Baltimore Orioles, who in 1970 had three with Palmer, Cuellar, and McNally; in 1971, four, with Palmer, Cuellar, and McNally again, and Pat Dobson; and my Oakland A's in 1973 with Hunter, Blue, and Holtzman.

Fifty years ago, some combination of your offensive and defensive skills decided your position in the lineup and on the field. Leniency was a factor in some instances, but the standards were more defined than they are today. Power and runs-batted-in were mostly provided by the corner outfielders, the corner infielders and the catchers, and least of all from the center fielders and the middle infielders. Exceptional defensive middle infielders like myself were given a reprieve from even the average offensive production expected, so although I was playing with the "no-hit" tag hung on me early in my career, I had some breathing room. Only a few players were recognized as a team's true home run hitters. Today, the home run is the much sought after offensive skill from everyone with hope that it is accompanied by at least some ability to catch the ball.

An experiment for many years had allowed each major-league club an additional three roster spots until May 15 when teams would trim back to the traditional limit of twenty-five. I was one of twenty-eight players with which the Athletics started the 1967 season. Whenever it was that I made the major leagues, I expected to be some club's everyday shortstop. Anything different was never something I considered, but that was not to be. Despite the doubts that were rumored about his ability to play the infield since his debut in 1964, because of his offensive explosiveness, Dagoberto Campaneris was going to remain Kansas City's shortstop. Considered the better defender, I was assigned to be his backup. As disappointing as that was, I understood.

What worried me about Kansas City's decision to put me in a part-time role was the amount of playing time I would be missing, playing time that I desperately needed to keep my defensive play respectable. One or two innings here and there were not going to be enough, and no amount of extra work was going to help maintain the competency of play I thought would be required to stay in the major leagues. No player can perform at his best without regular playing time, and I knew myself well enough to know how even one day off affected me. To think about being out of action for days at a time, maybe weeks, was not something I looked forward to, and if that continued, it was going to put any career I might have in jeopardy.

Baseball was in an era of "do it or else." It was not management's style to talk to players. There were no meetings to discuss our progress, offer advice, or map our destiny. We wrestled with our own neurotic suspicions about what the organization thought of us until whatever was to happen would. In that cold and callous atmosphere, it was perhaps foolish and naive of me not to realize I might have to play multiple positions, but it was something I had never considered. Not once had anyone even suggested that I workout at another position. Having played over 800 games and every single inning during my six minor-league seasons at only the shortstop position, including the two times I was optioned to other organizations, I was anesthetized about playing elsewhere on the infield. My goal and my only thoughts were to one day be the starting shortstop for the Kansas City Athletics.

Players being groomed to play more than one position is now commonplace; today's game prides itself on versatility. Many current executives consider having multifaceted athletes a crowning achievement. When it is decided that someone can play two or three positions, two for sure, it's as if gold has been discovered, eyes light up and smiles fill the meeting room. This happens early in the careers of more than a few players. No one realizes how unfair it might be to the player, or the organization, and that failure at a second position often occurs before there is maturity at the first. Competency at both gets compromised, but with today's easy acceptance of mediocrity, it doesn't matter; no one seems to notice; everything is fine. Patience is not much of a virtue in the game anymore.

Needless to say, my major-league career did not begin on a rousingly positive note. As a back-up, a utility man, a second-stringer, a bench, role, or platoon player, it was the first time in my life that I was not an everyday player on any team. I was not very happy. I had no idea how I would react to not playing every day, or how hard it might be, or what would be expected of me. I did not want to embarrass myself.

Had I been asked to define what a utility player was, my simple answer would have been that he was a good player, but with only enough talent to periodically help the team. There may have been those who were comfortable with the role, but not me. Maybe I was making too much of what I thought was going to be difficult, but it was frustrating, and I was not very pleased with my situation. Sitting night after night wondering when I might be called on was nerve-wracking. Never again would I feel the comfort that came from playing everyday.

There was no way to stay in touch with the pace and speed of the game without regular playing time. My longest period of inactivity with not one appearance on the field was eighteen days, an endless period of almost three weeks. During these longer periods of inactivity, I hated going to the ballpark. Not playing for two days, maybe three, was OK, but after that I began to first get irritated, and then mad. Each succeeding day on the bench made me feel more isolated, and not part of the team. Even playing for three lousy outs calmed me down. Looking back on what was a frustration situation, I realized two things that I'd never considered. One, was the mental strength I had to stay as prepared as I could despite my misgivings, and two, the emotional control it took to accept how irritated I was. It was years before I could accept the role with a modicum of comfort.

The utility role is an important position on a major-league club. To do it well requires acceptance, composure, perseverance, poise, and many of the same traits expected from a regular, every day player, but on a part time basis, they were greater challenges. What caused the most angst for me was wanting to play well under sporadic playing conditions. You had to be prepared to accept your own mediocrity and failure.

● ● ●

My defensive skills had peaked during my AAA season in Vancouver in 1966. I was the league's best shortstop, and honestly felt, though it might have taken a year or two, that I would have made a name for myself at the position in the major-leagues. However, the skills I'd worked so hard to achieve were slowly fading each day I did not get on the field, and I didn't know what to do about that. Worse, and frightening, was that the longer I did not get to play, the more I became gun-shy, and unsure of myself about playing the shortstop position that I at one time had mastered.

My play remained acceptable, but it was slowly deteriorating. Defensive skills that had been instinctive, now needed reminders. I was finding myself having to think too much about what I had to do. The ballpark was becoming a work place, rather than the fun place it was. Trying to cope with the competition while losing my edge, and playing part time, was difficult physically and emotionally.

For nine of my ten major-league seasons I was a utility infielder, playing when needed. That I remained employed meant I was adequately filling the role, but I had to live with never again being proud of how I played shortstop. It was scary to feel the movements and actions that I had so meticulously fine-tuned lose their involuntary, mechanical, and almost robotic ability to respond when called upon. Each day was one of doubt, of adjusting, coping, doing what I could, accepting, adapting, and aging, all while experiencing the shame of not being the player I believed I could be. I worked hard, did what I could, kept my mouth shut, and got by.

After sporadic activity during my first three years in the major leagues, playing second and, occasionally, third base for the first time, I was traded. It was the winter of 1969. The Seattle Pilots acquired me from Oakland to be their regular everyday shortstop in 1970. The Pilots had just completed their first season as an expansion ball club, but their future was bleak. It was questionable whether the franchise could survive even one more season. High ticket prices, a bad economy, a rundown stadium, an inaugural season of lower-than-expected attendance, and underfunding of the club by its investors had led to a situation that was jeopardizing its existence. With what had to be a mountain of legal filings, court-required affidavits, petitions, briefs, subpoenas, and more fiscal trouble than could seemingly develop in one year, the team was embroiled in a battle for its life.

The only thing we players knew as spring training progressed was that the team's situation was desperate. Where the club would be located for the upcoming season was up in the air. There were rumors about its future, but no one really knew what was happening. When camp ended, we were homeless. We had nowhere to go. The equipment trucks that left Arizona had no specific destination. They put up somewhere in Utah to await a court decision.

When it was discovered that the Pilots lacked the finances to continue paying the coaches or us players, the franchise was declared bankrupt, and the sale of the team was accepted to a Milwaukee group headed by Bud Selig. The Milwaukee car salesman had been looking for a team to replace his beloved Milwaukee Braves who had moved to Atlanta in 1966. This was the same Bud Selig who became baseball's commissioner in 1998 after being acting commissioner for six years.

The trucks that had been sitting in Utah turned and headed for Milwaukee.

A few days later, on April 7, 1970, I took the field for the first game ever played by the modern day Milwaukee Brewers, née the Seattle Pilots, wearing a Pilots hand-me-down uniform that now had "Brewers" across my chest. After three years of sitting on the sidelines, totally unsure of just how good I would be, my name was listed in a major-league opening-day starting lineup. I was batting eighth against the California Angels. We lost 12-0.

My life as a Milwaukee Brewer began on December 7, 1969. My wife and I had just walked into our house late one evening with my one-year-old daughter when the phone rang. It was Charlie Finley. One o'clock in the morning Chicago time meant this was not a personal call, one to wish me Merry Christmas, or to tell me to watch for his Christmas gift in the mail. Finley's late-night phone calls were business related. Straightforward and right to the point as he always was, he told me he had traded me to Seattle. My heart sank. Nothing could have ruined Christmas more. I listened for the couple of minutes it took for him to give me the particulars of the deal, hung up, and in a daze told my wife we'd be moving. The comfort of nine years with an organization and teammates I considered my baseball family vanished with just a few words. It was difficult to be leaving a club that was improving, and, obviously, on the verge of being very good, something I would not have the privilege of experiencing.

It's the rare player who does not get traded at some point in his career. The first time it happens your response is unpredictable, but it is emotional. You feel shunned, cast aside, unwanted, and though it may have justification, it's upsetting. You question your ability. I could not have been more disappointed or depressed that this was happening to me. My first thought was about moving my family, and what it would take to get them to Seattle, but I was quickly overwhelmed with a feeling that was more unsettling. Under normal conditions, the trade would have been a good thing because I was finally going to get my chance to play every day, but my situation was far from normal.

Ted Kubiak welcomed to the Seattle Pilots by
Marvin Milkes, the Pilots General Manager.

After three years of what I considered relative inactivity, I had no idea about what kind of player I was going to be. Seattle was expecting a major-league shortstop. I was not sure I was anymore. It was an honor that there were those who thought I was good enough to still to handle the position, but I knew I was not going to be what they expected, and, worse, what I knew I could have been. The task ahead was to prove that I still had enough ability to play in the major leagues; my battle had become personal and internal. If I could not compete, then what? I wasn't sure what I would do.

Seattle, of course, had no idea they were not getting the defender I had been for the Vancouver Mounties in 1966. Players in utility roles are given the benefit of the doubt, a sort of forgiveness is associated with the position, and though a certain quality of play is expected, a lot gets overlooked and accepted. Everyone understands the difficulty of a part-time position. The Seattle braintrust had apparently felt that my sporadic play had been more than adequate for three years. I knew differently, and was unsure of what remained of the old me.

Three seasons of multi-positional and part-time play had drained me of the great feel I had for the shortstop position. It did not matter what I had done in the meantime, how long I worked every day, how many ground balls I took, what drills I did, how many sprints I ran, I knew of no way to simulate the stress and actions of a game. Where at one time I felt capable of being able to cover almost the entire left side of the infield, that was now out of the question. I had become uncomfortable standing where I had at one time felt completely at home. The great reads I had been able to make of hitters' swings were no longer instinctive; they were riddled with unwanted hesitancies. Everything that had been unconsciously automatic now had to be scripted and rehearsed before-hand. Actions that were previously spontaneously made were delayed by critical split-seconds. It was all I could do to stay positive each time I took the field knowing that it was not the "me" who should have been there.

The Seattle club that had been assembled for what was to be the franchise's second season was not very good. Several of the original draftees when expansion in 1969 created the Seattle Pilots, the Kansas City Royals, the Montreal Expos, and the San Diego Padres had been replaced by me and others, hoping the franchise would have a more promising future, but it would be a long time before the organization would gain respectability. We finished the year with a record of 65-97 in a tie for fourth place in the American League West with the Kansas City Royals, ingloriously within three runs of scoring the least amount of any team during the season.

Though my year was nothing to rave about, the question of whether I had enough left to be deserving of major-league status was answered. I did. I hit .252, missed only two games all year, and held my own among some of the game's best ever. Though the year was not the fun it should have been, I had passed my own personal test.

Being traded often triggers a stream of similar transactions. When one organization sees you as deficient in some aspect of the game, others do also. As the athlete ages, those decisions are more right than wrong. As your career winds down, unless you are lucky to land where your talents mesh with those of the other players on the club, your tenure on any club is shaky. I was a Seattle Pilot/Milwaukee Brewer for only a year-and-a-half before I began hop-scotching the leagues. In July of 1971, the Brewers traded me to St. Louis. That November I was shipped to the Washington Senators, and, in a repeat of the Seattle-to-Milwaukee shift in 1970, the Washington club found itself a new home that winter, Arlington, Texas. I did not play one inning in our nation's capital, but, instead, kicked off the 1972 season for another new franchise, the Texas Rangers.

As with my other recent stops, my stay in Texas wasn't long, but this time the change could not have been sweeter. On July 20, 1972, after a night game, a little more than three months into the Ranger's first season with my career going downhill fast, as if someone was looking out for me, Ted Williams, the Texas manager, called me and first baseman Don Mincher into his office, and told us we had been traded to the Oakland Athletics! C'mon!! You're kidding, right? This could not be happening! Back to the A's! Had I been able to do a cartwheel, I would have done one right then and there in front of The Splendid Splinter. I was going home! How great was that?

Ted Williams, my Texas Rangers manager in 1972.

An hour later my wife and I were trying to figure out how to best get her, two kids, and two dogs back to Oakland when the phone rang. It was Finley. Welcoming me back, he said the A's had suffered several injuries, were short of infielders, and he needed me in Boston for the next day's doubleheader. My concern was getting everybody and everything to Oakland, not being in Boston in twelve hours. How was I supposed to catch a flight to Boston in the middle of the night anyway? Finley could sometimes be a little impetuous. After trying to browbeat me into leaving my family on their own, he said not to worry; he would pay for and take care of everything if I would get to Fenway Park as quickly as possible. I did not make the double-header, but was once again a very happy starting second baseman for my Oakland A's the next night.

As a member of the A's organization for almost ten years before being traded to Seattle, I was back where my heart was. Though frustrated to again be back on the bench, I had become tolerant of the role. The A's had matured. They were polished, still raw, with more to give, and were darned good. In just a few short months we would experience the first of our three historical consecutive World Championships. Thank you Charles O. Finley!

With the club poised for the success that was about to come, every player's role was important. There was still an unproductiveness associated with my utility role, but winning consistently trumped whatever ill feelings I harbored. Player injuries would get me into the lineup for days, sometimes weeks, and whether to find solace in my reserve position, or to keep my confidence up, I convinced myself that because of how I was used to finish games, I had been entrusted with their crucial late innings. Staying positive continued to be the hurdle it had always been.

Six years in the minor leagues was an unduly long apprenticeship, but it was what I needed to mature physically and emotionally. I would have loved to have progressed faster, but we do what we do as best we can. I had the good fortune to play in the major leagues, was honored to be a member of a team that won three world championships, and thankful to have played with, and against, some of the very best players the game has seen in an era many think was maybe the best ever. The memories I have are incredible and irreplaceable.

All in all, that's not a bad legacy for someone signed out of a tryout camp.

Winning the American League pennant in 1972 versus the Detroit Tigers. Mike Hegan, Vida Blue, Tim Cullen, Joel Horlen, Darold Knowles, Ted Kubiak, Joe Rudi

Victory over the Detroit Tigers in the ALCS in 1972.
Catfish Hunter, Dick Green, Dal Maxvill, Tim Cullen,
Ted Kubiak, Gene Tenace, Sal Bando, Bert Campaneris.

Clubhouse celebration after winning the American
League pennant in 1972. Joel Horlen, Ted Kubiak,
Dick Green, Dal Maxvill, and Tim Cullen.

**The on-field celebration after beating the
Cincinnati Reds in the 1972 World Series.**

**Clubhouse celebration after beating the Cincinnati Reds
in the 1972 World Series. Ted Kubiak and Dick Green**

Two stalwarts during the championship runs in 1972, 1973, and 1974. Sal Bando and Catfish Hunter.

Joe DiMaggio, Oakland A's coach in 1969.

19

MISSING THOSE YOU LOVE

Many of my former Oakland teammates would agree that we may not have had the very best players, but in the first half of the 1970s, no team played more consistent, mistake-free baseball than we did day after day. Having been a member of a few major-league teams that struggled, and witness to the poor play of others, it's hard to find fault with either of those observations.

As a member of the twenty-five man Oakland A's roster each of our championship years, there were extended periods of time when I was one of the "elite" starting nine that took the field every day, a proud time to be sure. My role was more properly defined as a utility player, a back-up infielder, one of the so-called extra men, a player who was more often relegated to watching my teammates from the dugout rather than playing alongside them on the field. From either vantage point, I can well vouch that Finley's boys knew what they were doing. Despite my limited role, I'm confident with having made significant contributions in those years when injuries to various teammates got me playing time. Many of us who were on the championship clubs of 1972, 1973, and 1974 matured together through similar minor-league seasons as we advanced from level to level in the Kansas City/Oakland farm system. The progress being made by a group of select individuals could hardly be missed.

As a typical first season in the major leagues might be for a rookie who did not play much, my career did not have an auspicious beginning. I was young, raw, anxious, and apprehensive on a Kansas City team in 1967 that was not very good. We lost 99 games, but we did so with future stars in the making such as Reggie Jackson, Sal Bando, Jim Hunter, John Odom, Chuck Dobson, Bert Campaneris, Joe Rudi, and Dick Green. That a handful of others were on the verge of success showed with our improved won-lost records in 1968 (82-80) and 1969 (88-74).

The first time you are traded is a shock, you feel discarded. It is a move from which you think you'll never fully recover, one that I first experienced during the winter of 1969. It could not have happened at a worse time. I had just completed my third season in the major leagues with a young A's team that was ready to win. What I didn't know was that though I was gone, I was not forgotten. Mr. Finley would bring me back to the organization in 1972 in time to become part of the club's remarkable three successive World Championships, a feat that has been accomplished by only a few teams in the history of baseball.

Being a member of those three teams was an incredible experience, something I have become prouder of as the years have passed. The success we had battling our way through those pressure-packed seasons slowly developed within me a sense of what it took to be a winner. I had no desire to manage or coach when I retired, but watching my teammates perform day after day made an indelible imprint on how I would ultimately instruct and manage players when I did. Their focus and commitment to winning and dedication to the fundamental details of the game were not easily forgotten. Everything they exhibited was an easily recognizable formula for success, and an invaluable foundation for my future.

Unfortunately, I had my own internal battles that were not going as well. I was making progress with my personal issues, but there was still a lot that needed attention, and many questions that required answers. Striving to understand how to better exist under the parental guidelines that had unintentionally suffocated my individuality, had me baffled and confused. If I was to ever gain the emotional freedom my life deserved, there had to be an awakening and an understanding of the changes I had to make. I was not sure I knew what they were.

As I matured—I was a late bloomer—I often wondered if there would ever be a day that would allow me to really know myself and understand what I wanted out of life. Would I ever be able to live every day with the clarity and wisdom I should have? Was it possible that I could eventually be the complete man in words and actions that I hoped to be? Decades have passed, and improvement is obvious, but, is there an end to this search?

Every new revelation or understanding is a pleasant surprise. I am much more accepting of who I am, much more cognizant of what is right and wrong, and no longer as influenced by others or outside forces. Events that in the past affected me because of some imagined fear, or that I just did not know how to deal with, are now lessons from which I learn. I look at situations more carefully, and assess their meanings more sensibly. Believing there is a purpose and a reason for everything we do, I am more receptive of the challenges and lessons that life presents.

The death of my parents, particularly my father, awakened me to some very interesting and unexpected admissions about who I am. With his loss, I measured myself against who he was, and discovered someone I never really understood. For the better part of his last two years I lived with him, and for his last six months did almost everything for him except feed him. I hadn't lived with my parents for any significant amount of time since I left home at eighteen in pursuit of a career in baseball, but returning to my childhood home fifty years later to care for him gave me an opportunity to see how he had impacted my becoming who I was. It wasn't something I sought nor was it immediately evident, but the longer I was with him, and the more I paid attention to what he did and said, the better I understood his influence.

He was still Dad, but as I peeled off his layers, I stripped away some of my own. He was sharp as a tack, spirited and lucid until his final day in 2008, two years after my mother passed. When questioned about his youth, his family, his play, his work, or life itself, I recognized that even as a young man he was an old soul, living with a pragmatic wisdom that belied his years. The calmness and surety of his words confirmed that he knew exactly who he was, where he was going, and what he wanted out of life. He made it all seem so simple. The man was as uncomplicated as I had thought him mystifying.

Had I been more discerning of him during the time I lived at home, able to understand the psychology of his actions, and more clearly able to decipher the dynamics between him and my mother, there's no doubt it would have positively altered my personality. Watching and listening to him during his final days in a way I had never done before made me realize that it was he who had silent control of our family, and that he, not my mother, as I had very mistakenly thought, was the greater influence on me as a man. That revelation was totally unexpected.

In no way do I mean to imply that I look upon my mother's death with any less emotion or remembrance, but I didn't need the same embedded time with her to clarify our relationship. Her influences were instilled through the daily control she had of me. The disciplinarian, the authoritarian, demanding and vocal, the impression was that she was the one in charge, but what was unmasked during the time I lived with Dad was the realization that hers was a superficial authority.

My father silently directed and guided her with his steadfastness, allowing her a freedom that had limits. He handled her moody, critical, and demeaning remarks in a way I did not understood. He stabilized her with a calm acceptance of her unpredictability, exhibiting a strength of character that I had for so long believed to be a weakness. Why wouldn't he ever just tell her off? Was he a milquetoast? Is that what I'd become? Those were my thoughts for years. He took almost every negative comment, ridicule, and frustration my mother threw at him without reprisal. Not that he was always tolerant, but rarely did he say much to her with even a hint of harshness. He apparently understood the frailties of the woman with whom he had chosen to live and love. He had the maturity to know who she was, and why she acted the way she did. Seldom did he retaliate, and turn it around on her.

My best explanation for their relationship was that it was inexplicably unique, but powerfully endearing. The occasional incidents of volatility were far, far overshadowed by their love and respect for each other. Any sudden burst of anger by Mom that triggered an explosive response from Dad was quickly dismissed without discussion. Neither apologized, nor was another word said. Each confrontation ended coldly and abruptly with no residual consequences. It was over, done.

Whether their silence was good or bad for them in their own relationship was hard to tell; it did me little good. Their behavior was an emotional stigma that did nothing to help me resolve issues with others in my own life. It was no role model for expression; I fell silent, turned inward, became isolated. Afraid of the consequences, I said nothing, not exactly a good example for psychological success as a lifelong practice.

Having to put my father in an assisted living facility for his final days was one of the toughest decisions I have ever had to make. The inevitable day of confrontation could not have been more dreadful. Traveling as I was at the time with my coaching duties, I could find no one trustworthy enough to stay with him as I had the previous summer. Convincing him it was the best thing for him, and that it had to be done was horrendously emotional. I agonized for days gathering the courage to tell him. Even though he didn't like the thought of it, and fought it as I had assumed he would, he ultimately understood the situation with the depth of maturity I should have expected.

Saying good-bye to him the night before I had to leave for Florida and our spring training meetings, he seemed in good spirits. I didn't expect to see him for another month, but leaving a team meeting one morning, not forty-eight hours later, I received a message from his nurse to call her. I did, and she told me that Dad had passed away.

Returning to handle the necessary funeral arrangements, I was informed by the staff caring for him that he had said the night I left that it would be the last time he would see me. He had decided he had had enough. There was an eeriness to our good-byes that hinted at something like this happening. He seemed to be content with me as his son, and though he couldn't say the words, with our last hug and words he showed a love for me I hadn't seen. It was the best he could do. I had a strange feeling as I left him. In tears as I write this, I find it strange how deep emotions can be despite being unable to express them to the people we love. My relationship with my own children and grandchildren will never be devoid of my expressions of my love for them.

Even in his last hours, Dad left this world with the same calm maturity he lived each day. He passed away peacefully in his wheelchair without pain at ninety-three, the same age at which Mom died. They were together for sixty-seven years, leaving me with tremendous lessons in love, compromise, acceptance, and tolerance. What immense gifts I inherited, many that so few understand, and even fewer will ever know, and they gave them to me unknowingly. They lived their lives the best way they knew.

Would that I could pass on to my children and grandchildren what they taught me in their quiet, dedicated time together.

With neither parent any longer in my life, the security that both provided became abundantly clear. That was something to which I had paid little attention. It mattered not where I was, or what I was doing, knowing that I could pick up the phone and hear their voices, one or both, was an available comfort I had not recognized or understood. With both now gone forever, I wasn't sure how I would respond, but an immediate strange sensation enveloped me that could not be ignored. I was no longer their little boy, but a man who now had to stand on his own two feet. How would this loss of emotional reliance affect me? There was no immediate answer, but there was no denying the overwhelming, instantaneous maturation I experienced.

All of a sudden I understood what growing up and being a man meant. I'd been stripped of my security blanket. I was on my own, in my sixties no less, no longer "Baby Teddy," the pet name given me by an aunt. Though embarrassing to admit, it was a jarring and sobering revelation. Whatever psychological growth and maturity I have achieved has mostly been self-inflicted as I have tried to right the emotional voids of my childhood. There were certainly positives to how I was raised, but the stoicism in my family's dynamics lessened their impact on me. What contradicted the doting love I was shown was how smothered it was by its lack of verbal expression. As I was growing up, I knew what I wanted from what I didn't get. I would not repeat that with my children.

My father's acceptance of my mother's foibles and imperfections showed his love for her, and despite her often cool attitude toward him, she loved him as deeply. Her eyes told of the safety she felt when she was around him and how, no matter what she did, she knew he was there for her. The reciprocal passion of their relationship was strange because it was not blatantly expressive, yet it was completely understood.

One of their very few displays of affection was when they would hold hands as they walked together. It was done furtively, as if they wanted no one to notice. They didn't look at each other, their fingers just naturally intertwined, as if a full grasp would be a risk. They were like two young lovers nervous in their first attempts at affection. That innocent clasp produced a glow that engulfed them, and their contentment was wonderful to see as they both mellowed in the silence of that moment.

What the connection was that my parents had, I may never fully understand. Theirs was a loyalty to each other that was beyond explanation. No matter what might have occurred between them on any given day, and though my mother may have just castigated him again for some silly reason, Dad would always kiss her before they went to sleep, always, even if he had to force her to accept it; he never failed to show his love for her.

Mom never refused this show of affection, but neither did she always make it easy for him. There was an old-school, undemonstrative understanding that they were there for each other. The reserved nature of their relationship, which was my model, made it hard for me to be any different. Knowing deep down that I wanted my life to be more expressive, the blueprint I was given kept my responses restrained and undemonstrative, and me in check. I love intensely as they did, and though similarly controlled for a long time, that is no longer a burden. Therapy has helped me to be more communicative, to understand and give more of myself, to reach out to people, and to value vulnerability. In their own way, and though I had to do a great deal of searching to uncover and make sense of its presence, Mom and Dad gave me a lesson about what true love is. What keeps me twisted is the difficulty of making it work, and accepting that it does.

The reason for revealing these very personal issues is because I recognized the similarity to a relationship I had with a teammate of mine on the A's. It was one I didn't really understand until it also involved his tragic death. Learning that Jim "Catfish" Hunter had contracted amyotrophic lateral sclerosis (ALS), better known as Lou Gehrig's disease, was crushing news. I didn't see him before he died in 1999, something I regret, and though his passing was not a complete shock, it was devastating, especially because of how I learned about it, and even more in how I responded to it.

His condition and its debilitating worsening had been widely publicized over the years, so I was aware of what was taking place. My one last chance to see him was at our 1994 World Series reunion in California, but for some reason I wasn't notified of its date until the day before it was to occur. Managing a club on the East Coast, it wasn't possible for me to get there in time. As the years passed and his health deteriorated, I thought of him often, and how difficult things had to be for him and his family. With less and less control of himself, he fell one day while entering his house, and after a brief hospitalization, passed away.

I was in Hudson Valley, New Jersey, when told of what had happened. My team was beginning its playoff series after having won its divisional title in the New York-Penn League. I had known Cat had fallen, but didn't know of his death until Phil Pepe, a New York sportswriter, matter-of-factly, and abruptly, asked me what I had thought of him as I sat in the dugout twenty minutes before game time. No players were present. I was by myself on the bench when Phil confronted me.

The way he proposed the question, his expression, and my knowing of Cat's recent hospitalization, I knew immediately that he had died, and when it was acknowledged that he had, I started to cry. I lost control of myself and was an emotional wreck the entire game. My reaction was instinctive, without thought or reason. I had felt bad for Cat, but the instantaneous emotional release I experienced with his death emphasized the deep admiration I had for him. It caught me completely by surprise. Because of the isolation, empty awareness, and lack of emotion in which I had lived most of my life, so often afraid to confront my feelings as I worried more about what others thought, my reaction was personally overwhelming.

My research, if correct, has found that only fourteen players were on all three of our Oakland A's World Championship teams. Our reunions have been spectacular gatherings of old friendships with the same sense of satisfaction and pride for what we accomplished decades prior still alive. Because of our time together on the field, and in the clubhouse, that seemingly totaled more hours than those I enjoyed with my own family, the team grew to be a second home away from home, Even in retirement, mellowed, and devoid of the green-and-gold garb, these past champions seemed no different.

The years had not dampened their competitiveness. It was neither dulled nor lost, and sparks of it remained in their spirit and good humor. The fire that once blazed could now only smolder, but were it possible to have these older and slower victors once again take the field with the focus and commitment I remembered, I would have to think twice about betting against them! The respect I had for each of them cannot be measured. They were winners; each and every one of them a leader in his own right. Nothing could be more rare on a ball club.

What I came to understand that day when confronted by Phil Pepe, and proudly so after being a member of the Oakland club for so many years, was the reverence I had for Catfish Hunter, not only as a baseball player and teammate, but as the individual he was, and how he conducted himself on the field. No one was more professional, and no one handled his job more maturely than he did.

Few pitchers in the history of baseball have accomplished what Cat did, and being able to say that I was on the field behind him in many of his twenty-win seasons is indeed an honor. He was the real "straw that stirred the drink" in Oakland, to plagiarize Reggie Jackson's supposedly famous quote. Off the field, he was devoted to his family and the farm he had in North Carolina. His baseball fortunes helped him buy acres and acres of land he worked on during the off-season, and his heart was always at home with those he loved.

After all these years, it is still difficult to talk about him without choking or tearing up, and writing about him now is not easy either. The more I thought about why I was so affected, the more I came to understand what I didn't understand about myself in my playing days. I had never viewed my teammates as anything other than baseball players. I knew them in the locker room and on the field, and had gotten to know their families, but only with a few did I really get somewhat close. Most players go their own way after a game, and after the season you would rarely see any of them until the following spring, so even though my children played with Cat's, I knew little about him or his wife, Helen.

Finding out that he had become afflicted with ALS was one of those things you never forget, I regret not knowing him better than I did, and feel badly to have not seen him before his last days. He was a man I had known as a stallion among us, a savior of sorts. That he was forced to his end so helplessly was tragic and unfair.

His passing made me realize that having feelings had no deleterious consequences. It was okay to be vulnerable, and free with my sensitivities. It made me look at others in a different light, one that was not judged or tainted by my own fears. It made me realize how much I cherish those years with my teammates, respecting each man for his contributions on the field. I may not have held them all in the regard that I did Catfish, but they were all special. To have been affected by his tragic death the way I was will always be a momentous event in my life.

Unable to attend his funeral is regrettable, and though I made several calls to the house, could understand why Helen wouldn't or didn't answer. I did write her and the family a letter that I hoped in some small way conveyed my respect, admiration, and love for her husband, and for all that I knew their family meant to him. To this day, whenever I think of the members of those three championship ball clubs, I remember Catfish as our horse, the reliable one who could stop the bleeding should we not be playing well.

Whenever he was handed the ball, he would get us the win we needed. He didn't miss a turn. I could watch any of his performances in review and not know whether it was a spring training game, or his relief appearance in Cincinnati in the World Series of 1972. His mound demeanor never changed. Time and time again his bulldog, noncommittal, and expressionless focus supported by a tremendous workmanlike commitment to excel was replicated on the mound. His stoic approach was a farm-boy's commitment to the job at hand; it was simply his turn to get it done, and he would. I can only imagine the quality of his upbringing. His pitching performances were probably no different from his times back home in North Carolina when, out with his dogs, he would plow his acreage, doing what was necessary without hesitation or reservation. Though he is greatly missed, his death had once again given me a new look at life.

The pressures of the game and everything surrounding it contributed to my not delving into who I was or how I was living. It's taken far too many years for me to finally feel that I have some grasp of myself, and what I should be doing, what I should have done with my life, how I should have treated the many people I've touched. Writing this book is one of the better things I have accomplished. What it has done for me is immeasurable.

Good things are happening, and I can only hope the progress continues. The death of my mother and father, the death of a great teammate, a divorce and the physical and emotional loss of my children because of it, various job situations I didn't handle as

I should have, and so many other events and decisions were all invaluable lessons of life, painful sometimes, and difficult overall to experience.

I will never quit trying to be a better person, just like I never quit trying to be a better ballplayer. Every happening in my life teaches me something because I'm now aware. I am not afraid to respond to what is happening. It's a shame that such sad events have led to my step-by-step enlightenment, but how can I not be grateful?

**Mom and Dad at Ted Kubiak Night
in Yankee Stadium in 1970.**

**Ted Kubiak Night in Yankee Stadium in
1970 with Highland Park fans**

**Highland Park City Council Portrait Presentation
at Ted Kubiak Night in Yankee Stadium in 1970.
Bus Lepine my high school coach on the right.**

20

What an Embarrassment

Baseball in its infancy was a gentlemen's game, more a social gathering than a competition. Those who played, in a show of decorum and respectability, were often nattily attired in white collared shirts with bowties, long, blue woolen pants, and a fashionable straw hat. Footwear was a pair of elegant two-toned spike-less high tops. Swinging bats that weighed up to fifty ounces, and were maybe three and one-half feet long while so elegantly dressed had to be challenging.

Sparking interest wherever it was played, and improved by several rule changes in the late 1800s, the game's popularity soared as the twentieth century approached. Not only did any number of cities and towns proudly boast baseball teams, it was common for various organizations and businesses to form their own in-house clubs. Teams had no shortage of players, but to play you had to be white. The Negro, black, African-American player, however he might be labeled, had difficulty finding a team that would accept him.

The first organization to formally govern baseball in America was the National Association of Base Ball Players in 1857. After a decade of supervision, a revision of its rules in 1867 banned black players, but the edict was flimsy and never fully enforced. A "grandfather clause" at the time allowed the few African-Americans already on major and minor-league rosters to continue playing. It was not until the late 1870s that a more formal vote by club executives closed the loopholes, and officially sanctioned the ban. That pronouncement was applauded by several white stars who unashamedly agreed with the racial divide. Future Hall of Fame player Cap Anson blatantly refused to play against any club that had a black on its roster.

A few blacks were able to find employment until about 1890 when a "gentlemen's agreement" among officials in the International League, the prominent minor league at that time, proposed its own rules officially adopting segregation. This mandate proved to be powerful enough that by the turn of the century the door that some had found open was effectively and permanently slammed shut, blacks were not allowed to play on any club. With that, pure and unconditional racism was born in baseball, and it remained solidly in place until Branch Rickey recruited Jackie Robinson from the Kansas City Monarchs in 1945.

The black players did not sit idle during all of this turmoil that decried their existence. Unwilling to accept that there were no other options, they organized and formed their own teams and leagues, and barnstormed the country consistently beating teams whose rosters were replete with their antagonists. The final scores usually left their opponents in awe of the competition they had faced, and chagrined to have lost.

The first African-American professional baseball team, formed in 1885, was an exceptionally talented group who held their own in competition for nearly twenty years. Calling themselves the Cuban Giants, they were not from Cuba, or anywhere near the Caribbean Island, but were a group of black waiters and porters working for a New York restaurant who passed themselves off as Cuban citizens. To further distance themselves from the perception that they were black, and because few people understood the language, they spoke a kind of gibberish on the field that was thought to be Spanish.

Several attempts were made in the late 1800s to organize these black leagues, but it was not until Andrew "Rube" Foster stepped forward in 1920 that anything significantly successful occurred. A fiery competitor, Foster had a stellar playing career. With that same passion he went on to manage numerous championship teams with his hard nosed, disciplined, hit-and-run style of play that included bunting, good defense, and solid pitching. But the more prominent contribution to his race and baseball, was his dedicated commitment to organize an eight-team league that became known as the Negro National League. That and a couple of other black leagues survived a bumpy road through the Depression Era, and into the 1940s.

The black player suffered almost thirty years of relative invisibility, isolated to his own kind with talents that would more than surprise the baseball world once unleashed. Jackie Robinson's debut in 1947 with the Brooklyn Dodgers was the first move made in the sloth-like integration of the American and National Leagues. It was a resounding call for the death of the Negro Leagues. As blacks were slowly added to major-league rosters, there was no further need for the Negro leagues, and by the end of the '40s they no longer existed.

Though the racial issues and the decades of solitude and shame endured by the black player that have scarred the game of baseball from its inception don't relate in any specific way to this writing, integrating the game holds such historic gravity that I believed it necessary to include certain remembrances and behaviors, including my naïve acceptance of the racial issues I lived through in the '50s and '60s, years that saw some of the strongest racial tensions ever in this country.

● ● ●

The decade of the '60s was one of considerable social upheaval. Racial injustices heaped on the black population included inhumane bombings, beatings, and murders. The Ku Klux Klan's hatred for the black race ran rampant. Many of a group of civil-rights activists called the Freedom Riders were beaten and killed for simply riding buses. Malcolm X was gunned down in 1965 for his speeches championing racial equality. Interracial marriages were rewarded with prison time, redlining restricted economic parity while perpetuating segregation, and the most prominent spokesperson of the time, Martin Luther King, was imprisoned time and again for his part in seeking political and social justice for the black man. His assassination in April of 1968 ignited rioting, and the burning and looting of downtown Baltimore, Maryland, delaying the start of my second major-league season. My Oakland club was forced to stay in nearby Towson during the days the city was under siege. Neither the earlier passage of the Civil Rights Act of 1964 nor the Voting Rights Act in 1965 could quell the hatred so many in this country had for the black man. The destruction of Baltimore was the culmination of the racial tensions that I had been witness to in many of my earlier minor-league seasons.

Long before the black race was referred to as "African-American," they were called Negro or colored people. Growing up I knew them as the latter. It always confused me why they were looked upon and treated so differently, but being young, I naively accepted what seemed right at the time though it made me uncomfortable. What I thought was a disparaging label, being called colored was accurate to describe their skin, but demeaning and inaccurate regarding their humanity. It was one of those slang identifiers that doesn't sit well with those to whom it is directed because it shows a lack of respect and approval. The term "honky," used in derogatory retaliation, no doubt makes some whites cringe. Being Polish, I've genuinely laughed at many Polish jokes. Some are very funny, and though I'd like to think I'm not affected by them, their reference to me being dumb does hit a nerve.

Aware of, but perplexed by segregation as a youngster, I could only react to it as I saw how it was dealt with by the adult world. What could a little kid do about it anyway? There was a small section of my hometown of Highland Park, New Jersey, that was seemingly reserved for the town's "colored population." I knew of no black person living anywhere else in town. There were no restrictions on my visiting or being in their neighborhood, but it made me uncomfortable when I was.

I felt awkward, not because I was among them, but because I was concerned about what others who degraded them would think of seeing me there, wondering perhaps why I was. I considered every colored person I knew in town a friend. As a youngster I found their race fascinating, much like I did members of the much larger Jewish population in Highland Park who were true isolationists governed by a much stricter culture, and following what I considered strange customs that never wavered. Because colored people were the more brazenly and blatantly singled-out segregated race throughout America, I looked at them more inquisitively trying to understand why they were so hated. What was it others were seeing that I didn't? Yes, their skin was different, often even among their own, and they lived a different lifestyle, spoke with a noticeable dialect, and had their own distinctive mannerisms, but every ethnicity had its eccentricities. Looking down on them made no sense.

There were no people of color living anywhere other than along those couple of avenues in Highland Park as far as I knew. That had me wondering if it was their choice to congregate in this area, or were they officially restricted to it by some local ordinance. No such edict was ever promulgated that I knew of. They may not have been considered poor, but not having much, they lived within their means. I sensed the inferiority in which they were held, and how they were overtly ostracized by society, yet they were not openly derided or disparaged in any way by anyone in town. As a race, they were congenial, and appeared, to my young eyes, to be treated respectfully.

That they were considered inferior was obvious by how they carried themselves. There was a deference in how those that were my friends responded to everyone, but it did not deter my playmates, or me, from making them the brunt of our jokes, or giving them the same good natured ribbing we gave everyone, and they had no trouble returning the jabs.

The only opinion I had of those my age was that they were good friends, teammates, classmates, and athletes. The occasional comments made by adults referring to them as lesser people simply because of their color baffled and embarrassed me as a Caucasian.

It was somewhat awkward and discomfiting that I allowed the contemptuous national opinion of this race of people taint mine, but as I said, I was young. Never did I treat them, or ever consider treating them with any less respect than I did others, yet I was affected by all the negatives spoken or written about them. I felt manipulated by public sentiment. Indoctrinated unfairly with this unwanted prejudice, it took a long time for me to realize that I did not have to accept the bigotry attached to their race, that I was fine having an opinion that differed.

With the colored neighborhood ironically located on the south side of Highland Park, it was a similarly compassed location to that part of our nation below the Mason-Dixon Line where the black race was more regularly humiliated, disparaged, and treated with considerably greater animosity and hatred, something I would one day get to see firsthand.

Neither Highland Park nor any of its surrounding communities had any overt or blatant segregational policies that I knew of. None of my colored friends were banned from doing anything I was allowed, barred from going anyplace in New Jersey, or relegated to separate eating or bathroom facilities, but I can't say that they may have voluntarily stayed away from certain venues. There may well have been signage prohibiting them from certain freedoms, but being a sheltered kid, I saw none. Just like the rest of us teenagers, they "hung out" at the Fifth Avenue Sweet Shop after school and on weekends downing hamburgers and cherry cokes. They were friends.

● ● ●

Civil rights laws and their decade's long fight for equal treatment notwithstanding, my own maturity would eventually allow me to accept African-Americans without the confusion of the guilt I had, but not before an incident in 1964 that bears mentioning. Playing for the Fort Worth Cats, the AA affiliate of the Chicago Cubs, I was unashamedly befriended by a black member of the team. He was freer with his opinion of me than I was with him. Admittedly, I was uneasy around him, and I wondered exactly what the intent of his obvious attention might be. What reasons were there for him to be so friendly? His friendship was shown with such openness and honesty that I truly wondered what motive he might have had, but there was never any hint of anything improper, including my suspicion of whether he might be gay.

My honest opinion was that he respected me as an individual, but self-conscious, shy and uncomfortable with anyone getting close to me, it was hard for me to let anyone into my world. I was emotionally much safer in isolation.

Fulfilling my military obligation during the pervious winter had wiped out any spring training I might have had in 1964, so when discharged, with no definitive place for me to be assigned, Kansas City sent me to their Pacific Coast League AAA club in Dallas. One month into the season, after rarely and mostly not playing well, I was optioned to the Cats of the Texas League.

During my brief time in Dallas, I had purchased a brand new Pontiac Bonneville which I took to Fort Worth. Knowing that I would be driving back to New Jersey at the end of the year, this teammate asked if I wouldn't mind dropping him off at his home in Chicago. His request shook my tendencies to remain aloof, and as my mind sifted through excuses why I couldn't, the fact that I had been raised to be polite made me quickly agree to help him out. For selfish reasons my initial response was to refuse him, but thinking that might appear to be a racial slur, I could not in all good conscience do that. I just wanted to get home. Going through Chicago would not only greatly increase my time on the road, but also the cost of the trip. When he generously offered to share the gas expense and driving time, not only did I feel more comfortable about accommodating him, I learned much more about his character. Despite having to revise my route, having him along made the drive much easier, and he was more than thankful when I dropped him off. The lesson in humility and tolerance he had given me was something for which I should have thanked him profusely.

For a week or two every summer until I entered high school, Mom, Dad and I vacationed in Daytona Beach, Florida, visiting my mother's sister, her husband, and my cousin. No matter how uncomfortable the 1000 mile drive was during the hottest and muggiest months of the year, I looked forward to every one of our visits. They were eye-openers for a little kid, especially in how I came to better understand the South, and its people.

The Interstate Highway System bill would not be signed into law by President Dwight D. Eisenhower until 1956, so without a direct unimpeded route south, Dad was forced to take the only major north-south corridor at the time, Route 301. This bumper-to-bumper, traffic filled, two-lane road took us through one small town after another, each one, thankfully, interrupting the monotony of the trip. The change in cultures were wonderful lessons in geography, history, architecture, sociology, and anthropology that put life into the otherwise boring ride.

Some of the more interesting sights along the way were the factories of the many major cigarette companies in Virginia and North Carolina. The acreage these factories covered was astounding, but considering how unashamedly the public was smoking, how it was so glamorously advertised in the media, and promoted in films and magazines, there size was justified. With a full carton being much cheaper in Virginia than in New Jersey—less than two dollars per—Mom never returned home empty-handed; she was never without a list of specific brands to bring back to my aunts and uncles.

Much of my time on these trips was spent watching the billboards, roadside signs, or mile markers telling us how much closer we were getting to the next town, restaurant, motel, or some point of interest. Two such popular businesses that you could hopscotch from one to the other going south were the twin-eateries known as Stuckey's and Horne's. Similarly constructed with their high pitched roofs, they would never equal the number of McDonald's franchises that would one day engulf the world, but one or the other of them seemed to pop up every few miles. Both were East Coast icons offering a variety of confectioneries, food and souvenirs. Stuckey's was famous for its pecan candies especially a Pecan Log Roll that my aunt in Florida loved. Horne's was more of a restaurant, but a copy-cat purveyor of similar sweets and unique gifts.

By far the most famous attraction was a restaurant just south of the imagined line that geographically separated North and South Carolina, aptly named "South of the Border." That it would one day blossom into the monster amusement stop it is now must have been anticipated because huge, colorful billboards advertised it states away from its location, and they all had the same message. "South of the Border" or 'SOB" was in big bold, multi-colored, animated, Mexican-styled letters, along with a large sombrero telling you how great the place was. You were warned not to dare not miss seeing Pedro, a mascot of sorts, who was also caricatured on every oversized billboard. Why a Mexican theme was mixed with the Southern Dixie motif made no sense, but such craziness was its draw. The place was a treasure chest of cheap oddball souvenirs with counters, shelves, and bins full of useless items just waiting to be turned into gifts. They were as tacky, and as useless as could be, but vacationeers bought enough of the weird stuff over the years that "South of the Border" grew from the one little original restaurant that I knew, into what is now its own little city of over 100 acres with multiple restaurants, gas stations, motels, an amusement park, and even a golf course. Not stopping to check it out at least one time is an impossibility. The signage that speaks of its eventuality on your trip begins hundreds and hundreds of miles away giving kids ample time to pester mom and dad into pulling in. And why wouldn't you want to take Aunt Mary an alligator head key chain, or Grandma Debby a stuffed frog dressed in Mexican attire playing a guitar? Better yet, how could you pass up a little heartburn?

Not to be forgotten were the enjoyable Burma Shave signs. Clever little jingles were segmented line by line on a series of successive rectangular highway signs that advertised the popular shaving cream. Once I saw my first set of them I was hooked, and on the lookout for others. An assemblage of six individual red and white wooden signs were strategically placed at locations along the highway, each with one short line of some catchy little rhyme that when pieced together in its entirety, was a cute message and an ingeniously created sales pitch for the product. Spaced maybe a hundred yards apart, their fun was trying to remember the whole slogan as you sped past them at sixty miles per hour. Allan Odell had convinced his father, Clinton, to erect the roadside advertising to boost lagging sales of the shave cream in the '20s, and they did the trick better than was expected. Passers-by were forced to give them greater attention than they would one lone billboard. It became impossible not to remember Burma Shave. Smart little sayings like "A shave, that's real, no cuts to heal, a soothing, velvet after-feel, Burma Shave" or "Every shaver, now can snore, six more minutes, than before, by using, Burma Shave" added a little lightheartedness to the ride. The last sign was always reserved for "Burma Shave."

Another roadside attraction, and the one I most desperately hoped we'd run across, was a group of men along the highway called a "chain gang." Whether a theatrical concoction or not, I wasn't sure, but there was always one such group characterized in every gangster movie on television that had anything to do with prisons. Known to be a Southern form of punishment, once we hit South Carolina, I began to look for a covey of individuals costumed in striped prison uniforms working on the side of the road.

These work gangs were a crude and conspicuous form of punishment. Despite the ball and chain—thus the name—attached to one or both ankles to prohibit any escape attempts, such duty may have been a form of penal charity in that it afforded the inmates a break from the monotony of their indoor incarceration. But when the entire group was banded together as one to further control their movement en masse, I wasn't convinced that it proffered a more lenient kind of labor than what might have been found within the prison walls.

The racial injustice of this forced bondage despite its appearance of leniency was that the inmates were always black, and always guarded by at least two shotgun-armed white men on horseback who could run down anyone who attempted to escape. A convicted workforce like this could not have been more indicative of the disparate and startling political and social agenda that so typically contrasted the North and the South.

Southern life was a step back in time. Not only did it move more slowly, nothing seemed urgent or important. The Southern blacks, just as they were depicted in movies, were slow-paced, never in much of a hurry to do anything, and it seemed their white counterparts, evidenced by how my relatives in Florida went about their daily lives, followed suit. From what I could tell, the only work available for any colored person were the typical menial jobs: house servants, gardeners, field workers, and grocery packers. At the local Piggly Wiggly grocery store, which seemed their most public place of employment, after they bagged everyone's purchases, they were required to carry and load them into the shopper's cars. Feeling it only right to tip them, I was told by my cousin not to because any kind of remuneration was not allowed, a humiliating sign that disavowed their efforts.

But what defined the South better than anything were the hundreds and hundreds of acres of cotton fields we would pass along the highway—the Carolinas might have a few, but they proliferated in Georgia—with dozens of farmhands slowly and tirelessly picking the little white puffs. Well-protected from the scorching sun by large brimmed hats, they filled bag after bag in the blistering sunshine and sweltering heat in a way that looked punishing. Not one of the pickers was white, it didn't matter what state we were passing through.

Somewhere on the acreage of these cotton fields, often not far from the highway would stand one lonely house. It was the only edifice rising out of the expanse of the cotton fields, somewhat the focal point of the acreage, and the gathering point for the colored field-workers and their families. Every one of these residences was weathered, rundown and more ramshackle the farther south we got until many appeared to be the skimpiest of shelters. Some were so dilapidated that whatever protection or comfort they provided from the elements could not have been much. As we passed them in the late afternoon or early evening, an entire family might be sitting on either the steps of their shabby sanctuary, or the edge of its rickety old porch recuperating from a day of laborious field work returning my looks with their own curious ones. I felt self-conscious looking so intently at their plight, but seeing their existence for the first time was startling. All they had were themselves, and the cotton that surrounded them.

What was rudely apparent about the South was how the entire southern populace looked at the black race with a disdain unlike anything I could imagine. There was no questioning how obviously inferior they were considered. Kept subservient in blatant and incontrovertible ways, there were demeaning written warnings everywhere that relegated them to their own rest rooms and drinking fountains. Separate entrances for the "Colored" or "Coloreds Only" were posted in many establishments. Seeing such placards announcing this degradation for the first time left me transfixed on them, and the people obeying them. Seating areas in parks and movie theaters might not have been labeled as such, but were unmistakably understood to be theirs.

The "Whites Only" signs seemed more flagrantly shameful. Blacks frequented no restaurants as far as I could tell, and they did sit in the back of the buses. Their conduct around town where they encountered the locals was deferential and submissive. On the sidewalks, they obediently stepped aside. They could work for "whitey," but had none of his luxuries. I looked upon this more shameless social exclusion and isolation with both disbelief and incredulous fascination. It was a blatant demonstration of racial injustice.

The Southern Negro, colored, black, African-American, whatever he might have been called, may not have been as controlled, tortured, and vilely treated as he was during the earlier harsher period of slavery, but he couldn't have felt much different. Segregation may not have been capital punishment, but it was, nonetheless, a living, breathing form of it.

One of the hallmarks of Daytona Beach was a ballpark built in 1914 called City Island Park. It was the home field to many different professional baseball organizations since the 1920s. In 1946 it gained the distinction of being the first ballpark in Florida to allow Jackie Robinson to play in what would be the first integrated professional baseball game since the establishment of the color barrier in the 1890s. How that came about was that the Montreal Royals, the Brooklyn Dodgers AAA farm team, of which Robinson was a member, was to play the parent Dodgers in an exhibition game at their Jacksonville spring training site. But the city of Jacksonville and every other nearby town, stood fast with Jim Crow and the segregation laws in place at the time. They were adamantly against the game being played, and refused to let Robinson and a fellow black teammate, Johnny Wright, take the field. Thanks in large part to Mary MacLeod Bethune who was a political activist and founder of an all-black girls school that later grew into Bethune-Cookman University in Daytona Beach, that city was much more progressive and accepted both players unabashedly. The Dodgers were so incensed by Jacksonville's refusal to stage the game that they moved their spring training site to Cuba the following year, and a year later, in 1948, they took over a Naval Station in Vero Beach, and Dodgertown was borne. The rest is history regarding that venerated venue.

City Island Park would eventually be renamed Jackie Robinson Ballpark inb 1989.

In the 1950s, my first experience with professional baseball was attending a game at this same ballpark on our southern vacations. It didn't matter that those on the field were not major-league players, but hopefuls wanting to make a career of the game beginning at this lowest rung of the professional ladder. I had as much curiosity watching the colored spectators being shepherded through their own separate entrance to their designated "Colored Section," usually well down the left or right field lines. They bothered no one, cheered for their own, and caused no problems. To a young boy like myself, trying to understand the reasons for them being deprived of everything to which I freely had access to, this was cruel.

In 1961, when my own professional baseball career began in the Florida State League, nothing had changed regarding the separation of the races. Playing in this same ballpark in which I was a spectator years before, there was no sign of any advancement in the social status of the black baseball fan. They remained relegated to the same segregated section of the ballpark well down each line as far from home plate as was possible.

The Florida State League which was my entry level into professional baseball, was a class D level minor league. As the year progressed, the warnings my dad had been given about how difficult life in the minor leagues would be were discovered to be definitely true, but I loved everything about it. The road accommodations my Caucasian teammates and I were given were decent, nothing spectacular, but more than acceptable. But the racial bias I saw with regard to where members of the team stayed on the road surprised me. On our first road trip, before my white teammates and I were housed, our little convoy of station wagons made a strange unannounced detour to drop off our colored players and dark-skinned Latinos—who were lumped in the same ostracized category—in "their" areas of town where sleeping arrangements had apparently been made for them. I had never considered they would not be staying where the rest of us did. Every day we would pick them up on our way to the ballpark, and drop them off again after the game. This arrangement had apparently been in place for years because my manager knew exactly where to take them. From what I could tell, they stayed in large homes, or what were called boarding houses.

With no knowledge of this ritual as we pulled into the first town on my first trip, something wasn't right. I didn't expect we'd be staying at the best place, but crossing the railroad tracks, and going into a considerably less affluent side of town seemed rather odd. I had no idea what was happening. Because our manager was driving the lead car, I figured he knew what he was doing. When I finally realized what was going on, I could not believe that we were banishing teammates to inferior accommodations because of the color of their skin. Exiling them like this was unbelievable when every day we dressed next to each other, traveled together crammed elbow to elbow, sweaty as we were, piled almost on top of each other in overcrowded cars or buses. Isolating them was an undignified affront to their humanity, and that it was condoned was an embarrassment.

When Jackie Robinson opened the door for blacks in the major leagues in 1947, it was not pushed open very wide, maybe no more than the tiniest of cracks. Full integration, at least at the big-league level, was a long way off, but no evidence of its restriction was found in the minor leagues. Not that the treatment received at the lower levels by those blacks I played with shouldn't have been better, but employment was at least available to them.

My Sarasota club was rostered with only one African-American player who, at twenty-three, was five years older than me. He was the kind of player organizations kept around to stabilize a club and, with a team full of high school and other first-year professionals, he was our best asset. I knew nothing about him, but never did I or any of my teammates disrespect or treat him differently. Consumed and focused as I was with baseball and the beginning of whatever career I was to have, his unique situation in the world wasn't one of grave concern to me. That he was black didn't really phase or matter to me, he was one of our outfielders, and he could hit. With little interest to explore relationships or develop a racial understanding—things were what they were—more important to me was being able to hit .314 as he did that year. I did notice that when asked for his autograph, all he could pen was a scratchy, printed last name. That was sad and somewhat startled me. Didn't everyone go to school?

His apparent lack of education had me wondering more about him, but the pitchers I was facing, who were bigger than any I'd ever seen, were of greater concern. When I learned of his age, I thought it remarkable that he was as young as he was. He easily looked to be thirty years old or older. Life had taken its toll on him. That he was aloof also didn't faze me. I figured his self-inscribed isolation was just his way. Hell, I was as shy as could be myself. Unfortunately, though I chose mine, his solitude was thrust upon him. It was also obvious that he knew his place, and what was expected of him.

What I would come to learn about the abuse black players suffered whenever they pioneered a particular league was beyond comprehension. The taunts, insults, threats, and indignities they had to endure were unmerciful. Carl Long, whom I met in Kinston, North Carolina, when I managed there, shared his experiences while playing for the Kinston club in 1955. Carl was an outfielder who played for a couple of years in the Negro Leagues with the Birmingham Barons before joining the Pittsburgh Pirates organization in Kinston.

Sitting with him for about an hour one evening, listening to story after story of the animosity that he and other black players were made to suffer could not have been more disheartening. He told of knowing and playing with Willie Mays, Ernie Banks, Frank Robinson and country Western star, Charlie Pride, all before their stardom. It was an incredulous and unbelievably well-spent historical hour listening to this polite, funny and well-mannered gentlemen tell of the vitriolic degradation hurled at his manhood while trying to make a living playing the game he loved.

Towns were asleep when our road games ended so finding something to eat was usually an adventure. Anything to calm the rumbling stomachs of a bunch of hungry athletes sufficed, it didn't matter what. Crammed into a small bus on one of our trips instead of our usual mini-fleet of station wagons, we stopped at a bar on the outskirts of the town of Palatka, figuring we could grab a hamburger and something to drink, and be on our way.

With most of the team underage and unable to go inside, our food orders were taken by the manager and the older players while we "young-uns" waited on the bus. Not more than five minutes passed when all of a sudden someone burst from the bar, and came running toward the bus. One of the inebriated patrons had somehow found out that there were a couple of blacks on the team, and was now trying to climb on board frantically waving a gun, sloppily hollering, "Get all those damn n-----s off the bus." My heart started pounding and I froze in my seat. I had just turned nineteen, was new to all of this racial stuff, and scared stiff. Before this maniac could make it up the stairs of the bus, our manager and a few other men corralled and wrestled him back inside. We got out of there as fast as we could, hamburgers or no hamburgers. This incident was the ugly highlight of my first professional season.

I couldn't help but wonder how my two teammates were feeling, and will never forget our outfielder huddled and cowering in the last row, afraid to move. As frightening as the incident had to be for him, it took some heavy breathing for me to calm down.

Kansas City was very impressed with the year I'd had, and added me to the forty-man big-league roster for the next season. This earned me an invitation to the organization's major-league spring training camp in West Palm Beach, Florida, in 1962. As a pseudo "major-leaguer" for at least a week or two until I was sent back to the minor-league camp, I was privileged to be housed in one of the better hotels in town along with the rest of the major-league roster, everyone, that is, but the colored players.

Jackie Robinson had taken verbal and emotional abuse far beyond belief to supposedly make things easier for those of his race who followed, but here, fifteen years after his sacrifice, in a major-league camp, a colored player was still not allowed to be in the same hotel with his white teammates. Where they were housed or fed was a mystery, and I could only wonder if their treatment was equivalent to the kind the rest us received. Were they able to order two shrimp cocktails and a large steak with the extras every night for dinner like I did, and just sign the check?

Two years later, in 1964, racial progress was still stalled; it was just as demeaning and flagrant. Robinson's sufferings and pioneering had still not done much if anything to change what I was seeing. His efforts remained nothing more than a bunt in the game of life and integration. Traveling that summer with the AA Texas League's Austin Braves, we stopped for lunch one day at a small diner in San Antonio, Texas, hoping to get in and out quickly, not wanting to waste any more time on the road than we had to. We were in Texas, not the South, or so I thought, but no sooner had we entered when someone behind the counter hollered, "They can't eat in here." This blatant refusal in a place I'd never expected it to happen underlined the national bias against the African-American.

Jumping ahead forty years, as a manager in the Oakland Athletic's and Cleveland Indians' organization, I met and worked with several black coaches, all of whom I considered good friends. I became especially close to a few, one specifically. There was a mutual bond in our outlooks, our personalities, and our instructional styles. He was conscientious, smart, a tremendous worker, and an outstanding teacher who would do anything to help our young players succeed. Polite and compassionate, he was one of those instructors who are so hard to find who always seemed to know what to say, when or when not to say it, and how to say it for its greatest effect. From a baseball standpoint, he knew the game inside and out, and was a positive influence for everyone. How he conducted himself was not a lesson lost on me. Billy Williams, and his wife Gloria, were the type of people anyone would be proud to call friends. Billy has unfortunately passed away but remains vividly in my memory, not for the baseball man he was, but the person.

As Billy and I got to know each better, he opened up to me about his own career. I sat for hours listening to him tell me about how he was treated, the abuse he suffered, and the difficulties he faced as the lone colored pioneer on a couple of minor-league teams.

The man endured some horrible indignities for years. He may have deserved more of a chance than just the twelve major-league at-bats he had for the Seattle Pilots in 1969 at age thirty-seven, but I believe, and he did too, that his color held him back. He was an outstanding hitter, leading the minor leagues in which he played in several offensive categories. As he freely told me of the injustices he suffered during his early playing days, and how they had scarred him, the effects were obvious. The inner strength he had to have to handle what he did I can only imagine. To have fought and clawed his way through all the abuses while pursuing his lifelong dream, to still become the human being he was to me and to his family, says so much more in his favor than about those who looked at him with unreasonable disdain and scorn.

Is baseball free of prejudice, probably not? Should it be? Of course. I can't say I've seen any blatant abuses, but there have been situations from which I believed the antagonistic feelings of some have surfaced against others because of their racial differences. Behind closed doors, in private conversations, in intimate thought, I am sure it still smolders. What a shame it is that we are not yet at a place of total acceptance.

21

THE BASEBALL GLOVE

Doing what it does silently and anonymously, rarely noticed, and expecting nothing in return, its reward is being thrown around like a rag, oiled, greased, spit on, pine-tarred, pounded, beaten, and often kicked. Having made a hero of its wearer for yet another season, it gets set aside, tossed into a dark closet, a dingy basement corner, a musty attic, an old trunk, under a bed, some out of the way place to recuperate. Only when old and flimsy, well beyond its proudest days, its worth exhausted, will it be revered, and looked upon with the respect it deserves.

This is the baseball glove.

The game of baseball is purported to have first been seen in the United States in the late 1700s. It gained prominence in the early to mid-1800s, and when in 1846 the first recorded game with rules was played, interest in it grew. Every contest was a roller-coaster of emotions, providing its diehards with moments of incredulous joy and devastating heartbreak, often within seconds of each other. Credit could understandably be given to either the bat or the glove for the game enduring as it has, but without a ball there would be nothing we know as "America's pastime."

It is a ball that elicits the gleeful sounds coming from children on a playground engaged in a lively game of baseball, one-eyed cat, or stick ball, allows two friends, alone on a field, the fun of taking turns hitting fly balls to each other, and provides one lone youngster the competitive joy of attempting to hit a spot on a wall with his throw. And what better way could there be to bond a dad to his son or daughter than with a simple game of catch?

Imagine there being no baseball. What would we have done without a Willie Mays, a Joe DiMaggio, a Ted Williams, or a Mickey Mantle to worship? What would the impassioned fan do, who believed it sacrilegious to abandon his team of perennial losers, when once again his heroes may have faltered, knowing that "there is always next year" never comes? And what would a dedicated fandom do to replace its commitment to sit through rain delays and doubleheaders when there would no longer be any? Without a baseball game, summer would be nothing but one sweltering, lazy day after another. And, "Good Lord!" What if there had been no Babe Ruth!?"

It is difficult to conceive that something as innocuous as a little ball is single-handedly responsible for giving America more than its fair share of unforgettable moments, fulfilling, and, in some cases, transforming as it has the days and lives of so many. No one could have predicted that the greatest compilation of statistical information ever assembled, memorable or not for any one vocation, and accountable for an overwhelming number of historically significant achievements, would result from the use of such an inconsequential plaything.

Fascinated as I have been with the history of the game, no baseball statistic has ever much mattered to me. Many of the game's greatest feats and records, interesting as they are, have sparked only a curiosity of how they were achieved. The overwhelming compilation of numbers, percentages, and rankings that put things in perspective for legions of baseball fanatics do nothing for me. I remain unamused by how many of this, how few of that, how high or how low a number is of a past accomplishment. Even less exciting is the present fascination with the technological findings and scientific reasonings that have inundated and usurped the purity of what I consider "the" game. I am unappreciative, and unmoved, by miles per hour, exit velocity, launch angle, spin rate, or any scientific computation that camouflages a baseball ability that is not there. They are trivialities that rasp at what I find more disturbing than intriguing about the game.

Batting averages are interesting, but who accomplished them, and how they did, is more appealing. My restlessness does not allow me to sit still in the stands for any game, at any level, for more than an inning or two. No player, no game, and no team has ever received the committed allegiance I gave the baseball diamond. My joy was playing the game, not creating its history.

● ● ●

As long as I can remember, baseball has been my favorite of the three major seasonal sports. Football and basketball were fun, but my skills were more adaptable to Doubleday's creation. My size and strength did not compliment the athleticism and dexterity required of the gridiron or a basketball court, but they worked well on the baseball diamond. My movements and actions coordinated more easily with what had to be done after a ball was hit rather than kicked, passed or shot. I was far from being the best of hitters, and though the batter's box was not intimidating, being within its boundaries was a bit unnerving. On the other hand, when attempting to catch or field the ball, I had none of the physical handicaps that I did trying to hit it. The glove was more naturally a part of me than was the bat.

In time I would become so skilled and accomplished with a baseball glove that anything I might do with a bat was an afterthought. To this day, with a collection totaling more than 100, ranging in age from well over a century to today's "Cadillac" versions, the baseball glove galvanized me to the game, and ignites my passion even today. As a work tool, it is an undeniably, artfully designed additional use for leather that made playing catch with my dad so special. Though others will reverently defend the baseball bat as the piece of equipment that most significantly affects the outcome of a game, the glove can be just as accountable, and will do so just as quickly, and with more unbridled flare.

The transformation of the baseball glove from the first fingerless designs to the exquisite nets of today, is a fascinating journey of ingenuity. When first conceived the glove was ridiculed and derided, and even when finally its purpose was acknowledged, it remained nothing more than an unheralded appendage to the game. As its functionality improved, so did play. It is only during the past few decades that a decline in its successful use has been evident. Those failings rest almost entirely with its wearer, but sharing the blame, and unrecognized, is the glove itself.

The glove long provided nothing more than hand protection, but with more required from it as the power and speed of the game increased, it metamorphosed out of necessity. As glove designs changed, so did the game. Exciting and spectacular plays became more common as the athletes and their new defensive equipment joined forces to maybe not end, but to make more even what had been an offensive-minded game. The glove began to affect the game's outcomes.

When the bat became a weapon of sorts for its performance-enhanced users in the '80s, a disturbing trend began. Defensive play that had been steadily improving began to suffer as the game turned its attention to the surge of "fence-busting" clouts. Gloves, and/or their wearers, were failing to hold on to the baseball as well as they once did, but fault could not be completely laid on the baseball finding ways to avoid the clutches of those trying to catch it. That responsibility lay in a complicated mix of the reshaping of society, a lessening of expectations within the game, an acceptance of mediocrity by the game's caretakers, and most significant of all, a very different kind of player whose complacency and competency were not constructively challenged. And never, even remotely, was it considered that the new glove designs were playing a consequential part in the miscues and errors being committed.

As closely connected as I've been to the defensive world of baseball ever since my playground days, I find that the glove has mystified many when it comes to being used properly. As the famous comic actor Rodney Dangerfield so aptly said about so many things, the baseball glove "gets no respect!" And that should not be. With what seems to be a lack of emphasis on its use, something that stems from ignorance, its casual acceptance, and a lackadaisical hierarchy to understand its value, the glove remains nothing more than an appendage. The many times a baseball either nestles easily into its pocket or jumps from its grasp, what the glove may have contributed is never recognized. Had this chapter on it been excluded, it would have been an omission in this book that itself could have been considered nothing less than a thoughtless error.

Putting on a baseball uniform almost every day for more than forty years never got old. Every time was just as thrilling as it was for me to put on the very first full flannel uniform I received as a member of the Hub Motors Little League team in Highland Park. Having to shower and change clothes no less than twice a day for all those years was a psychological comfort as was having a number on my back. Without one, something just didn't seem right.

My life has been consumed by sports. My buddies and I played all three of the major ones—football, basketball, and baseball—as their seasons dictated. As a youngster, my routine was school, a couple of hours of playtime, dinner, homework, and bedtime, every day. During the summer when school was out, I spent all day on some playground around town playing baseball. At night there would be a game in one or another of the leagues I might be in. I played baseball around the clock. The days were never long enough.

It was a time when the only special days, other than birthdays, were Christmas, and Easter. Going to a ballgame, a movie, or even a school event such as a dance or a play was something to look forward to.

One of my favorite childhood memories is the first time Dad took me to "Cheap John's," the popular outdoor/sporting goods store across the Raritan River from Highland Park in New Brunswick. I was seven years old. Officially known as "John's," I knew it by the economic title Dad gave it because of the discount he was given. Welcomed as he always was by certain of the salespeople—enough to warrant the markdowns he got—he must have frequented the store more often than I knew.

John's was a Shangri-La for anyone who loved the outdoors. The place was stocked with aisle after aisle of everything anyone needed to hunt, fish, or camp. There was a large variety of canvas and rubberized rain gear; red-and-black hunter's clothing; guns, pistols, and rifles; camping stoves, tents, and sleeping bags, and knives of all shapes and sizes. It was fascinating for a young boy to see it all for the first time, but my only interest in the place was its sporting goods, and the baseball gloves it sold.

While Dad was on his own hunt for what fishing gear he needed, I roamed the aisles, fascinated by the endless assortment of merchandise. Sprinkled among the glut of outdoor equipment and other paraphernalia was an array of stuffed animals that, whether hanging on the walls or posed and standing lifelessly, always seemed to be looking at me somewhat ominously. Seeing them up close, silent as they were, was thought-provoking, and somewhat sad.

Fishing may not have been Dad's favorite sport, but I do believe he liked it better than baseball. What he found so fascinating about standing alone and casting his line monotonously again and again into the rough surf at Ocean Beach, New Jersey, with no results, hoping something from the Atlantic would take pity on his patience, was something I never understood. It was nothing for him to spend a couple of hours after dark with just a flashlight waiting for just the slightest of nibbles. Should he hook the occasional bluefish or flounder that seemed to have sacrificed itself to be sure his time had not been wasted, his night was a success.

Just the possibility that he might catch something was enough entertainment for him. His patience was admirable, unlike mine. I would stand quietly by his side as long as I could wanting desperately to see him hook something, but when I finally tired of watching him reel in one empty hook after another, I scampered up and down the beach to see what the other anglers might have caught. The fact that so many others had caught something made me wonder what Dad was doing wrong. Was it his bait, the spot he had chosen, or just his misfortune? He never caught much, but I was never happier for him than when he came home with anything that had scales. Should he return with only his pole and leftover bait, he was fine; he'd had a good time, fish or no fish. And I was happy to have had the opportunity just to spend time with him.

For a sport that I believed required no coordination or athleticism, the grace Dad exhibited when he cast his line was unexpected. His easy manipulation of the the long surf rod he used was actually beautiful to watch. With each cast his bait splashed down well beyond the crashing waves, thrown there with a poise and elegance that was remarkable.

Starting with a half-turn, he would point the tip of his pole with its weighted and baited hook dangling loosely as far behind him as he could. At the moment he felt it provided him the right amount of leverage, when he considered the pole's alignment and the tension on his line adequate to maximize the power of his cast, he would lean backward just a bit more to fully cock his readiness, and then swiftly whip the pole's tip forward with a little bit of a looping motion. It was an unexpected artful cast that exhibited the skill required the way true athletes do, effortlessly. Compared to the other fishermen, there was a rhythmic dance to Dad's technique; everyone of his casts perfectly executed.

John's inventory of sports equipment included everything you could want to play football, basketball, baseball, golf, tennis, or to swim, ski, or boat. When Dad promised to take me there one day to pick out my first baseball bat, school that day could not have been more boring, or moved more slowly. When I was finally in the sports department, the first things I saw were two circular revolving bat racks filled with models branded with the names of Hank Greenberg, Ralph Kiner, George Kell, Ted Kluszewski, and other major-league stars, bats too big for me to swing at the age of seven or eight. Removing one and then another, inspecting each one, testing its weight and feel while running my hands over its high-gloss sheen, for what little I knew, I was holding the exact bat once swung by the player whose boldly inscribed name I was reading.

From those more my size, the one that caught my eye was a Little League "Babe Ruth" model, easily identified because of the decal of Babe Ruth's face pasted on its barrel. Only the best players were afforded such idolatry. Though Ruth was unquestionably considered better than anyone ever, he was not the only one to have his photo on a bat. Other greats like Hank Greenberg, Ted Williams, Mickey Mantle, and Jackie Robinson had their own. Was it possible that this Ruth bat would be significantly better than the others; would it make me a better hitter? I was going to find out because it was the bat I intended to take home.

The earliest baseball bats were thick-handled little monsters, many weighing forty or more ounces. Those swung today may be as light as thirty-one ounces. Ted Williams was reported to have swung one 35 inches long weighing 34 ounces, and I swung a 36 inch, 36 ounce model one year, and hit .295 with it. The Ruth bat that caught my eye was a little on the heavy side, but I pestered Dad, insisting how perfect it was for me. He finally relented, but I had again done what I would do over and over in my lifetime which was to decide on something because it was thought to be the best, looked better than the rest, was the most expensive, but which was in no way practical. Neither I, nor any of my friends, were comfortable swinging it because it was too big for us little guys, something I knew when I bought it, yet, I had to have it. When it got thrown down on the street in front of my house during one of our games, and a quarter of its knob broke off, I never used it again.

As early as I can remember, certainly at the age of seven when Dad first took me to John's, I was fascinated with baseball gloves. I don't know why. So, as great as it was to handle and hold the bats, it was the gloves that I wanted to see and touch, and the display John's had did not disappoint. I'd never seen so many brand new, mint condition baseball gloves all in one place; I couldn't help but stare at the different models. Many of them stood on top of a plain and drab-colored box that had "Fielder's Mitt," "Fielder's Glove," or "Catcher's Mitt" stamped on one of its sides. Some were boxed and shelved, others stood proudly in front of a box that featured a picture of the player whose model glove it supposedly was, or so a seven year old thought. I had no idea at the time that companies had players endorse gloves to increase sales.

I put my hand into every glove that I could reach. Not only were there the expected Rawlings, Spalding, and Wilson models, but also some made by Nokona, a company I'd not heard of, that were surprisingly very nice. Manufactured in Nocona, Texas, the gloves carried their name spelled with a "K" instead of the "C" because the U.S. Patent and Trademark Office would not sanction the name of a town to be trademarked.

It was at John's that I first discovered, and marveled at the smell of a brand-new baseball glove, and its wonderful, fresh-out-of-the-box feel.

During the '50s there was no Toys "R" Us to run to for a new toy or two. Buying or being given anything was a surprise, a treat, left more for the days of gift giving like birthdays and Christmas. Whether it was a toy, a book, or even clothing, everything you received was treasured. Had I a list of wants, a new baseball glove would have topped even a new bike. On my eleventh birthday, while sitting on the floor of our living room opening presents, Dad dropped one of the best presents I've ever received over my shoulder and into my lap, a "Carl Erskine" Nokona model fielder's glove.

The glove was Nokona's best, its top-of-the-line model that year, that at a cost of maybe twenty dollars had to be a huge sacrifice for Mom and Dad, and, no doubt, a large portion of Dad's monthly salary. It was a big glove, with a thickly padded thumb, little finger, and heel. Even today it's a popular model with collectors, and comes up for sale from time to time on various Web sites. I have a couple of them in my glove collection, unfortunately, not the one that was my birthday gift.

Until the 1880's baseball was a polite game, played with a sense of chivalry, often more a leisurely social contest. Every hitter had the prerogative to ask the pitchers, who were throwing underhanded at the time, to throw the ball either high or low to a spot they felt they had the best chance to hit it. Trying to catch the softer balls used in these early contests wasn't much of a challenge. No ball hit went very far or fast, and with no gloves yet, a player used his feet to sometimes stop the ball. But when a more-tightly wound and harder baseball was introduced, and lighter bats began to hit it farther, and at a greater speed, something was needed to protect the hands of the fielders; thus the "invention" of the baseball glove. Though the very simple hand protection first used was looked at with contempt, and the players using such things considered "sissies," a glove of some design would soon become an important part of every player's equipment.

Once the obvious utilitarian purpose of the glove was recognized, their use, though grudgingly, was accepted. This revolutionized the game, quickened its pace, and dramatically affected its outcome, not to mention significantly diminishing the bruised, battered, and calloused hands of players. It was nothing for the earliest infielders to make any number of errors, often fifty or more a year. Field conditions contributed to the miscues, but even with the introduction of the glove, it was not uncommon to see individual yearly totals approaching 100. Today's young minor-league players make forty or fifty, and I personally made forty or more my first couple of seasons.

The first known use of anything resembling a glove was in 1870 when a young catcher by the name of Doug Allison used a soft buckskin mitten to protect his hand after an injury. He was chided, ridiculed and considered weak for doing so. In 1875, Charles Waitt, a first baseman, tried to sneak a flimsy, flesh-colored glove past everyone to protect his hand only to be similarly mocked and taunted.

A few years later, Albert Spalding, who pitched almost every game for the Boston Red Stockings, and later briefly for the Chicago White Stockings, elected to pad his non-throwing hand to protect it from the abuse it was taking from all of his time on the mound. Spalding was a well-respected competitor, and had earned a lofty standing in baseball circles because of his phenomenal pitching record. His total of 252 wins versus 65 losses, twice logging over 500 innings in a season and once over 600, were amassed in a relatively short span of seven years, an incredible accomplishment. Deferentially treated because of his prowess on the mound, he did not meet with the same hostile reaction Allison and Waitt received when they wore their "protective device."

Further reason for Spalding using a glove was that he and his brother were selling them through the sporting goods company they had started. Using one made perfect sense. What better advertising could there be than having him play with a glove he had made? When other players saw the value not only in the protection the glove provided Spalding, but also in the advantages it provided him defensively, it became popular very quickly. In 1885, the Rawlings Company applied for its first patent allowing for more padding to be put into the thumbs, fingers, and palms of the gloves they were making, and by the turn of the century every player was taking advantage of using this new and unique defensive tool.

Three months prior to my architectural classes beginning at Pratt Institute in Brooklyn, New York, the possibility of having a career in professional baseball materialized. That someone was willing to pay me to play made my decision a no-brainer. It wasn't long before I was a nervous eighteen year old flying, for the first time, to Florida to begin life as a professional baseball player. My luggage included a glove, a pair of spikes, some underwear, a jock and cup, and a pair of sliding pads.

Neither the Erskine glove that had been a welcomed birthday gift when I was a Little Leaguer, or the subsequent 1950s Rawlings "Playmaker" that I used in high school were going to meet what I thought would be the demands of a professional infielder. The Erskine was too big, and too well-padded, and after a few workouts I knew the Ballhawk had to go. I needed a new glove, but, stranded as I was in camp, I wasn't sure how I'd find one; that had me concerned. My problem was quickly solved when sales representatives from the major sporting goods companies began showing up with their different models. Walking into camp one morning, I was surprised to find Rawlings model gloves spread out on a cafeteria table, and three or four' large duffle bags on the floor that were full. I thought wow! This was better than John's. I had no idea what kind of glove I was looking for, but, surely, there had to be one to my liking out of the dozens laid out before me.

The more familiar I became with the various model gloves displayed by the Rawlings, Spalding, and Wilson sales representatives, the more I realized that not every glove had the quality of leather I expected. What surprised me was their overall inconsistency. No two models stamped from the same pattern from the same company were ever the same. Some were constructed of excellent, high quality leather while others had a rubbery or vinyl-like feel. Many of the better quality models, those made from the best portion of the animal's hide, those that were stiffer, stronger, and would seemingly hold their shape better, and last longer, were not models I liked, but being desperate with the season starting, I settled on a small glove from the Spalding company just before camp broke.

What the model number of that Spalding glove was has long been forgotten, but having heard so often that good middle infielders used small gloves, it was the smallest I could find. One of the major-league's best shortstops at the time was a flamboyant Venezuelan named Luis Aparicio, a future Hall of Fame member playing with the Chicago White Sox. As so many other Latin infielder's did, he formed his glove to have a long pocket by folding the thumb and little finger together. Believing that he knew what he was doing, I followed suit. But the glove shaped that way forced me to field the ball too often with one hand which I did not want to do. With the glove shaped vertically with its long, narrow pocket, I had to think too much about whether it could be opened enough to field or catch the ball, and I did not want that worry.

Midway through the season, after seeing him play a number of times, I was impressed by the play of a young infielder for the Tampa Tarpons, the Cincinnati Reds affiliate. I had been watching him carefully every time our teams met because of the glove he used that was very different looking than those being used by other infielders. Were Tommy Helms's quick hands because of the completely wide-open, flat glove he used? I wasn't sure, but knew immediately that it was the type of glove I needed if I was to perfect the two-handed style of play I hoped to teach myself. The question was finding one.

At the end of every minor-league season, the major-league organizations held special instructional camps to which they invited their top prospects. They still do today. Impressed with my first year of play, Kansas City invited me to be part of their Florida Instructional League team based in Clearwater, Florida, in September, 1961. As the salesmen from the different glove companies came through these camps as they did in the spring, I had another chance to find a replacement for my "Aparicio" model. Rummaging again through bag after bag of the different models from all three companies, again finding nothing I liked, it was a Rawlings rep who finally showed me an innovative design his company had introduced a few years earlier, and it looked to be exactly what I needed. It was a small, open-designed infield glove that looked able to be easily flattened even more.

When I opted to use the Spalding glove during spring training, the sales rep asked me to sign a merchandising contract with the company which gave them the exclusive rights to use my name on any future gloves they might want to put up for public sale—much like those I saw at John's—should I become an established major-league player. As an inducement, in return, they would provide me with a couple of gloves and a pair of spikes each year. This was a common practice with all the companies. But now, liking the Rawlings model as much as I did, and with no intention of ever using the Spalding glove again, I was not sure how to respond to Rawlings' request to sign with them. What trouble would I be in if I signed a similar contract with another company? I could have refused and just bought the Rawlings glove whenever I needed one, but I did not want to miss out on the "freebies" every year.

Whether right or wrong, legal or illegal, I decided to double-dip. What I counted on was that neither company would make a fuss about a teenaged rookie just out of high school doing such a thing. Being light-years from playing in the major leagues with no assurance I ever would, why would either one of them care anyway? And with a career that was average at best, the endorsement issue never materialized thereby avoiding any potential legal problems. As it turned out, Spalding bought Rawlings in 1960, making my concerns moot.

Rawlings considered this new line of gloves Experimental Player Gloves, and cleverly used the acronym XPG on each of the different variations of the model. I figured the "S" on the model I used (XPGS) meant "small," because it was. It is a very rare glove to find today. Rawlings had first agreed to manufacture a new and unprecedented design in 1920 when Bill Doak, a highly successful major-league pitcher, persuaded them to make a glove that featured a longer thumb, extending it to be more even with the glove's index finger, with lacing that tied it to that finger giving the glove what today is called its web. This made it easier for the ball to be caught. With the new XPG models, Rawlings had come up with the perfect design for me.

The XPGS became the extension of my hand that I was hoping some glove would. Being partially "open" when brand new and very stiff, it presented some challenges because it did not have a deep pocket. It took about two weeks to soften it a little, and turn it into the "pancake" I wanted for the games, but for the next fifteen years I used either the XPGS or an XPG5 Rawlings model glove. Gloves were not cheap in 1961—twenty-five dollars was a lot of money—but I would buy one or two extra every year to be sure I had one on hand when my "gamer"—what my teammates and I called the gloves we used in a game—got too flimsy. I liked my gloves to have a stiff feel to them.

My Rawlings XPGS model glove.

With what I thought to be the glove I needed, I began to study every movement I made when fielding a ground ball. Believing each one to be important, and that there was a logical and sequential order to their execution that, if perfected, would make fielding it much easier, my workouts became disciplined, militaristic-like, detailed studies of what the ball was doing. Over a period of the next few years, I developed what I thought was the most comprehensive analysis possible of the fundamentals and techniques that were necessary to field ground balls consistently.

Teammates laughed and joked about how flat my glove was, but it was all in good fun. Their tongue-in-cheek remarks were the same that could happen over anything any one of us might find humorous. None of it was bothersome, and I was actually glad no one liked it. I hated when someone put their hand in my glove because it altered how I had it shaped.

With my glove as wide open as it was, there were some uneasy moments with it for a few years, and more than a few uncalled-for errors. Adjusting to the unique way I formed the glove took some time. The easiest of ground balls would occasionally bounce out of it. What I was attempting to do was just stop the ball, and then quickly grab it with my throwing hand. That was nothing difficult, and probably nothing different than what most infielders do, but it took on another meaning with a flat glove. I never "caught" a routine ground ball in the true sense of the word.

When I began coaching and my young infielders saw the type of glove I used, they snickered just like my teammates had. None of them used anything similar, or the same way. That was fine, but what bothered me was that when questioned about their own gloves, they had nothing to say. They looked at me as if to say, "What do you mean, what kind of glove am I using?" The disregard they had for their own glove's importance, and their own play, was disappointing. No player, nor my bosses, understood my concerns about balls being dropped, or not fielded because of the glove, or how the player used it. To know that a different glove might help someone became a frustration when there was no interest shown in knowing why or how.

The gloves used in the early 1900s increased the possibility of the ball being caught, but without a defined pocket, two hands had to be used. As glove designs improved, and their size increased through the '30s, '40s, and '50s, along with them being more profusely padded, sometimes overly so, a more-pronounced pocket was developed. Gloves remained simple and presented no notable problems while the player was given greater control. It was eventually possible to catch a ball with one hand because the glove could be sufficiently manipulated, but using two hands remained the better and more secure way.

Every glove made prior to 1930 put a majority of the responsibility on the player to make whatever catch or play had to be made as opposed to many of today's models that actually do the catching for its user. Today's player does not realize that the glove dictates how it must be used, and that he doesn't have the control of it that he thinks he does. That statement would stir quite a debate, but many of today's gloves are something akin to a net that snares the ball. Their size and configuration make this possible.

Using a glove properly has never been thought to need the kind of instruction as does swinging a bat, but I wanted my glove to work for me in specific ways. Not only did I expect it to not give me any problems, I did not want to have to think that it might. Whether others gave theirs the same thoughtful consideration, I don't know. It appears that players use, and do the best they can with what they have.

Too many position players—first basemen and catchers excluded—wear their gloves incorrectly, and not at all according to how they are constructed. The fact that their construction forces them to be used as they are makes this a catch-22 situation. Gloves have five finger stalls into which five fingers should be correctly inserted. What appears now common is for players to put both the little and ring fingers in the little finger stall of the glove and the middle and index finger in any one of the next adjacent stalls. That leaves one, or sometimes, two stalls open. This is not to say that this is a wrong way to use the glove, but imagine putting on a cold winter-weather fur-lined glove this way. What control would you have of it?

Not using all the finger stalls, incorrect as it is, is how many players control today's leathery monsters. The construction, in particular, the long fingers of many outfielder's gloves makes controlling them difficult. When a stall or two is left open, the ball is caught more with the fingers of the glove in what could be considered its webbing rather than it slamming into, or near the palm or pocket of the glove, over which the player has control. Watch games carefully to see how often an outfielder's glove affects play. The design of a glove should in no way hinder how a ball should be fielded or caught.

Modern gloves should not be as uncomfortable as they are. That is, of course, my opinion, but my style of play would have been greatly affected had I had to use one. Any attempt I might make to simply catch a thrown ball with any of them, an act that should require no thought, would have, instead, been a concern. So many of today's designs force the player's hand to adapt to their shape and size, dictating how it should be worn and used, often not to its best advantage. Is there a possibility that this affects today's fielders without them realizing it? Credit must be given to the players who have endured their designs, and make them work as efficiently as they do.

Every time I caught a thrown ball, line drive, or pop-up with my flat glove—and I do mean every time—it hit the area of the glove between my thumb and index finger just below the glove's webbing in what I considered the crotch, or pocket, of the glove. If my hand was properly inserted into the glove, one finger in each stall, the ball would be hitting the part of my hand that was the pad of my palm below the index finger. In this way, using my thumb, index, and middle finger, I was able to "grab" and hold onto the ball with just one hand when necessary. Doing this for more than sixteen years pounded my left index finger into submission. It was always colder than the others—I presumed a blood supply issue—that, in the long run, was a minor inconvenience.

As easy as it should be for the ball to enter a glove, so should it be easily removed. This is most important for infielders, primarily the shortstops and second basemen. "Quick hands" are an asset to these middle of the diamond defenders. Many of today's gloves require more work to do that than should be necessary because of their extremely deep pockets, and the seconds that are lost in the transfer becomes significant on certain plays. Quite often you will see someone who can't quite "find the handle," and he will have difficulty making his throw. Being able to manipulate the glove properly is something young infielders should consider.

The ball should never be purposely caught in the webbing of the glove, yet glove construction now makes that routinely possible, and often demanded. Even when I dove for a ball, I had such control of the glove that I caught it in the pocket as I've explained.

It is impossible not to see the number of misses, drops, bobbles, double-clutches, tipped, and even poor throws made either directly or indirectly because of the glove that occur at the major-league level. A lack of athleticism plays a part in fly balls that bounce off an outfielder's glove, or escape an infielder's, while what the glove contributes goes unnoticed. The most obvious example of how the glove itself, or a lack of it being controlled, affects the ball being caught is to watch today's major-league catchers during any televised game. The gloves for these defenders used to be round and well-padded, requiring the use of two hands, a greater focus, and more effort to catch every pitch. Catchers are now squatting first basemen; both receive the ball with one hand. The present designs of catcher's mitts make that easier to do, but the one-handed catcher is only half-invested in the act of catching the ball; half of his body is not involved in the process. When the speed of the game combines with an athletic imbalance, and a catcher's mitt that folds almost in half, the result is less than satisfactory backstopping.

Deriding the one-handed catcher, or the design of the modern catcher's mitt, may seem unfair, but should not everything be considered at such an important position, especially at the major-league level?

Modern gloves present a dichotomy in their effectiveness. Some designs improve the skills of their users; others highlight their deficiencies. Many are designed with gimmicks meant to improve their use—and sales—but what benefits they portend to provide, I don't see. Short-fingered infielder models have pockets formed by the thumb being bent awkwardly outward. Supposedly to facilitate catching the ball, this instead causes the player to lose control of the important opposable thumb, especially if his fingers are not properly put into each of the finger stalls. This thumb configuration is annoying. It forces my hand into an uncomfortable and awkward position.

Most gloves are stiff when new, some uncommonly so, which is usually a good thing. Some are so heavily strung that they are almost immune to being broken in as they should be. Many outfielder's gloves appear larger than the game's rules allow with fingers so long they make the glove uncontrollable when the glove softens. Too many others are formed so they can be opened just barely enough to allow the ball to enter the pocket. Most are impossible to reshape. Pockets are too deep, and the webbing or its lacing tears or breaks more quickly than it should. Manufacturers have designed gloves that are basket-like with player performance in mind, but they apparently do not realize how difficult it is to manipulate their creations. Where I wanted width to my gloves, many of today's models emphasize length. Being vertically constructed rather than horizontally, balls are easily, and mostly, caught in the glove's webbing, or what could be more accurately considered its netting, rather than in the pocket. "But the ball was caught!" rationalizes every one of the patented features. Yes, it was if you are just as willing to accept the times it wasn't to be followed by the excuse, "That was too tough to handle."

● ● ●

If someone was to tell me that I would one day think about the baseball glove as highly as I do, or that I would make a living with it, I would have probably told them they were crazy.

Is it not strange that glove is spelled- "g —l o v e"!

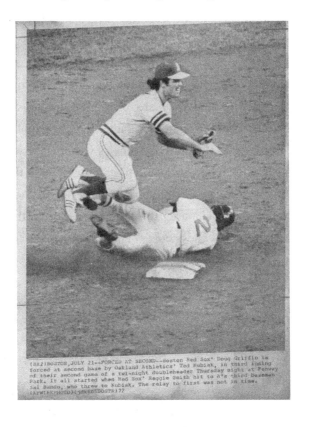

(AXZ)BOSTON,JULY 21--FORCED AT SECOND--Boston Red Sox' Doug Griffin is forced at second base by Oakland Athletics' Ted Kubiak, in third inning of their second game of a twi-night doubleheader Thursday night at Fenway Park. It all started when Red Sox' Reggie Smith hit to A's third baseman Sal Bando, who threw to Kubiak. The relay to first was not in time. (APWIREPHOTO)(jtk60SDOSTR)72

451

A Personal Postscript

Thoughts in Passing

Growing up an only child, and the center of my parent's world was a good thing. But with no brother or sister to bounce things off, or to be bounced around by, my life had neither tints nor shades; it was black or white. I knew but one way, my way, and quietly and silently admired my friends who had siblings, and a family life that seemed more comfortable and relaxed, not the tightrope I walked.

Missing in our household were two or more kids whose identity was dependent on their order of birth. The firstborn, if the only child, receives the best or worst from parents who are learning to become responsible guardians, and can grow to be a jealous little adult while becoming an ambitious leader. The siblings that follow—no matter the number— given increasing space and freedom, may feel left out, but are easy-going and independent; and the last born, because of parental exhaustion and less-cautious guidelines, tends to be free-spirited, social and spoiled, and possibly irresponsible.

With no sibling, and doted on by two loving and well-meaning parents, I muddled through the confusion of being a self-confident, neurotic perfectionist in my own privatized and imagined world while trying to make as much sense as I could of maturation and pubescence. There was no one to offer judgments, share ideas, or challenge my thoughts. I knew only what I lived, and much of that was misunderstood. I wrestled too often with my self-imposed passionate conclusions, attempting to untangle right from wrong the best I could, wondering constantly what life was all about.

Raised as well as I was, the verbal approvals that would have redirected my life were missing. I knew I was loved. As a kid, it's easy to know that you are. If you aren't, you do what you can to fill the void while never understanding the dynamics of that emotion until you have to give it yourself. When my mother would sometimes look at me and start to cry, I tried to muffle my laugh, confused by her emotions, and a little embarrassed by the magnitude of the love she had for me. I didn't understand it. Now I feel the same depth of emotion when I think of my own children.

Nothing is more compelling than the love or passion you have for someone or something, and the range of events that prove that can be surprising. It's why athletes get emotional when they have accomplished something difficult; why I broke down after completing my first marathon; why I cried when told of Catfish Hunter's death. And why, as my mother did with me, I tear up just thinking about my daughter and son.

After one minor-league championship run, my team lost the title in a hard-fought final game of the playoffs. It took me twenty minutes wandering around the field, choking on the defeat before I could join and address the team in the locker room. Even in losing, I was so proud of what they had come so close to accomplishing. When another of my clubs won its league championship, even after the celebration had subsided, again my words would not come easily. There could not be enough said to have them feel what I did about what they had achieved, or to satisfactorily praise their efforts.

I still get emotional about my Oakland teammates of fifty years ago, the memories of our days together, and winning three World Series in a row. I am so proud of what we accomplished. It's a special feeling that I was fortunate to have had in triplicate.

Why I say all this is because of how deeply I love the game of baseball; it's been my life. That passion makes much of what I've written seem contradictory, and it wasn't easy to do. I miss what I had, what the game was, and I don't like that feeling.

Just as I wish to experience again the delight my three year old daughter had riding her little pink tricycle, or the joy of recalling my son at age four sitting patiently on our front porch waiting to go trick-or-treating on Halloween wearing a caped Superman costume and his blue rubber rain boots, so do I wish the game of baseball could have stayed as it was when I was an active player. It's hard to let go of things when you love them so much.

Printed in the United States
By Bookmasters